Prison Readings

Prison Readings
A critical introduction to prisons and imprisonment

**Edited by Yvonne Jewkes and
Helen Johnston**

WILLAN
PUBLISHING

Published by

Willan Publishing
Culmcott House
Mill Street, Uffculme
Cullompton, Devon
EX15 3AT, UK
Tel: +44(0)1884 840337
Fax: +44(0)1884 840251
e-mail: info@willanpublishing.co.uk
website: www.willanpublishing.co.uk

Published simultaneously in the USA and Canada by

Willan Publishing
c/o ISBS, 920 NE 58th Ave, Suite 300,
Portland, Oregon 97213-3786, USA
Tel: +001(0)503 287 3093
Fax: +001(0)503 280 8832
e-mail: info@isbs.com
website: www.isbs.com

First published 2006

Paperback
ISBN-10 1 84392 148 0
ISBN-13 978 1 84392 148 6

Hardback
ISBN-10 1 84392 149 9
ISBN-13 978 1 84392 149 3

British Library Cataloguing-in-Publication Data

A catalogue record for this book is available from the British Librar

Cover photo copyright Christian Bailey. This photograph was taken at Kilmainham Gaol Museum, Kilmainham, Dublin, Ireland.

Typeset by GCS, Leighton Buzzard, Bedfordshire, LU7 1AR
Project managed by Deer Park Productions, Tavistock, Devon
Printed by TJ International, Padstow, Cornwall

Contents

Acknowledgements   ix

Introduction: prisons in context   **1**

Part A   The emergence of the modern prison   **13**
Introduction   13
1   The body of the condemned   18
   Michel Foucault
2   The prison chaplain: Memoirs of Reverend John Clay   22
   Walter Lowe Clay
3   Women, crime and custody in Victorian England   30
   Lucia Zedner
4   Grinding men good? Lancashire's prisons at mid-century   39
   Margaret E. DeLacy
5   Victorian prison lives   45
   Philip Priestley
6   The well-ordered prison: England, 1780–1865   51
   Randall McGowen

Part B   Theoretical approaches and emerging trends   **55**
Introduction   55
7   Prison privatization: panacea or Pandora's box?   60
   Michael Cavadino and James Dignan
8   Can prisons be legitimate? Penal politics, privatization, and
   the timeliness of an old idea   71
   Richard Sparks
9   Legitimacy and order in prisons   79
   Richard Sparks and Anthony Bottoms
10   The rise and rise of supermax: an American solution in search
   of a problem?   84
   Roy D. King
11   Softly does it   94
   Sally Weale

12 The abolitionist approach: a British perspective   98
     Joe Sim

Part C   Prison populations   **105**
Introduction   105
13 Tougher than the rest? Men in prison   109
     Joe Sim
14 Analysing women's imprisonment   121
     Pat Carlen and Anne Worrall
15 From the inside   129
     Ruth Wyner
16 Racism in prisons   135
     Ben Bowling and Coretta Phillips
17 Paramilitary imprisonment in Northern Ireland:
     resistance, management, and release   138
     Kieran McEvoy
18 From Borstal to YOI   150
     John Muncie

Part D   The prison community   **159**
Introduction   159
19 The society of captives: a study of a maximum security prison   164
     Gresham M. Sykes
20 Asylums: essays on the social situation of mental patients
     and other inmates   174
     Erving Goffman
21 Time and deterioration   181
     Stanley Cohen and Laurie Taylor
22 The defences of the weak: a sociological study of a
     Norwegian correctional institution   193
     Thomas Mathiesen
23 Mind games: where the action is in prisons   202
     Kathleen McDermott and Roy D. King
24 Doing prison work: the public and private lives of prison officers   209
     Elaine Crawley

Part E   Current controversies   **223**
Introduction   223
25 Social characteristics of prisoners   229
26 Suicides in prison: ten years on   230
     Alison Liebling
27 The drugs economy and the prisoner society   237
     Ben Crewe
28 Radical risk management, mental health and criminal justice   245
     Philip Fennell
29 Life as a woman: the gendered pains of indeterminate
     imprisonment   253
     Stephanie Walker and Anne Worrall

30   United States of America: prison labour: a tale of two penologies   268
     James B. Jacobs

31   Prisoners' rights in the context of the European Convention
     on Human Rights   276
     Stephen Livingstone

Conclusion: prisons, public opinion and the 'new punitiveness'   **283**

Index   **295**

Acknowledgements

We have made every attempt to obtain permission to reproduce material in this book. Copyright holders who we may have inadvertently failed to acknowledge should contact Willan Publishing.

We are very grateful to the following for permission to reproduce material in this volume:

Part A
1. Penguin Books (London) for Michel Foucault, 'The body of the condemned', pp 3–7 from *Discipline and Punish: The Birth of the Prison* (1991); **2.** Patterson Smith (Montclair, NJ) for W. Clay 'The prison chaplain', pp 272–82 from *The Prison Chaplain* (1861); **3.** Clarendon Press (Oxford) for Lucia Zedner 'Women and penal theory', pp 105–30 from *Women, Crime and Custody in Victorian England* (1991); **4.** Croom Helm (London) for Margaret E. DeLacy, 'Grinding men good? Lancashire's prisons at mid-century', pp 182–211 from V. Bailey (ed.) *Policing and Punishment in Nineteenth-century Britain* (1981); **5.** The author and Pimlico (London) for Philip Priestley 'Prisoners', pp 59–63 from *Victorian Prison Lives: English Prison Biography* (1999). Reprinted by permission of The Random House Group Ltd; **6.** Oxford University Press (New York) for Randall McGowen 'The well-ordered prison: England, 1780–1865', pp 95–8 from Norval Morris and David J. Rothman (eds.) *The Oxford History of the Prison: The Practice of Punishment in Western Society* (1998).

Part B
7. Sage Publications Ltd (London) for Michael Cavadino and James Dignan, 'Prison privatization: panacea or Pandora's box?', pp 228–236 from *The Penal System: An Introduction 3rd edn* (2001); **8.** Oxford University Press (Oxford), for Richard Sparks, 'Can prisons be legitimate? Penal politics, privatization, and the timeliness of an old idea', pp 14–28, *British Journal of Criminology, vol. 34, special issue* (1994); **9.** The authors and British Journal of Sociology for J. R. Sparks and A. E. Bottoms, 'Legitimacy and order in prisons', pp 56–60, *British Journal of Sociology, vol. 46. no. I* (1995); **10.** Sage Publications Ltd (London) for Roy D. King 'The rise and rise of the supermax: an American solution in search of a problem?', pp 163–186, *Punishment and Society, vol. 1,*

no. 2 (1999); **11.** The Guardian Newspapers Ltd for Sally Weale 'Softly does it' (2001); **12.** Manchester University Press (Manchester) for Joe Sim, 'The abolitionist approach: a British perspective', pp 263–84 from A. Duff et al. (eds.) *Penal Theory and Practice: Tradition and Innovation in Criminal Justice* (1994).

Part C

13. Taylor and Francis (London) for Joe Sim, 'Tougher than the rest? Men in prison', pp 100–17 from T. Newburn and E. Stanko (eds.) *Just Boys Doing Business? Men, Masculinities and Crime* (1994); **14.** Willan Publishing (Cullompton) for Pat Carlen and Anne Worrall, 'Analysing women's imprisonment', pp 54–74, *Analysing Women's Imprisonment* (2004); **15.** Aurum (London) for Ruth Wyner, 'From the inside', pp 16–23 from *From the inside,* (2003); **16.** Pearson Education (Harlow) for Ben Bowling and Coretta Phillips, 'Racism, crime and justice', pp 195–205 from *Racism, crime and justice* (2002); **17.** Oxford University Press (Oxford) for Kieran McEvoy 'Paramilitary imprisonment in Northern Ireland: resistance, management, and release', pp 233–49 from *Criminalisation* (2001); **18.** Sage Publications Ltd (London) for John Muncie 'Youth and crime', pp 283–90 from *Youth and Crime 2nd edition* (2004).

Part D

19. Princeton University Press (Princeton, NJ) for Gresham M. Sykes 'The society of captives: a study of a maximum security prison', pp 65–79 from *The Society of Captives* (1971); **20.** Penguin Books (London) and Random House Inc (New York) for Erving Goffman 'Asylums: Essays on the social situation of mental patients and other inmates', pp 24–36 from *Asylums: Essays on the Social Situation of Mental Patients and Other Inmates* (1991); **21.** The authors for Stanley Cohen and Laurie Taylor 'Psychological survival: the experience of long-term imprisonment', pp 87–105 from *Psychological Survival: The Experience of Long-term Imprisonment* (1972); **22.** Taylor and Francis (London) for Thomas Mathiesen 'The defences of the weak: a sociological study of a Norwegian correctional institution', pp 124–34 from *The Defences of the Weak: A Sociological Study of a Norwegian Correctional Institution* (1965); **23.** Oxford University Press (Oxford) for Kathleen McDermott and Roy D. King 'Mind games: where the action is in prisons', pp 357–77 from *British Journal of Criminology, vol. 28, no. 3* (1988); **24.** Willan Publishing (Cullompton) for Elaine Crawley 'Doing prison work: the public and private lives of prison officers', pp 95–115 from *Doing Prison Work: The Public and Private Lives of Officers* (2004).

Part E

25. Social Exclusion Unit Report *Reducing Re-offending by Ex-prisoners* for 'Social characteristics of prisoners' reproduced in Prison Reform Trust Factfile (December 2004); **26.** Prison Service Journal for 'Suicides in prison: ten years on', pp 35–41 from *Prison Service Journal, no. 138* (November 2001); **27.** Prison Service Journal for 'The drugs economy and the prisoner society', pp 9–14 from *Prison Service Journal, no. 156* (November 2004); **28.** Cavendish (London) for Philip Fennell 'Radical risk management, mental health and criminal justice', pp 70–2, 80–3, 95–7 from N.S. Gray, J.M. Laing and L. Noaks (eds.) *Criminal Justice, Mental Health and the Politics of Risk* (2002); **29.** Prison Service Journal for 'Life as a woman: the gendered pains of indeterminate imprisonment', pp *27–37* from *Prison Service Journal, no. 132* (2000); **30.** Ashgate (Aldershot) for James B. Jacobs 'United States of America: prison labour: a tale of two penologies', pp 269–79 from D. van Zyl Smit and F. Dunkel (eds.) *Prison Labour: Salvation or Slavery?* (1999); **31.** Sage Publications Ltd (London) for Stephen Livingstone 'Prisoners' rights in the context of the European Convention on Human Rights', pp 309–10, 313–17 from *Punishment and Society, vol. 2, no. 3* (2000).

In addition to acknowledging the permissions granted by publishers, the editors would like to offer their sincere thanks to those individual authors who hold copyright for allowing us to reprint their work, specifically; Joe Sim, Stanley Cohen, Laurie Taylor, Alison Liebling, Ben Crewe and Anne Worrall. Thanks also to Gerry Johnstone and Tim Newburn for offering us advice and encouragement on the project at an early stage, and to Brian Willan for his enthusiasm in seeing it through.

Finally thanks to Kilmainham Gaol for permission to use the cover image.

Introduction: prisons in context

Prison Readings provides a critical introduction to some of the main debates and dilemmas associated with prisons and imprisonment, and acquaints students with some of the most relevant literature on the subject. Specifically, it charts the history and development of prisons, discusses contemporary theories and current controversies relating to prison populations, examines sociological and psychological literature on the 'effects' of imprisonment, and introduces readers to debates about the management and privatization of the prison estate and emerging trends in the use of imprisonment. Although each reading has been chosen on its own merits, we have organized some of the material in such a way as to set up interesting debates between particular approaches that differ theoretically or methodologically, in order to indicate the varied and conflicting research on prisons, as well as its current debates. Our aim is not to provide a set of 'definitive' readings, but rather to offer a mixture of historical and more contemporary pieces that are representative of the issues and perspectives that have shaped the study of prisons, imprisonment and penal policy in the modern period. As with any reader, the extracts we've chosen are inevitably subjective; they reflect our interests and likes, what we think is important, and, hopefully, what will be of interest and value to students and other readers.

The principal aim of this Introduction is to offer a context for the readings that will follow. Our intention is to provide a broad overview of the development of prisons throughout the nineteenth century and into the twentieth, and examine notions of visibility and invisibility as a thread to understanding the historical development of the prison. We discuss key issues in the late twentieth century, including the 'prison crisis' referred to by some of the authors in the extracts selected, and the classification system for prisoners implemented 40 years ago and still in use today. Finally, we offer a few words on the organization and structure of the book.

Prisons from the late eighteenth to the early twenty-first century: turned full circle?

In recent prison scholarship it has been proposed that current penal policy is returning us to a Victorian model of punishment, whereby the bureaucratic and technical requirements of the institution overshadow the needs and rights of the individual prisoner (Pratt *et al.* 2005). But what were the characteristics of the Victorian prison and, as penal institutions have developed over the last two centuries, what remnants of their early incarnations have been retained?

Our analysis begins with the period from the late eighteenth century to the end of the nineteenth century when there were a number of fundamental changes in punishment, including the dwindling use of transportation of offenders to the colonies and the increasing use of prison as a method of punishment in its own right. Public execution also declined at this time, from around 7,000 executions in England between 1770 and 1830, to 347 between 1837 and 1868 (Gatrell 1994). Emsley (2005) notes that, whilst in practice no one was executed for crimes other than murder from the 1840s, it was not until the Offences Against the Person Act 1861 that Parliament formally abolished the death penalty for all crimes except murder and treason. Executions were moved inside prisons in 1868, the last one in public occurring on 26 May outside Newgate. The first execution behind prison walls happened later the same year in Maidstone. There is some contention as to why public execution ended, but reasons suggested include concerns about the 'carnival' atmosphere that surrounded them, growing sympathy on the part of the crowd for the condemned, and pressure from reformers and middle-class intellectuals who viewed the spectacle as particularly distasteful (Pratt 2002).

Prisons in the eighteenth century were much more a part of the community than prisons as we recognize them today. Gaols and houses of correction of this period were places that held, in general, petty offenders, debtors, and those awaiting trial, transportation or execution. More serious offenders were, at this time, shipped off to America, and later to Australia, or were publicly executed. The prisons of the eighteenth century were not the high-walled secure buildings of the modern period, but places where people from the wider community would freely come and go, associating with prisoners and trading produce within the prison walls. As McGowen (1998) notes these prisons were characterized by neglect, disorder, smell and noise, and it was not always easy to distinguish who the prisoners were. But as Part A of this reader shows, there was a dramatic transformation in the nature and use of imprisonment in the early to mid-nineteenth century. Increasingly, prisoners became cut off from wider society (and, during the separate/silent systems, from each other). Nevertheless, a period of reform had begun that would continue well into the nineteenth century, and prison conditions and regimes were discussed widely in parliamentary debates, newspapers, prisoner and staff autobiographies and in various novels and other fictional writings (Johnston 2006).

During the nineteenth century a number of changes took place in the disposal of offenders. The transportation of serious criminals to North America ended in 1776, sparking the first major government initiative concerned with imprisonment. Under the Penitentiary Act 1779 it was the government's intention to build one or more penitentiaries. However, the penitentiary was never built and the problem was alleviated by the discovery of Australia and its perceived suitability as a convict colony (Webb and Webb 1963; also see Hughes 1996; Shaw 1998). But despite the utilization of Australia as a penal colony, a proper place of confinement was still required to hold convicts prior to their transportation, and in 1812 the government set about the construction of Millbank Penitentiary. Millbank opened in 1816 and was constructed to hold around 1,000 prisoners, although it was never used to its full capacity. By the 1840s, there was growing concern about the severity of the regime and the effect it was having on the mental health of inmates. Growing numbers of prisoners were becoming insane and the committee was compelled to introduce prisoner association after deeming long periods of separation unsafe. By 1843 Millbank had become a convict depot where prisoners were assessed and sent to other institutions, or to the hulks (prison ships) to await transportation (McConville 1981).

It was only at the beginning of the nineteenth century, then, that the government began to get involved in the management of prisons. There were, however, a large number of gaols and houses of correction, which we will broadly call 'local prisons' (termed this from the Prisons Act 1865) that existed across the country and were administered by local authorities. Thus, at the beginning of the century, prisons existed in two forms: the government-run penitentiary and a range of local prisons. Locals held prisoners serving shorter sentences, but the introduction of government inspectors in the 1830s was the start of a long process of increasing government involvement in local prisons which culminated in their nationalization in 1877. During the demise of Millbank the government had already decided to move its reformatory effort elsewhere and Pentonville Model Prison was opened in 1842. Pentonville had been constructed with the separate system in mind and the regime was one where prisoners would spend all their time alone in cells, sleeping, working and eating. Prisoners only left their cells to attend chapel or for exercise and in these circumstances they were still to have no contact with other prisoners and had their faces covered with masks to avoid recognition. Initially the regime at Pentonville was based on 18 months solitude, but as with Millbank, there was public concern over the high rates of insanity amongst prisoners (for a discussion of representations of the separate system, see Johnston 2006). The periods of solitude were reduced to 12 and then 9 months, but by the end of the 1840s, 'Pentonville sank under the weight of public disapproval' (McConville 1981: 209) and, like Millbank, became a convict depot.

By the mid-nineteenth century transportation was again under threat, for Australia no longer wanted British convicts 'contaminating' their country. There was also concern about the nature of transportation since it varied greatly in character, from severe penal labour in chain gangs to the assignment system where convicts worked for colonists (a relationship that could encompass anything from slavery to a formal employee/employer contract). Thus the British government was once again forced to find a solution to holding prisoners in this country, and the convict system emerged. Initially based on a four-year minimum sentence, the convict system entailed one year in separate confinement (thought to be the maximum prisoners could endure) and three years on the public works. The first Penal Servitude Act

1853 had introduced the sentence of penal servitude alongside that of transportation. Four to six years' penal servitude represented seven to ten years' transportation, six to eight years' penal servitude represented ten to fourteen years' transportation, but those sentenced to fourteen years' to life transportation were still sent abroad (Tomlinson 1981). Pentonville, Millbank and Perth were used, alongside cells that were rented in local prisons. Public works prisons were constructed or adapted from existing facilities at Portland, Dartmoor, Portsmouth, Chatham and Borstal between 1847 and 1874 (Tomlinson 1981).

However, by the second Penal Servitude Act in 1857 the sentence of transportation was abolished and the minimum sentence reduced to three years, a move which fuelled public anxiety and led to demands for more deterrent forms of punishment. Disturbances occurred in a number of convict prisons, the most notable of which was at Chatham Convict Prison where a riot broke out involving over 800 men and the military were called on to regain control of the prison (Brown 2003). Public anxiety about convicts was also heightened by a panic in London after a number of garottings which were thought to have been carried out by convicts on tickets of leave (an early form of parole). In 1864 a further Penal Servitude Act increased the minimum sentence to five years for the first conviction and seven years for any subsequent convictions. Stricter controls were implemented on the ticket -of-leave system and the photographing of convicts was introduced to trace repeat offenders. The new system of penal servitude was to be administered by Edmund Du Cane who hoped it would be 'the last and most dreaded result of a heinous offence against life and property, short of capital punishment' (quoted in Tomlinson 1981: 141).

Therefore, by the mid to late nineteenth century the prison had become the predominant form of punishment in England and other Western societies. This change in punishment has been examined by a number of historians and criminologists from different perspectives. Orthodox or Whig historians, such as Webb and Webb (1963), Whiting (1975) and Stockdale (1977), have explained this change in terms of humanitarian progress and benevolent advancement; the barbaric and public bodily punishment of torture and execution and the filth and decay of unregulated institutions being replaced by cleaner, healthier, more ordered prisons which then became punishment for the majority of offenders. However, revisionist historians such as Foucault (1977), Ignatieff (1978, 1985), Melossi and Pavarini (1981) and Rothman (1971) have explained these changes in terms of the ability of the prison (and other disciplinary institutions such as the school and the factory) to control and regulate populations. Thus revisionist accounts are concerned with power and power relations, economic motives, the interests of the governing class and the operation of state power to regulate and control society (although they have been criticized for their focus on government-run penitentiaries, their neglect of the mass of local prisons that were administered by local authorities before 1877 and for their failure to discuss female convicts). As Muncie (2001) points out, by the late 1980s the limitations of such a polarized debate were obvious and other authors put forward a more integrated approach (Garland 1990; Wiener 1990).

Pratt (2002) argues that the prison increasingly disappeared from public view throughout the nineteenth century. As high walls and gates became a barrier to the outside world, the presence of the prison began to provoke a growing distaste: another arena of punishment (in addition to execution and forms of public punishment) 'to be pushed behind the scenes of the civilised world' (2002: 35). Pratt (2002) notes three forms of architectural design of prisons during the period from the late eighteenth to the mid nineteenth century which reflected differing views on the purpose of imprisonment and public sentiments regarding inmates (which were somewhat fickle and, as we have seen, susceptible to outside influences, including the media of the day). Prison facades thus fell into the categories of neoclassical, gothic revivalism or functional austerity. The neoclassical designs were grand and formal, sending messages to the public about the prison's interior, but closing the building off from outside scrutiny. Gothic revival designs had turrets, towers, battlements and extravagant gargoyles invoking images of medieval confinement in towers and dungeons. But both these designs were imposing in size and gave the impression of luxury and extravagance, as 'the idea of imprisonment broke free from its associations of squalor and disorder' (Pratt 2002: 39). However, both architectural styles were relatively short lived. The opening of Pentonville prison in 1842 began the dominance of 'functional austerity' in prison design that would continue throughout the nineteenth century. With the exception of the gatehouse, these prisons had no exterior decoration. For Pratt, the use of prison clock towers also symbolized the modern prison, indicating regularity and order inside, and the deprivation of time rather than physical punishment (see Reading 21 by Cohen and Taylor for a more recent analysis of the management of time in prison). Prison buildings 'had to be sufficient to inspire remorse and trepidation about what they contained within, but at the same time would leave unspecified the exact nature of the deprivations occurring inside – the observer could only imagine these' (Pratt 2002: 44).

Unlike the older prisons which were located in the centre of towns and cities, these new prisons were more likely to be built in outlying, elevated sites, slightly removed from the local community. Pratt argues that these changes in architectural design and location were:

> to transform the prison, both from its place as an unremarkable feature of everyday life … and from its place as a kind of extravagant theatre of punishment … to a place where it would be set back from but elevated above modern society: looming over it, but at the same time closed off from it, with its windowless high walls and secure gate. Its size made it unmistakable, and the austerity of its design provided a chilling and sombre threat (2002: 46).

However in the late nineteenth century there were growing views that this 'prison look' – Wormwood Scrubs in London, built in 1884 – was too austere, too threatening and too unpleasant. Pratt notes that the prison authorities in the civilized world sought to beautify the exterior of the building, not with turrets or gargoyles, but with landscape gardening, fountains and flowerbeds, 'attempting to draw a more attractive veil across what they now thought to be the unnecessarily spartan exterior of their own institutions' (2002: 48).

By the early twentieth century there was little public knowledge about the 'hidden' world of the prison. There were, of course, particular types of prisoners who drew attention to the system and its operation, notably, suffragettes, conscientious objectors to compulsory military service and other political prisoners (for example, Irish Republican prisoners) who wrote pamphlets and biographies of their prison experiences (Brown 2003). But by this time a range of non-purpose-built buildings were being utilized by the prison authorities, including army camps, airfields and country houses, as plans for new prisons were rejected by the communities in which they had wanted to place them. These new locations further assisted the camouflage and disguise of the prison and only served to make imprisonment even more remote and cut off from the rest of society (Pratt 2002).

Today, in the UK, most people – if asked to conjure up a mental image of a 'typical' prison – might imagine an institution such as HMP Shrewsbury or HMP Leicester; Victorian prisons with impressive, and sometimes austere, facades, fortress-style turrets and very visible barbed wire. Yet the prisons that have been built in this country over the last few decades are somewhat different in appearance although, with their cell-lined wings, narrow corridors and communal areas veiled with netting over the stairwells to prevent suicides, their interiors may not be as different from their Victorian predecessors as many prison reformers would wish. But just as the architectural designs of prisons built in the nineteenth century reflected the penal thinking of the time, more contemporary prison designs have mirrored recent penal evolution. It has taken a very long time, however. In the early 1960s, as attitudes to prisoners were moving from detention and retribution towards training and rehabilitation, HMP Blundeston in Suffolk opened its doors. Resembling a public school with four T-shaped cell blocks each housing just 75 inmates (as opposed to the hundreds held in the wings of prisons like Pentonville), Blundeston proved to be something of a blip in twentieth-century prison design, and most prisons dating from the 1960s conformed to the traditional model of regimented rows of corridors lined with cells – thought to be a suitable design to hold notorious 'super-criminals' such as the Krays and the Great Train Robbers (Glancey 2001).

Through the 1980s and 1990s many newly built prisons looked rather like private hospitals, no-frills chain hotels or the kind of corporate HQ you might expect to find in a business park. Run by the private security company UK Detention Services, HMP Peterborough is the first purpose-built prison in modern times to hold both men and women. Instead of the usual green-grey paintwork, Peterborough has a bright colour-coding system to identify the purpose of different parts of the prison – orange workshops, lilac activity areas and a segregation unit painted a deep red (Travis 2005). With its low-rise design, natural lighting, healthy living and alternative therapy centre, and artificial trees placed in the workshops and education block, Peterborough prison more closely resembles a shopping centre than an archetypal jailhouse. Cells have been designed with as few ligature points as possible to reduce suicide, each cell is fitted with an intercom linked to the wing office, rather than the more usual simple call button, and prisoners can control the lighting in their cells. Following an enthusiastic endorsement from the Chief Executive of the National Offenders Management Service, HMP Peterborough may become a blueprint for future prison design in the UK.

Whilst the design of new-generation prisons seems a great deal more enlightened than their austere (not to mention leaky and ill-ventilated) predecessors, it should not be forgotten that many thousands of inmates are still housed in prisons like Pentonville that were built more than a century ago. Not only are many of these institutions inadequate but, in some cases, they may even be dangerous environments for their occupants. In the last few years, several prisons in the UK have introduced measures designed to alleviate some of the worst aspects of incarceration, particularly in the first days and weeks of a sentence. These initiatives include 'first-night units' where new inmates can spend at least two nights on reception to prison in bright and comfortable surroundings, and 'listening schemes' where trained inmates provide a 'Samaritans' role for each other. But, as the readings in this collection will show, the UK has a long way to go before it can claim to have an enlightened policy on imprisonment and the legacy of Michael Howard's infamous 'Prison Works' speech (delivered in October 1993) still looms large over discussions of prisons and penal reform. Whilst the American 'supermax' is arguably the Western world's most extreme example of state-administered punishment (excluding capital punishment, of course), prisons throughout the 'advanced' world are returning to nineteenth-century models of punishment (including long hours of lockdown, segregation of prisoners, sensory deprivation, and unproductive and psychologically destructive regimes) – only, now, prison authorities have a range of sophisticated technologies at their disposal to carry out their tasks with brutal efficiency (Pratt *et al.* 2005).

Types of prison and prisoner

In this Introduction, we thought it worth providing a brief explanation about the types of prison that exist, and how inmates end up being sent to a particular prison on grounds of their security classification. Categorization of convicted offenders based on their perceived security risk is a system that has underpinned the allocation of offenders to prisons since 1966, when a committee headed by Lord Mountbatten published its findings into prison security (HMSO 1966) following a series of high-profile escapes. The system of classification proposed by Mountbatten and still in operation today is that those prisoners whose escape would be 'highly dangerous to the public or police or to the security of the State' should be classified as Category 'A' inmates. Those for whom 'escape should be made very difficult but without recourse to the highest security conditions' are Category 'B' prisoners. Category 'C' inmates are those 'who lack the resources and will to make serious escape attempts but would abscond from open prisons and should be kept in semi-secure closed custody'. Finally, Category 'D' inmates are those 'who can be reasonably trusted to serve their sentences in open conditions'. The Mountbatten Committee made another key recommendation which was that all Category A inmates should be housed together in a purpose-built, maximum-security, fortress-style prison, not dissimilar to the American supermax of today (Reading 10). However, the potential risks inherent in containing all Britain's most dangerous criminals within a single establishment 'known to all involved as the end of the road' (Home Office 1979: para. 2.33), and in recruiting officers to staff such a prison with fairness and integrity, were subsequently considered too great to overcome. The proposal was rejected two years later by the Radzinowicz Committee and instead it was proposed that Category A offenders should be 'dispersed' throughout a low number of high-security prisons where they would be a relatively small minority absorbed into the general population of mainly Category B inmates.

In addition to being of different security categories, prisons in England and Wales are of different 'types', some of which are drawn from the historical construction of the system in the nineteenth century already described. 'Local' prisons service the courts by holding those remanded in custody awaiting trial as well as sentenced prisoners. Often thought of as little more than 'transit camps' (Fitzgerald and Sim 1979) because of the constant movement and high turnover of inmates, many short-term prisoners nevertheless end up serving their entire sentences in a local prison, and increasingly even medium and long-term prisoners (that is, those serving four years or more) are housed in a 'local'. The other main type of prison is the 'training' prison, which can be 'open' or 'closed' depending on the category of prisoners being held there. The emphasis at these institutions (which include the 'dispersals'), is on work and training. Prisons which wholly or partly accommodate women may also be open or closed. In addition to these main types of prison are remand centres which may be either purpose built or part of a local or youth prison, and which have a specific brief to hold those awaiting trial or conviction, and young offenders institutions for offenders who are between 15 and 21 years of age. Finally, although most prisons are under the jurisdiction of the prison service, increasing numbers of prisons of various types and categories are run by private companies.

As well as the formalized categories outlined above, there may be other, less formal factors that contribute to the differences between prisons. Indeed, two institutions of identical security category and type can differ quite markedly, as a result of their individual histories, geographic locations, management ethos, physical (or 'situational') security measures and commitment to 'social' methods of containment and control. The experience of individual prisoners can also vary quite significantly, not least because there is a further categorization system in place which determines the level of comfort and amenities they are entitled to when serving their prison sentence. The Incentives and Earned Privileges (IEP) scheme was introduced in 1995 following the publication in 1991 of the report of the inquiry into the disturbances at Strangeways by the Chief Inspector of Prisons, Lord Justice Woolf. During the 1980s and 1990s the visible nature of the prison to the wider public was most marked through riots, disorders and prisoners protesting on the roofs of prison buildings, which were widely shown on television news and reported in the newspapers. Disturbances in prisons had begun in the 1980s and were located within the maximum-security 'dispersal' system and the long-term adult male 'training' prisons, but by 1990 there were a number of protests in local prisons. Woolf concluded that the scale and intensity of the disturbances in prisons could only be attributed to a widely shared sense of injustice (see Readings 8 and 9).

One of Woolf's key recommendations was that prisoners' rights should be formally established in the form of 'contracts' or 'compacts' between governors and inmates, setting out the legitimate expectations to which an inmate is entitled. It was Woolf's intention that institutions would have to provide, in writing, the reasons for any decisions which would adversely affect any prisoner, such as being placed in an institution of significant distance from his home or being transferred to a new prison without warning or explanation, both of which are reasonably common occurrences. However, when it came to policy formulation, the Prison Service interpreted the findings of its Chief Inspector rather loosely, so that the basic entitlements which Woolf thought that prisoners have a right to expect were, in the end, designated 'privileges' to be earned by compliance and good conduct, or withdrawn for bad behaviour or misconduct. There are essentially three categories which inmates may fall into, which determine the type and amount of privileges they can expect: Basic, Standard and Enhanced. In most prisons, inmates enter the institution on Standard regime (although in some prisons inmates may start on either of the other two levels). After a period of time (which varies from prison to prison) Standard prisoners may advance to Enhanced status if they meet the prerequired criteria. If, however, they disobey the prison rules, they may be put on to Basic regime, and in some prisons isolated in a specially segregated Basic Regime Unit (BRU), with consequent loss of status and privileges. One of the key intentions of IEP was to achieve some uniformity in the prison system as a whole. However, the anticipated coherence in policy has only been partly achieved because some acceptable earned privileges can be devised locally and some prison governors have interpreted privilege entitlement policy more liberally than others (Liebling *et al.* 1997). In fact the scheme is frequently interpreted loosely enough for the staff of some institutions to talk of a 'Super-enhanced' regime for the especially well behaved, and a 'sub-basic' regime for the especially troublesome. In the case of the former, accommodation is often separated from the main wings, and might afford inmates particular 'luxuries': carpets, washing machines, satellite television and the like. The latter usually refers either to the prison's segregation unit or 'punishment block', or to the threat of being moved to another wing or even being 'shipped out' to a more notorious prison.

Prison readings

Finally, let us introduce you to the book itself. As we already hope to have demonstrated, the establishment of the prison as the main form of punishment during the late eighteenth and early nineteenth century is central to any understanding of imprisonment and the philosophies underpinning it. The opening part of *Prison Readings,* 'The emergence of the modern prison', thus provides a contextual framework for the remainder of the book, and contains extracts elaborating on different aspects of imprisonment between the end of the eighteenth and the middle of the nineteenth century. This section is concerned to chart the fundamental changes in punishment at this time, the movement away from public torture and execution to the ordered and highly regulated prison that focused on the mind of the prisoners rather than the infliction of pain on the body. It is also concerned with the operation of prison regimes and how penal theory was applied to different types of prisoners and in different kinds of prisons. In particular, the extracts are concerned with the role of the prison chaplain and religion within the prison regime, the application of Victorian penal theory to female prisoners and the operation of local prisons in the nineteenth century.

Part B, 'Theoretical approaches and emerging trends', is concerned broadly with the use, management and operation of imprisonment and prisons. Thus the section examines key issues and recent trends in the management of prisons, through an examination of prison privatization and the rise of the 'supermax', together with theoretical perspectives on key current debates and reflections on longer-standing issues within prison research. It is also, therefore, concerned with the operation of prison regimes, and raises questions regarding legitimacy, order and control, and therapeutic communities. In examining the various approaches to the operation of prisons, it also asks questions about whether prison regimes can work effectively to reform or rehabilitate and indeed questions whether we should retain prisons at all.

Part C brings together a number of readings on 'Prison populations'. The section includes statistics on the demography of the prison population as a context for discussion, but is also concerned with the qualitative experience of life in custody, a theme which is developed further in Part D. The extracts cover various groups of prison inmates, initially focusing on gender. We start with a discussion of men and issues relating to masculinity (prisons are frequently said to be 'hyper-masculine' environments) and then move on to concerns relating to the imprisonment of women, reflecting key issues of drug use, bullying, violence and the imprisonment of women with young children. An autobiographical account of one woman's experience in prison is also included. Subsequently, the section provides extracts concerned with the rising number of inmates from ethnic minority backgrounds and the problems of racism and racist victimization in prison. Incarceration is then examined in relation to paramilitary prisoners and, finally, the imprisonment of children and young people.

Having established the diversity of the prison population, Part D, 'The prison community', explores the extent to which the purposes and aims of imprisonment impact upon the lived experience of incarceration. In other words, the section explores prison conditions and inmate responses to them via a selection of classic and contemporary texts. Focusing primarily on the prison's punitive function, Part D is concerned with the 'effects' of imprisonment and the various strategies that prisoners employ in order to cope with, and adapt to, a period of confinement. This section also examines aspects of the prison community from the perspectives of prison staff, a 'prison population' who are frequently overlooked or lacking prominence in the prisons literature.

The final section, Part E, is concerned with 'Current controversies'. It explores some of the most controversial issues that are currently affecting prisons and shaping penal policy. Unsurprisingly, there are a large number of 'current controversies' that – because of limitations of space – have been missed out, but some of these are picked up and discussed in the Conclusion of this collection. The controversies discussed in Part E include: social exclusion; suicide and self-harm; the drugs economy in prison; mental health issues and the authorities' attempts to control 'risky populations'; gendered experiences of indeterminate sentencing; prison labour; and prisoners' rights within the context of the European Convention on Human Rights.

As a final point before you delve into the extracts we've chosen, we would encourage you to follow up your reading of this book by going to the original texts from which these pieces have been selected and seeking out some of the research cited in the commentaries and by the authors represented in this collection. In this way, we would hope that *Prison Readings* will stand as a stimulating introduction to the key dimensions and debates which characterize the field of prisons and imprisonment and act as a springboard for further, and enriched, study.

References

Brown, A. (2003) *English Society and the Prison – Time, Culture and Politics in the Development of the Modern Prison, 1850–1920*. Woodbridge: Boydell.

Emsley, C. (2005) *Crime and Society in England 1750–1900* (3rd edn). Harlow: Longman.

Fitzgerald, M. and Sim, J. (1979) *British Prisons*. Oxford: Blackwell.

Foucault, M. (1977) *Discipline and Punish – The Birth of the Prison*. London: Penguin Books.

Garland, D. (1990) *Punishment and Modern Society: A Study in Social Theory*. Oxford: Clarendon Press.

Gatrell, V.A.C. (1994) *The Hanging Tree: Execution and the English People 1770–1868*. Oxford: Oxford University Press.

Glancey, J. (2001) 'Within these walls', *Guardian* (1 February) (www.guardian.co.uk).

HMSO (1966) Report of the inquiry into prison escapes and security by Admiral of the Fleet, the Earl Mountbatten of Burma, London: HMSO.

Hughes, R. (1996) *The Fatal Shore: A History of the Transportation of Convicts to Australia, 1787–1868*. London: Harvill Press.

Ignatieff, M. (1978) *A Just Measure of Pain: The Penitentiary in the Industrial Revolution 1750–1850*. Basingstoke: Macmillan.

Ignatieff, M. (1985) 'State, civil society and total institutions: a critique of recent social histories of punishment', in S. Cohen and A. Scull (eds) *Social Control and the State*. Oxford: Blackwell.

Johnston, H. (2006) ' "Buried alive": representations of the separate system in Victorian England', in P. Mason (ed.) *Captured by the Media: Prison Discourse in Popular Culture*. Cullompton: Willan Publishing.

Liebling, A., Muir, G., Rose, G. and Bottoms, A. (1997) *An Evaluation of Incentives and Earned Privileges: Final Report to the Prison Service. Vol. 1*. July.

McConville, S. (1981) *A History of Prison Administration. Volume One. 1750–1877*. London: Routledge & Kegan Paul.

McGowen, R. (1998) 'The well-ordered prison: England, 1780–1865' in N. Morris and D.J. Rothman (eds) *The Oxford History of the Prison: The practice of punishment in western society*. New York: Oxford University Press.

Melossi, D. and Pavarini, M. (1981) *The Prison and the Factory – Origins of the Penitentiary System*. Basingstoke: Macmillan.

Muncie, J. (2001) 'Prison histories: reform, repression and rehabilitation', in E. McLaughlin and J. Muncie (eds) *Controlling Crime*. London: Sage.

Pratt, J. (2002) *Punishment and Civilisation*. London: Sage.

Pratt, J., Brown, D., Brown, M., Hallsworth, S. and Morrison, W. (2005) *The New Punitiveness: Trends, Theories, Perspectives*. Cullompton: Willan Publishing.

Rothman, D.J. (1971) *The Discovery of the Asylum: Social Order and Disorder in the New Republic*. Boston, MA: Little, Brown.

Shaw, A.G.L. (1998) *Convicts and the Colonies: A Study of Penal Transportation from Great Britain and Ireland to Australia and Other Parts of the British Empire*. Irish Historial Press.

Stockdale, E. (1977) *A Study of Bedford Prison, 1660–1877*. London: Phillimore.

Tomlinson, M.H. (1981) 'Penal servitude 1846–1865: a system in evolution,' in V. Bailey (ed.) *Policing and Punishment in Nineteenth Century Britain*. London: Croom Helm.

Travis, A. (2005) 'Ministers say new private jail means end for prison ship', *Guardian* (10 March) (www.guardian.co.uk).

Webb, S. and Webb, B. (1963) *English Prisons under Local Government*. London: Frank Cass.

Whiting, J.R.S. (1975) *Prison Reform in Gloucestershire, 1776–1820*. London: Phillimore.

Wiener, M. (1990) *Reconstructing the Criminal: Culture, Law and Policy in England, 1830–1914*. Cambridge: Cambridge University Press.

Part A

The emergence of the modern prison

Introduction

Part A of this reader develops some of the discussions and debates set up in the Introduction, offering a more focused account of the prison's historical context. The part is principally concerned with the end of the eighteenth to the mid-nineteenth century, a period which has been identified as crucial in the development of the modern prison and is often referred to as the time when the prison was 'born' and when imprisonment became the predominant form of punishment in Western society.

Before the late eighteenth century, the prison existed in two predominant forms: the gaol and the bridewell (or house of correction). The gaol was purely a place of detention for those awaiting trial, execution or committed for debt. It was a profit-making enterprise with fees charged for admission, discharge, food, lodgings and the 'tap' (an alehouse for prisoners and visitors), which meant that those with money or family support were able to ameliorate the circumstances of their imprisonment. However, as the majority of prisoners were relatively impoverished, 'starvation, intimidation, disease, and desperation were the lot of the poor prisoner certainly until the late eighteenth century' (McConville 1998: 275). The bridewell or house of correction had existed from the mid-sixteenth century to receive prisoners for punishment and reformation through hard labour and discipline. It mainly held those found guilty of petty crime such as disorderly behaviour, begging and vagrancy – precisely those crimes associated with the poor (Innes 1987).

Reformers such as John Howard travelled throughout Britain and Europe in the late eighteenth century visiting gaols and bridewells, and wrote extensively about the deprived conditions within them. As some local magistrates, and later the government, took on board Howard's criticisms at the beginning of the nineteenth century there began the establishment of a different kind of penal institution in which prisoners were classified or (later) held in separate cells and routinized through a timetable. The new institutions were clean and were constructed around the belief that, through hard work, religion and solitude, the prisoner could be transformed into a law-abiding citizen. By the mid to late nineteenth century, public execution had ceased and capital punishment was retained only for murder and treason. The transportation of convicts to

13

the colonies had also ended by the late 1860s and so the prison became the predominant form of punishment in England and many other Western societies.

This shift in the use of imprisonment and the changing nature of prisons have thus been of particular interest to historians and criminologists. The orthodox or Whig histories of this period have broadly located the developments at the end of the eighteenth century in terms of humanitarian reform and progress. The decline in the use of execution and the rise of imprisonment as the predominant form of punishment are seen as a more humane and 'civilized' method of punishment replacing the barbaric and arbitrary system of old (Emsley 2005). From this perspective, the disorder and squalor of the old gaols and bridewells were replaced by the new regimented, healthy and orderly prison of the nineteenth century. However, revisionist historians, such as that from which our first reading is chosen, have criticized the Whig accounts for their purely progressive, humanitarian account of this transformation and have broadly argued that the changes that occurred in punishment during this period were based around notions of greater social control (see the Introduction).

The first extract, then, is taken from Michel Foucault's *Discipline and Punish* and clearly illustrates the change the author is addressing in his thesis on the birth of the prison, contrasting the horrific public torture and execution of Damiens, hung drawn and quartered for attempted regicide in 1757, with the minutely detailed timetable of a reformatory for young offenders at Mettray in France 80 years later. For Foucault this demonstrates a fundamental change in punishment, from the public bodily punishment of the offender in the eighteenth century, to the highly regulated prison in which the mind and soul of the offender are the central concern of the institution by the mid-nineteenth century. This extract is just the starting point for Foucault's work in this area, and we would urge you to follow this extract by reading *Discipline and Punish* – and its many critiques and commentaries – more fully.

Central to the prison regime in the early to mid-nineteenth century was religion. During the 1820s and 1830s there was national and international debate over two contrasting methods of reformatory prison regimes. First, the separate system, which had already been implemented in some prisons in the USA, and which was receiving strong approval from the recently appointed government inspectors in England. Under the separate system prisoners would be kept apart at all times, held alone in separate cells where they would work, sleep and take meals. The only time they would leave their cell was to attend chapel, when their faces would be masked, or for exercise during which they might be sent to separate exercise yards. The aim was to avoid any contact with other prisoners, particularly for young or first-time offenders who were thought more prone to 'contamination' from more hardened criminals. Prisoners may also have been visited by the prison chaplain, whose sermons and preaching were used to encourage offenders to reflect on their criminal activities, repent and 'look to God' in order that they would be religiously and morally transformed on leaving the prison. The second system was the silent system, whereby prisoners were to be silent at all times. They were allowed to associate but would work at hard labour. Again, non-communication was a preventative method to avoid the corrupting influences of the more hardened prisoner, but also the system was constructed to deter offending behaviour and to instil habits of industry.

The next reading in this section consists of two extracts taken from the memoir of Reverend John Clay, written up by his son Walter as *The Prison Chaplain*, and published in 1861. Clay was the chaplain at Preston House of Correction in Lancashire and was active in mid-nineteenth-century penal debates. These extracts, from the reports of 1846 and 1847, are included for a number of reasons; first, they provide the reader with original documents from the period, including Clay's reports to the magistrates in Lancashire which were part of his administrative duties at the prison. Secondly, they demonstrate the way in which penal philosophies and practices operated in one prison during this period, and Clay provides some comparison with other local and government-run prisons of the time. Thirdly, they offer the views of one prison chaplain on reformation and deterrent principles. Clay, clearly an advocate of reformatory principles, argues that all prisoners, except a few whose disposition allowed no hope, would benefit from the reformatory principle. Through religious and moral instruction, periods of separation to reflect and protection from the contaminating influences of other prisoners, Clay and other commentators believed that the reformatory system could have a lasting effect on transforming the offender and reducing crime.

Feminist writers have since criticized both the Whig and revisionists accounts for their lack of discussion of women's imprisonment during this period. Few authors have attempted to 'redress the gender imbalance which remained after the new social histories of the 1970s revised the story of nineteenth and early twentieth century penal systems' (Howe 1994: 133). However, over recent decades there have been some contributions to the field which have provided a revisionist history of punishment and imprisonment of women (e.g. Freedman 1981; Rafter 1985; Dobash *et al.* 1986). Reading 3 is taken from one such contribution, Lucia Zedner's 'Women and penal theory'. Zedner examines the application of nineteenth-century penal theory to women prisoners and the role of female reformers and Lady Visitors within this process. She argues that women were not, as some authors have argued, absent from penal discussions, but that they posed a particular problem to prison administrators, as policies and practices (predominantly constructed for male prisoners) often had to be adapted or modified when applied to women.

A number of authors have also challenged the revisionist accounts of the birth of the prison through their examinations of local prisons (e.g. Forsythe 1983; DeLacy 1986; Johnston 2004). To summarize, these authors broadly argue that many of the key strategies within the prison regime discussed by Foucault and other revisionist historians were only gradually incorporated into local prisons. Regimes and practices in local prisons remained diverse and often 'fell short of government showpieces such as Pentonville' (Saunders 1986: 79). Research by these commentators seems to suggest that the transformation of the prison to the minutely organized 'total' institution was a more protracted and gradual process than Foucault and others within the revisionist perspective have argued.

Reading 4, entitled 'Grinding men good? Lancashire's prisons at mid-century', is taken from Margaret E. DeLacy's research on local prisons. She is concerned with the extent to which the revisionist theories of 'social control' describe the circumstances of prison life in Lancashire at this time. The extract examines the implementation of prison discipline, highlighting some of the views of prison officials and the chaplain, the Reverend John Clay, on the operation of these regimes. DeLacy argues that Lancashire was quite 'lacklustre' in its approach to the separate system. Delays were caused by the financial costs of altering the prison buildings and, by the time suitable cells were constructed, the separate system had fallen from use. When built, the numbers of prisoners committed to these prisons often meant that prisoners shared cells and thus were not completely separated. DeLacy maintains that although the prisons of the 1840s were very different from those existing at the end of the eighteenth century they were 'never quite "those machines for grinding men good" that the reformers have claimed and the critics have charged'.

Reading 5 is taken from Philip Priestley's 'Prisoners' and gives us some insight into those who were subject to these prison regimes during the nineteenth century. Drawing on prisoners' biographies, prison chaplains' accounts, views of penal commentators and government inquiries, this extract offers a descriptive account, piecing together a picture of the Victorian prison population. For reasons of space an extract that discusses broad views on the working classes, and the dangerous and criminal classes, has been chosen rather than one that focuses on specific groups of prisoners such as women, juveniles or middle/upper-class prisoners.

The final reading in this part examines the prison during the mid-Victorian period. In 'The well-ordered prison: England, 1780–1865', Randall McGowen argues that from the 1850s and 1860s the focus of the prison regime became increasingly concerned with deterrence as the ability of the prison to reform criminals was brought into question. There are a number of factors that influenced the changes in penal philosophy during this period, as we saw in the Introduction to this reader. McGowen summarizes these changes and discusses the contradictions that emerged in highly regulated prison regimes whereby the detailed rules and regulations, already alluded to by Foucault in Reading 1, which governed every aspect of the prisoners' life, had the effect of defeating the reformers' aspirations to transform the offender. This extract also discusses the ways in which prisoners tried to subvert this oppressive regime by communicating through the prison piping system, learning ventriloquism or mastering tricks to ease the demands of hard labour. McGowen argues that, paradoxically, many aspects of the prison regime that were implemented to aid the reformatory endeavour became part of strategies to ensure severe conditions and improve management. But by far the most important and enduring legacy of this period was to sever the prison from the rest of society. The changes that were established in the prison system by the 1860s would have a lasting effect on the way in which prisoners were treated and on the operation of the prison system, at least until the Gladstone Committee at the end of the nineteenth century.

References

DeLacy, M. (1986) *Prison Reform in Lancashire, 1700–1850 – A Study in Local Administration.* Manchester: Manchester University Press.

Dobash, R.P., Dobash, R.E. and Gutteridge, S. (1986) *The Imprisonment of Women.* Oxford: Blackwell.

Emsley, C. (2005) *Crime and Society in England 1750–1900* (3rd edn). Harlow: Longman.

Forsythe, W.J. (1983) *A System of Discipline – Exeter Borough Prison 1819–1863*. Exeter: Exeter University Press.

Freedman, E. (1981) *Their Sisters' Keepers: Women's Prison Reform in America 1830–1930*. Ann Arbor, MI: University of Michigan Press.

Howe, A. (1994) *Punish and Critique: Towards a Feminist Analysis of Penalty*. London: Routledge.

Innes, J. (1987) 'Prisons for the poor: English bridewells, 1555–1800', in F. Snyder and D. Hay (eds) *Labour, Law and Crime: An Historical Perspective*. London: Tavistock.

Johnston, H. (2004) 'The transformation of imprisonment in a local context: a case-study of Shrewsbury in the nineteenth century.' Unpublished PhD thesis, University of Keele.

McConville, S. (1998) 'Local justice: the jail', in N. Morris and D.J. Rothman (eds) *The Oxford History of the Prison – The Practice of Punishment in Western Society*. Oxford: Oxford University Press.

Rafter, N.H. (1985) *Partial Justice: Women in State Prisons 1800–1935*. Boston, MA: Northeastern University Press.

Saunders, J. (1986) 'Warwickshire magistrates and prison reform, 1840–1875', *Midland History*, XI: 79–99.

1. The body of the condemned

Michel Foucault

On 2 March 1757 Damiens the regicide was condemned 'to make the *amende honorable* before the main door of the Church of Paris', where he was to be 'taken and conveyed in a cart, wearing nothing but a shirt, holding a torch of burning wax weighing two pounds'; then, 'in the said cart, to the Place de Grève, where, on a scaffold that will be erected there, the flesh will be torn from his breasts, arms, thighs and calves with red hot pincers, his right hand, holding the knife with which he committed the said parricide, burnt with sulphur, and, on those places where the flesh will be torn away, poured molten lead, boiling oil, burning resin, wax and sulphur melted together and then his body drawn and quartered by four horses and his limbs and body consumed by fire, reduced to ashes and his ashes thrown to the winds' (*Pièces originales …*, 372–4).

'Finally, he was quartered,' recounts the *Gazette d'Amsterdam* of 1 April 1757. 'This last operation was very long, because the horses used were not accustomed to drawing; consequently, instead of four, six were needed; and when that did not suffice, they were forced, in order to cut off the wretch's thighs, to sever the sinews and hack at the joints …

'It is said that, though he was always a great swearer, no blasphemy escaped his lips; but the excessive pain made him utter horrible cries, and he often repeated: "My God, have pity on me! Jesus, help me!" The spectators were all edified by the solicitude of the parish priest of St Paul's who despite his great age did not spare himself in offering consolation to the patient.'

Bouton, an officer of the watch, left us his account: 'The sulphur was lit, but the flame was so poor that only the top skin of the hand was burnt, and that only slightly. Then the executioner, his sleeves rolled up, took the steel pincers, which had been especially made for the occasion, and which were about a foot and a half long, and pulled first at the calf of the right leg, then at the thigh, and from there at the two fleshy parts of the right arm; then at the breasts. Though a strong, sturdy fellow, this executioner found it so difficult to tear away the pieces of flesh that he set about the same spot two or three times, twisting the pincers as he did so, and what he took away formed at each part a wound about the size of a six pound crown piece.

'After these tearings with the pincers, Damiens, who cried profusely, though without swearing, raised his head and looked at himself; the same executioner dipped an iron spoon in the pot containing the boiling potion, which he poured liberally over each wound. Then the ropes that were to be harnessed to the horses were attached with cords to the patient's body; the horses were then harnessed and placed alongside the arms and legs, one at each limb.

'Monsieur Le Breton, the clerk of the court, went up to the patient several times and asked him if he had anything to say. He said he had not; at each torment, he cried out, as the damned in hell are supposed to cry out, "Pardon, my God! Pardon, Lord". Despite all this pain, he raised his head from time to time and looked at himself boldly. The cords had been tied so tightly by the men who pulled the ends that they caused him indescribable pain. Monsieur Le Breton went up to him again and asked him if he had anything to say; he said no. Several confessors went up to him and spoke to him at length; he willingly kissed the crucifix that was held out to him; he opened his lips and repeated: "Pardon, Lord."

'The horses tugged hard, each pulling straight on a limb, each horse held by an executioner. After a quarter of an hour, the same ceremony was repeated and finally, after several attempts, the direction of the horses had to be changed, thus: those at the arms were made to pull towards the head, those at the thighs towards the arms, which broke the arms at the joints. This was repeated several times without success. He raised his head and looked at himself. Two more horses had to be added to those harnessed to the thighs, which made six horses in all. Without success.

'Finally, the executioner, Samson, said to Monsieur Le Breton that there was no way or hope of succeeding, and told him to ask their Lordships if they wished him to have the prisoner cut into pieces. Monsieur Le Breton, who had come down from the town, ordered that renewed efforts be made, and this was done; but the horses gave up and one of those harnessed to the thighs fell to the ground. The confessors returned and spoke to him again. He said to them (I heard him): "Kiss me, gentlemen." The parish priest of St Paul's did not dare to, so Monsieur de Marsilly slipped under the rope holding the left arm and kissed him on the forehead. The executioners gathered round and Damiens told them not to swear, to carry out their task and that he did not think ill of them; he begged them to pray to God for him, and asked the parish priest of St Paul's to pray for him at the first mass.

'After two or three attempts, the executioner Samson and he who had used the pincers each drew out a knife from his pocket and cut the body at the thighs instead of severing the legs at the joints; the four horses gave a tug and carried off the two thighs after them, namely, that of the right side first, the other following; then the same was done to the arms, the shoulders, the arm-pits and the four limbs; the flesh had to be cut almost to the bone, the horses pulling hard carried off the right arm first and the other afterwards.

'When the four limbs had been pulled away, the confessors came to speak to him; but his executioner told them that he was dead, though the truth was that I saw the man move, his lower jaw moving from side to side as if he were talking. One of the executioners even said shortly afterwards that when they had lifted the trunk to throw it on the stake, he was still alive. The four limbs were untied from the ropes and thrown on the stake set up in the

19

enclosure in line with the scaffold, then the trunk and the rest were covered with logs and faggots, and fire was put to the straw mixed with this wood.

'... In accordance with the decree, the whole was reduced to ashes. The last piece to be found in the embers was still burning at half past ten in the evening. The pieces of flesh and the trunk had taken about four hours to burn. The officers of whom I was one, as also was my son, and a detachment of archers remained in the square until nearly eleven o'clock.

'There were those who made something of the fact that a dog had lain the day before on the grass where the fire had been, had been chased away several times, and had always returned. But it is not difficult to understand that an animal found this place warmer than elsewhere' (quoted in Zevaes, 201–14).

Eighty years later, Léon Faucher drew up his rules 'for the House of young prisoners in Paris':

'Art. 17. The prisoners' day will begin at six in the morning in winter and at five in summer. They will work for nine hours a day throughout the year. Two hours a day will be devoted to instruction. Work and the day will end at nine o'clock in winter and at eight in summer.

Art. 18. *Rising*. At the first drum-roll, the prisoners must rise and dress in silence, as the supervisor opens the cell doors. At the second drum-roll, they must be dressed and make their beds. At the third, they must line up and proceed to the chapel for morning prayer. There is a five-minute interval between each drum-roll.

Art. 19. The prayers are conducted by the chaplain and followed by a moral or religious reading. This exercise must not last more than half an hour.

Art. 20. *Work*. At a quarter to six in the summer, a quarter to seven in winter, the prisoners go down into the courtyard where they must wash their hands and faces, and receive their first ration of bread. Immediately afterwards, they form into work-teams and go off to work, which must begin at six in summer and seven in winter.

Art. 21. *Meal*. At ten o'clock the prisoners leave their work and go to the refectory; they wash their hands in their courtyards and assemble in divisions. After the dinner, there is recreation until twenty minutes to eleven.

Art. 22. *School*. At twenty minutes to eleven, at the drum-roll, the prisoners form into ranks, and proceed in divisions to the school. The class lasts two hours and consists alternately of reading, writing, drawing and arithmetic.

Art. 23. At twenty minutes to one, the prisoners leave the school, in divisions, and return to their courtyards for recreation. At five minutes to one, at the drum-roll, they form into work-teams.

Art. 24. At one o'clock they must be back in the workshop: they work until four o'clock.

Art. 25. At four o'clock the prisoners leave their workshops and go into the courtyards where they wash their hands and form into divisions for the refectory.

Art. 26. Supper and the recreation that follows it last until five o'clock: the prisoners then return to the workshops.

Art. 27. At seven o'clock in the summer, at eight in winter, work stops; bread is distributed for the last time in the workshops. For a quarter of an hour one of the prisoners or supervisors reads a passage from some instructive or uplifting work. This is followed by evening prayer.

Art. 28. At half-past seven in summer, half-past eight in winter, the prisoners must be back in their cells after the washing of hands and the inspection of clothes in the courtyard; at the first drum-roll, they must undress, and at the second get into bed. The cell doors are closed and the supervisors go the rounds in the corridors, to ensure order and silence' (Faucher, 274–82).

We have, then, a public execution and a time-table. They do not punish the same crimes or the same type of delinquent. But they each define a certain penal style. Less than a century separates them. It was a time when, in Europe and in the United States, the entire economy of punishment was redistributed. It was a time of great 'scandals' for traditional justice, a time of innumerable projects for reform. It saw a new theory of law and crime, a new moral or political justification of the right to punish; old laws were abolished, old customs died out. 'Modern' codes were planned or drawn up: Russia, 1769; Prussia, 1780; Pennsylvania and Tuscany, 1786; Austria, 1788; France, 1791, Year IV, 1808 and 1810. It was a new age for penal justice. [...]

From Discipline and Punish: The Birth of the Prison *(London: Penguin Books), 1991, pp. 3–7.*

References

Faucher, L., *De la réforme des prisons*, 1838.
Gazette d'Amsterdam, 1 April, 1757.
Pièces originales et procédures du procès fait à Robert-François Damiens, III, 1757.
Zevaes, A.L., *Damiens le régicide*, 1937.

2. The prison chaplain: Memoirs of Reverend John Clay

Walter Lowe Clay

From the Report for 1846

'… It was once a truth so fully recognised as to become proverbial, that *"a criminal came out of prison worse than when he went in"'*. To the young criminal the proverb bore a special application. His vicious education, begun in parental poverty, or neglect, or bad example, was completed in Gaol. Leaving that finishing school of crime, he carried out with him a spirit which contaminated the companions of his labour, or his idleness, and even the members of his family. He became a local centre and agent of demoralization. If unable to renew the associations which he had formed in prison, he organized new ones from fresh materials; he gathered round him a gang of idle or neglected lads, who, interested in his prison stories, and emulous of the heroes of them, without either parents or principles to save them from the danger awaiting them, soon became active in crime … So far back as 1831, when the population from which they were derived was only 286,400, of sixty-four boys under twenty years of age indicted at these sessions for felony, thirty-seven were *associated in gangs*. In 1837, forty-four boys were so connected; in 1838, forty-two; and each group of young criminals comprised a leader duly qualified for his post by a previous training in Gaol. On conviction, the adept was transported, and his pupils sentenced to a short imprisonment, which sufficed, however, to complete their training in crime, and in due – i.e. a very short – time to render them ripe for transportation. It was thus that crime was propagated and punished, and a stream of demoralization poured into some of our most valuable colonies. I am unconscious of the slightest exaggeration in the foregoing statement. For more than twenty years I have seen a House of Correction operating as a seminary of sin; and wherever the association of prisoners is permitted, there the work of corruption is still going on! But if I have often deplored my inability to stimulate attention to the subject, and procure a remedy for the evil, I have, at last, the satisfaction to know that whatever lingering or caution there may have been in moving along the path of reform, the authorities of this Gaol were not only, among the first to recognise the necessity for abolishing association among convicted prisoners; but, as I believe, were *the first* to take the most momentous step ever yet taken in prison reform, by sanctioning *the individual separation of the untried*. Let us look at the result of this separation, and we shall find the moral condition of the discharged prisoner *now*, in most happy contrast with what I have attempted to describe above. The prisoner is not now dismissed from his confinement with an imagination heated by the tales of successful plunder which he has heard in 'the yard', and with a determination to rival the exploits of Turpin and Sheppard. Now, instead of exciting others to crime he is himself desirous to forsake it. He has no stories for his acquaintance redolent of the treadwheel and trial yard; but when he speaks of prison, he speaks of stern, but wholesome, restraint; of friendly admonition, of the good thoughts which came into his mind when alone in his cell, of his grief for the grief he has caused to those who loved him, of his penitence for his fault, of his prayers for forgiveness, and of his resolution, by God's grace, to sin no more ...'

[After referring to the good accounts received from the police concerning forty-two out of sixty prisoners liberated from separate confinement] ... 'I have yet further evidence in support of the views I advocate, which, if not more convincing than what I have already brought forward, is perhaps more interesting, – that of the prisoners themselves. During the process of self-examination which a prisoner, capable of exercising it, must undergo in his cell, he is encouraged to review his past life, and to trace to their source his faults and sufferings. Many of the prisoners have availed themselves of this encouragement in a way which, while useful to themselves, will be, I think, also useful to those who inquire into the mental and moral state of the labouring classes. They have written, and sometimes dictated to me or to the schoolmaster, short narratives of their lives, their delinquencies, their self-convictions, and their penitence. Of these narratives I possess a volume consisting of more than 300 folio (MS.) pages; and it is scarcely too much to say that while evincing the beneficial process going on in the writers' minds, every page illustrates a history of which we are yet too ignorant, – the actual social and moral state of our poor fellow-subjects. Yet the native strong sense of the Anglo-Saxon character shines through almost every tale of temptation and sin, and must add to our regret that such materials for building up a "great nation – an understanding people", should lie neglected and exposed to influences equally injurious to their physical and moral state. We see them, boys or men, as they appear at one period, sinking beneath the moral evils which, sometimes surrounding them at their birth, sometimes involving them afterwards, too often beset their position in the *world*; and again, after a time of chastening, we see them prepared to occupy a better and happier place in the community, their mental and religious capabilities having been developed in *prison!* ...

'Within the last year an improvement has been made with regard to the *dress* of the prisoners. From a very early period convicts under sentence of imprisonment were distinguished by a costume of red and yellow, and those under sentence of transportation by one of blue and yellow. To many of the prisoners such a dress was a great and useless aggravation of punishment, and must have militated in some degree against the disposition of mind which it was our endeavour to induce; while at the same time it intimated to all the prisoners the nature of the offence for which each one was incarcerated.

23

The dress now for all classes is grey, with such slight distinctions as are equally inoffensive to the eye and the feelings, and are only intelligible to the officers.

'Before dismissing this subject, I would beg it to be remembered that the discipline here was instituted and is continued as an *experiment*. Based, like that of Pentonville and Reading, upon what I am fully convinced is the essential principle of a reformatory system – *encellulement* – separation; it differs in some not unimportant particulars from the plans pursued in those prisons, by permitting the prisoners to *see each other* at exercise and during Divine worship in chapel. After three years' trial of this mode of treatment, and considering the results as detailed in the present Report, I presume to recommend its continuance. The great, if not the only, objection to the prisoners seeing each other on these occasions, is that it may lead to *future recognition*: and that an ill-disposed offender may attempt or drive again into crime another who may be endeavouring to live honestly, – that a malicious criminal may denounce a reformed one to the master who has given him work, and so procure his dismissal from his situation. I admit and lament the possibility that such things *may* occur. But there are recognitions equally, if not *more* injurious to a reformed prisoner's future welfare which *cannot* be guarded against. To say nothing of the practice which cannot, without a great sacrifice of time and convenience, be dispensed with, of swearing the jury to a great number of arraignments at the same time, the dock being sometimes crowded with prisoners, – each individual prisoner, on taking his trial, is exposed to the gaze of hundreds of spectators; most of whom are idle or profligate characters, attracted to the Court House by sympathy with the accused. The recognition of the prisoner by these persons is unavoidable, so long as justice is administered publicly; and the probabilities of such recognition are much more numerous than those which relate to fellow-prisoners. But the recognitions most prejudicial to a reformed prisoner take place when, at the expiration of his sentence, he returns, as most prisoners do from this gaol, home. There he is recognised by all his former profligate associates; who, having so far escaped justice, or having been made more wicked by prison association, are much more likely to tempt him again into crime, than the former fellow-prisoner, even should he meet with him, in whom wholesome discipline and reflection may have wrought a good work; and from whom he is more likely to find encouragement in well-doing than in sin. And again, recognition even by those of his own rank who have borne comparatively good characters may be – *is*, – prejudicial. Too often their pride or ill-nature, their sarcasms or ridicule, drives the liberated prisoner from the situation which a wise and kind master, cognisant of his past misconduct, but with faith in his future steadiness, may have placed him in; and causes him to incur the temptations which accompany idleness or distress. I have known injurious consequences from this kind of recognition, but never from the recognition of one who had been a fellow-prisoner under the separate system. But it may be said, – the prisoners see each other in chapel, where they are seated so closely together that communication may take place, though it cannot do so at exercise, where they are separated by intervals of nine or ten yards. I believe the arrangements in the chapel render communication among the prisoners impracticable; and such is the earnest and unfeigned attention to the purposes for which they are met, that I feel assured there is little or no inclination to attempt it. Besides, the prisoners assemble and meet together "for *common prayer*"; "with *one accord* to make their *common* supplications" unto Him who "pardoneth and absolveth all them that truly repent". Does this association in prayer consist with complete local isolation? And is it not desirable, whenever it can be done, to cultivate congregational feeling? As a congregation the behaviour of the prisoners in this Gaol is not merely decorous but exemplary: it is a weekly and daily test of their power of self-control, an evidence of their soberness of thought, if not of their pious feelings. It is a proof that when gathered together to worship God, they may be freed from almost all restraint but that of their reverence for Him. Their meeting in chapel is a privilege (and I know it is highly esteemed) which *I never see* abused, and to which I think they are entitled so long as they manifest such a full and grateful sense of it. I have always considered and urged that the great objects to be accomplished by the individual separation of prisoners were the abolition of all intercourse among them, and giving them opportunities for self-examination and the cultivation of better feelings; but if, in addition to these views, it is deemed right to enforce isolation at exercise and in chapel, in order to prevent the possibility of future recognition, then, I submit, it is necessary to go much further, and not only to screen prisoners from each other and from the public, when put upon their trials, but, on their discharge, to send them to neighbourhoods where they will not be known.

'I feel that there are other points in this matter deserving of consideration. The prisoners here, unlike those of Pentonville, are *suddenly* taken from the agitation of common life, and after a certain period *suddenly* thrown into it again. Both changes must have a powerful effect on ordinary minds. Take the case of a railway labourer. His removal from coarse associations and pleasures and great personal liberty to a state of perfect external quietude and restraint must produce a great mental effect, sometimes irritating, sometimes depressing the spirits. But as the first unpleasant effects of an efficacious medicine are followed by a restoration to health, so the moral remedy in this case, though at first distressing, eventually induces better and happier feelings. The desired effects of his treatment become visible in the prisoner; his dormant intelligence awakes, the Divinity stirs within him, he is born again to a higher and more spiritual existence, a sober calm settles upon his heart, and his cell is no longer a dreary and unfruitful solitude. But he has now to return to his former life, to his active labour, to his unthinking, if not brutal, companions; and *without any intermediate step or preparation*. Here is a second change as great as the former one, – and more critical. Now, I think that the first change is alleviated, and that the preparation is made for the second, by the daily view which a prisoner has of his fellows, undergoing the same treatment which, even if he does not feel it, he is assured is intended to benefit both himself and them: his proper gregarious feelings are kept alive, and he is better prepared to resume his place in the world than he would be if isolated entirely, and up to the moment of his liberation. And I must say, that even with the daily habituation to the sight of each other, the mental and physical state of separated prisoners requires careful attention. Few can conceive the nature of those feelings which bring daily tears from eyes that never wept since childhood, and prompt the disturbed or penitent sinner to lay open to his minister a mind which it is almost awful to contemplate!

'Such, in short, is cellular discipline when applied to the subjects I have described – to those who have been brought suddenly from active life to be suddenly restored to it – that, convinced as I am of its extraordinary power in producing, by God's grace, amendment and reformation, I am yet unwilling to recommend a more rigid application of it, by depriving prisoners of the view of each other either when at exercise or when engaged in "common prayer".'

From report for 1847

'… Adopting the main principle of individual separation, other and minor features of discpline are different in different prisons. In the Model Prison at Pentonville, where separation is enforced in its fullest integrity, a course of superior religious instruction is combined with instruction in a trade. To the attainment of these important objects twelve or eighteen months can be devoted, so that the prisoner on his removal as an "*exile*" is qualified, in every sense, to begin a "new life". In the prison at Reading, where "*encellulement*" is also most strict, the prisoners are employed "*in nothing but education*". In the Glasgow Bridewell the paramount aim of the plan pursued, is the self-maintenance of the establishment.[1] Here, in Preston, while the personal discipline is severe enough to deter such as give no hope of something better, our chief efforts are used to produce permanent amendment of character, by rousing into life and action the religious principle originally planted in the breast, and never altogether effaced. Order, cleanliness, and obedience, are enforced to a degree which must be irksome to persons accustomed only to irregularity and dirt; two hours of active exercise, daily, preserves the bodily health, and keeps up elasticity of mind: instruction in reading, writing, arithmetic, &c., is given – and received – as a valuable privilege; work is supplied to all – except when compulsory idleness is inflicted for breach of prison rules, – and the value of regular occupation thereby taught; – and those who can exercise their trade in a cell, are permitted to do so, – a boon which is most highly valued. The prisoners assemble for daily and Sabbath worship, under circumstances which make them regard the Holy service as the greatest solace and advantage of their condition. Fully recognising, as we do, the importance of instruction, and communicating it as far as possible, it must be remembered that the great majority of prisoners come to us with minds to which the limited period of their confinement will scarcely permit the conveyence of much technical learning. Yet though there may not be time, in a two or three months' imprisonment, properly to cultivate any capacity for letters, opportunities may be seized for awaking whatever good feeling or tendency may exist, or for reviving some holy impression given in childhood. Our prisoners may be ignorant to a lamentable degree of the merest elements of evangelical doctrine, but there are few of them on whose hearts a law is not written which, they know, forbids lying, blasphemy, drunkenness, and such like; and most of them are still capable of filial and parental affection. It is by appealing to this knowledge and this affection, that we strive to render fruitful the short time available for the purpose. We are aided in our endeavours by the prisoner's separation from all influences which might counteract it. In his cell he has no temptations from without; and many salutary monitions from within. Active memory collects and brings before him "everything that ever happened to him since he was a child"; reflection traces painful consequences back to their sinful causes; the sense of sin and the sorrow for it succeed; he is directed to Him who bore our sorrows and atoned for sin; then rises up the prayer for pardon – *that* is followed by the consolation which answers prayer; and when about to leave the scene of his probation, and try the stability of his new impressions, he says, in a voice which does not permit a doubt of the sincerity of his intentions – "By God's help I'll be a different man for the future". Here, then, are such symptoms of reformation as justify the belief that a great change has taken place, in the criminal's heart; and of the permanency of such change we have numerous and most satisfactory proofs. When the time allowed, or the disposition of the prisoner, will not permit us to hope for reformation, his fears of being again subjected to the severe discipline of the cell, or the yet more severe discipline of the work-room, may *deter* him from such conduct as would expose him to it. The intimation that this inferior – deterring – principle has taken hold, is also evinced by the language used on leaving us – "I'll take good care I don't come *here* again!" A declaration even like this, shows an immense advance in the science of gaol discipline; and if the promised "care" be really observed, society will profit by it. But looking only to the external quiet of the community, I am satisfied that the deterring motive produces much less benefit than the reformatory principle. Two men, both parents, quit the Gaol: the one reformed – purposing, influenced by the love of God, to lead a new life; the other, only deterred, merely determined to keep his evil inclinations within safe limits. Which of these men is the more likely to preserve his children in the right way? to promote order and good living among those within the reach of his example? We never hear, from the merely deterred parent, what is often said by the reformed one – "I'll show my children a different example to what I have done". Here are some of the "prison thoughts" written down in a cell: – "I find in the second commandment that all the sins of my children rest on my shoulders. O! would to God that I was with them! If it should please God to restore me to them, my wife will find as much enjoyment in one month as she has found in twenty years. Now you see *it has not done good to me only, but to my wife and children*, should it please the Almighty to let me live until I go to them again." A deterred criminal is only a more cautious one, and the history of his prison sufferings, told to his companions, will have no better effect than to excite them to the practice of greater cunning. They all flatter themselves that by using more circumspection in their dishonest courses, they may still pursue them safely; and when they discover their mistake they call themselves "*unlucky*". "I'll not come here again" – betrays, at least, a compromise with duty. Whatever errors there may be in these views, the *Chaplain* of a Gaol will have every apology for thinking that a reformatory course of discipline is most likely to be effectual in lessening the amount of crime: it certainly is best for the criminal, and, I believe, for the community.

'The services of the chapel are, by the Divine blessing, greatly instrumental in bettering the feelings and principles of the prisoners: and it will, I think, be conceded that nothing of a deterring character should have place there. The chapel brings, now, the acceptable hour – the welcome and interesting occupation which relieves the severe monotony of a prisoner's daily life. I wish the chapel service – and especially that of the Sabbath, to be so consolatory, so agreeable, so necessary to the prisoners, that, participation in Divine worship, begun under compulsion, may be continued ever after from choice and affection. I would, therefore, have the chapel present, as far as practicable, – even in the minutest particulars – the appearance of a well-ordered church; so that some who enter it may be beneficially reminded of the Sundays of a more innocent and happier time; and that many may be so trained, during imprisonment, to the observance of Sabbath duties, that they may resort, when at liberty, to their own house of prayer, with hearts still grateful for the comfort received in a similar place, and at a time, when almost everything else spoke sorrow and disgrace.

'I submit these observations in support of the argument introduced in my last report, in favour of dispensing with the cellular arrangement in the *chapel*, which forbids the feeling of *social* worship, and shuts out that contagious emotion which spreads through, and softens, a *congregation*; and to which the mind could not afterwards revert, with that feeling which it is so desirable to create.

'I must advert, for a moment, to our modification of the separate system – which consists in permitting the prisoners to exercise, and attend the chapel service, in sight of each other – for the purpose of pointing out this advantage in it – viz. its adaptation to *boys* as well as to adults. Two hours' brisk exercise daily, preserves their bodily health; and, being taken in company, though without communication, keeps also their minds in vigour. At Wakefield "the boys were put in close confinement at first; and afterwards, on their suffering from debility and contraction of the joints, it was obliged to be relaxed, and the boys were permitted to play at leap frog and other similar recreations". In the Juvenile Reformatory, at Parkhurst, it was also found necessary to resort to the same rather anomalous course in order to obviate the effects of excessive *encellulement*. The most satisfactory proof exists that the Preston system is safe for boys [...]

'Having, on several occasions, represented what I conceive to be the advantage of making – except in some special cases – three months the minimum term of imprisonment, – especially if, when sentence is pronounced, the *reformation* of the prisoner to be held in view, – I presume, now, to press this point more formally. On the supposition that the powers given by a recent act, which permits summary proceedings in trifling cases of felony, will be generally exercised in such cases, and proportionally short terms of imprisonment be assigned, – offences tried at the sessions may be considered of a graver character, and as authorizing heavier sentences. With regard to boys – neglected, ignorant, vicious, – it is seldom that any good impression can be made on them by a treatment of less than three months' duration. I would add, too, that, with scarcely any – if any – exception, all the evidence recently given before a Select Committee of the House of Lords on the execution of the criminal law is opposed to short imprisonments. On the other hand, I fully concur in the opinions of those experienced persons who would not extend *separate confinement* beyond 12 or 15 months.

'The circumstances of our Gaol, during the last year, have incidentally shown that, with many characters, periods of separation, alternated with periods of labour in the open air, may be given, not merely with safety, but with decided advantage. The works carried on in the Gaol found employment for 30 or 40 – sometimes for 80 men. These men, working under a superintendence which made intercourse – and still more contamination – impracticable, suspended their labour to attend the daily prayers, and to wash themselves before their meals, which were taken in their cells. Here, then, was combined labour – made all the more agreeable and wholesome, because it had a visibly useful object – with cleanliness, daily prayer, and total separation for some hours of the day, and all the night. The effects of this incidental modification of discipline have been satisfactory. The bodily health thus promoted has communicated a healthy tone to the mind; and many of the prisoners who had no spirit of systematic profligacy to be rooted out, have given proofs that, for them, it was not so much that strict *encellulement* was needed, as the preservation from contaminating agency, uninterrupted time for thought, and daily religious exercise and instruction.' […]

From The Prison Chaplain *(Montclair, NJ: Patterson Smith), 1861, pp. 272–82.*

Note

1. According to the last report of Frederick Hill, Esq. Inspector of Prisons, it appears that while the earnings of 503 prisoners (exclusive of work done for the prison), in February last, amounted to nearly 150*l.*, the *recommittals* within the year exceeded 28 per cent. In the Manchester New Bailey, in which, unlike the Glasgow Bridewell, there are no means of separation, the recommittals in a year are under 20 per cent. My impression has ever been that in proportion as economy or profit is aimed at, the probability of reformation is sacrificed.

3. Women, crime and custody in Victorian England

Lucia Zedner

Advocates of the silent system, of whom perhaps the most notable was George Laval Chesterton, Governor of Coldbath Fields House of Correction, Middlesex, argued that the main purpose of imprisonment was reform.[1] This was most readily achieved by developing powers of self-control and an unquestioning obedience to discipline. Although prisoners were to work 'in association', that is, together, communication was forbidden. Silence was enforced by a large supervisory staff who could employ a wide range of punitive measures to discipline transgressors. The system was based on a profoundly pessimistic view of the offender as corrupt, defiant, and lacking self-control.[2] The system therefore allowed for immediate, severe punishment of any transgression of the silence rule, and so, as Chesterton saw it, forced prisoners to recognize the pains of indiscipline. The silent system also had other advantages – it required no structural alterations to prison buildings and was, therefore, relatively cheap to introduce. More importantly, it was relatively humane, allowing prisoners to associate with one another whilst minimizing corruption. […]

In fact, as Matthew Davenport Hill, Revd J. Kingsmill, Henry Mayhew, and many others pointed out, it was often impossible to enforce silence amongst prisoners held together in association. Prisoners could and did evolve subtle and sophisticated means of secret communication which effectively undermined the entire system. Cynics observed that prisoners were more likely to acquire a facility for deception than habits of obedience. Moreover, since women were believed to be more impressionable than men, they were thought to suffer particularly from the corrupting effects of association. Relatively innocent women, convicted only of some petty crime, would, it was argued, be irrevocably corrupted when fellow prisoners unashamedly whispered details of their sexual exploits or extolled the advantages of prostitution. The adverse effects of association among women were highlighted by the close attention paid to the individual moral character of female convicts. According to evidence given by Revd G. de Renzi, Chaplain of Millbank Convict Prison, to the Royal Commission into the Penal Servitude Acts 1878–9: 'the injurious effects of the women being placed in association are immediately seen; there is less disposition to attend to the scripture reader, there is not the same desire to see the Chaplain, the evidence of deterioration is palpable.'[3] […]

In England, despite widespread and trenchant criticism, the silent system, or a poorly supervised variant of association, was still common well past mid-century. […] Association evidently persisted even up to the end of the century; as late as the Paris Prison Congress of 1895 delegates were still condemning the damage done to women by associating in prison with 'thieves, brothel-servants, prostitutes'.[4]

The 'separate system'

The separate system, as its name implies, sought to isolate prisoners from one another as far as possible by holding them in individual cells and, when bringing them together was unavoidable, by reducing contact to a minimum. As early as 1791, Sir George Onesiphorus Paul, High Sheriff of Gloucestershire, had pioneered the containment of prisoners in separate cells at a penitentiary in Gloucester.[5] His initial impetus was the desire to prevent prisoners from corrupting one another. In the free association allowed in unreformed prisons corruption was so rife that it seemed that incarceration encouraged rather than eliminated vice. Even in prisons which attempted to classify prisoners and to separate the comparatively innocent from the 'hardened offender', the possibilities for contact were considerable. Paul's experiment had a further, more ambitious aim in that it hoped that isolation would provide the prisoner with an opportunity for self-examination and reflection. Under the separate system, prisoners were completely isolated from one another. Locked in individual cells for most of the day, they slept, worked, and ate alone, for it was believed that reflection was most effective if the individual was held apart from the distraction of associating with other prisoners. […]

The benefits of limiting contact with other prisoners were widely accepted as even being greater in relation to women. Whitworth Russell advised: 'with Women … I would have Silence and Separation strictly observed, for Women contaminate one another even more than the Men do.'[6] Yet again the supposed vulnerability of women demanded even greater protection from the adverse influences of other inmates than was deemed necessary for men.

Only when absolutely necessary were prisoners brought together for prayer or for hard labour which could not be done in the cell. Even then, elaborate devices were employed to maintain isolation. Prisoners walked in single file, chapels were partitioned into hundreds of tiny stalls, and face masks (or, as in Pentonville, long peaked caps) were issued to reduce any possibility of recognition to a minimum. Though every effort was made to prevent corruption under the separate system, in practice the prisoners found new and ingenious ways to communicate. […]

After preventing corruption, the second aim of separation was moral reform – a goal that was even more difficult to achieve. The theory was that, denied the companionship and approbation of fellow prisoners, inmates would become more receptive to the good influence of the chaplain. Even the most hardened offenders, once burdened with solitude would become crushingly aware of their sins. […] On the common assumption that women were more impressionable than men, some optimistic observers suggested that they must, therefore, be more susceptible to reform. For example, the Chaplain at Stafford County Gaol argued that young female offenders benefited particularly. Such women, he claimed, 'under the old system, must have gone out corrupted and ruined by association with the most depraved and basest of their sex, have under that now in operation (the separate system) been discharged from prison impressed with better principles, and possessed of a real desire to retrieve their characters and to become useful members of society'.[7] The supposed intensity of women's emotions meant that a successful appeal to the heart might win a woman's trust and secure her enduring loyalty to a higher ideal. [...]

As supposedly reformed characters reappeared for second and third sentences, faith in the efficacy of moral reform was badly shaken. The historian William Forsythe rightly points out that women in particular 'were seen as a problematic group whose conduct was frequently "uninfluenced by the word of God"'.[8] Despite its continuing commitment to moral reform, even the Howard Association recognized that: 'It is well-known that the least hopeful subjects of moral influence are habitual criminals, and most of all, criminal and debased *women*.'[9] By the end of the century, confidence in the feasibility of reform was greatly undermined. This was partly due to the increasing penological interest in the 'habitual offenders' who defied all reformatory efforts, returning to the prison time and again. [...]

The third and perhaps most important facet of separation was deterrence. The deterrence principle relied on the assumption that its subject was a rational man who could estimate the consequences of his actions and who was capable of weighing up the pains of imprisonment against the possible benefits of crime. In practice, offenders rarely operated on the basis of such calculations. Women, considered to be emotional and impulsive in all their actions, were thought to be less prone to such rational calculus and less likely, therefore, to be deterred.

Deterrence was less frequently the subject of debate amongst penologists. This may have been because this purpose was so long established as to be uncontroversial. [...] And yet the writing of penal reformers and administrators up to mid-century seem to reflect considerable unease about the damage done by imprisonment. They questioned prisoners' capacity to withstand, physically and more especially mentally, the pains of solitude. Callous or obdurate characters might become more hardened still, whilst those of more ordinary human frailty might collapse into melancholy or even madness.[10] Men had such terrible nightmares they screamed in their sleep and even fell prey to daytime hallucinations. Many considered women even less able to cope, whilst young girls especially were said not to have the mental equipment to benefit from solitude at all. Elizabeth Fry was particularly concerned about the adverse effects of separation on 'very nervous' women. She urged that separation should be applied very cautiously, with matrons given full discretionary powers over its application.[11]

Despite the doubts expressed by those actually working in local prisons, policy makers at the national level were surprisingly sanguine about imposing separation on women, even arguing that the impact of close confinement was less harmful to women than men. They considered women to be 'naturally' more sedentary and passive in their habits, and therefore better able to withstand this restriction of their mobility.[12] The troubling vision of active men caged like beasts pacing behind bars simply did not apply to women since they were thought to be inherently lethargic and used to the confines of the home. Many of the witnesses called to give evidence to the Commission into the Working of the Penal Servitude Acts (1878–9) concurred that women stood separation better than men, suffering less from 'depression of the spirits' and 'physical deterioration' and, according to some, even preferring solitary confinement to association.[13]

After the appointment of Sir Edmund Du Cane, a former military than, to head the penal system in 1869, reform undoubtedly took second place to the more readily achievable purposes of deterrence and punishment.[14] A Royal Commission appointed in 1863 to investigate the implementation of penal servitude had expressed a widely held feeling that the regime needed to be tightened up. Whilst Du Cane recognized the importance of reform, he was most concerned to increase the deterrent impact of the prison on the wider population.

Any efforts by humane authorities to alleviate the burden of isolation by implementing a careful reformatory programme might achieve success only at the price of deterrence or punishment. [...] The Poor Law Amendment Act 1834 had laid down in relation to paupers that conditions provided in workhouses should be of a lesser standard than those enjoyed by the poorest workers outside. 'Less eligibility', as this injunction was known, had implications for every aspect of penal provision. [...] For, given the example set by the workhouse authorities, they could hardly justify treating the criminal to better conditions than those of the 'honest' poor.[15]

In practice, to implement a 'less eligible' regime posed an absurd dilemma: to provide conditions lower than those of the honest poor would be to impose filth, squalor, and starvation, so endangering the very lives of the prisoners. And yet to provide decent, clean accommodation and food sufficient to ensure good health would be to provide conditions of relative comfort, and the extremely poor with a positive incentive to crime. Basic humanitarian instincts set the level of provision in many cases; for example, a sufficient diet was considered essential for women as it was feared that their reproductive system would be irreparably damaged by prolonged privation of food.[16] Rusche and Kirchheimer claim that, erring on the side of deterrence, standards were kept at an inhumanely low level, causing malnutrition and even death.[17] Yet, [...] some women undoubtedly regarded the conditions of prison life as preferable to absolute destitution and certainly better than the more punitive level of provision in some workhouses. [...]

Elizabeth Fry and the Ladies' Prison Associations

[...] Since the pioneering work of Elizabeth Fry had forced the plight of women prisoners into the nation's conscience, their treatment had been the subject of continuing debate. Fry, 'the more than female Howard', became widely known throughout Britain and abroad for exposing the appalling conditions of 'riot, licentiousness, and filth' suffered by women in the female wards of Newgate, and for their lauded efforts to improve the condition of women prisoners generally.

Shocked by her first visit to Newgate in 1813, Fry and a growing number of other Quaker women launched a radical experiment to reform both prison conditions and, by personal influence and religious instruction, women prisoners themselves. The high profile given to their efforts and the enthusiastic publicity awarded their claimed successes drew much public attention to the plight of women in prison.[18] This, in turn, led to the setting up, in 1817, of the pioneering Ladies' Association for the Reformation of Female Prisoners in Newgate; soon to be followed by the wider reaching British Ladies' Society for the Reformation of Female Prisoners. [...]

Fry's own position as a wealthy and highly connected member of an influential group of Quakers meant that she was particularly well placed to promote the non-sectarian religious education of women prisoners. And it was in this emphasis on religious instruction, personal influence, and individual attention from voluntary Lady Visitors that Fry's approach differed most markedly from that proposed by Bentham. Whereas Bentham's scheme advocated uniform treatment, formal direction, rigid adherence to rules, and no individual differentiation between prisoners, Fry went so far as to suggest that willing co-operation and cheerful submission to rules by the women was a prerequisite to their reform.[19] Her insistence on the need for individualization became widely accepted as the most distinctive feature of the treatment of women.

Later in the century, the Directors of Convict Prisons accepted this as a crucial difference between prison regimes for women and men and stressed: 'Male convicts must be treated in masses rather than according to their individual characters. Individuality must be more regarded with female convicts.'[20] This view was generally accepted and reflected the common belief that women would benefit from close, personal attention. That this must be provided by women was perhaps the most influential of Fry's tenets. She insisted: 'It is absolutely essential to the proper order and regulation of every prison, that the female prisoners should be placed under the superintendence of officers of their own sex.'[21] Quite apart from pointing out the appalling examples of corruption and exploitation which occurred when female prisoners were guarded by, or even merely accessible to, male warders, Fry emphasized the positive role a 'respectable' woman might fulfil as 'a consistent example of propriety and virtue'.[22] [...] Significantly, the responsibilities that this imposed on the female warder were far more exacting than the mere wording of the legislation suggested, and certainly more so than those imposed on her male counterpart. Though male officers were also expected to be honest and to demonstrate qualities of integrity and impartiality, in women's prisons the character and conduct of the warders became the very means of effecting reform and had, therefore, to be exemplary.

A report by the predominantly Quaker Society for the Improvement of Prison Discipline, published the year after this Act, indicates the very high expectations this placed on the female warder: 'In the exercise of her duties she is at once the representative and guardian of her sex, and she ought to be a bright example of its purity, disinterestedness, and love.'[23] The aim was to make the female warder a maternal figure who would, by benevolent encouragement, engender in inmates a strong desire to please. There was a marked gap between the informal and subtle process of modifying women prisoners' behaviour and the highly symbolic tariff of punishment that officially applied, and which was indeed generally enforced in male prisons. [...]

A role for 'Lady Visitors'

Debate concerning the role of women in official posts within the female prison was paralleled by a more controversial debate over voluntary women workers or 'Lady Visitors'. Their work was based on the fundamental assumption discussed above that women had special powers of influence. It was felt that bringing female prisoners into contact with their benevolent 'betters' would provide them with concrete demonstration of qualities to which they might aspire. [...] This stress on the social standing of Lady Visitors clearly differentiated their personal qualities, and therefore the high example they set, from the less exalted attributes of the lower-class women actually employed as prison warders. It also suggested that merely by association with such 'pure, high, and holy women', inmates would somehow be spiritually uplifted. And, throughout the literature on prison visiting, the language of 'raising up' intermingled imagery of religious salvation with the more prosaic purpose of 'bettering oneself'.

If, in this respect, the purpose of visiting was as much based on class as on gender, the means by which Lady Visitors were to exert their influence was peculiarly feminine, and it is no doubt significant that there was no male equivalent of the Lady Visitor. Modelled on the devoted, emotionally charged relations common between upper-class Victorian women, the close relation between Lady Visitor and female prisoner was intended to break down the latter's stubborn resistance to external influences which so often obstructed the rather less energetic efforts at reform carried out by overworked or ill-qualified staff. It was argued: 'Official staff may do their duty and achieve much, but it is not possible for them to give the individual sympathy and patient attention to every member of a community ... needed to win the confidence of persons made suspicious and distrustful by years of guilt, and maybe of ill-usage too.'[24] A philanthropic lady with little call on her time might devote sufficient attention to win confidence and so establish a friendship which would continue throughout the sentence and, ideally, even after discharge. They operated on a one-to-one basis in the belief that 'confidence can only be won through the medium of the sympathy of woman with woman'.[25] [...]

Debate about the appropriate prison treatment of women was stepped up in the last quarter of the century by the growing number of feminists who not only saw social and welfare issues as a female province but who like women reformers earlier in the century, saw women prisoners in particular as demanding attention. They, too, decried the consistent failure of penal policy makers to take sufficient account of women in prison. But whereas earlier women reformers had demanded only a supervisory role, by the end of the nineteenth century women were seeking to establish their influence over prison administration and the wider development of penal and social policy. Such claims became intimately bound up with demands for their participation in all aspects of government. [...]

Criminal women were seen by many feminists as victims of a social structure that provided few opportunities for all women and was especially inhospitable to those who sought to support themselves. Consequently, much feminist thinking on penal policy opposed prevailing views on the deterrent and primarily punitive role of the prison. Instead, like earlier moral reformers, the feminists argued that the primary purpose of penal treatment should be to bring about some good in its charges. Yet, since they saw criminal women not so much as innately evil but as socially disadvantaged, they placed far less emphasis on moral improvement and more on a practical programme intended to equip women better to lead an honest life once released. They deplored the overriding concern amongst prison administrators to reduce running costs, for example by employing women prisoners in drudge work around the prison, as a false saving. And they called instead for proper industrial training which would fit women for careers in skilled work on release.[26] By thus providing women with the means to self-sufficiency, such a regime would strike at the very source of much crime.

In addition to the economic reasons for female crime, it was increasingly recognized that many women in prison suffered from mental or physical incapacities which left them unable to survive unprotected in society. Such women, it was argued, should be removed from prisons to specialized institutions orientated towards dealing with their particular problems. [...] To ensure recognition of that class of women who should not have been in prison at all, feminists called for the appointment of female medical officers in women's prisons and of female medical inspectors at national level.[27] It was not by chance that the first Lady Inspector of Prisons, Mary Gordon, appointed after persistent demands from various women's organizations, was herself a qualified doctor and a committed feminist.[28]

Perhaps the greatest influence on the treatment of women prisoners came as a quite indirect result of the suffragette campaign for votes for women. When suffragettes turned in desperation to militant and often violent tactics in the pursuit of their cause, they quickly found themselves in the hands of the criminal justice system. The repeated imprisonment of militant suffragettes between 1905 and 1914 gave numbers of educated and influential women personal experience of conditions in prison for the first time.[29] Despite the fact that they insisted that they were not ordinary criminals but political prisoners, they nonetheless took a keen interest in the criminal women confined alongside them. The suffragettes gave unprecedented publicity to the plight of women prisoners. They continually barraged the Home Office with demands for the differential treatment of women. And they made many specific recommendations for changes to practices and regulations, not least those they regarded as unnecessarily humiliating and degrading to women (such as the requirement that they have their hair shorn off).[30] Critics as vociferous as these could not easily be ignored and a frantic, private correspondence between top Home Office officials gave 'grave consideration' to their 'weight and importance'. Perhaps surprisingly, the officials admitted that 'the superior training and culture of many of them have induced useful criticisms as regards the treatment of women prisoners'.[31] [...]

Despite the general silence of penal historians on issues of gender and despite the belief of at least one historian that these issues failed to generate anything that might be identified as gender-specific policy, such policies did exist. As William Forsythe rightly recognizes, 'the almost exclusive male world of prison discipline theorists and analysts was never entirely at ease in its attitude to women prisoners'.[32] It was this very unease that led them to adapt, to modify, and often to mitigate the regime developed for women's prisons. The most coherent sources of penal policy for women lay mainly outside official government policy-making circles and arose from highly publicized but largely voluntary endeavours. They were not without influence in promoting a general acceptance that women required separate and different treatment from men – so pressing further demands on a system already fraught with contradiction and controversy.

From Women, Crime, and Custody in Victorian England *(Oxford: Clarendon Press), 1991, pp. 105–30.*

Notes

1. G.L. Chesterton, *Revelations of Prison Life* (1856), 2 vols.
2. Ibid. ii. 40.
3. Royal Commission into the Working of the Penal Servitude Acts, Minutes of Evidence, *Past and Present*, 37 (1878–9), 540.
4. Madame d'Abbadie d'Arrast, 'Women in Prison', in Howard Association, *The Paris Prison Congress 1895* (1895), 8–9.
5. William J. Forsythe suggests that penal reformers such as Jonas Hanway, Samuel Denne, and John Howard were promoting such ideas as early as the 1770s, see his *Reform of Prisoners* (1987), 19.
6. W. Russell to Select Committee of the House of Lords on Gaols and Houses of Correction, Minutes of Evidence, *PP*, 11 (1835), 124.
7. Nineteenth Report of the Inspector of Prisons: Southern and Western District, *PP*, 34 (1854); see also Mary Carpenter, *Our Convicts* (1864), i. 42.
8. Forsythe, *Reform of Prisoners*, 64.
9. Howard Association, *Annual Report* (1880), 11.
10. Such consequences were widely feared [...] see the writings of Joshua Jebb, for example, letter from J. Jebb to H. Waddington, 'On the Testament of Female Prisoners' (11 April 1855), Jebb Papers Box 7; W.L. Clay, *The Prison Chaplain* (1861), 218–19; H. Mayhew and J. Binney, *The Criminal Prisons of London and Scenes of Prison Life* (1862), 103–5.
11. Evidence by E. Fry, Select Com. of the House of Lords on Gaols and Houses of Correction, Minutes of Evidence (1835), 527.
12. For example, see evidence given by Prison Inspector J.G. Perry, Select Committee on Prison Discipline, Minutes of Evidence, *PP*, 17 (1850), 153.
13. See, for example, evidence given by W. Morrish, a Director of Convict Prisons, and by Mrs. S. Seale, Lady Superintendent of Fulham Prison, RC on the Working of the Penal Servitude Acts, Minutes of Evidence (1878–9), 264, 381–3.
14. E. Du Cane, *The Punishment and Prevention of Crime* (1885).

15. The development of a 'less eligible' regime was a major concern of the Select Committee on Prison Discipline in 1850, see especially its Report, *PP*, 17 (1850), 5 and 6.
16. This fear was frequently a subject for discussion in the reports of the Surveyor-General, the Inspectors of Local Prisons and the directors of Convict Prisons. It also concerned several of those giving evidence to the two Royal Commissions on the Penal Servitude Acts, see especially *PP*, 21 (21 (1863), 457, 463, 684; *PP*, 38 (1878–9), 846–8. On the issue of diet more generally, see V. Johnston, 'Diet in Workhouses and Prisons 1835 to 1895', D.Phil. thesis (1981).
17. G. Rusche and O. Kirchheimer, *Punishment and Social Structure* (1939), 107–8.
18. See accounts by T. Timpson, *Memoirs of Mrs Elizabeth Fry* (1847), M. Wrench, *Visits to Female Prisoners at Home and Abroad* (1852), and Clay, *Prison Chaplain*.
19. E. Fry. *Sketch of the Origins and Results of Ladies' Prison Associations* (1827), 7–8.
20. Reports of the Directors of Convict Prisons, Millbank for 1856, *PP*, 23 (1857), 48. Some went so far as to argue for the 'complete individuality of treatment' for women – A Prison Matron, *Prison Characters drawn from Life with Suggestions for Prison Government* (1866), i. 297.
21. E. Fry, *Observations on the Visiting, Superintending and Government of Female Prisoners* 2nd edn. (1827), 27.
22. Ibid. 31.
23. Society for the Improvement of Prison Discipline, *Sixth Report* (1824), 65.
24. Davenport-Hill, 'Women Prison Visitors', 542.
25. M. Wrench, *Visits*, 30.
26. E. Orme, 'Our Female Criminals', *Fortnightly Review*, 69 (1898), 793–4, and S.M. Amos, 'The Prison Treatment of Women', *Contemporary Review* (June 1898), 809.
27. Such demands, remaining largely unmet, continued into the 1920s – see the mass of letters, proposals, and petitions from leading bodies such as the Consultative Committee of Women's Organisations and the Women's Freedom League in PRO HO45/16184.
28. Though the medical orientation of her work was denied by the Home Office and her very appointment derided as a mere 'sop to feminism'. E. Troup, 21 December 1919, in PRO HO45 10552/163497.
29. B. Harrison, 'The Act of Militancy: Violence and the Suffragettes, 1909–1914', in his *Peaceable Kingdom* (1982); 'The Political Offender', Ch. 13 in L. Radzinowicz and R. Hood, *A History of English Criminal Law and its Administration from 1750*, v (1986). Papers, petitions, reports, and correspondence relating to the imprisonment of the suffragettes held at PRO HO144 were kindly made available for consultation by agreement of HO Notice Office.
30. See, for example, PRO HO144 1042/183256/20; see also the later account in M. Gordon, *Penal Discipline* (1922), 37–9.
31. PRO HO144 1042/18325/17. Correspondence between Sir Evelyn Ruggles-Brise, the Director of Prisons, and Sir Edward Troup, the Permanent Under-Secretary. The impact of the suffragettes on the imprisonment of women in the longer term falls beyond the period of my study but is very clearly enunciated in Gordon, *Penal Discipline*. Overlooked by most accounts is the startling fact that Gordon was not only sympathetic and supportive of suffragette militancy but that she secretly contributed to the women's Social and Political Union Defence Fund. Her involvement was uncovered and vehemently condemned by the Home Office after a surprise raid on the offices of the WSPU in 1914. PRO HO45 10552/163497.
32. Forsythe, *Reform of Prisoners*, 131.

4. Grinding men good? Lancashire's prisons at mid-century

Margaret E. DeLacy

In recent years, beginning with the appearance of Gertrude Himmelfarb's 'The Haunted House of Jeremy Bentham' in 1965, historians have presented a new view of nineteenth-century prison reform.[1] In place of the traditional respectful accounts of such reforming heroes as John Howard and Elizabeth Fry, these writers have suggested that most prison reform was misconceived and manipulative, designed to increase the 'social control' that members of the 'middle class' could exercise over the dangerous classes. In place of the squalor and capricious cruelty of early-modern sanctions, they suggested, prison reformers created a systematic and pervasive 'machine for grinding men good', a design for controlling not merely the body but the mind. The Panopticon, with its 'big brother' inspection system, its exploitative work, its codified rules, its fertile inventions for altering men's bodies and minds, has entirely eclipsed as a cautionary symbol those two great 'gothic' monuments to royal arbitrariness and official neglect, the Bastille and Newgate; our progress towards 1984 has become more important than our retreat from the Dark Ages.[2]

Before the many theoretical objections to the theory of social control can be aired, it seems reasonable to enquire whether it has in fact accurately described the phenomenon it seeks to explain. Just who did this controlling and who was controlled? Were these measures in fact applied and, if applied, did they work? The radical historians have tended to rely on the writings and speeches of the very men they are so anxious to discredit: middle-class reformers, for their depiction of prison conditions in the mid-nineteenth century. On the whole, however, these reformers neither ran the prisons nor inhabited them. It is time for a closer examination of the evidence available from all sources if the debate is to progress.

The purpose of this reading is to examine the evidence on one prison system – the county system of Lancashire – to see what qualifications it may suggest to the 'social control' theory. I do not intend either to demolish the theory or to erect a new one, but merely to see how well it describes the actual circumstances of nineteenth-century prison life and to suggest areas in which it needs to be qualified in the light of further investigation. Lancashire's system is appropriate for this examination because it was a very large system: by mid-century the four county prisons together contained an inmate population second only to that of Middlesex. Together with the borough gaols, they contained about one-fifth of England's total prison population. Moreover, Lancashire was the heart of that industrial capitalism which has drawn so much radical criticism. Preston's Gradgrinds and Manchester's economists epitomised, both for contemporaries and for their descendents, the economic, political and social values of the utilitarian state.[3]

This analysis covers the middle of the century because radical historians have chosen that period to represent the apotheosis of the strictly regimented prison. To Michael Ignatieff, 'the opening of Pentonville in 1842 represents a point of culmination in the tightening up of social controls underway since 1820'.[4] Michel Foucault, with unwonted precision, fixed the 'date of completion of the carceral system' on 22 January 1840, the day when Mettray opened.[5] Nevertheless, since every prison was different and since each changed at a different rate, the choice of period is neither simple nor unimportant. Similar arguments could take place over an earlier period or several later ones. [...]

The efforts of reformers and, in particular, the introduction of the silent and separate systems constituted a sustained attack on this prison community. However lax Lancashire's other prisons had become, Preston symbolised for the whole nation the fluctuating currents of reform, from 'benthamite' labour regimes to 'evangelical' isolation. The chief local proponent of the separate system and a figure of national importance was the Reverend John Clay, Preston's chaplain, whose social theory and apparent success in implementing it make Preston central to the case for a social control approach during the Pentonville era. We will examine the implementation of Preston's new regimes in some detail; if they were limited there, they are unlikely to have been more fully enforced in most other local prisons.

[...]

Like many prison chaplains, Clay preferred the separate to the silent system, arguing against the latter because it did not produce 'that deep and earnest self-examination which is the necessary prelude to self conviction and conversion'.[6] After Crawford's visit to the American prisons in 1834, he began an intense and prolonged effort to persuade the Preston justices to adopt the separate system, or the silent system as second best. In 1834 he persuaded the Bench to agree to the adoption of a 'modified American system' but the agreement was not implemented.[7] In subsequent reports he continued to hammer at the subject. In 1840 he could report some progress. A number of solitary cells had been made, though they were only certified for one month's confinement, and the silent system was in use in much of the rest of the prison. In 1841 he noted that after another year's trial the system seemed to be working. In 1843, a year after Pentonville opened, a corridor of separate cells appeared at Preston. In the report for that year Clay commented on the continuous improvement in the discipline of Preston in the years since 1828 (the year of Liddell's departure) and a dramatic improvement over the last 18 months. The silent system was now 'fully enforced'. In 1845 the treadwheel was removed and for the first time all prisoners before as well as after trial were separated. By 1848 Clay proudly pointed to a decrease in committals and of crime in North Lancashire that was greater than that in any other county over the past five years and attributed the trend to the introduction of the new system at Preston.[8]

Although Clay referred to the discipline he introduced as the 'separate system' and argued vigorously for its advantages over the silent system, in fact the separation was so modified that it is difficult to assign it to either category. Clay was appalled by the high suicide rate at Pentonville although Crawford was prepared to write off a few extra deaths as the cost of more effective reformation. Accordingly, Clay altered the system to permit a good deal of silent contact between the prisoners. They exercised together, took their lessons together, gathered together in an open chapel and often worked together in large shops.[9]

Clay had originally opposed the imposition of prison labour on prisoners sentenced to short terms and was later to argue against Maconochie's mark system (differing for once from M.D. Hill, the Unitarian Recorder of Birmingham) on the basis that it devoted all its efforts to making men industrious. Preston's convicts, according to his figures, were already industrious. By 1851, however, he changed his mind and argued that industrial occupation was essential to preserve mental health and prevent depression.[10]

Like Hill, Clay began to think of prisons as 'moral hospitals' where prisoners would come to be cured of the moral aberrations brought about by a lack of religious training and education.[11] If prisons were reformative rather than punitive and if crimes were symptoms of a diseased state, then clearly the answer was to send more people to prison earlier in order to nip the evil in the bud and to protect these convalescents while there from any further contamination. Clay originally expressed doubts about the value of incarcerating offenders, juveniles in particular, because it just made them worse. As Preston more and more nearly conformed to his ideal, however, by preventing prisoners from corrupting each other, he felt able to recommend incarceration as a universal panacea.

Since imprisonment was no longer imposed as a sort of social vengeance, the idea of simple justice, of a fitting of the punishment to the crime, became less relevant. Clay believed that only a long spell of reformative imprisonment could truly rehabilitate the criminal and break him of his bad habits, so he advocated ever longer sentences. He was perfectly willing to countenance sentences which, had they been imposed merely for punishment, would have seemed utterly disproportionate to the original offence. The culprit would remain until he had undergone a complete cure. It is possible, though it cannot be proved, that Clay's success in convincing the justices that imprisonment was beneficial increased their readiness to sentence offenders to gaol for petty offences such as public drunkenness – especially since the number of drunken offenders already in gaol proved the seriousness of the problem. (Lancashire had the highest commitment rate for drunkenness in the country, amounting to approximately half of all county committals.)[12] This was the danger from reform that Sir George Paul had feared in the late eighteenth century.

It was probably owing to Clay's growing influence that the separate system was also partially introduced into Kirkdale and Salford. William John Williams strongly supported the silent system, which had the additional recommendation of cheapness. Frederic Hill, an adamant opponent of silence, also disliked the complete imposition of separation.[13] Several local leaders believed, in the words of the chaplain of Kirkdale, that gaol reform was hopeless 'as long as the state of society remains what it is outside'.[14] Nevertheless, old cells were altered and new ones built to make at least partial separation possible.

At Lancaster, where architectural barriers made large-scale adoption of the separate system impracticable, Captain Hansbrow was converted by his experiments with his more quarrelsome and difficult charges. He began 'putting apart' offenders against prison rules on full diet in their cells as a way to evade the rule that restricted gaolers' punishments to three days of solitary. Hansbrow frequently found the justices' decisions frustrating; on one occasion a prisoner repeatedly and brutally kicked another, splitting his lip and knocking out a tooth, but the justices refused to punish him on the grounds that he had committed only a single offence, while their jurisdiction was limited to *repeated* infractions of the prison rules.[15] Several of these isolated offenders came to thank him for the period of reflection. By 1849 he was noting in his journal that Crown prisoners improved 'rapidly and perceptibly' in health and appearance when put apart, attributing the change to the absence of irritation and the inability of prisoners to part with their food. In 1850 he wrote with regret that a felon newly released from solitary had begged to be put apart but that he had no space to do so.

The Home Office was increasing its pressure on the local prisons to tighten their discipline and introduce separation. The prison inspectors for the Home District had long since agreed that the separate system should be enforced throughout England, but it is difficult to know what effect they had since they and the Surveyor General were on very bad terms with Williams.[16] Nevertheless, it seems likely that it was Clay's work that was decisive in persuading the Committee of Justices appointed in 1846 to adopt the separate system completely in Kirkdale and Preston and to convert Lancaster into a women's and debtors' prison. No immediate plans could be made for Salford because the Borough of Manchester and the Hundred had not come to an agreement about city prisoners. It was on the basis of the Committee's work that the county embarked on a building programme that soon aroused loud protests from the ratepayers. By 1851, the county was firmly committed to a policy of separation.[17]

The official adoption of separation by the government, the commitment of the magistrates and the triumph of the reformers, should not be allowed to obscure the limited way in which the separate system was actually implemented. The storm of controversy over the idea has concealed its tenuous existence in fact. The expense of total conversion and the ratepayers' revolt acted as important brakes on its introduction, as did the delay common to all governments and especially those dependent on committees of amateurs. By the time Lancashire was actually prepared for conversion, the separate system was again falling out of fashion, replaced by the mark system. Another difficulty was the unpredictability of prison populations: in 1851 Preston contained 168 cells certified for separation, 108 cells which could not be used for separation and 34 cells too dilapidated for use. Since Preston's average population in that year was 367, it is difficult to see how more than about two-thirds, at most, could have been separated even at night. Only 168 prisoners could have been separated by day as well.[18] While the municipalities of Manchester and Liverpool were able to introduce separation into their newly-completed prisons in the 1850s, matters changed little in the county prisons. In 1863, Preston still had only 168 separate cells. Kirkdale, despite much building, had only 162 and Salford, with a population of nearly 500, had 101. The new inspector, Herbert P. Voules, now responsible for half of England, supported separation only at night; by day he encouraged industrial labour and open schooling. Lancashire prisoners spent up to five hours a day in associated schooling even when they were nominally separated.[19]

Lancashire was not atypical in this lacklustre approach to prison reform. Only one prison in all Wales had any separate cells at all. The Committee of 1863 complained that 'there are so many interruptions to the regularity of prison discipline, instruction is given at such various times, and the communications which pass between prisoners and other persons are so frequent, that separation, though it exists nominally in many, is really to be found in few gaols'.[20]

Lancashire was both the industrial and the ideological heart of the new order, yet with the partial exception of Preston for a short period, Lancashire's prisons bore no more resemblance to the highly regimented model of Pentonville than Lancashire's Poor Law did to the rigorous visions of the New Poor Law commissioners. As with the New Poor Law, Lancashire's foot-dragging suggests that the theory that links the development of industrialisation with the rise of repressive institutions is in need of some qualification.

This is not to suggest that change and reform did not take place. It did. The prisons of 1845 were very different places from their predecessors of three to six decades before. They were larger, more highly and formally organised, more firmly controlled by a professional staff headed by a more powerful governor. On the whole, reformers won their most important battle; after a reverse in the late teens and early twenties they succeeded in improving conditions far enough to reduce the death rate. While prisoners paid for these changes in loss both of freedom and of community life, the prisons never quite became those 'machines for grinding men good' that the reformers have claimed and the critics have charged.

From V. Bailey (ed.) Policing and Punishment in Nineteenth-century Britain *(London: Croom Helm), 1981, pp. 182–211.*

Notes

1. Himmelfarb's essay, which originally appeared in *Ideas in History*, was reprinted in *Victorian Minds* (New York, 1970), pp. 32–81.
2. See e.g., L.J. Hume, 'Jeremy Bentham and the Nineteenth-Century Revolution in Government', *Historical Journal*, vol. 10, no. 4 (1967), pp. 361–75 and idem., 'Bentham's Panopticon, an Administrative History', part one, *Historical Studies*, vol. 15 (1973), pp. 703–21; part two, *Historical Studies*, vol. 16 (1974), pp. 36–54; Barbee-Sue Rodman, 'Bentham and the Paradox of Penal Reform', *Journal of the History of Ideas*, vol. 29 (1968), pp. 197–210;

Robin Evans, 'Bentham's Panopticon: An Incident in the Social History of Architecture', *Architectural Association Quarterly*, vol. 3, no. 2 (1971), pp. 21–37, and idem., 'Panopticon', *Controspasio*, vol. 10 (1970), pp. 4–18; William C. Bader, 'Jeremy Bentham: Businessman or "Philanthropist"?', *Albion*, vol. 7, no. 3 (1975), pp. 245–54. See also Gordon Hawkins, *The Prison, Policy and Practice* (Chicago, 1976), Ch. 1; David J. Rothman, *The Discovery of the Asylum* (Boston, 1971); Michel Foucault, *Madness and Civilization* (London, 1967) and *Discipline and Punish* (London, 1977); Michael Ignatieff, *A Just Measure of Pain* (New York, 1978); and Rod Morgan, 'Divine Philanthropy: John Howard Reconsidered', *History*, vol. 62 (1977), pp. 388–410. For a more extensive discussion of this interpretation see my thesis, 'County Prison Administration in Lancashire, 1690–1850' (Univ. of Princeton, Ph.D. thesis, 1980), pp. 1–33, 207–11 and 467–9. See also, Ursula Henriques, 'The Rise and Decline of the Separate System of Prison Discipline', *Past and Present*, 54 (1972), pp. 61–93.

3. For Lancashire's committal rate see V.A.C. Gatrell and T.B. Hadden, 'Criminal Statistics and their Interpretation', in E.A. Wrigley (ed.), *Nineteenth-Century Society* (Cambridge, 1972), pp. 336–96. On Preston's Gradgrinds see Philip Collins, *Dickens and Crime* (London, 1965) and Norris Pope, *Dickens and Charity* (New York, 1978). For Manchester's economists see Michael J. Cullen, *The Statistical Movement in Early Victorian Britain* (Hassocks, 1975); Asa Briggs, *Victorian Cities* (Harmondsworth, 1968); and V.A.C. Gatrell, 'The Commercial Middle Class in Manchester, c. 1820–1857' (Univ. of Cambridge, Ph.D. thesis, 1971). For Lancashire, see Eric C. Midwinter, *Social Administration in Lancashire, 1830–1860* (Manchester, 1969) and John Foster, *Class Struggle and the Industrial Revolution* (London, 1974).

4. Ignatieff, op. cit., p. 193.

5. Foucault, op. cit., p. 293.

6. Walter Lowe Clay, *The Prison Chaplain* (Montclair, 1969), Report for 1842.

7. *The Prison Chaplain*, p. 120.

8. Reports for years named in text.

9. Report for 1849; *The Prison Chaplain*, p. 196.

10. Report for 1851. See also *The Prison Chaplain*, pp. 311 and 396–8. Alexander Maconochie, *General Views Regarding the Social System of Convict Management* (Hobart Town, 1839). Maconochie's 'mark system' allowed a convict to work his way out of prison by assigning him so many 'marks' each day for industry and good behaviour. When he accumulated enough marks he was released. In the later stages of their sentences, convicts worked and earned their marks in groups. This system became popular with educational reformers such as Dickens and M.D. Hill, who brought Maconochie to Birmingham prison where his experiment failed tragically. See Peter W.J. Bartrip, 'The Career of Matthew Davenport Hill' (Univ. of Wales, Ph.D. thesis, 1975); Collins, op. cit., ch. VII; S.J. Webb and B. Webb, *English Prisons under Local Government* (London, 1963), pp. 165–74.

11. *The Prison Chaplain*, p. 211. For the implications of this belief see Steven L. Schlossman, *Love and the American Delinquent* (Chicago, 1977); Charles Silberman, *Criminal Violence, Criminal Justice* (New York, 1978), ch. 9; Bartrip, op. cit.; and David J. Rothman, *Conscience and Convenience* (Boston and Toronto, 1980), ch. 1.

12. Gatrell and Hadden, op. cit.

13. Third and Thirteenth Report of the Inspectors for the Northern and Eastern District.

14. LCRO, QGR/3/45, Richard Appleton, Chaplain's Report for Kirkdale, 1850. See also S. Greg, 'Notes on Criminal Statistics', ms. copy of a paper read before the Manchester Statistical Society, sess. 1837–8, Manchester Central Library, ms. F. 310.6. m5. I am grateful to the City of Manchester Cultural Services, archives dept., for providing me with copies of this and other Statistical Society papers. Kay-Shuttleworth also believed that environmental improvements and education were the only solution to the problem of crime: James Phillips Kay-Shuttleworth, *The Moral and Physical Condition of the Working Classes Employed in the Cotton Manufacture in Manchester*, 2nd ed., reprt. (Didsbury, 1969).

15. PRO, PCom 2/444, 17 June 1847.

16. PRO, HO 20/4, Williams to Lord John Russell, Wakefield, 18 Nov. 1837 and 14 Dec. 1837. For Jebb, see Eric Stockdale, 'The Rise of Joshua Jebb, 1837–1850', *British Jour. of Criminology*, vol. 14 (1976), pp. 164–70, I am grateful to Judge Stockdale for providing me with a copy of this article.

17. LCRO, QGR/5/1, *Report of the Committee on Prison Accommodation and Discipline* (1853).

18. Ibid.

19. Report from the Select Committee of the House of Lords on the Present State of Discipline in the Gaols and Houses of Correction, P.P. 1863, vol. 9.

20. Ibid.

5. Victorian prison lives

Philip Priestley

The working classes

A more settled portion of the English population formed the major recruiting ground for Victorian prisons. In his *Chapters on Prisons and Prisoners* Kingsmill reproduces 'the means of living' of the first one thousand men to be received at Pentonville: '67 had been employed in office of trust, 71 as in door and out door servants, 388 were tradesmen and mechanics, 50 weavers and factory labourers, 100 farm labourers, 25 colliers, 15 boatmen, 10 common sailors, 18 in the army and navy, and 256 general labourers and hawkers.'[1] 'One is astonished', he says, 'at finding in that return so small a proportion of the most ignorant and neglected part of the whole community – factory labourers, colliers, and boatmen ... the causes of the small proportion of criminals in those classes being, rather that their wants are few; that they are accustomed from their childhood to the hardest toil, and that, worn out by overwork, they have little energy left for good or evil.'[2]

When it first opened, Pentonville accepted only convicts sentenced to transportation, so their convictions were for 'more serious' offences. A different occupational picture presented itself at the county gaols. The daily 'male' reception at Northampton amounted to 'six or seven, most of them drunken shoe hands, poachers or tramps';[3] and at Cardiff 'The population of the prison consisted largely of miners and sailors'.[4] 'The great mass of the prisoners' at Stafford were 'taken from among the colliers, boatmen, potters, and the ironwork men and tin plate workers – people who are brought up in the roughest and most miserable manner as to morals, who are rarely or never accustomed to come in contact with any educated people, whose knowledge of right and wrong is of the most limited kind, and whose value of human life, from the perilous trades many of them pursue, amounts to nothing. They come in here perfect savages'.[5] These 'savages' were actually working class men who worked in the new heavy industries, and who lived in the fast-growing industrial towns. But many of them remained psychologically rooted in a countryside that was never very far away geographically either. It was also a theatre in which scenes from a continuing drama of class war were acted out.

The Reverend John Clay once accompanied a group of justices on an inspection of Preston prison.

> I had occasion to point out to them some sleeping cells so damp that the water lodged on the floors, when one of the inspectors observed, 'Oh, they're good enough for poachers'. This was the first intimation I had of the light in which the poacher is viewed by a large portion of the country magistrates. In their eyes he is the worst of criminals, and to put him down the law may be strained a little beyond its equitable limits.

This was done, in Lancashire at any rate, by sentencing men to terms of imprisonment for poaching and, when they were released, putting them in front of a commissioner of taxes for 'taking game without a licence'. They were then recommitted to prison as being unable to pay a monetary penalty. Clay protested to the Home Secretary, Sir James Graham, who put a stop to it; but under Lord Palmerston, his successor at the Home Office, he says, 'the practice has revived of discharging both (legal) barrels at the poaching offender.'[6] It was not only 'legal' barrels that were discharged in this rural warfare. Clay 'found in the hospital two poachers in very severe pain, from having in the late affray with Mr F—'s gamekeepers, been shot in the legs. I was sorry to observe that the wounds were not made by round pellets, but by angular pieces of lead about the size of shot'.[7]

The intimate relation between crime and the countryside is underlined by the testimony given to the Royal Commission which in 1854 enquired into discipline at Leicester County Gaol. A series of prisoners and former prisoners was asked why they were in prison: William Burton – 'I went from Croxton Park races for gambling. I won a sovereign. They took me up, and I had a month in half an hour';[8] William Pratt – 'Getting turnip tops ... Two calendar months';[9] Isaac Weston 'for shooting at a stuffed pheasant. Three months';[10] Frederick Holyoake – 'For standing by and seeing a dog fight. Three months'.[11] This list of trivial offences, and the trivial sentences they were thought to merit, typify one aspect of petty crime in the mid-century Midlands. But the altercation that subsequently developed between Frederick Holyoake and his inquisitors typifies another:

> Have you ever been in trouble before? – Many a time. ... Let me see if I can give you a list . ... September 18th, you were charged with rescuing a prisoner from the police, and fined, 1 *l* or one month's imprisonment again? – So would you for your own brother. I would not see him taken. ... August 15th, 1844, again taken before the magistrates for assaulting the police. Fined 10s. or three weeks' imprisonment? – You have got it all down. ... February 3d, 1845, you were again taken before the magistrates for fighting, and ordered to find sureties to keep the peace? – I did not break it; I kept the peace. ... But you were taken before the magistrates? – Do not you put it on so thick, it is not of any use.[12]

Frederick Holyoake's testimony breathes truculence in every line; he is not intimidated by the Royal Commissioners, or their proceedings, and is determined to give as good as he gets. From the evidence of his criminal record it was an attitude he carried onto the streets and into his dealings with the humbler functionaries of the newly formed police force. His disrespect for their persons, and for the older 'legality' they represented, was not however universally shared by members of the lower orders. When George Jacob Holyoake – no relation – was awaiting his turn to be tried at Gloucester, he saw 'a man sentenced to transportation for life to Norfolk Island. His offence had arisen in ignorant and depraving circumstances, yet, when he heard the ferocious sentence, in genuine and awkward humbleness he made a rustic bow to the Bench, saying "Thank you, my Lord". Ignorance had never appeared to me before so frightful, slavish and blind. Unable to distinguish a deadly sentence passed upon him from a service done to him, he had been taught to bow to his pastors and masters, and he bowed alike when cursed as blessed'.[13]

The criminal classes

Frederick Holyoake and his cronies were rude and unruly members of Leicestershire civil society, but their offences against it were no more than by-products of the gaming, drinking and fighting that characterized their own traditional, semi-rural ways of life. As the countryside was invaded by a more densely settled townscape and as city slums flourished, these habits and attitudes began to cross the boundaries surrounding an area of society in which individuals made their entire *livings* by thieving and cheating. These were inhabited by the criminal classes, within which there existed a recognizable hierarchy of technical skill, of 'moral' commitment and mutual regard. At the bottom end of the ladder were men not too dissimilar in character from the Leicester roughs, but with a more predatory turn of mind that led them to pursue careers as footpads. A street robber describes his last offence:

> I had a bit of luck and had plenty on me, had been to see my mother and had given her some money and was on my way to my own place, when a young lady that looked like a school teacher girl passed me with a watch hanging outside her dress; I said to myself, 'I've got enough. I will let her off,' so let her go by. I hadn't gone 200 yards before a feeling came over me, 'I must have that ticker,' so I turned round, followed her up, knocked her down, collared her watch and rings and made off.[14]

Equally rough characters could be culled from every prison register. There was a Lancashire man called Braithwaite, who had, 'it was said, a head that was as hard as iron, and would, for a quart of ale, undertake to break with it any mantelpiece before which he was placed'.[15] Also in Lancashire was a prisoner in the Salford New Bailey who 'had been a prize-fighter, he had fought more than 20 pitched battles, and he was generally backed by the publicans to fight'. He told the Reverend Bagshaw he 'had been for many years so employed, that he would fight for 20*l.* a battle; that he had fought 150 rounds on one occasion'.[16] The face of a man known to Dr Quinton told a similar story: he had 'a broken nose, rupture of one tympanic membrane, and a generally battered look about his face, but he had, further, dozens of tiny cicatrices like the pitting of small-pox, only more irregular, on both cheeks. These were caused by killing rats with his teeth against time, an occupation which he had recourse to in his declining years, and out of which he made "a good bit".'[17]

Pickpockets

Alongside these crude operators at the bottom of the criminal ladder were the sneak thieves, amateur pickpockets, and snatch purses; some of them mere children like 'Elizabeth P., aged eleven ... committed for pocket picking':

> The first time I ever took money was in Byrom Street; there was a fire in that street, and I saw a lady with three sovereigns in a purse. I went up to her and said, aye? do you see that woman on fire? I then put my hand in her pocket and took out her money, and ran off with it.[18]

Proper pickpockets considered themselves a cut above the snatch-thieves and crude footpads; they saw themselves as skilled craftsmen, and often operated with one or more accomplices. Some such men could not resist an opportunity to demonstrate their skills in prison. When Major Blake was in training at Chelmsford Prison, the then governor, Captain Conor, 'was the possessor of a very valuable gold watch and chain which he was in the habit of wearing, and which he very highly prized. When he came to look at the time one morning after inspecting the prison he found that he was not wearing his watch. He could not find it anywhere until a prisoner was brought in at his own request.' 'The first thing he did was to hand the Governor the missing timepiece, complete with chain. "I 'ope you won't be angry with me sir," he said apologetically. "I never meant to keep it. But you were wearing it as you were going your rounds and – well – I just wanted to keep my hand in".'[19]

Professional pickpockets not only had to keep their 'hand in'; One-who-has-endured-it for instance, asked 'a man who had the reputation of being a most expert hand at "slinging his hook," ... if the hard work of prison did not spoil his hands for delicate manipulations. "Oh, bless you, no!" he replied, "a few bread and water poultices followed by wearing well greased gloves will set all that to rights. In a week or two a man can bring his hooks and feelers into full working trim again and no mistake".'[20] 'Trained thieves and pick-pockets,' says the Reverend John Clay, 'differ from the mere tramps, both as requiring a far greater amount of plunder to support them, and as more constantly and actively seeking it. While the tramps are always pedestrian, and are content to herd in the most sordid lodging houses, the professional thieves resort to alehouses and taverns, travel by rail, and altogether maintain a style of living unattainable by meaner rogues. They differ again from the "resident bad characters", inasmuch as they *never* work; but live entirely upon the fruits of their daily villainy.'[21]

Almost at the top of the criminal tree were the men who undertook audacious robberies and burglaries requiring degrees of planning and daring, of the sort displayed by a 'professional "cracksman"' who was met by 'Merchant' – another pseudonymous gentleman prisoner: 'He was a man of fair education, good appearance, and considerable natural ability; much above the average of his professional brethren. He had been living luxuriously in London, on the fruits of his professional industry and skill.'[22] Another of Merchant's prison acquaintances engaged in the same trade when at liberty:

> My brother and I and another bloke went out 'chance screwing', one winter, and we averaged three pounds a night each. My brother had a spring cart and a fast trotting horse, so when it began to grow dark, off we set to the outskirts of London. I did the screwing in this way. Wherever I saw a lobby lighted with gas, I looked in at the key-hole. If I saw anything worth lifting I 'screwed' the door – I'll teach you how to do it – seized the things, into the cart with them, and off to the next place.[23]

One of the marks of the truly professional criminal was a determination to foil the efforts of the law, at almost any cost. Two men had effected an entrance to a house in Bedford Square, but were discovered and apprehended. Both were removed to the nearest police office. '"On me", said one of the pair, "nothing was found", but from his pockets some money and articles were removed. To this he offered no opposition, but he steadily refused to open one of his hands, which he kept firmly clenched in spite of every attempt that was made to relax it. It was struck with a baton, trodden on the ground by an iron heel until the blood was streaming, yet not for a moment did he loosen his grip. He succeeded in keeping it, but his disappointment was extreme when he discovered afterwards, from his knowledge of *stones*, that his firmness had been exerted in preserving a paltry counterfeit.'[24] […]

From Victorian Prison Lives: English Prison Biography, 1830–1914 *(London: Pimlico), 1999, pp. 59–63.*

Notes

1. Kingsmill (1854), 44.
2. Ibid., 49.
3. B. Thomson (1925), 150.
4. Ibid., 152.
5. Fulford (1852), 148.
6. W.L. Clay (1861), 564.
7. Ibid., 567.
8. Leicester Inquiry (1854), 215.

9. Ibid., 236.
10. Ibid., 225.
11. Ibid., 220.
12. Ibid., 223.
13. Holyoake (1893), I, 163.
14. Half-Times (1917), 78.
15. Bent (1891), 71.
16. Drunkenness Inquiry (1834), 355.
17. Quinton (1910), 16.
18. Joseph (1853), 45–6.
19. Blake (1927), 18.
20. One-who-has-endured-it (1877), 259.
21. W.L. Clay, 522.
22. Henderson (1869), 29.
23. Ibid., 68.
24. Ritchie (1854), 163.

References

Select committees and royal commissions

Select Committee on Inquiry into Drunkenness. *PP* 1834 (559), VIII, 315.
Royal Commission Appointed to Inquire into the Condition and Treatment of the Prisoners Confined in Leicester County Gaol and House of Correction. *PP* 1854 (1808), XXXIV, 197.

Other sources

Bent, James (1891) *Criminal Life: Reminiscences of Forty Two Years as a Police Officer*, Manchester, J. Heywood.
Blake, Wallace (1927) *Reminiscences of a Prison Governor*, London, Hodder & Stoughton.
Clay, Walter Lowe (1861) *The Prison Chaplain – A Memoir of the Rev. John Clay*, London: Macmillan.
Fulford, Captain (1852) 'On prison discipline', in *Meliora*, ed. Viscount Ingestre, London, J.W. Parks.
Half-Timer (1917) *Prison Reminiscences*, London, Eliot Stock.
Henderson, Frank (ed.) (1869) *Six Years in the Prisons of England by 'A Merchant'*, London, R. Bentley.
Holyoake, George Jacob (1893) *Sixty Years of an Agitator's Life*, 2 vols, London, T. Fisher-Unwin.
Joseph, Rev. Henry Samuel (1853) *Memoirs of Convicted Prisoners*, London, Wertheim & Co.
Kingsmill, Rev. Joseph (1854) *Chapters on Prisons and Prisoners*, 3rd edn, London, Longmans.
One-who-has-endured-it (1877) *Five Years' Penal Servitude by …*, London, Richard Bentley.
Quinton, Dr R.F. (1910) *Crime and Criminals*, London, Longmans Green.
Ritchie, Dr. Daniel (1854) *The Voice of Our Exiles; or Stray Leaves from a Convict Ship*, Edinburgh, John Menzies.
Thomson, Basil (1925) *The Criminal*, London, Hodder & Stoughton.

6. The well-ordered prison: England, 1780–1865

Randall McGowen

The Mid-Victorian prison experience

While reformers and retributivists tried to shape the prison regime to suit their purposes, both the reality of the prison and the use made of imprisonment by the judicial system displayed the substantial limits of their achievement. Judges and magistrates used the prison, but not in a way that cooperated with the ambitions of the designers of penal regimes. Both reformers and retributivists believed that long sentences were needed to reform or deter offenders. But sentencing policy moved in the opposite direction. Of some 74,000 sentenced by magistrates to imprisonment by the early 1860s, 52,000 were for terms of one month or less. Of the 12,000 sentenced to jails by higher courts, nearly 7,000 were for a period of six months or less. Only 2,100 were subjected to the harshest penalty, penal servitude. By contrast some 9,000 debtors were sent to prison, where they remained, as debtors had a century earlier, a separate group subject to special rules. The Carnarvon Committee acknowledged that little could be done for the typical prisoner beyond a short, sharp sentence. The average occupant of the prison – the drunkard or the individual who could not pay a fine – was seldom the professional criminal who was so graphically described in popular debate.

If the central features of the eighteenth-century prison had been abolished by 1865, the various penal ideals of the reformers had been only imperfectly realized. This failure made imprisonment a different kind of experience from what had been imagined. For instance, the reformers believed in the power of a rationally planned and minutely articulated architecture to transform human character. Far from being neutral and anonymous, however, the actual mid-Victorian prison building possessed a distinctive personality. The smell of the prison was offensive. The cold produced a level of suffering that approached cruelty. The silence was incomplete, broken by the sobs and cries of prisoners at night or the movements of guards and the constant opening and closing of doors. Although the goal of separation led to refinements in the prison, these changes often only complicated the task of moving large numbers of prisoners about the building. Convicts were given only a few minutes in the bathroom in the morning, and it could take up to an hour to get prisoners in and out of the stalls at chapel.

Similarly the rituals of prison life often worked differently than had been desired. Reformers introduced a regime whose ambition was to erase the old identity of the offender and to destroy the immoral sociability that was thought to sustain bad habits. Imprisonment was supposed to create this change by the combined action of stone, routine, labour, and religion. No aspect of life was thought too insignificant to contribute to this result. The initiation into prison life symbolized this quest. New prisoners were given a bath and a haircut. They were clothed in uniforms and assigned a number in place of their names. These measures were intended to facilitate the creation of a new identity, but numerous prisoners testified to a different outcome. They felt demeaned and humiliated. The bathwater was foul. The uniforms were coarse and ill-fitting. The shoes were cheap and uncomfortable. The physical inspection of the prisoner's body established from the outset that he had no right of privacy, a lesson reinforced every day by the spy hole in the cell door.

Whatever high-minded goals inspired the regime, these aims tended to be lost in the multiplication of rules and rituals that governed prison life. Both reformers and their opponents agreed that comfort and pleasure had no place in the prison, that privation was a necessary element of any penal scheme. In practice this agreement led to a relentless hunt to check communication or deny any petty pleasure. The threat of punishment hung over every proceeding. The ex-military men who staffed prisons were far better at detecting infractions than at contribution to moral reform. The morning inspection of the cell became a contest during which the discovery of poorly folded blankets or a stained cup resulted in a mark against one's name. During the early part of their terms, prisoners slept on a plank bed. Their food was monotonous, unpleasant, and barely adequate. Short-term prisoners received bread and an oatmeal gruel. Those confined for more than three weeks were given in addition potatoes and soup. Prisoners sentenced to hard labour and long sentences were provided with a few scraps of meat. The food was often of dubious quality and ill-prepared. Hungry prisoners were ready to eat anything they came across, whether weeds, candles, or paper. The deprivation of food was the mainstay of punishment within the prison. Convicts who failed to fulfill their work quota, were caught talking, or proved sulky might find themselves on a diet of bread and water. The pettiness and spitefulness of these measures did far more to set the tone for imprisonment than any of the lofty words of spiritual consolation.

One of the main aims of the reformed penal regime was to render prisoners passive so that their characters could be reshaped. But the evidence offered by prison memoirs told a different story. Prisoners were inventive in discovering ways to subvert penal discipline. Only the new convicts challenged the regime head-on, and a beating or a week of reduced diet demonstrated the folly of such attempts. The old hands avoided direct confrontations; they were the model prisoners whom many commentators suspected of hypocrisy but against whom nothing could be proved. They taught new prisoners methods for communicating with each other, shortcuts in finishing work, and the names of guards who could be played upon. Convicts shared food and warned of the approach of guards. They developed a form of ventriloquism, the art of talking without moving one's lips. The prison at night was filled with the sound of tapping as pipes became the medium for telegraphic communication. Some prisoners created chat holes through which they could speak to each other. They relayed information on where to find nails that would make oakum picking, the separation of strands of old rope, easier. They told how to step on the treadwheel so as to make that ordeal less exhausting. Some engaged in an illegal trade with guards and among themselves for tobacco and other small luxuries. Witnesses before parliamentary committees testified to the intransigence of prison culture and the solidarities formed among prisoners.

No other area of prison life exposed the contradictions and tensions of imprisonment so much as health. The reform of incarceration had arisen out of a concern with the sickness and suffering that existed in the old jails. The claim that modern prisons protected health served to justify their existence. The critics worried that too much relaxation of a necessary severity had crept into the regime under this banner. Prison officials were often skeptical of reports of sickness, yet they were afraid of the scandal that arose from illness and death. Since the prison surgeon had considerable authority to grant a prisoner release from labour or a better diet, convicts had a powerful incentive to take advantage of this chink in the penal order. Some were so desperate that they deliberately injured themselves to avoid dangerous or unpleasant work. Others became masters of feigning illness to gain access to the relaxed discipline of the hospital. The reformers and retributivists who debated possible forms of imprisonment always imagined reducing the autonomy of the prisoners and the guards to a minimum. Prison memoirs revealed how elusive this goal could be.

Conclusion

In the period between 1780 and 1865, confinement was given a more uniform and exacting shape. The ideals of reformers often played a decisive role in defining this shape, even though the penal practices fostered by reformers long survived the decay of their ideals. For instance, the classification of prisoners was born from a desire to limit the spread of moral contagion. It came to constitute a way of organizing the prisoner's progression through his sentence and enlisting his cooperation. All too often strategies that were intended to reform prisoners found acceptance because they increased the severity of confinement or aided in the management of convicts. The most enduring accomplishment of these years was the creation of the prison as a place apart from the world. It was a realm defined by an ever more thorough loss of freedom. Prisoners suffered few physical punishments, but they were denied any control over their days. They were permitted almost no visitors. Even their letters were censored. Communication was conducted under a constant threat of punishment. Any contact that might resemble normal sociability among prisoners or with the outside world became a target for controls and prohibitions.

Even as the prisoners were more closely controlled and observed, punishment disappeared from the experience of most people. The general public became less familiar with the inside of the prison. Society came to rely on the wide dissemination of literary and journalistic reports about the prisons. Here was the other enduring consequence of this period. The prison loomed even larger in the public's imagination as the prisoner disappeared from view. The prisoner out of sight produced more, rather than less, anxiety. The public was alarmed at the occupant of the 'other' world and the possibility of his return to their world. This separate time and space had been created for the benefit of the offender, as a way of reforming him. The order and morality of the prison world was supposed to mirror that of respectable society. But the prison regime remained an order of unfreedom and severity. And as such, it branded those who had passed through it. The witnesses before the Carnarvon Committee returned time and again to the power of the stigma that attached to those who came out of prison. The prison was supposed to individualize treatment, to produce a 'new man'. But the public never came to accept this claim. On the contrary, they regarded the prison as discovering the true identity of those who passed through its gate. Thus the prison, far from curing crime, created a uniform criminality whose taint clung to anyone who had been confined. Prisons were supposed to civilize their occupants, but it was difficult for most in society to admit that the institution or its residents belonged to the civilized world. Yet this was an effect that no one who contributed to the penal debates had intended. The prison regime of 1865 not only was the product of the ideals of reformers and the practices of prison administrators, of local initiatives and government intervention, but also was the outcome of an institution that had created its own logic and powerful necessity.

From Norval Morris and David J. Rothman (eds) The Oxford History of the Prison: The Practice of Punishment in Western Society *(New York, NY: Oxford University Press), 1998, pp. 95–8.*

Theoretical approaches and emerging trends

Introduction

Part B is concerned with some of the theoretical approaches to imprisonment and emerging trends in the use and organization of imprisonment in recent decades. As Sim (2001) notes, liberal approaches to the prison are built on a number of competing and contradictory goals – for example, rehabilitation, general prevention, incapacitation, punishment and individual and collective deterrence. These various theoretical approaches have underpinned the use, management and organization of the prison system, and the operation of prison regimes, throughout the modern era. The following extracts focus on the organization and management of prisons, prison privatization, order and control, and legitimacy, and collectively question the extent to which prisons can rehabilitate or reform prisoners. This part also asks whether we should question more deeply the use of the prison as punishment, with a view, as Sim has suggested, to replacing it with a more 'reflexive and integrative strategy for dealing with these complex social phenomena' (2001: 2).

Privately contracted prisons raise many philosophical, empirical and policy questions that cover a wide range of issues. For example, is it proper for prisons to be administered by anyone other than government? Can private companies improve the *quality* of imprisonment through new innovations or will they cut corners to save costs? How might the *quantity* of imprisonment be affected? Is *accountability* decreased because prisons are less accessible to public scrutiny, or increased due to legal controls in the private sector (Logan 1990)? The privatization of prisons in the UK and USA since the late 1980s is one particular trend that is examined by Michael Cavadino and James Dignan in the first extract chosen. In this reading, they discuss the various forms that privatization takes, from the 'contracting out' of services like education, healthcare or prison escort services, to the running and management of entire prisons by a private operator. They discuss the development of the debate concerning privatization in England and Wales in the 1980s, which eventually led to the 'contracting out' of Wolds Prison (as a remand centre) and a new prison, Blakenhurst, opened to hold remand and sentenced prisoners, in the early 1990s. Other prisons were rapidly contracted out, followed by three purpose-built private institutions at Fazakerley, Bridgend and Salford; the first prisons to be designed, constructed, managed and financed by the private sector. The latter part of Cavadino and Dignan's argument explains the continued development of privatization within the prison system – its establishment a 'seemingly well entrenched multimillion pound market' – and provides a review of the theoretical foundations on which prison privatization is based.

Privatization is also a key theme of Reading 8. In 'Can prisons be legitimate?' by Richard Sparks anticipates several of the forthcoming readings, including Sim on abolition (Reading 12), Sykes on the 'society of captives' (Reading 19) and Mathiesen on 'the defences of the weak' (Reading 22). In the full article from which this extract is taken, Sparks utilizes the concept of legitimacy drawing on a definition by Beetham (1991) who advocated that power can be said to be legitimate to the extent that it conforms to established rules; the rules can be justified by reference to established beliefs shared by both the dominant and subordinate; and there is evidence of consent by the subordinate to the particular power relation. In this piece Sparks explores some of the current problems with legitimacy in Western penal systems, particularly focusing on privatization and the 'new penality'. He argues that the problem of legitimacy is of central importance in writing about prisons. He suggests that all prison systems confront severe legitimacy deficits, but that these are not universally experienced: 'for as long as we must have prisons, it is ... possible to distinguish clearly between better and worse, preferable and less preferable, stronger and less strong justifications both in the conditions which externally govern their use and in their internal practices.'

Readings 8 and 9 are inter-related, each examining questions of legitimacy, order and control in prisons. Continuing the discussion of the previous reading in, 'Legitimacy and order in prisons', Richard Sparks and Anthony Bottoms compare problems of order and modes of regulation in two English maximum security prisons for men, Albany and Long Lartin. Their research found that the regimes operating in these two prisons were markedly different. At Albany the regime was stringently controlled in comparison to other long-term prisons, restrictions on association and movement were more pronounced and there was a higher recorded rate of minor disciplinary offences. However, the interpersonal skills of the staff helped to maintain good relationships with prisoners, and consistent procedures and 'service delivery' may have helped limit the prison legitimacy deficit. On the other hand, Long Lartin operated a regime where there was more time out of cells, more association, freedom of movement and lighter supervision by the staff. Sparks and Bottoms argue that this regime, which had a history of stability, a favourable regime, and good staff relations, made Long Lartin appear, superficially at least, more 'legitimate' than Albany. However, the regime also offered more opportunities for deviance, predatory behaviour, bullying and risks in day-to-day life. Prisoners who were afraid of victimization felt unsupported by staff, and there were concerns about procedural treatment.

Reading 10 examines the recent 'Rise and rise of supermax' – a facility Roy D. King argues is one 'of the most dramatic features of the great American experiment with mass imprisonment'. Super maximum security prisons were constructed to deal with those prisoners reported to be so disruptive or dangerous that the 'normal' maximum security prisons were unable to cope with them. King dates (in the full article from which this extract is taken) the origins of the modern idea of the supermax to US Penitentiary Marion, Illinois, after the killing of two prison officers, Kluts and Hoffman, in October 1983. This incident followed a 'summer of escalating violence against inmates and staff in the prison, punctuated by lockdowns, shakedowns and suspended activities', resulting in a state of emergency and the permanent lockdown of the facility. King also discusses the 'proliferation of supermax' facilities which has resulted in an estimated 20,000 prisoners held in such conditions in the USA in 1998 (although their use varies in different states) and a system in which these prisons are 'significantly and inappropriately over-used'.

This extract provides us with a discussion of the development of prison policy in Europe as regards dealing with violent and difficult-to-manage prisoners. In the UK, King notes the government's concerns during the 1990s, after high-profile escapes from Whitemoor and Parkhurst, and considers the different approaches to dealing with high-security prisoners in England and Wales as compared with the USA. England and Wales have predominantly favoured the dispersal of these prisoners to secure units within prisons with good to high security, as has the rest of Europe. America, on the other hand, has preferred to concentrate the 'worst of the worst' prisoners in large prisons surrounded by lethal electric fences, perimeter guards and watch towers (see the Introduction and Conclusion to this volume for a fuller discussion of dispersal prisons in the UK and supermaxes in the USA).

Reading 11 is an article from the *Guardian* written by Sally Weale. 'Softly does it' provides a stark contrast with the previous reading on the supermax by examining the success of the therapeutic regime at HM Prison Grendon in Buckinghamshire, England. Grendon is the only prison in the country providing a 'unique regime in its therapeutic care of offenders'. Housing up to 230 inmates in Category B secure conditions, the prison operates using its six wings as 'autonomous therapeutic communities' (www.hmprisonservice.gov.uk). There are five other 'Democratic Therapeutic Communities', at HMP Dovegate (200 places for Category B men), HMP Gartree (23 places for Category B lifers), HMP Aylesbury (22 places for young offenders), HMP Blundeston (40 places for Category C men) and HMP Send (40 places for women). Weale claims that Grendon is evidence of how prison can work. Reconviction rates are lower than elsewhere, prisoners and staff benefit from positive relationships, and many prisoners are changed by their experiences there. The regime observes three key policies: no drugs, no sex and no violence. A breach of any of these rules results in an inmate's peers deciding whether he or she should be allowed a second chance or should be kicked out. The therapy sessions are crucial – prisoners confront their criminal behaviour, past life and childhood, and try to address why they have committed such offences. But equally important is a prisoner's motivation to want to change her- or himself.

The latter part of the article refers to HM Prison Dovegate in Staffordshire which is, at the time of writing, due to open a unit for 200 prisoners based along similar lines to Grendon. The therapeutic community unit at Dovegate (run by the private company Premier Prison Group) received a positive report from Anne Owers, Chief Inspector of Prisons in September 2004, along with Grendon. However, as Allison (2004) notes, these progressive practices are often 'under siege from reactionary elements ... seen as heresy in the eyes of the Old Guard.

They see Grendon and Dovegate as a soft touch, a million miles away from the "lock 'em and count 'em" mantra, which, they believe, has served the system well thus far (appalling reconviction rates are conveniently ignored)' (www.guardian.co.uk).

The final reading is by Joe Sim: 'The abolitionist approach: a British perspective.' Abolitionism is a theoretical perspective that seems to have been somewhat lost within the discussion of imprisonment in recent years, despite the large and growing numbers of people in prison and seemingly perennial problems relating to the use of imprisonment. As Sim informs us elsewhere, abolitionism is a 'sociological and political perspective that analyses criminal justice and penal systems as social problems that intensify rather than diminish crime and its impact' (2001: 2). In the full article from which this extract is taken, Sim discusses the origins of abolitionism and particularly refers to the British abolitionist contribution. The first British abolitionist group, Radical Alternatives to Prison (RAP), was established in 1970. This group contributed to a number of early campaigns including opposition to the rebuilding of Holloway women's prison as a secure hospital and to the psychiatric control units to discipline prisoners labelled as 'subversive troublemakers'. They also highlighted the use of drugs to control prisoners, the role of the Prison Medical Service, defended the regime of the Barlinnie Special Unit in Glasgow, widely regarded as a successful therapeutic unit which was closed in 1994 (see also Readings 11 and 13), and were involved in the formation of 'Inquest', established to draw attention to deaths in custody (see www.inquest_org:uk for further information on current issues and campaigns).

In Reading 12, Sim argues that some may see abolitionism as a failure in the current penal climate, but he maintains that the campaigns noted above, although not all successful, have succeeded in making the issue more visible to the public. Sim also sets out the abolitionist critique of the 'reforms' outlined in the reports published in the aftermath of prison disruption in the 1980s, *Opportunity and Responsibility* (Scottish Prison Service) and the Woolf Report (see the Introduction to this volume). He argues that these reports marginalize or heavily qualify prisoners' experiences, shifting the debate from wider structural questions of power, collective rights and democratic control, to a more narrow focus on individual prisoner contracts and emphasizing coercion and militarization as a strategy for maintaining order. For Sim, these reports have also missed the central issue raised by abolitionists and others, namely, that 'unconditional support for limited change mystifies broader structural questions around prevailing definitions of criminality that operate in this society, and who is punished as a result of these definitions'. These points seem particularly pertinent when one examines the characteristics of social exclusion in the prison population of England and Wales (Reading 25) and the features of 'mass imprisonment' in the USA, outlined by David Garland (2001); namely, the vast numbers of people in prison and, particularly, the predominance of young black urban males within the American prison population (see the Conclusion to this volume).

References

Allison, E. (2004) 'Therapy behind bars', *Guardian*, 22 September (www.guardian.co.uk).

Beetham, D. (1991) *The Legitimation of Power*. Basingstoke: Macmillan.

Garland, D. (ed.) (2001) *Mass Imprisonment: Social Causes and Consequences*. London: Sage.

Logan, C. (1990) *Private Prisons: Pros and Cons*. Oxford: Oxford University Press.

Sim, J. (2001) 'Abolitionism', in E. McLaughlin and J. Muncie (eds) *The Sage Dictionary of Criminology*. London: Sage.

7. Prison privatization: panacea or Pandora's box?

Michael Cavadino and James Dignan

Meaning and forms of privatization

Privatization involves 'the systematic transfer of government functions and programmes into the private sector' (Adam Smith Institute, n.d.: 17–18).[1] The first candidates for privatization comprised previously nationalized industries that were involved in the manufacture of goods,[2] followed by some of the former public utilities (telecommunications, gas, electricity and water) that are responsible for providing major public services. It was not long before some on the right began calling for an extension of the policy into the social sphere, including the delivery of punishment (Adam Smith Institute, 1984; Young, 1987) and other aspects of the criminal justice system including certain police functions and even some court services.

Private sector involvement in the penal system may take a variety of forms. In the case of prisons, it could in theory extend to selling off the entire prison system as a going concern, which was the approach adopted for many of the other formerly state-owned monopolies (Shaw, 1989: 56). In practice, however, the government has so far opted for a more limited form of private sector involvement, comprising the 'contracting out'[3] of specific functions to private operators in relation to individual institutions. There are at least five distinct sets of functions relating to the activities of the prison service that could in principle be contracted out in this way.

First there are the various *ancillary* services which do not form part of the 'core function': activities such as catering, education, health care, prison workshops and farms, and also prison escort services. A great many prison ancillary services have now been contracted out both in the United Kingdom and elsewhere. A second function involves the *design and construction* work for new prisons, rather than relying on in-house services as in the past. A third relates to the *financing* of new prisons – by raising money through investments, private loans or the stock market – as an alternative to directly using taxpayers' money. This has become increasingly common in the United States, where voters' demands for more punitive sentences have not always been matched by a willingness to pay for these out of current revenue (Shichor, 1995: 142–6). Fourth, the most controversial form of contracting out to date involves the *management and operation* of all or part of an entire institution. We describe the extent to which this has happened to date in England and Wales in the next section. In all the above options, the involvement of the private sector is limited to the *delivery of services* while the government retains responsibility for allocating the contract, monitoring its performance and also determining prison policy at least at a strategic level (and, of course, ultimately footing the bill through contractual payments to the private firms). In theory at least, a fifth option might be to contract out some of these functions as well.[4]

Finally, a useful distinction is sometimes drawn regarding the 'depth of penetration' by the private sector into the 'prisons market'. This refers to the kind of institutions that may be considered suitable for privatization. These vary considerably from so-called 'shallow-end' institutions – which are those housing relatively low security-risk inmates such as juveniles, remand prisoners and those in open prisons at one extreme – to those which operate at the 'deep-end', catering in the main for high-risk or even maximum-security adult prisoners at the other. As we shall see in the next section, the tendency has been for privatization to involve mainly shallow-end institutions, at least initially, though in England and Wales both the pace and 'depth' of its immersion have increased rapidly after a somewhat hesitant start.

[...]

Strictly speaking, the recent antecedents of prison privatization in England and Wales can be traced back to 1970 when the government entered into a contract with the private security firm, Securicor Ltd, to operate detention centres at the four principal airports for the purpose of holding the growing number of suspected illegal immigrants.[5] This novel arrangement, which extended to the provision of associated escort services, excited little interest at the time, even though by 1988 nearly half of all detained immigrants were said to be held in these and a small number of other private facilities (Joint Council for the Welfare of Immigrants, 1988: 13, quoting Green, 1989). The next tentative step towards prison privatization appears to have been unrelated to this development. However, it too, was prompted by pragmatic rather than ideological concerns, in response to growing alarm over the use of police cells as temporary accommodation for remand prisoners, for whom no room could be found in the chronically overcrowded prisons of the late 1980s. One temporary expedient which the Home Office resorted to in May 1988 involved the use of the Alma Dettingen military barracks near Camberley. Although the prisoners were guarded by military police and troops, the catering service was contracted out to a small company in Surrey in what has been described as 'virtually the first breach in the state monopoly of imprisonment since "nationalization" of the county gaols and recidivist prisons in the late 1870s' (Shaw, 1992).

The contracting out of prisons themselves was first advocated in England and Wales in a pamphlet published by the Adam Smith Institute (a right-wing think-tank) in 1984 but was not taken seriously in either government circles or the Home Office at the time. Indeed, Home Secretary Douglas Hurd informed the House of Commons on 16 July 1987 that: 'I do not think there is a case, and I do not believe that the House would accept a case, for auctioning or privatizing the prisons or handing over the business of keeping prisoners safe to anyone other than government servants' (HC Deb. 16 July 1987, vol. 119, col. 1299).[6] By this stage, however, the cause of prison privatization had been taken up by a small number of Conservative back bench MPs and peers who began to promote it with almost evangelical zeal, backed by tireless and ultimately highly effective lobbying by the would-be providers of private prisons themselves. The result was a policy U-turn, the scale and speed of which was only exceeded by the government's contemporaneous law and order 'counter reformation' [...].

One important precursor of this policy shift was a report by the House of Commons Home Affairs Select Committee (1987) which called for private firms to be allowed to tender for the construction and management of custodial institutions, and particularly those in the remand sector 'because it is there that the most overcrowding in the prison system is concentrated'. Their three-page report followed a brief visit by the Committee to visit a number of private prisons in the United States, which 'profoundly impressed' the Conservative members of the Committee.[7] Shortly afterwards, its chairman, Sir Edward Gardner, was recruited to serve as chairman of Contract Prisons, a company founded 'to exploit the new opportunities' (Windlesham, 1993: 288), following his retirement from Parliament at the 1987 General Election. His new appointment set in motion a 'revolving door' through which other senior Conservative politicians[8] together with growing numbers of senior staff formerly employed by the prison service, senior civil servants and even members of the prison inspectorate (see below) were to pass as the momentum towards privatization gathered strength. Thus, a powerful combination of personal self-interest and corporate self-aggrandizement has been another important factor in the recent resurgence of prison privatization, reinforced by a close overlap between the political and commercial interests associated with senior members of the Conservative Party (Windlesham, 1993: 288–9).

The report by the Home Affairs Committee was followed by a much more ideologically partisan report by Peter Young (1987), of the Adam Smith Institute, who advocated prison privatization partly as a means of breaking the 'monopolistic provision' of imprisonment by the state but also, more specifically, to counter trade union influence on prison policy. As we shall see, such ideological considerations have proved crucial on more than one occasion in the campaign to promote the policy. The first real signs of a change in the government's attitude towards privatization came with the publication of a Green Paper in the autumn of 1988 (Home Office, 1988). This specifically proposed the contracting out of court and escort duties that had hitherto been carried out by police and prison officers, and also recommended an experiment to assess the scope for greater involvement by the private sector in the management of remand prisons. The latter recommendation was partly in response to a dramatic increase in the size of the remand population over the previous decade.[9] Moreover, this sector of the prison estate was felt to raise fewer operational difficulties or issues of principle than those sectors responsible for holding sentenced prisoners. Management consultants were appointed to make detailed recommendations, and a legislative opportunity presented itself in the shape of the Criminal Justice Bill which was being drafted to implement the government's 1991 reform programme.

By this stage, however, the largely pragmatic considerations favouring the introduction of contracting out in relation to remand prisons had become much less compelling following a fall in the overall remand population. Since the proposal was not expected to produce substantial savings, Home Secretary David Waddington's initial inclination was against the inclusion of a power to contract out certain remand prisons (Windlesham, 1993: 297). Before dropping it, however, he sought confirmation from Prime Minister Margaret Thatcher who insisted that the move towards privatization should go ahead.[10] Even so, the original wording of the Bill made it clear that, apart from court escort services,[11] the power to contract out was to be limited first, to remand centres; and second, only to those established after the implementation of the Act. Existing remand centres and prisons housing sentenced prisoners were not initially covered by the Bill. In the end, however, these restrictions were overturned by a 'sub plot ... to which at least one Home Office junior minister was sympathetic, and which only came to light as the Bill progressed' (Windlesham, 1993: 420). This involved a back bench Conservative MP tabling an amendment extending the power to contract out any type of prison, whether holding remand or sentenced prisoners, and whether new or existing.

Although this went far beyond official government policy at the time, the substance of the amendment was retained in section 84 of the 1991 Criminal Justice Act,[12] with the connivance of junior Home Office Minister Angela Rumbold. Nevertheless she assured the House that '[i]f, and only if, the contracted remand centre proves a success might we move towards privatization of other parts of the prison service' (HC Deb. vol. 186, col. 720, 7 Feb. 1991). This assurance counted for little, however, for even before the first remand centre to be contracted out – Wolds Prison – had taken its first inmates in April 1992, Home Secretary Kenneth Baker unexpectedly announced in December 1991 a second candidate for contracting out. This was to be another new prison at Blakenhurst, which would cater for both remand *and* sentenced prisoners.[13] As Lord Windlesham (himself a supporter of contracting out, at least in respect of remand centres) has pointed out (1993: 426): 'To claim that the tendering exercise had been a success in showing how much the private sector had to offer fell well short of fulfilling the undertaking to evaluate the actual experience of private sector management in practice.'[14]

Not long after this there was another even more significant extension to the contracting out policy when it was announced that the management of the existing prison at Strangeways, rebuilt after the 1990 riot, would also be contracted out, though in the event the tender was won by the in-house Prison Service bid.[15] The third private prison – Buckley Hall, near Rochdale – had previously been mothballed but was recommissioned and put out to tender. The next three private prisons (at Fazakerley, Bridgend and Salford) were the first 'DCMF' prisons – designed, constructed, managed and financed by the private sector – which is the model that has subsequently been adopted for all new private prisons. Under these contracts, the private contractors arrange finance to meet the capital costs and only start to receive payments when the first places become available. Thereafter, the Prison Service pays a set fee for each available place over a 25-year period.

In September 1993 Home Secretary Michael Howard announced that the government was planning for about 10 per cent of the prisons in England and Wales (12 prisons in total) to be contracted out during the 'initial phase' of the process, with the aim of creating a sufficiently large private sector to be able to provide sustained competition (HM Prison Service, 1993).[16] At that time it was envisaged that up to seven existing prisons would be contracted out, and a 'market-testing' programme to identify suitable candidates was launched, involving over 20 prisons. However, in October 1994 the Prison Officers' Association (POA) successfully complained to the Central Arbitration Committee that they had not been properly consulted about the market testing exercise. The initial result was to seriously delay the whole process, which was later abandoned by Michael Howard, who was said to have been advised that he would be exceeding his powers if he were to grant leases to private companies in respect of properties that he did not own (Nathan, 1996).

Another setback to government plans to contract out existing prisons was caused by uncertainty surrounding the effect of European Union laws designed to protect the jobs and conditions of workers affected by take-overs and mergers. Under the European Commissions Acquired Rights Directive[17] contractors are obliged to maintain existing jobs and conditions in respect of any contracts they win. Assuming this applies to the contracting out of existing prisons and ancillary services such as court escorts,[18] it would seriously undermine their profitability since this largely depends on contractors being able to reduce the size of both the workforce and the wage bill.[19]

In other respects, however, prison privatization proceeded at an even faster pace under the Conservative government. Thus, by May 1997 the process of contracting out had been extended to include all prison–court escort services, and a wide range of other ancillary services, such as education and some catering services. Of even greater significance was the launch of the Private Finance Initiative in November 1992, the aim of which was to prevent any new public expenditure from being agreed by the Treasury unless the use of private finance has first been considered. In May 1995 the Prison Service appointed a firm of management consultants to find out how much further privatization could be extended under this initiative. The report concluded that the scope was considerable, and recommended that private finance could be used *inter alia* for: major refurbishment projects involving whole prisons,[20] projects for the replacement or refurbishment of individual ancillary service functions (such as catering, prison industry workshops, health care, non-core administration and so on), self contained projects such as new CCTV systems, IT or communication projects. This paved the way for 'Project Quantum', which was launched in July 1996 with a view to privatizing 1200 administrative jobs within the prison service involving finance, personnel and inmate record systems (*Guardian*, 30 July 1996). The project aimed to save £50 million per annum and reduce the Prison Service's administrative budget by 30 per cent.

Thus, within a remarkably short space of time, prison privatization in

England and Wales had progressed from being a seemingly outlandish proposal to a fiercely competitive and seemingly well-entrenched multi-million pound market. For a brief period immediately following the 1997 General Election, the longer term future of prison privatization in England and Wales seemed more doubtful since the victorious Labour party had pledged repeatedly and unequivocally while in opposition, to take private prisons back into public ownership.[21] However, this 'principled opposition' began to melt away within days of the election victory. One week later Jack Straw, the new Labour Home Secretary, announced that he would be prepared to sign contracts that were already in the pipeline if this proved to be the only way of providing new accommodation quickly. Just over one year later he confirmed[22] that a complete *volte face* had taken place when he announced that, in the wake of two internal (and therefore secret) Prison Service reviews, all new prisons in England and Wales would be privately built and run. The reviews were said to have concluded, first, that the option of using private finance to build new prisons while retaining the management function within the public sector was not affordable and did not offer value for money; and second, that the immediate transfer of private prisons back to the public sector could not be justified for the same reasons.

The only consolation offered to the public sector was a commitment to allow the Prison Service to tender for private management contracts when these expired,[23] and over the next four years it successfully tendered for three contracts in the face of competition from the private sector.[24] These individual set-backs for the private sector did not in any way signal a weakening in the Labour government's new-found enthusiasm for the policy of prison privatization as a whole, however. By the end of January 2001 nine prisons were being managed by the private sector (though two of these were due to revert to public sector management), five of which were also designed, constructed and financed by the private sector.[25] A further four 'DCMF' prisons were either in the pipeline or at the planning stage. Moreover, in July 1999 the prisons minister, Paul Boateng had announced that Brixton prison was to be market tested with a view to privatizing it after it was publicly denigrated as a 'failing' prison, and he subsequently indicated that other prisons felt to be failing in terms of regime quality and costs would follow suit (Prison Reform Trust, 2001: 2).[26] Then in December 2001 the Director General of the Prison Service announced plans to sell off to developers a number of the 37 English prisons which are no longer fit for modern use and replace them with larger and more modern facilities. Consequently, the policy of encouraging private sector involvement in the design, construction, financing and operation of prisons in England and Wales now appears unassailable, at least for the foreseeable future.[27]

[...]

Panacea or Pandora's box?

The main philosophical justification for prison privatization derives from the *laissez-faire* free-market economic theories championed by right-wing governments in the 1980s and 1990s. Various economic 'nostrums' are invoked by 'true believers' to support the case for privatizating areas of public provision. (See particularly, in relation to prison privatization, Young, 1987; Hutto, 1990; and Logan, 1990.) They include a reliance on 'free competition' through the market-place as the best spur to efficiency and quality of service, and also as the most effective scourge of restrictive practices and vested (trade union) interest; a split between the producers and purchasers of public services and a rhetorical belief in 'rolling back the frontiers of the state', at least to the extent of reducing its 'social rôle and responsibilities' (Kamerman and Kahn, 1989: 256).[28] To put it crudely, the seductive appeal of prison privatization is that it offers more (prison capacity) and better (quality of service) for less money. On the face of it, however, one of the strongest arguments deployed by supporters of prison privatization is the lamentable and all-too-obvious failings associated with the publicly-run prison service […]. Before examining the specific claims advanced on behalf of prison privatization, we wish to comment on the theoretical foundations underpinning the programme.

First, whatever sentimental attachment some might feel towards a mythical bygone era in which a free and unregulated market supposedly delivered the best of all possible outcomes in response to the laws of supply and demand, such a model is singularly inappropriate today, whether in relation to the provision of social services in general or the practice of punishment in particular. For whatever the position might have been in the past, today there is no such thing as an unregulated market. Instead, the size of the custodial 'market' itself, the nature of the services to be supplied, and also the terms in which this is to happen, including even (to some extent) the identities of the 'players' are all determined by the state, which is quite at liberty to forbid public sector institutions from submitting a bid should it choose to do so. Indeed, this is precisely what happened with both the Wolds and Blakenhurst prison tenders. Moreover, the government has it in its power to alter the balance of advantage between the public and private sectors,[29] for example by starving the one of the resources it might need to implement the Woolf reforms across the board, while ensuring that the other is given the opportunity to develop a limited number of 'show-case' institutions, intended to show off the private sector in the best light.[30]

Governments are not the only ones who are capable of 'rigging the market', however. For, as Sutherland (1956: 90) pointed out, 'big business does not like competition, and makes careful arrangements to reduce it and eliminate it'. This is most easily done where there are relatively few powerful corporations, the 'entry price' is high, and opportunities for reallocating the contract are limited, all of which applies to the privatized prisons market. Despite an increase in the number of companies aspiring to join the 'corrections–commercial complex'[31] (Lilly and Knepper, 1990, 1992), the market itself is dominated by a small handful of multinational corporations or conglomerates for whom various mechanisms might be available to limit competition. One is that of price-fixing; another is the taking over of rivals.[32] One danger is that once a government comes to depend on a small number of private companies, it may be 'held to ransom' and have little choice but to pay the higher prices charged to increase profitability. The risk would appear to be even greater where private operators are licensed not only to operate a particular institution but also to build, own and run it, as is now to be the case with all future tenders in England and Wales.

Second, the classical free market model in which the laws of supply and demand ensure responsiveness by the producer to the needs of the purchaser is difficult to apply in the context of prison privatization (Shichor, 1995: 71–3). For instead of the traditional dyadic relationships linking vendor and purchaser or even provider and client, with prison privatization there are three parties to the relationship – the third being the state, which provides the money. At the very least this is likely to distort the 'normal' operation of supply and demand mechanisms. Thus, the inmates for whom the contractor's services are ostensibly provided are not free to shop around or 'take it or leave it' (Palumbo, 1986), and are therefore much more dependent on the contractor than would normally be the case, particularly given their political, economic and social impotence (Geis, 1987). Conversely, the service providers are much less dependent on the 'consumers' of their services for their economic success than they are on their primary customer or paying client, the government. Consequently, inmates may have even less control over their fate in a privatized prison system than in one provided directly by the state itself. At the very least there may well be a conflict of interest between the needs and desires of the parties to this triadic relationship, which underlines the importance of not accepting at face value the free-market rhetoric that is usually used in support of prison privatization.

Third, while the deplorable state of the publicly run prison system has to be acknowledged, it may be as well to remember that the principal reason why it came into being in the first place was because of the excesses and shortcomings associated with an earlier era of private provision. It may well be that, as Sparks (1994: 26) has argued, all prison systems by their very nature suffer from legitimacy deficits even at the best of times. But then the crucial question raised by prison privatization is not whether it is capable of 'delivering more for less' […] but whether, in the light of the available evidence, it is likely to alleviate or aggravate the crisis of legitimacy, as well as the other pressing problems confronting the English prison system.

[…]

From The Penal System: An Introduction *(London: Sage), 3rd edn 2001, pp. 228–36.*

Notes

1. We use the terms 'private sector' and 'privatization to refer to the commercial (profit making) sector, as distinct from the 'voluntary sector' (charities etc.) and the 'informal sector' of active but unpaid citizens. Voluntary organizations run 'intermediate treatment' and other non custodial projects, and the voluntary sector was invited to bid for the government's secure training centres for 12 to 15 year olds, an invitation it declined. Within the criminal justice system as a whole certain activities have also been transferred to what has been described as the informal sector, as in the case of 'neighbourhood watch' (see Mawby, 1989; Nellis, 1989).

2. Rolls Royce, British Steel, British Shipbuilding, British Leyland and British Aerospace were among the first government-owned concerns to be privatized.
3. Technically, the government does not regard this as 'privatization', which may result in misleading answers being given to parliamentary questions on the subject unless they are very carefully phrased (Nathan, 1995a: 18).
4. This has not yet happened anywhere, as far as we are aware. However, Nathan (1994: 16) reported that in 1994 the Department of Justice in the Australian state of Victoria was planning to privatize the contracting out process itself, by appointing consultants Coopers and Lybrand to oversee the bidding process relating to three new prisons which were to be financed, designed, built and operated by private firms.
5. See McDonald (1994), citing Green (1989) and Rutherford (1990). Interestingly, an increase in the number of illegal immigrants during the 1970s, combined with a of funding for new facilities to house them, has also been linked to the develop of privatization in the corrections sphere in the United States (Windlesham, 1993: 281).
6. Mr Hurd did, however, accept the need to consider how private sector skills knowledge might be used to supervise and accelerate the delivery of the prison-building programme, in response to concerns expressed by the Comptroller Auditor General and also the House of Commons Public Accounts Committee the government's ambitious and costly prison building target might fall short of its target of matching available places with the total prison population by the end of the decade (Windlesham, 1993: 279).
7. According to a press statement issued by Sir John Wheeler MP on 31 October 1986.
8. Most notable of whom was Conservative Party Chairman Sir Norman Fowler, who was a non executive director of Group 4 until he resigned in September following an outcry over his dual role. In addition, Sir John Wheeler MP, succeeded Sir Edward Gardner as Chairman of the Home Affairs Committee a former Chairman of the British Security Industries Association, many of whose members have bid for contracts.
9. In the ten year period between 1979 and 1988, the remand population increased 76 per cent from 6,629 to 11,667, compared with a much more modest rate of increase (18 per cent) in the overall size of the prison population (James and Bottomley, 1998: 223).
10. The episode sheds interesting light on Mrs Thatcher's approach to criminal justice policy, which appears not to have been particularly interventionist at this time though this did not stop her from giving free rein to her ideological instincts in response to a specific enquiry, without reference to Cabinet Committee or even other Home Office ministers (Windlesham, 1993: 298).
11. The first contract for these was awarded to Group 4 Securitas with effect from 5 April 1993.
12. The legislative scope for prison privatization has since been extended still further by section 96 of the Criminal Justice and Public Order Act 1994, which allow the contracting out of *parts* of public sector prisons. Moreover, section 99 authorizes the contracting out of any functions or activities at state run prisons, which raises the prospect of private sector prison staff being brought in to undertake duties in prisons that have not themselves (yet) been privatized.
13. N.B. Wolds prison was itself recategorized as a prison catering for both remand and sentenced prisoners in 1995.
14. In the event, the evaluation of Wolds prison (by Professor Keith Bottomley of the University of Hull) which was supposed to have been successfully completed before other parts of the prison service were privatized, did not appear until April 1 and then only in summary form (Bottomley et al., 1996).
15. For a time this placed HMP Strangeways in a somewhat anomalous position since the terms on which it was managed by the Prison Service closely resembled the model adopted for private corporations. This included the incorporation of a 'Service Level Agreement' between the Governor and the Prison Service, and the appointment of a 'Compliance Manager', with a role akin to that of 'controller' in contracted out institutions [...]. However, the Prison Service has subsequently proposed the introduction of similar 'Service Delivery Agreements' for all prisons, with a view to encouraging the adoption of concepts such as financial efficiency and contract compliance, which are associated with the private sector (Jago and Thompson, 1999: 231).
16. In 1998 it was predicted that this 'target' would be achieved by March 2002, by which time the certified normal accommodation of the prison service as a whole was forecast to be 67,700, 6,600 of which (9.7 per cent) were expected to be managed by the private sector (Hansard, 17 July 1998, as reported by Nathan, 1998: 15).
17. Directive (77/187), which was implemented in the UK in 1981 by the Transfer of Undertakings (Protection of Employment) Regulations (TUPE) (Crabbe, 1993: 34–5).

18. The High Court ruled in 1993 (*Kenny v. South Manchester College* (1993) IRLR: 265) that Prison Service education lecturers' pay and conditions should remain as they were before the service was put out to tender (Nathan, 1993b: 14). Moreover the government was forced to concede (after taking legal advice) that existing staff contracts and conditions of employment at Strangeways would be honoured even if a private operator were to secure the contract (Nathan, 1993a: 12).
19. Subsequently, the Labour government has altered the term of the Private Finance Initiative [...] to ensure that it complies with the Directive (*Guardian*, 14 March 2000).
20. In which the contractor would first refurbish (and/or extend) and then take over and manage its entire operation.
21. Both John Prescott (who was to become Deputy Prime Minister) and Jack Straw (who was to become Home Secretary) had reiterated the party's clearly stated opposition to the policy of prison privatization in speeches to the annual conference of the Prison Officers' Association (in 1994 and 1996 respectively). See Prison Reform Trust (1998: 1).
22. In a speech delivered, ironically, at another annual conference of the Prison Officers' Association on 18 May 1998 (Prison Reform Trust, 1998: 1).
23. The Prison Service had not been allowed to bid for the Wolds and Blakenhurst tenders.
24. The first of these – Buckley Hall – had previously been managed by Group 4 since it reopened in 1994. In October 1999 it became the first privately operated prison to revert to public sector control. Then in January 2001 the Prison Service was named as preferred bidder to take over the management of Blakenhurst prison from United Kingdom Detention Services (UKDS). The third successful public sector bid was to continue running Strangeways prison when its contract came up for renewal, also in January 2001.
25. They were Parc, Altcourse, Lowdham Grange, Ashfield and Forest Bank.
26. It remains to be seen whether any private concern will show any serious interest in taking on such a challenge, let alone succeed with it. A far better solution in our view for failing prisons of this kind would be to close them.
27. In marked contrast to the position in other jurisdictions such as New Zealand and the Australian state of Victoria, which appear to have concluded that prison privatization is a 'failed experiment' (Cavadino and Dignan, forthcoming).
28. It has often been observed that the attitude of the new right towards the role of the state is not entirely consistent, however, and that the conservative agenda in relation to crime control has been to extend the reach of the law and extend the power of the state to enforce it while cutting back on its responsibilities for health, welfare and other social programmes (Shichor, 1995: 59).
29. As, arguably, happened in both the educational and health services under the post-1979 Conservative governments.
30. Similar criticisms have been voiced against certain privately run correctional institutions in the United States, particularly the Silverdale Detention Centre in Tennessee, which is operated by 'market leaders' Corrections Corporation of America, and which has been described as 'the most researched correctional facility in the United States' (Shichor, 1995: 177).
31. Various terms have been coined to express the same idea including 'criminal justice–industrial complex' (Quinney, 1977; Maghan, 1991; Shichor, 1995) and 'correctional industrial complex' (Bronstein, 1993/4).
32. For example, the US 'market leaders' Corrections Corporation of America was reported to have acquired one of its major US competitors, Concept Inc., which was described at the time as the third largest company in the corrections industry (Nathan, 1995b: 19).

References

Adam Smith Institute (1984) *Justice Policy*. London: ASI Research.
Adam Smith Institute (n.d.) *Privatizing America*. Washington DC: Adam Smith Institute.
Bottomley, A.K., James, A., Clare, E. and Liebling, A. (1996) *Wolds Remand Prison: An Evaluation*. Home Office Research Findings No. 32, London: HMSO.
Bronstein, A.J. (1993–4) 'More Prison Less Crime?', *Criminal Justice Matters*, 14: 8–9.
Cavadino, M. and Dignan, J. (with others) (forthcoming) *Penal Systems: A Comparative Approach*. London: Sage Publications.
Crabbe, T. (1993) 'Private Profits in the Public Sector', *International Union Rights* (Journal of the International Centre for Trade Union Rights), 1 (4): 34–5.

Geis, G. (1987) 'The Privatization of Prisons: Panacea or Placebo?', in B.J. Carroll, R.W. Conant and T.A. Easton (eds), *Private Means, Public Ends: Private Business in Social Service Delivery*, pp. 76–97. New York: Praeger.

Green, P. (1989) 'Private Sector Involvement in the Immigrant Detention Centres'. London: Howard League for Penal Reform.

HM Prison Service (1993) 'Michael Howard Unveils Plans for More Private Sector Involvement in the Prison Service', News Release, 2 September 1993.

Home Office (1988) *Private Sector Involvement in the Remand System*, Cm 434. London: HMSO.

House of Commons Home Affairs Select Committee (1987) *Contract Provision of Prisons* (Fourth Report, Session 1986/7, HC291). London: HMSO.

Hutto, T.D. (1990) 'The Privatization of Prisons' in J.W. Murphy and J.E. Dison (eds), *Are Prisons any Better? Twenty Years of Correctional Reform*, pp. 111–27. Newbury Park, CA: Sage Publications.

Jago, R. and Thompson, E. (1999) 'Privatisation of Prisons', in M. Leech and D. Cheney, *The Prisons Handbook 2000* (4th edn), pp. 229–31. Winchester: Waterside Press.

James, A. and Bottomley, K. (1998) 'Prison Privatisation and the Remand Population: Principle versus Pragmatism?', *Howard Journal of Criminal Justice*, 37: 223–33.

Joint Council for the Welfare of Immigrants (1988) *Annual Report 1988*. London: Joint Council for the Welfare of Immigrants.

Kamerman, S.B. and Kahn, A.J. (eds) (1989) *Privatization and the Welfare State*, Princeton, NJ: Princeton University Press.

Lilly, J.R. and Knepper, P. (1990) 'The corrections–industrial complex', *Prison Service Journal*, 87: 43–52.

Logan, C. (1990) *Private Prisons: Cons and Pros*. Oxford: Oxford University Press.

McDonald, D.C. (1994) 'Public Imprisonment by Private Means: the Re-emergency of Private Persons in the United States, the United Kingdom and Australia', *British Journal of Criminology*, 34: 29–48.

Maghan, J. (1991) 'Privatization of Corrections: Anticipating the Unanticipated' in D.E.J. Macnamara and R.J. Kelly (eds), *Perspectives on Deviance: Dominance, Degradation and Denigration*, pp. 135–91. Cincinnati, OH: Anderson.

Mawby, R.I. (1989) 'The Voluntary Sector's Role in a Mixed Economy of Criminal Justice', in R. Matthews (ed.), *Privatising Criminal Justice*, pp. 135–54. London: Sage Publications.

Nathan, S. (1993a) 'Privatisation Factfile 1', *Prison Report*, 22: 12–14.

Nathan, S. (1993b) 'Privatisation Factfile 3', *Prison Report*, 24: 11–18.

Nathan, S. (1994) 'Privatisation Factfile 7', *Prison Report*, 28: 11–18.

Nathan, S. (1995a) 'Privatisation Factfile 9', *Prison Report*, 30: 13–20.

Nathan, S. (1995b) 'Privatisation Factfile 10', *Prison Report*, 31: 13–20.

Nathan, S. (1996) 'Privatisation Factfile 16', *Prison Report*, 27: 13–16.

Nathan, S. (1998) 'Privatisation Factfile 23', *Prison Report*, 44: 15–18.

Nellis, M. (1989) 'Juvenile Justice and the Voluntary Sector' in R. Matthews (ed.), *Privatizing Criminal Justice*. London: Sage Publications.

Palumbo, D.J. (1986) 'Privatization and Corrections Policy', *Policy Studies Review*, 5: 598–605.

Prison Reform Trust (1998) *Prison Privatization Report International*, Volume 21. London: Prison Reform Trust.

Prison Reform Trust (2001) *Prison Privatization Report International*, Volume 38. London: Prison Reform Trust.

Quinney, R. (1977) *Class, State and Crime: on the Theory and Practice of Criminal Justice*. New York: David McKay.

Rutherford, A. (1990) 'British Penal Policy and the Idea of Prison Privatization' in D.C. McDonald (ed.), *Private Persons and the Public Interest*, pp. 42–65. New Brunswick, NJ: Rutgers University Press.

Shaw, S. (1989) 'A Bull Market for Prisons' in P. Carter, T. Jeffs, and M. Smith (eds), *Social Work and Social Welfare Yearbook 1*. Buckingham: Open University Press.

Shaw, S. (1992) 'The Short History of Prison Privatization', *Prison Service Journal*, 87: 30–2.

Shichor, D. (1995) *Prisons for Profit: Private Prisons/Public Concerns*. Thousand Oaks, CA: Sage Publications.

Sparks, R. (1994) 'Can Prisons Be Legitimate? Penal Politics, Privatization, and the Timeliness of an Old Idea', *British Journal of Criminology*, 34, Special Issue: 14–28.

Sutherland, E.H. (1956) 'Crime of Corporations' in A. Cohen, A. Lindesmith and K. Schuessler (eds), *The Sutherland Papers*, pp. 78–96. Bloomington, IN: Indiana University Press.

Windlesham, D. (1993) *Responses to Crime, Volume 2: Penal Policy in the Making*. Oxford: Clarendon Press.

Young, P. (1987) *The Prison Cell*. London: Adam Smith Institute.

8. Can prisons be legitimate?
Penal politics, privatization, and the timeliness of an old idea

Richard Sparks

Penal problems as legitimation problems

I think it makes a great deal of sense to try to think through many of the current problems of western penal systems in terms of the concept of legitimacy. Indeed I suspect that the tradition of sociological study of 'captive society' can be read very largely in terms of the competing views it throws up of issues of legitimacy and legitimation problems (see also Sparks and Bottoms 1992). Furthermore this has a crucial bearing on our interpretation of such central matters as prison disorders and prisoners' rights campaigns. By the same token legitimacy is also central to the understanding of official discourses generated in response to prison problems.

In principle legitimacy is an issue for every practice of punishment or sanctioning, as it is for all distributions of power and resources (see Beetham 1991, chapter 2). This is true on various levels. These include the endlessly recurrent arguments about which philosophical principles might animate or justify the imposition of criminal sanctions, or about the failure of such principles.[1] Any genuinely full discussion would also have to deal with the equally extensive and contentious problem of the relations between practices of punishment and the sources of social power.[2] I cannot extend or revise the discussion of these big issues here. Rather I will use the concept of legitimacy in an exploratory way to discuss some more particular and topical questions (already quite large enough in themselves).

[...]

Legitimacy is not an abstruse concern. Quite the contrary – it is intimately and practically implicated in every aspect of penal relations. For this reason it has recently begun to attract the attention of commentators speaking from a variety of differing vantage points, such as Cavadino (1992), Sim (1992), Sparks and Bottoms (1992) and arguably Woolf himself (1991). Its conceptual power lies in the connections which it illuminates between the interior life of penal systems, and the social relations that characterize them, and the centrally important 'external' issue of the conditions under which it is judged appropriate to impose prison sentences in the first place. Neither is this to forget the larger economic and political settings in which penal institutions are embedded. Rather it is to look at the connections between the 'interior' and the 'exterior' aspects of penal problems from a slightly altered vantage point.

A number of recent interventions in penal affairs (notably Lord Justice Woolf's report on the 1990 disturbances) implicitly depend on some such idea but in a way that is generally unspoken, or at least inadequately defined. I suggest that it is right to view Lord Justice Woolf's inquiry and other recent documents as seeking to restore the legitimate basis of the system in the face of a near terminal crisis of order and moral credibility. One of the objectives of such interventions is to prevent the re-emergence of the kind of violent upheavals which prompt them, and in so doing to forestall their delegitimating effects. To emphasize the problem of legitimacy, therefore, is to inspect such attempts through the lens of social and political theory as a way of evaluating their adequacy, their progressive credentials. and their likely success. Ultimately it may also help to refine our general ways of thinking about penal problems and to move beyond certain received ideas and distinctions – for example the tension on the 'radical' side between reforming and abolitionist projects. More immediately, to operate *without* the kind of intellectual grounding which such concepts provide is to continue to allow some versions of official discourse and the claims of other interests to define many prison problems as being separate, contingent, and individual matters, and hence as being open to merely technical and/or repressive 'fixes', whether these be lodged in terms of architecture and hardware or indeed of management technique and ownership (the level at which current debates about privatization often appear stuck).

It would seem that for a host of reasons the resulting questions (which I have summarized in the one question 'can prisons be legitimate?') are not likely to receive an overwhelmingly positive answer. Indeed, the attendant sense of intractability is a part of what has motivated some observers to take the view that to seek any positive answer to such questions is inevitably both futile and collusive. Thus the arguments that Mathiesen sets out in *The Politics of Abolition* (1974) and *Prison on Trial* (1990) in favour of prison abolition are in large measure a radicalized consequence of the conclusions he originally reached in *The Defences of the Weak* (1965). That is, that a legitimate distribution of power and authority in prisons is impossible and that attempts to discover one are inevitably *post hoc* rationalizations for the persistence of the 'prison solution' to social problems. It follows for Mathiesen that any 'positive reform' is open to being seized upon by the prison institution as an opportunity for relegitimation (1974: 174–6). Consequently, Mathiesen argues, the only reforms which should be pursued are those which are 'negating', 'exposing', and 'of the abolishing kind'. They must seek to demonstrate once and for all that the prison solution is a 'fiasco' and to unmask its supporting ideologies (Mathiesen 1990: 141–2).

On the other hand, Mathiesen is also explicit in *The Politics of Abolition* that his concepts of negative reforms within the horizon of 'the unfinished' are precisely intended to cut through any settled reform/revolution dichotomy by keeping the direction and destination of progressive change deliberately open. On my argument, the very generality and open-textured nature of the concept of legitimacy fits it for a similar job. This is because it is double-edged: it is always in question in the present, yet always apparently unrealized. It therefore has an inherent dialectical energy. Yet, I will conclude by arguing, it is thereby also open to rather different and more politically feasible inferences than those which Mathiesen would wish to draw.

   […]

Privatization, legitimacy, and the 'new penality'

Of all the arguments advanced in support of privately managed prisons I will deal here briefly with only two closely related ones. These are:

(i) whether the sharp distinction between the allocation and delivery of punishment which advocates of privatization are compelled to draw is defensible; and
(ii) the assumption on the part of Clarke and others that advocating privatization on technical or managerial grounds does not commit one to a view of the penal realm which is fundamentally altered in other respects.

As we have seen the response of the private prisons lobby to the first of these questions is simple. There is no problem – merely a set of technical issues which can be dealt with by setting up the appropriate systems for regulation and oversight, specifying contractual obligations, retaining state-appointed ombudspersons and inspectors, and so forth. Indeed McConville suggests that those who insist on raising such matters of principle are posing questions which completely escape rational adjudication (1990: 94). (If he is right then of course those who oppose privatization have an argument that is just as strong as those who advocate it.) For Logan the matter is beguilingly simple: private and public prisons face all the same problems:

> It is primarily because they are prisons, not because they are contractual, that private prisons face challenges of authority, legitimacy, procedural justice, accountability, liability, cost, security, safety, corruptibility, and so on. Because they face no problems that are both unique and insurmountable, private prisons should be allowed to compete (and cooperate) with government agencies so that we can discover how best to run prisons that are safe, secure, humane, efficient and just. (Logan, 1990: 5)

Of course Logan knows that this view is open to an interpretation deeply uncongenial to, indeed disregarded by, most of his fellow travellers in the privatization camp – namely that privatization in and of itself settles none of the prior questions about the legitimacy of the penalty of imprisonment in any given case. One can turn this logic to the view that neither public nor private prisons were ever likely to be safe, secure, humane, efficient, and just enough to warrant their continued use on anything like their present scale. This is clearly not what is intended, however. Rather, the sharp distinction between allocation and delivery of punishment serves rhetorically to insulate the two areas of discussion from one another. It protects the original act of sentencing (a judicial specialism – one sphere of expertise) whilst at the same time it presents the delivery of imprisonment in a moderated and sanitized language (a correctional specialism – another sphere of expertise – nothing to do with the intended delivery of pain).

These manoeuvres serve to nudge the questions which have classically preoccupied political philosophers interested in punishment away from the centre of penal debate. Lacey raises the traditional issues in a sharp form. It is inherent in the definition of punishment that it involves the deliberate imposition of unpleasant consequences. Hence its intrinsic need for the strongest possible justification. Otherwise it could only be a *'prima facie* wrongful exercise by state officials of state power'* (Lacey 1988: 14).

This leads us into the second area of concern, namely the ways in which privatization itself alters the contours of the penal realm. I am arguing that the allocation/delivery split tends to sandpaper away the contested and 'dismaying' (Garland 1990: 1) nature of state punishment. In that sense it makes it appear *more* akin to other spheres of ordinary administrative activity (hence 'governmental' in Foucault's sense of the term rather than Logan's). To this extent the delegation of penal service delivery to private agencies only serves to accelerate and intensify tendencies which are in any case characteristic of modern institutions of punishment. These tendencies have been identified with particular clarity by Garland when he writes of the 'rational, passionless terms' increasingly characteristic of modern penality 'wherein moral evaluation is displaced by scientific understanding' (1990: 186). Such developments clearly predate the advent of privatization as such, but the ascendancy of consequentialism and quantification in the language of private correctional management decisively shifts the terrain of debate in this direction. Thus the construction of complex input–output models of correctional efficiency (Garland 1990: 188) and the construction of refined actuarial techniques of risk management (Simon 1988) in criminal justice all bespeak a dominant form of managerialism identified by some as a 'new penality' which tends to displace older normative concerns and anxieties. This in turn corresponds closely to the more general regulation of social life under conditions of modernity by 'expert systems' to which Giddens alludes (1990: 27–8).

Here we can do no more than sketch a couple of the possible consequences of this. First there is the inherent likelihood that expert systems of punishment, whether 'public' or 'private' and however formally accountable, will tend to escape any public sphere of informed debate and decision (with the possible further consequence that lay opinion is left to roam free in a realm of imagination and mythmaking with only the most tenuous connection to what happens inside the system (Garland 1990: 188; Sparks 1992: 160–2)). Secondly, there is the question of the scope and extent of the system itself.

This latter issue returns us very directly to the question of privatization as such. It is unconvincing, indeed even inconsistent, for advocates of privatization to argue that their position is not wedded to growth in the prison system. Logan merely argues weakly that:

> Contracting need not always be aimed at increasing the number of available prison cells. If the need for secure confinement should decline, or if a viable alternative is developed, it should be easier to alter contracts or change contractors than to restructure entrenched public bureaucracies. (1990: 10)

There are several reasons why this view is both at odds with observable trends and contrary to the logic of privatization initiatives in general. First, as Lilly and Knepper (1992a) point out, privatization has to date only seriously taken root in those jurisdictions with the highest proportionate prison populations amongst Western countries (Britain, the United States, and Canada). Within the United States it is strongest amongst those southern states whose existing prison systems are most decrepit, most overcrowded, and most fiscally overburdened. It begins, that is to say, as an emergency measure. Secondly, Logan's position rests on a naive and falsely transparent conception of elasticities of demand for imprisonment. Both the 'need' for prison places and the 'viability' of alternatives are matters of political decision and ideological preference – and in any case the free market preferences of governments sympathetic to privatization and their high demand for prison places are more than accidentally related (Hale 1989; Pease 1990; Greenberg 1991). Thirdly, serious corporate investors in private prisons will not commit capital to prison construction and management unless there are realistic prospects of growth and long-term returns (Lilly and Knepper 1992b), and in any case (as Lilly and Knepper further point out (1992a)) the construction of new prisons and the provision of their hardware is by far the most profitable sector of the business. Fourthly, as recent British experience culminating in the sentencing provisions of the Criminal Justice Act 1991 suggests, serious governmental pressure on sentencers to treat prisons as a scarce resource only tends to arise where the existing system has become a real economic and political burden, a circumstance which private investment is precisely designed to obviate. Fifthly, and by no means least, many of the companies most keenly interested in prison privatization are defence contractors experiencing a 'negative peace dividend', whose lobbying skills and ties to government are already strong and whom governments may experience a strong political pressure to assist.

If one takes the strong analogy of private provision of health services, the whole strength of the privatization case turns on the notion of an indefinitely large demand which public provision alone can never in principle satisfy. In examining privatization discourse the term which routinely arises is *supplement* (Fulton 1989; Gardiner 1989; Logan 1990). Private prisons are explicitly conceived as *supplementary to* an existing system which has reached or exceeded even the most permissive estimation of its capacity. They are extremely unlikely, for reasons of economic and political logic, to reduce the overall dimensions of any such system. Moreover, there is a powerful tradition of criminological analysis which suggests that *supplementarity* is precisely the mechanism whereby criminal justice institutions are most likely to extend their scale and their sphere of operations (see e.g. Cohen 1985; Nelken 1989).

For these reasons alone, though there are numerous others, there is reason for extreme scepticism over whether the current preoccupation with privatization in any sense presages a renewed concern with the normative legitimacy of the system, or whether it will in any sense creatively focus public anxiety on the justifications for imposing penal sanctions.

Conclusions – towards a 'utopian realist' politics of imprisonment

The problem of legitimacy has received rather short shrift in writing about prisons, despite the central importance which, I have argued, it possesses, or should possess. Too often it has been defined (as at times in Mathiesen's writings – 1990: 141–2) as *nothing but* the ruses of statecraft whereby a bankrupt system seeks to perpetuate and protect itself. Of course this negative, ideological sense of the term is important, and examples of it are everywhere to be found.

Yet the idea of legitimacy also carries a deeper and more challenging implication. On a proper understanding of its significance, as a problem that is chronically implicated in all penal practices, it delimits in large measure the very arena within which penological debate must take place. What I have tried to indicate by considering some current prison problems and examples of official discourse in response to them is the growing necessity of reinstating this concern at the centre of penal politics. The concept of legitimacy carries an open and dialectical awareness of change, such that every time an attempt at legitimation (such as Lord Justice Woolf's reform agenda) appears to promise a new settlement one can begin to discern within it the outlines of another emergent set of issues and possibilities and to reach towards them.

In his recent writings Giddens speaks of the inherent 'institutional reflexivity' of modernity, defined as 'the routine incorporation of new knowledge or information into environments of action that are thereby reconstituted or reorganised' (1991: 243). Such a reconstitution is continual and has no necessary stopping point. I am arguing that the debate about the legitimacy of imprisonment must now become of this kind. In a post-traditional social order it is open to us to review our institutional environment in a more sceptical and more thoroughgoing way than may have been possible in the past. In the case of an institution such as the prison we may ultimately come to the conclusion that its intrinsic design faults are such that it rarely or never achieves its stated objectives, or that it routinely produces unintended 'perverse consequences' (Giddens 1990: 152) which may be so severe that it must either be transformed or abandoned.

In such a case the appropriate form of engagement lies in what Giddens terms a stance of 'utopian realism' (or alternatively 'a critical theory without guarantees' – i.e., one grounded in rigorous practical reasoning and without recourse to an implicit teleology or determinism (1990: 154)). On this view it may indeed be open to us to imagine a future without prisons as we currently know them or in which our reliance on them is radically reduced, provided only that we can show that we are not thereby increasing the level of 'high consequence risks' by courting a perverse outcome (say by increasing the public's real risk of exposure to serious victimization or by inviting the substitution of some other more noxious form of social control) and that this course has some grounding in 'immanent institutional possibilities' (1990: 155).

'Power in its broadest sense,' Giddens comments, 'is a means of getting things done.' The question of legitimacy focuses our attention on which distributions of power we are prepared to accept and which we come to define as divisive, exploitative, or oppressive (1991: 211) in the light of norms of justice which we regard as valid and with which we hope to persuade others to agree (1991: 212–3). Hence, 'justifiable authority can defend itself against the charge of oppression only where differential power can be shown to be morally legitimate' (1991: 212).

All prison systems confront severe legitimacy deficits, especially from the vantage points of the confined. But such deficits are not always total. Nor are they everywhere equally severe. This being so, for as long as we must have prisons, it is indeed possible to distinguish clearly between better and worse, preferable and less preferable, stronger and less strong justifications both in the conditions which externally govern their use and in their internal practices.

From 'Can prisons be legitimate? Penal politics, privatization, and the timeliness of an old idea', British Journal of Criminology, *Vol. 34, Special Issue, 1994, pp. 14–28.*

Notes

1. In modern times this means the still unfinished disputes between the claims of Kantian high retributivism and Benthamite utilitarianism and the various inheritors and critics of these positions. See, for discussions, Walker (1991), Lacey (1988), Mathiesen (1990).
2. I have in mind here the literature that effectively begins with Rusche and Kirchheimer (1939) and extends through Mathiesen (1974), Melossi and Pavarini (1981) and Ignatieff (1978) to Foucault (1979), Garland (1985, 1990), and others.

References

Beetham, D. (1991), *The Legitimation of Power*. Buckingham: Macmillan.
Cavadino, M. (1992), 'Explaining the Penal Crisis', *Prison Service Journal*, 87: 2–12.
Cohen, S. (1985), *Visions of Social Control*. Cambridge: Polity Press.
Foucault, M. (1979), *Discipline and Punish*. London: Penguin.
Fulton, R. (1989), 'Private Sector Involvement in the Remand System', in M. Farrell, ed., *Punishment for Profit?* London: ISTD.
Gardiner, E. (1989), 'Prisons – an Alternative Approach', in M. Farrell, ed., *Punishment for Profit?* London: ISTD.
Garland, D. (1985), *Punishment and Welfare*. Aldershot: Gower.
Garland, D. (1990), *Punishment and Modern Society*. Oxford: Oxford University Press.
Giddens, A. (1990), *The Consequences of Modernity*. Cambridge: Polity Press.
Giddens, A. (1991), *Modernity and Self-identity*. Cambridge: Polity Press.

Greenberg, D. (1991), 'The Cost-benefit Analysis of Imprisonment', *Social Justice*, 17: 49–75.

Hale, C. (1989), 'Economy, Punishment and Imprisonment', *Contemporary Crises*, 13: 327–49.

Ignatieff, M. (1978), *A Just Measure of Pain*. London: Penguin.

Lacey, N. (1988), *State Punishment*. London: Routledge.

Lilly, J.R. and Knepper, P. (1992*a*). 'The Corrections–Commercial Complex', *Prison Service Journal*, 87.

Lilly, J.R. and Knepper, P. (1992*b*) 'An International Perspective on the Privatization of Corrections', *Howard Journal*, 31/3.

Logan, C. (1990), *Private Prisons: Cons and Pros*. Oxford: Oxford University Press.

McConville, S. (1990) 'The Privatization of Penal Services', in Council of Europe, *Privatization of Crime Control*. Strasbourg: Council of Europe.

Mathiesen, T. (1965), *The Defences of the Weak*. London: Tavistock.

Mathiesen, T. (1974), *The Politics of Abolition*. Oxford: Martin Robertson.

Mathiesen, T. (1990), *Prison on Trial*. London: Sage.

Melossi, D., and Pavarini, M. (1981), *The Prison and the Factory*. Basingstoke: Macmillan.

Nelken, D. (1989), 'Discipline and Punish: Some Notes on the Margin', *The Howard Journal*, 28: 245–54.

Pease, K. (1990), 'Punishment Demand and Punishment Numbers', in D.M. Gottfredson and R.V. Clarke, eds, *Policy and Theory in Criminal Justice*. Aldershot: Avebury.

Rusche, G., and Kirchheimer, O. (1939), *Punishment and Social Structure*. New York: Columbia University Press.

Sim, J. (1992), '"When You Ain't Got Nothing You Got Nothing to Lose": The Peterhead Rebellion, the State and the Case for Prison Abolition', in K. Bottomley, T. Fowles, and R. Reiner, eds, *Criminal Justice: Theory and Practice*. London: British Society of Criminology.

Simon, J. (1988), 'The Ideological Effect of Actuarial Practices', *Law and Society Review*, 22.

Sparks, J.R. (1992), *Television and the Drama of Crime*. Buckingham: Open University Press.

Sparks, J.R., and Bottoms, A.E. (1992), 'Order and Legitimacy in Prisons,' Paper presented to the American Society of Criminology Meetings, New Orleans, November 1992.

Walker, N. (1991), *Why Punish?* Oxford: Oxford University Press.

Woolf, Lord Justice (1991), *Prison Disturbances, April 1990*. London: HMSO.

9. Legitimacy and order in prisons

Richard Sparks and Anthony Bottoms

Legitimacy and order in two prison regimes

How directly does [a] discussion of legitimacy bear on the analysis of social order in prisons? In earlier work (Bottoms *et al.* 1990; Hay *et al.* 1990; Hay and Sparks 1991a) we have compared the problems of order and modes of regulation encountered in two adult male English maximum security prisons whose regimes differed markedly.

At the risk of reducing that comparison to unduly simple terms we can summarize briefly:

Albany

At the time of our study (1988/9) Albany operated a regime which was stringently controlled relative to other English long-term prisons. This involved, in particular, restrictions on association and movement within the prison which were more pronounced than in the comparison prison. Prisoners in general were well aware of these differences: indeed prisoners in Albany probably had a slightly exaggerated perception of their relative disadvantage. Accordingly, many felt aggrieved at having been located there, and felt that they had been given no adequate explanation of their differential treatment by comparison with their peers elsewhere. Some went further and interpreted their allocation as deliberately and personally punitive. Throughout the 1980s Albany regularly generated higher recorded levels of minor disciplinary problems (refusals to work, disobedience, fighting) than other 'dispersal' prisons, giving rise at least to the suspicion that attending to the risk of disorder on one level might serve to exacerbate it on another (Hay and Sparks 1991b).

The Albany regime was therefore in the main rather unpopular with prisoners, except among older men who often welcomed its restraining effect on the noisiness and bumptiousness of the younger majority. However, with few exceptions (and somewhat against our initial expectations) prisoners drew a rather sharp distinction between the regime as such and the staff who administered it, whom they considered in the main to be reasonable, fair, 'just doing their job' and so on. Our impression was that, aware that they were administering a disliked system (albeit one which they strongly supported themselves) staff at Albany took some pains to counter their own potential unpopularity by cultivating a rather discreet and amenable interpersonal style. They did this in the hope – realized to some extent – that good relationships would help them retain a degree of legitimate authority. Moreover, the regime at Albany was quite highly procedurally explicit and relatively consistent in its operation, and emphasized good 'service delivery' in matters such as food and pre-release programmes. Assuming Tyler's (1990) views to be correct, all these factors may have helped limit the scale of the prison's legitimacy deficit.

Long Lartin

The regime at Long Lartin was widely regarded by prisoners as having a number of benefits over those of other 'dispersal' prisons. Prisoners had significantly more time out of cells than at Albany, more association, more freedom of movement within the prison, more frequent access to the gymnasium. They also noted and mostly approved the staff's cultivation of a rather relaxed and friendly way of working and a light and unobtrusive style of supervision. The use of first names between prisoners and staff was fairly general, and staff took pride in being able to manage the prison without formally sanctioning every 'petty' infraction of the rules. Amongst the successes claimed for Long Lartin's liberal approach were the avoidance of riots, and hence an unbroken line of continuity with the founding principles of the 'dispersal' prison system (Sir Leon Radzinowicz's 'liberal regime within a secure perimeter': see Advisory Council on the Penal System 1968). It was widely accepted that a number of prisoners who had rejected regimes at other long-term prisons and been reckoned unmanageable had settled successfully at Long Lartin. It was also clear that Long Lartin used its rather favoured status in the eyes of most inmates as a device for influencing prisoners' behaviour. Thus the prison had enjoyed some success in integrating sex offenders and other vulnerable prisoners into the main body of the prison's population, calling on potential predators' fears of being transferred elsewhere. By the same token vulnerable prisoners were more ready to tolerate the risks involved in mixing with other prisoners for the sake of the perceived benefits of the regime. Yet it was also clear that such people were by no means free from fear. Moreover, the level of *sub rosa* economic activity (especially in the supply of drugs, and gambling) was rather high; there was evidence from hospital records and numbers of alarm bells to suggest that the level of back-stage violence might have been much greater than the official picture of calm would indicate; and when incidents did occur those within our sample were more likely than at Albany to involve numerous people and the use of weapons. The history of stability (assessed in terms of the absence of large scale collective unrest), the favourable regime and the generally approved staff practices lent to Long Lartin an appearance of much greater legitimacy in the eyes of the majority of prisoners than was the case at Albany. Yet it also seems probable that the regime gave rise to opportunities for deviance, and predation on fellow-inmates, not found to the same degree elsewhere, and hence to some risks in day-to-day inmate life. It is certain, from our evidence, that some of the victims of predation felt not only afraid but angry and unsupported. Meanwhile some of those alleged to have caused trouble, and in consequence transferred from the prison on the Governor's authority,[1] felt they had been unfairly treated procedurally. Hence there were two kinds of legitimacy questions raised by some prisoners against the liberal regime at Long Lartin: one concerning the provision of safe custody, and one concerning its scope for procedural discretion and consequent injustice.

Conclusions

In our view this discussion clearly confirms that Woolf was correct in his implicit stress on the need for prisons to seek legitimation from prisoners, and on the importance of humane regimes and procedural justice in the process of doing so. He was also correct in his emphasis on the necessity to achieve improved staff–prisoner relationships, with important implications for staff training and conduct. We have sought to extend those concerns and to provide them with a developed theoretical basis. The perspectives on which we have drawn argue strongly both for the extension of procedural justice in prisons and for sensitivity to the relational and specifically social aspects of prisoners' treatment.

In the course of preparing this paper, we were asked informally by a prison governor: 'Does all this mean that legitimacy is just about pleasing the prisoners?' It is an important question, and one can easily see how it arises – not least for those who have explicitly or implicitly imbibed the Weberian view of legitimacy simply as subjects' 'belief in legitimacy'. But if, on the other hand, we adopt Beetham's formulation that power relationships are legitimated (in part) when they can be 'justified in terms of [subjects'] beliefs', then subtly different considerations are introduced within the 'dialectic of control' (Giddens 1984) that continually takes place in all prisons. For, [...] Beetham's formulation injects a moral judgment into the dialogue, and the moral judgment will inevitably be grounded principally in the shared moral beliefs of the particular society in question. Hence, prisoners making far-fetched demands (for example, for luxury accommodation, or waiter-service at all meals) will be easily rebuffed by prison management, who will know that such demands have no basis of moral support in that society. By contrast, the protesting prisoner may not infrequently (as Thomas and Pooley (1980) pointed out) be asserting standards and expectations of fair and humane treatment now taken for granted in the world beyond the wall (cf. [...] Tyler (1990) on the importance of fair procedures, and the representational importance of the behaviour of officials). Where this is so – or where the prisoner is able successfully to 'point the finger' at prison officials for not following their own rules or proclaimed principles (Mathiesen's (1965) 'censoriousness') – then paying attention to prisoners' critiques of prison regimes has to be judged as *not* being simply about 'pleasing the prisoners';

rather, such critiques may be pointing to moral issues which will, sooner or later, carry real social weight both within the prison system and in wider political debates.

If this is correct, then a defensible and legitimated prison regime demands a dialogue in which prisoners' voices (as to what is 'justified in terms of their beliefs') are registered and have a chance of being responded to.[2] Moreover (as Woolf recognized with a clarity unfamiliar in English penal debates), legitimacy, thus understood, demands reference to standards that can be defended externally in moral and political argument. In the first instance this stipulates attention both to procedural and relational dimensions of prison regimes; in other words, to the recognition of prisoners in terms both of their citizenship and their ordinary humanity. (More ultimately it also calls for accounts both of the justice of the laws and procedures which put them in prison, and of the rationales which claim to justify their confinement.) Where any of this can be achieved, prisoners are to that extent more likely to acknowledge the legitimacy of the regime, as the positive dimensions of our Albany/Long Lartin evidence show.

We have argued elsewhere (Bottoms *et al.* 1990: 91–2) that an analogy can be drawn between approaches to the maintenance of order in prisons and approaches to crime prevention in other contexts, be they mainly situational or mainly social in emphasis. Prisons impose higher levels of situational control than are usually present elsewhere. But an exclusive focus on the situational questions of environmental management and surveillance carries both diminishing returns and possible counter-productive consequences. Obtrusive situational controls irritate and grate, and are likely to stimulate resistance, especially when applied to places where people live. The social level of control is therefore also inherent – but any social crime prevention initiative makes assumptions about the legitimate nature of the community which aspires to integrate the offender within it. For these reasons, we believe, it is important that the situationally controlling aspects of the prison environment be as unobtrusive as possible, and impede the normalization of its interior life to the least extent compatible with safe custody. But it is also vital that the prison be made habitable in other ways. For considerations of fairness and respect are not just normatively desirable, they are central to the achievement and reproduction of social order itself. Clearly, neither of the two prisons in our own study had achieved a fully satisfactory synthesis of these priorities. Albany's heavily situational approach was regarded by most prisoners as onerous, even provocative. Long Lartin's strongly social emphasis left open opportunities for victimization which we found unsettling. We hope however that the comparison between them clarifies some of the dilemmas.

Even in a somewhat speculative reading there are points that we feel able to state with some certainty. These include that every instance of brutality in prisons, every casual racist joke and demeaning remark, every ignored petition, every unwarranted bureaucratic delay, every inedible meal, every arbitrary decision to segregate or transfer without giving clear and well founded reasons, every petty miscarriage of justice, every futile and inactive period of time – is delegitimating. The combination of an inherent legitimacy deficit with an unusually great disparity of power places a peculiar onus on prison authorities to attend to the legitimacy of their actions. This underlines the necessity of acting legitimately in terms of formal rules at all times, and attending to those elements of shared moral beliefs existing between staff and prisoners (for example in terms of humane regimes, distributive and procedural fairness and supplying meaningful rationales for the exercise of power) so as to maximize the residual sense in which prison authorities may be entitled to call upon prisoners to confer consent.

From 'Legitimacy and order in prisons', British Journal of Sociology, *Vol. 46, No. 1, 1995, pp. 56–60.*

Notes

1. At that time Home Office Circular Instruction 10/74 empowered the Governor of any maximum security 'dispersal' prison to remove a prisoner from his prison to another prison (normally to reserved cells in a specified local prison) summarily (and under restraint if necessary) for 28 days. This procedure was officially styled a 'cooling off period', but its sudden and highly discretionary character frequently had rather the reverse of that effect on those subjected to it. This measure has since been replaced by Circular Instruction 37/90 which introduces certain procedural safeguards, but leaves the effective power itself substantially unaltered. Curiously Woolf 'reluctantly concluded that this power should remain in place' (paras 12.254, 12.256). For us and for other commentators (King and McDermott, 1990) it is at best uncertain whether the tactical benefits to prison managers of this measure outweigh either the arguments of principle against it from the vantage point of prisoners' rights or its possible delegitimating effect.
2. Compare also the views of J.R. Lucas (1980) that persons in power who are concerned to avoid injustice need (i) to consider situations from the point of view of those who may be disadvantaged; or disappointed by decisions they (the powerful) are about to make; and (ii) to reach decisions that are adverse to those citizens only for reasons that they (the citizens) ought rationally to acknowledge as cogent.

References

Advisory Council on the Penal System (1968) *The Regime for Prisoners under Conditions of Maximum Security* (Radzinowicz Report), London: HMSO.

Bottoms, A.E., Hay, W. and Sparks, R. (1990) 'Situational and social approaches to the prevention of disorder in long-term prisons', *The Prison Journal 70*: 83–95.

Giddens, A. (1984) *The Constitution of Society*, Cambridge: Polity Press.

Hay, W., Sparks, R. and Bottoms, A. (1990) *Control Problems and the Long-term Prisoner*, Unpublished report submitted to the Home Office Research and Planning Unit by the University of Cambridge Institute of Criminology.

Hay, W. and Sparks, R. (1991a) 'Maintaining order in the English dispersal system' in A.K. Bottomley and W. Hay (eds) *Special Units for Difficult Prisoners*, Hull: University of Hull.

Hay, W. and Sparks, R. (1991b) 'Vulnerable prisoners: risk in long-term prisons', Paper presented to the British Criminology Conference, University of York, July 1991.

King, R.D. and McDermott, K. (1990) '"My geranium is subversive": some notes on the management of trouble in prisons', *British Journal of Sociology 41*: 445–471.

Lucas, J.R. (1980) *On Justice*, Oxford: Clarendon Press.

Mathiesen, T. (1965) *The Defences of the Weak*, London: Tavistock.

Thomas, J. and Pooley, R. (1980) *The Exploding Prison*. London: Junction Books.

Tyler, T.R. (1990) *Why People Obey the Law*, New Haven, CT: Yale University Press.

Woolf, Lord Justice (1991) *Prison Disturbances, April 1990*, Cm. 1456, London: HMSO.

10. The rise and rise of supermax: an American solution in search of a problem?

Roy D. King

Introduction

One of the most dramatic features of the great American experiment with mass incarceration during the last quarter of the 20th century (Zimring and Hawkins, 1991) has been the proliferation of the so-called super-maximum security facility – hereinafter referred to as 'supermax'. These institutions usually purport to deal with the 'worst of the worst' prisoners who are said to be so dangerously predatory, or so disruptive, that they are impossible to manage in the more open general population settings of 'normal' maximum security prisons. On the basis of the research reported here, some 20,000 prisoners were housed in these kinds of facilities in the United States in 1998 – about 1.8 percent of the prisoners serving sentences of a year or more in state and federal prisons. This is about equivalent to the entire sentenced prison population of Oklahoma – or the population of the City of Bangor, UK, where the present author lives and works. This compares to fewer than 50 prisoners held in the very highest security or close supervision centres in the prison system of England and Wales at the beginning of 1999 – less than 0.1 percent of prisoners serving sentences of a year or longer – or, to get these things in perspective, about the size of an honours criminology class in the University of Wales, Bangor.

However, it is by no means clear what is meant by expressions such as 'supermax' and 'worst of the worst', a situation compounded by the virtually complete absence of independent research in this field. Just as Jacobs (1983–4) once complained that we knew all too little of the politics of prison expansion because it had been ignored by researchers, so we know all too little of the politics of proliferation for supermax. Despite this lack of research, or perhaps because of it, by 1997 at least 34 states of the union and the Federal Bureau of Prisons claimed to have identified a need for one or more such facilities and proceeded to develop them. At least four other states are poised to follow suit, and several plan to increase existing provision. Some jurisdictions have left the term 'supermax' vaguely defined and the circumstances of its use, for an equally ill defined population of 'worst of the worst' prisoners, poorly specified.

But what is assumed to be self-explanatory, or unnecessary to explain, can sometimes carry very different meanings for the producers and consumers of these expressions. Even where these terms are clearly specified, it can be a moot point whether these intended specifications are appropriately reflected in the criteria which govern entry to, and exit from, such facilities, or in the policy and procedure documents which shape their daily operation. Yet, arguably, the proliferation of such units has been both cause and effect of a major change in the justification of American prisons in the late 20th century, which has come about with all too little discussion. Nevertheless, there can be no doubt that prisoners who fall within the remit of such institutions suffer far-reaching consequences which have already tested the limits of the protections provided under the US Constitution (*Madrid* v. *Gomez*, 1995) and will almost certainly continue to do so. The National Institute of Corrections has recently warned Departments of Corrections that 'generally, the overall constitutionality (of supermax programs) remains unclear' and that they should proceed with caution (NIC, 1999).

Although the effective reach of international human rights standards governing the treatment of prisoners remains uncertain, there seems little doubt that what goes on in a number of supermax facilities would breach the protections enshrined in these instruments (Amnesty International, 1994, 1998; Fellner and Mariner, 1997). The International Covenant on Civil and Political Rights, which the United States has ratified, for example, has a more extensive ban on 'torture, cruel, inhuman or degrading treatment or punishment' than the Eighth Amendment prohibition of 'cruel and unusual' punishment, and requires no demonstration of intent, or indifference to the risk of harm, on the part of officials. Yet some officials seem unaware of the Covenant or the guidelines laid down in the United Nations Standard Minimum Rules for the Treatment of Prisoners, adopted in 1957 by the Economic and Social Council, or the Body of Principles for the Protection of All Persons Under Any Form of Detention or Imprisonment, or the Basic Principles for the Treatment of Prisoners, adopted by the General Assembly in 1988 and 1990 respectively. At least one official, aware of these guidelines and acting on behalf of the Commission on Accreditation for Corrections in rejecting Amnesty International's findings on Oklahoma State Penitentiary, self-consciously set them to one side as of no relevance compared to the decisions of US courts and the will of the American people.[1]

This is not to suggest, as some campaigning organizations do, that supermax or control unit prisons are part of a conspiracy aimed at silencing dissent among politically active minorities and should be necessarily closed down (Campaign to End the Marion Lockdown (CEML), no date). But simply that the nature and circumstances of their use demands proper scrutiny and independent evaluation in the context of an informed public debate.

What is no less striking than the American embrace of supermax is the lack of resonance of these notions in Europe. Apart from an important, but temporary, flirtation with the possibility of building one or even two supermax prisons in the United Kingdom, there has been remarkably little interest in these developments in Europe. This may have something to do with the effectiveness of bodies such as the European Committee for the Prevention of Torture and Inhuman or Degrading Treatment or Punishment whose critical reports can profoundly embarrass governments.

The European experience

British interest in supermax was most recently brought to the fore by the report of the Learmont Inquiry (Home Office, 1995) into prison service security in England and Wales. This followed the escape in September 1994 by six Category A (exceptional risk) prisoners – the highest security rating in the system – from the Special Security Unit, effectively a prison within a prison, at Whitemoor (Home Office, 1994); and a further escape by three Category A (standard risk) prisoners from Parkhurst in January 1995. The first escape was from the country's newest high security prison, opened in 1991, and involved five IRA prisoners. Although all were quickly recaptured, a prison officer was shot and wounded in the course of the escape. The second escape was from one of the country's oldest maximum security prisons, and, although the prisoners concerned were deemed to be somewhat less dangerous and were soon recaptured without further serious incident, major escape equipment had been manufactured and a toy firearm had been used.

The Director General of the Prison Service did not survive the political fall-out from these incidents, despite being able to refer to a creditable record in implementing important reforms which had been recommended by Lord Justice Woolf (Home Office, 1991) following a far-reaching enquiry into the prison service occasioned by the riots at Manchester and other prisons in 1990. Woolf had attributed the riots, in part, to legitimate grievances on the part of prisoners about the lack of fairness in their treatment, and the failure of the system to balance the needs of security and control with justice.

Whitemoor and Parkhurst were two of six so-called 'dispersal' prisons which formed the bulk of the high security estate. As indicated earlier, a policy of dispersing high security risk prisoners in comparatively small numbers throughout a number of maximum security prisons had been adopted following the report of the Radzinowicz sub-committee of the Advisory Council on the Penal System in 1968. This overturned the recommendation of Lord Mountbatten (Home Office, 1966) that high security risk prisoners should be concentrated in a single, newly planned, 'fortress-style' prison on the Isle of Wight. It is important to recognize, however, that there has always been a major difference between British and American applications of the concepts of dispersal and concentration. In the United States, armed guards in control towers and perimeter patrol vehicles, assisted nowadays by lethal electric fences, have largely factored out the prospect of escapes; thus the growth of high security institutions has been driven by the fear of riots, assaults and predatory behaviour. In Britain, a country where the police have only recently and reluctantly, and still not routinely, had recourse to arms, the prison service has operated entirely without the use of lethal force or, indeed, of chemical agents or other incapacitants. High security custody was driven largely by the fear of the consequences of escapes, and inmate behaviours have been controlled by direct supervision involving high levels of staff operating in a comparatively relaxed atmosphere.

Nevertheless, one of the arguments which convinced the British government in favour of dispersal over concentration in 1968 was the fear that locking up all the escape risks together would produce an unmanageably dangerous prison that would be impossible to staff – a powder keg waiting to blow up. Ironically, the dispersal prisons had a very troubled history of riots and disturbances throughout the 1970s and the early 1980s. The response to this over the years has been twofold. On the one hand, the number of dispersal prisons at first expanded – in an attempt to dilute the problem further – and then in more recent years contracted with a greater concentration of high risk prisoners in each. What had originally been four temporary special security wings evolved into three special security units (SSUs), two of which were purpose-built, including the one at Whitemoor, to deal primarily with the highest risk terrorist prisoners. The original concept of dispersal which involved a relaxed regime within a secure perimeter was tightened considerably, though none of the dispersals has ever run on anything remotely resembling a lockdown regime, and prisoners even in the SSUs have always been able to be out of cells for several hours every day on work, education or other programmes. (For an account of the development of one of the first dispersal prisons see King and Elliott (1978); for a comparison of a dispersal with Oak Park Heights see King (1991); and for a study of maintaining order in two dispersal prisons see Sparks et al. (1996).)

On the other hand, there have been ongoing attempts to deal directly with the problems of violent and difficult to manage prisoners. In 1974, there was a brief attempt to introduce control units utilizing a two-stage behaviour modification programme: in the first stage, lasting 90 days, the prisoner did not associate with other prisoners except during exercise periods; in the second stage, lasting a further 90 days, he was permitted to work and attend education classes with other prisoners. Misbehaviour, however, could mean starting the process again from the beginning. Two control units were planned, but one was closed down after a public outcry and the other never received any prisoners. Instead, a comparatively small group of very difficult prisoners was transferred from segregation unit to segregation unit on what became known officially as the Continuous Assessment Scheme and unofficially as the 'magic roundabout' or 'merry-go-round'.

In 1984, the Control Review Committee (Home Office, 1984) developed an alternative strategy, pending the possible development of two new generation prisons rather like Oak Park Heights which it hoped might one day replace the dispersal system and deal with both the escape problem and the control problem. The new strategy emphatically rejected the behaviour modification approach of the ill-fated control units. Instead, it involved the development of a series of small units to which difficult prisoners would be transferred: while one of these units was intended to be 'austere' and 'highly structured', the others would offer a good deal of psychiatric or psychological support with both work and cognitive programs.[2] Considerable attention was paid to selection criteria, because, while it was accepted that removing difficult and dangerous prisoners from the general population could have a beneficial effect on the rest of the system, it was deemed important that institutions as far as possible should 'consume their own smoke' and not simply try to get rid of nuisance prisoners. Accordingly allocation to the units was controlled from headquarters by a Special Unit Selection Committee (SUSC). A group of officials and academics was appointed to a Research and Advisory Group (RAG) to have oversight of the small unit strategy,[3] and the use of the units was to some extent evaluated by consultants (Bottomley, 1995). In practice, the special units were not extensively used, and the Continuous Assessment Scheme continued to operate.

After the escapes from Whitemoor and Parkhurst, Learmont made a great many recommendations for upgrading the security at the existing dispersal prisons to prevent further escapes, but also took on board some questions about the maintenance of order and control even though these fell somewhat outside his terms of reference. Among his principal recommendations were proposals to build two new prisons: a 200-place high security prison for the most dangerous escape risks (Home Office, 1995: paras 5.14–16), and a 200-place control prison to accommodate the most disruptive prisoners including those who were mentally ill and a group of what Learmont described as 'highly volatile' young prisoners serving relatively short sentences in medium security (Category C) institutions (paras 5.41–52). Not surprisingly, these proposed prisons were quickly dubbed 'supermax' prisons and, even before the report was published, the Prison Service established a small project team to consider the feasibility of the Learmont proposals for supermax prisons and to make recommendations.[4]

Members of the project team visited the Federal ADX at Florence, Colorado and Oak Park Heights in Minnesota – as had the then Home Secretary, Michael Howard, and both the outgoing and the incoming Directors General of the Prison Service, Derek Lewis and Richard Tilt. It is an open secret that the Home Secretary preferred what he saw at Florence, while prison service personnel, including the project team, preferred Oak Park Heights. The project team eventually recommended that it would be feasible to build one supermax prison of about 400 beds, to accommodate, in separate units, the most dangerous escape risks on the one hand and the most serious control problems on the other, and including a mental health unit. However, Learmont's group of volatile young prisoners from lower security establishments were explicitly excluded from consideration as candidates for supermax. The project team initially took the view that supermax custody would offer distinct advantages in tackling the security problem provided it was not simply an additional tier: it would help clarify the security classification process which had been clouded by dispersal policies, and take the de facto process of concentration already under way one stage further. However, it would be worth while only if economies could be achieved by taking one or more dispersal prisons out of the high security estate. The project team only reluctantly came to the view that it would be right to concentrate the control risk prisoners by transferring existing small units into the new facility, and then largely on grounds of cost effectiveness. They rejected any idea of having a lockdown facility in favour of a somewhat more programme-rich environment, while nevertheless advocating a very high security specification.

The work of the project team was conducted against the backdrop of the emerging peace process in Northern Ireland and the possibility that many of today's 'terrorists' might soon be released. Indeed, by February 1999, about 250 such prisoners had been paroled. Moreover, work had already begun on upgrading security in the existing dispersal prisons according to Learmont's other proposals making the economics of removing a dispersal prison to make way for a supermax more questionable. The report of the project team was delivered to the Home Secretary of the outgoing Conservative Government, but after a long hiatus was finally considered by the incoming New Labour Government. By then, the development of the peace process and the relative calm in the system had made the idea of adopting supermax seem more or less irrelevant, and the idea was publicly abandoned. Meanwhile, the old CRC special units for difficult to manage prisoners had been reorganized into a more integrated system of close supervision centres. Under the new scheme, instead of unrelated free-standing units, five small centres offered a graduated system in which prisoners might progress from a very restricted regime through to a transitional unit with a heavy concentration of programmes before returning to the general population in the dispersal system. It was the intention to run down the Continuous Assessment Scheme, under which prisoners were transferred from one segregation unit to another, and indeed the numbers on this have been reduced to a trickle. A monitoring group, including an academic, two forensic psychiatrists, a chief probation officer and an independent lay person, as well as officials, has oversight of the system. The Director of the leading prison reform NGO – Prison Reform Trust – has had access to the units and his written comments have been formally considered by the monitoring group, and in some cases acted upon.

What is remarkable about the system in England and Wales, compared to what has happened in the United States, is its economy. The system looked very closely indeed at supermax but in the event drew back from the brink. In a system containing about 45,000 prisoners serving sentences of a year or longer, fewer than 50 are held in the very highest levels of security either in the special secure units on grounds of escape risk or the close supervision centres on grounds of their prison behaviours. As at February 1999, one of the SSUs at Full Sutton provided eight places and was used for other purposes (witness protection); the other two at Whitemoor and Belmarsh provided a total of 60 places of which 36 were operational, but following the release of prisoners under the peace process they housed only 11 prisoners between them. The close supervision centres provided 64 places but housed only 29 prisoners, and only a handful of those in the bottom tier of the graduated regimes experienced lockdown status. The system also had seven high control cells for prisoners who must be kept separate from the rest of the population, of which two were in use, and two other prisoners remained on the Continuous Assessment Scheme.

Nor is the situation in other European jurisdictions very different. According to a review of European practice carried out for HM Prison Service in England and Wales, 'no European country has any experience of running complete institutions on a super-maximum security basis: ... [instead] ... the tendency in Europe has been to operate highly secure units within prisons that otherwise have average to good security' (Vagg, 1995: 1). Vagg's review included France, which did create a series of special high security units in 1975 but abandoned them in 1982; Germany, which from time to time has experienced terrorist problems in response to which some Länder have created special security units in addition to operating a transfer system like the English 'magic roundabout'; and Belgium, The Netherlands and Sweden, all of which have operated small, highly secure units either for escape risks, or for prisoners exhibiting dangerous behaviour, including in recent years for gang related activities, or both.

Sometimes the regimes operated in these units have been extremely isolating and have had to be changed or abandoned following reports of the European Committee for the Prevention of Torture (Council of Europe, 1992, 1993). For the purposes of this, as yet incomplete, study, research visits have been made to Western European jurisdictions in Sweden, and Berlin and Hanover in Germany: other visits are planned. Although Vagg cites a working expectation that perhaps 1 percent of the prison population in these jurisdictions would be in special high security accommodation on grounds of escape or control risks, such units were operating below that level during my visits.

Vagg suggests that one of the reasons why small unit strategies have been more popular in Europe is that many jurisdictions are quite small and that the numbers have not warranted specialization at the level of whole institutions. But the prison population in Sweden is currently a little over 5000 – one-and-a-half times the size of Nebraska which has 164 supermax beds; The Netherlands has a prison population of over 13,000 – comparable to Colorado which has 750 supermax beds; and Belgium has a prison population of over 8000 – comparable to Nevada with 430 supermax beds.

Further research visits have been conducted in Russia and Eastern Europe. Russia does have a history of using whole institutions as the basis of a system for correcting the behaviour of prisoners seen as disruptive of the wider prison system, in particular at Byely Lebed (the White Swan) at Solikamsk. Byely Lebed has the express task of breaking the resolve of prisoner leaders – known as 'thieves in law' – who have been transferred there for periods of six months or a year on grounds that they had proved intractable at other locations, and it has a poor reputation among human rights organizations. Even though there are a number of other institutions serving a similar purpose, the total number of such places in Russia is very much smaller than in the United States as a whole, despite the general comparability in the size of the overall systems. Vologda, a converted monastery, houses its prisoners whose death sentences have been vacated two to a spacious cell and provides them with daily work programmes. Despite the terrible conditions which generally prevail in Russian prisons, the authorities there have cooperated with the United Nations Special Rapporteur on Torture and with the European Committee for the Prevention of Torture (CPT).

Conclusion

It is safe to assume that all prison systems will find some of their prisoners much more difficult to manage than others. Britain, too, has its share of serial killers; the prisoners typically housed in the special security units have been responsible for multiple deaths in bombing outrages; and some prisoners in its close supervision centres have killed in prison and openly threaten to kill again, while others have repeatedly taken hostages or assaulted staff. But, in response to these and similar problems, the United States has embraced the idea of super-maximum security custody to a quite extraordinary degree, whereas, in Europe, the concept has fallen largely on stony ground.

There can be no question that both federal and some state prison systems have had to cope with some extremely violent and seemingly unpredictable prisoners, some of whom have been involved in gangs whose sub-cultures appear to be governed by racially motivated or other 'hate' crimes involving extreme violence. Some response has been necessary if only as a temporary and tactical measure to protect both staff and prisoners. But it is hard to resist the conclusion that the use of supermax custody has become at best a pre-emptive strategy that is almost certainly disproportionate in scale to the problems faced and at worst a routine and cynical perversion of penological principles.

The sheer scale of the contrast between the American embrace of supermax and its lack of appeal in Europe is the more striking in light of recent comparisons in criminal statistics. The latest evidence from both official police statistics and academic crime surveys shows that crime rates even for serious crimes such as assault, burglary and auto theft are actually higher in England and Wales than in the United States (Langan and Farrington, 1998). Crime surveys already show that robbery is higher in England and Wales although the police still record more robberies in the United States despite a rapid convergence between the two rates. It is true that the murder rate is six times higher in the United States than it is in England and Wales, but the British experience suggests that people who are sentenced for murder do not constitute particular control problems in prison. Although it is always tempting to succumb to the popular imagery of the United States as a much more violent society, in accounting for these trends, it would be hard to account for the magnitude of the difference on these grounds. While European systems have been taken to task by the Committee for the Prevention of Torture, the conditions thus exposed have been much less onerous than those typically found in the United States, and have applied to very small numbers of offenders.

There seems to be little doubt that American prisons have been, and continue to be, much more violent than their British counterparts: but before jumping to the extreme levels of response currently adopted in the United States it would be prudent to pose the question as to why this should be so. It seems most unlikely that this is simply a matter of national character, or the product of a society still dominated by the frontier. The way in which people behave in prisons is known to be a product of many factors: their length of sentence, their likelihood of getting out, their ties to the community, the nature of incentives to good behaviour and disincentives to bad behaviour, and whether or not they are treated fairly by staff and by 'the system'. Recent developments in sentencing policy in the United States have arguably had the effect of boxing prisoners into situations both where they have less and less to lose and where their chances of being reintegrated into the community have been reduced. Such developments have placed prison administrators in a difficult situation. In the United Kingdom, where similar trends have occurred, albeit in a minor form, the response of administrators has been to look to research for a better understanding of the circumstances in which order is maintained in prisons without resort to coercion. There seems to have been a complete absence of such research in the United States. Instead, cash-strapped administrators seem to have colluded with their political masters in defining all problems as the result of an increasingly intransigent and impossible to manage minority of prisoners. One of the most disturbing sights for a European visitor to American supermax facilities is to watch parties of school children being indoctrinated with the notion that it is somehow necessary and appropriate for dehumanized prisoners to be moved from 'living pods' to 'dog run' exercise yards in handcuffs, leg-irons and waist chains. The possibility should at least be examined that the reason for the high levels of violence in American prisons may have as much to do with the way in which prisons have been managed and staffed on the cheap, and the fairness and dignity with which prisoners are treated, as it has with the qualities that criminals bring with them into prison. It is at least a plausible hypothesis that the ever more repressive response to violence – of which supermax is but the latest expression – sets up a vicious circle of intolerance which is doomed to make matters worse.

From 'The rise and rise of the supermax: an American solution in search of a problem?', Punishment and Society, Vol. 1, no. 2, pp. 163–86.

Notes

1. For example, the report by the Monitor, appointed by the Commission on Accreditation for Corrections to re-examine the conditions in H Unit at McAlester, in Oklahoma, following the report by Amnesty International (1994) ended as follows: 'In this monitoring report, there is not a discussion or discourse on philosophical issues, nor is there a reference to international standards or prisoner treatment or care. The Oklahoma Department of Corrections and the Oklahoma State Penitentiary ... is operating under United States law and following the requirements for decent, humane care of prisoners which has evolved from court decisions, ACA standards, state legislative laws, and the will and expectation of the citizens of Oklahoma.'
2. Despite the recommendations of academic advisors, the Prison Service stopped short of establishing a unit run along the lines of Barlinnie in Scotland, where prisoners were involved in negotiating aspects of the regime and enjoyed a degree of self government (see Cooke, 1989). After a long, but chequered, history, the unit was disbanded and has not been replaced (Bottomley et al., 1994).
3. In addition to the present author, the other external members were Professor A.E. Bottoms of the Institute of Criminology, Cambridge and Professor John Gunn of the Institute of Psychiatry, London.

4. The author was appointed as academic advisor to the project team, and participated in all the discussions and the preparation of the first two drafts of the report.

References

Amnesty International (1994) *Conditions for death row prisoners in H-Unit, Oklahoma State Penitentiary*, AMR 51/35/94. London: Amnesty International.

Bottomley, A.K. (1995) *CRC Special Units: a general assessment*. London: Home Office Research and Planning Unit.

Bottomley, A.K., Liebling, A. and Sparks, R. (1994) *The Barlinnie Special Unit and Shotts Unit*. Edinburgh: Scottish Prison Service.

CEML (no date) *Close Marion and Lexington Control Unit Prisons*. Chicago: Committee to End the Marion Lockdown.

Cooke, D.J. (1989) 'Containing violent prisoners: an analysis of the Barlinnie Special Unit', *British Journal of Criminology* 29(2): 129–43.

Council of Europe (1992) *Report to the Swedish Government on the visit to Sweden carried out by the European Committee for the Prevention of Torture and Inhuman or Degrading Treatment or Punishment from 5–14 May 1991*. Strasbourg: Council of Europe.

Council of Europe (1993) *Report to the Dutch Government on the visit to The Netherlands carried out by the European Committee for the Prevention of Torture and Inhuman or Degrading Treatment or Punishment from 30 August to 8 September 1992*, Section 3, Special Detention Units. Strasbourg: Council of Europe.

Fellner, J. and Mariner, J. (1997) *Cold storage: super-maximum security confinement in Indiana*. New York: Human Rights Watch.

Home Office (1966) *Report of the Inquiry into Prison Escapes and Security* (Mountbatten Report), Cm. 3175. London: HMSO.

Home Office (1984) *Managing the long-term prison system* (The Report of the Control Review Committee). London: HMSO.

Home Office (1991) *Prison disturbances April 1990* (Report of an Inquiry by the Rt. Hon. Lord Justice Woolf (Parts I and II) and His Honour Judge Stephen Tumim (Part II)), (The Woolf Report), Cm. 1456. London: HMSO.

Home Office (1994) *The escape from Whitemoor Prison on Friday 9th September 1994* (The Woodcock Enquiry), Cm. 2741. London: HMSO.

Home Office (1995) *Review of Prison Service security in England and Wales and the escape from Parkhurst Prison on Tuesday 3rd January 1995* (The Learmont Inquiry), Cm. 3020. London: HMSO.

Jacobs, James B. (1983–4) 'The politics of prison expansion', *New York University Review of Law and Social Change* 12: 209–41.

King, R.D. (1991) 'Maximum-security custody in Britain and the USA: a study of Gartree and Oak Park Heights', *British Journal of Criminology* 31(2): 126–52.

King, R.D. and Elliott, K.W. (1978) *Albany: birth of a prison – end of an era*. London: Routledge & Kegan Paul.

Langan, P.A. and Farrington, D.P. (1998) *Crime and justice in the United States and in England and Wales, 1981–96*. Washington, DC: Bureau of Justice Statistics.

Madrid versus Gomez (1995) No. C90–3094–TEH, Class action: findings of fact, conclusions of law, and order, US District Court for the Northern District of California, January.

NIC (1999) *Supermax prisons: overview and general considerations*. Longmont, CO: US Department of Justice, National Institute of Corrections.

Sparks, R., Bottoms, A.E. and Hay, W. (1996) *Prisons and the problem of order*. Oxford: Clarendon Press.

Vagg, J. (1995) 'The management of disruptive prisoners – a literature review of European practices', unpublished report prepared for the Home Office Research and Planning Unit.

Zimring, F.E. and Hawkins, G. (1991) *The scale of imprisonment*. Chicago and London: University of Chicago Press.

11. Softly does it

Sally Weale

Prisoners are queuing up to get into Grendon, Britain's only therapeutic jail. Why? Does it simply offer them 'easy time' – or is it their best hope of escaping from a life of crime? [...]

Special report: prisons

If you stand outside the perimeter of HMP Grendon on an icy grey winter's morning, it's not that different from any other modern prison. It's not Pentonville or Wormwood Scrubs – it's 60s brutalist, rather than Victorian monolith – but there are the same blank walls, not as high, not as austere, but faceless, windowless, topped with the same loops of razor wire that keep the community inside apart from us outside.

There are the same *Porridge*-style prison gates with a spyhole; the same prison staff in the same uniforms, carrying the same jangling keys, with which they methodically unlock and lock, unlock and lock, day in, day out, all day, every day.

It's not until you are inside that you start to notice the difference. At first it is subtle, it creeps up on you: an unexpected camaraderie between inmates and prison staff. They chat about forthcoming events in the prison; they call each other by their first names; there is a mutual respect. The prisoners seem relaxed, the atmosphere is calm. There is none of the edgy us-and-them atmosphere that pervades other prisons – there is no sense of imminent danger. It is more like a student hall of residence than a category B prison.

On the governor's walls hang Christmas cards from inmates, former and current. 'Thank you for giving me this chance to change,' reads one. 'I don't have that long to go now until I'm released. I'm very confident about me and my future.' Also posted on the wall are these words: 'If you want to know what someone is really like, give him some authority.'

For the old lag who has spent his entire life in and out of prison, Grendon must come as a dramatic culture shock. Inmates move around with comparative freedom: their cells are unlocked at 8am, they remain open all day, prisoners eat together and talk together, with lock-up at 9pm. Most crucially they attend daily group therapy sessions. There they confront their crimes, take responsibility for their actions and explore their lives, their pasts, their childhoods, to try to uncover why they have done what they have done and how to avoid doing it again.

For Grendon is a therapeutic prison – the only one of its kind in the country. It opened in 1962 as an experiment in the psychological treatment of prisoners, and today it is proof that prison can be humane, constructive and life-changing. It is proof that prison can be more than sheer containment, benign or otherwise. It is proof that prison can work.

Mark Leech served almost 20 years in 62 prisons, but since Grendon has become an award-winning journalist, author and leading campaigner for penal reform. 'It certainly worked for me. Once you get locked into being a criminal, you just accept it. Grendon made me realise there were other options I could choose.'

Not everyone will leave Grendon a model citizen, but many prisoners undergo radical change. When they walk out of the gates, the hope is that they will be at least a little less aggressive, a little less hostile, a little less dangerous and a little less likely to reoffend.

The reconviction rates are encouraging. For those prisoners serving life sentences elsewhere, there is a 24% reoffending rate; at Grendon it is 8%. For non-lifers the reoffending rate is 10% lower at Grendon than elsewhere, and if prisoners complete the therapy, which ideally runs for at least 18 months, reoffending is slashed by 20–25%.

Set in the rolling Buckinghamshire countryside near Aylesbury, Grendon houses some of the most dangerous criminals in Britain, many of whom have severe personality disorders – 95% of inmates have committed offences of violence against the person, 27% have committed sex offences. Out of the 200 current inmates, 94 are lifers, and many have come to Grendon because traditional prisons, or 'the system', as it is called, cannot deal with them.

The prison is divided into therapeutic wings. Each wing is a democratised community that selects its own officials and sets its own rules. There are three key policies that everyone is expected to observe – no drugs, no sex, no violence. If you breach any of the three, your peers can decide whether you should be allowed a second chance or kicked out.

Sean, 37, is 10 years into a life sentence for rape. He has done time in prisons all over the country; now at Grendon, he is determined to turn his back on crime. 'I led a very active criminal lifestyle. That's been one of the things I've struggled with. It's trying to switch that off and not see things in a criminal way.

'I committed the rape. That was the point in my life when I thought, I've got to do something. I can't go on like that. The first six months I was put on remand I thought, I can't go on – no more hurting people and totally destroying another human's life. I needed to stop.'

He, like all of Grendon's inmates, had to volunteer to go there – motivation is crucial. Prisoners have to want to change. 'Grendon has taught me how to deal with people, how to communicate. Four years ago I would not have known how to communicate properly. I would have been quite intimidated, but now I feel quite confident about who I see I am as a person.

'I can't do with having the victims on my conscience any more. Before I could not see the victims. Now I can. I feel when I'm in other prisons that it's just reinforcing my old behaviour – me against the system. In other prisons I feel like I'm an inmate. Here I feel I'm part of a team who are working towards my progress.'

If Grendon works, Sean benefits, the taxpayer benefits, society benefits – arguably even his victims benefit, by knowing he is not hurting anyone else in the way they have been hurt by him.

Daryl, 35, is serving 10 years for conspiracy to commit an armed robbery. 'I'd been a thief all my life. When I got nicked for this I thought to myself, I've got to try and sort my life out. I was sick of my own behaviour but I didn't know how to break away from it.'

Grendon gave him the chance. To some it looks like a cushy number – more freedom, a softer regime, an easy way to do your time. Others in the prison system can be scornful (prison officers at Grendon are called the Care Bears by colleagues elsewhere). But staff and inmates at Grendon insist it's the toughest way 'to do your bird'. The therapy is intensive, gruelling, demanding work.

'This has been one of the hardest things I've done,' says Daryl. 'If you are really determined to change all aspects of your life, you have to do things you never thought you would do here. It's hard. You've got all sorts of peer pressures going on. People thinking you are a grass. It's hard to live with all that. Here you've got a chance to change your life. You just couldn't do this in a normal establishment. I believe in myself this time. I want it. That's the most important thing. You've got to want it.'

But what of Gary Watkins, who spent time in Grendon after being convicted of a vicious sex attack? He volunteered for Grendon; perhaps he too was determined to change. Within a month of his release on parole he kidnapped a 17-year-old girl at knifepoint, dragged her into his car, bound her with ropes and sexually assaulted her. He told Oxford crown court that he had maintained fantasies of assaulting and killing a young girl throughout his treatment.

John Shine, Grendon's director of research and development, is realistic about the prison's achievements. 'Some people here make enormous changes. Other people we have to be extremely cautious about when assessing the real impact of therapy. We don't know what goes on in their head.'

Mark Morris, the prison's director of therapy, adds that the Grendon way is not necessarily the right way for every prison or every prisoner. 'One of the problems we have is the issue of people who are here to genuinely work on themselves and people who are here because they see it as an easy route. There are people trying to manipulate the structure, trying to get on top of the therapeutic community process to work in their own nefarious ways. Where that manipulative, destructive impulse is at its height, we need settings which are more control-focused.'

A second therapeutic prison is finally opening later this year, almost 40 years after Grendon began taking in prisoners. HMP Dovegate, at Marchington, east Staffordshire, will offer a further 200 places for prisoners who want to undergo therapy (there are currently 200 prisoners on a waiting list at Grendon), but unlike its role model it will be attached to a 600-bed traditional prison and run by a private company.

Maybe that is progress, but it is abysmally slow, and it is against a backdrop of a spiralling prison population and a persistently punitive atmosphere. The prison officer who shows me round Grendon tells me at the end of my visit that he is in favour of bringing back hanging. Perhaps he is kidding.

'How can you think that when work in a place like this?' I ask. 'I'm a professional,' he says. He does his job according to the rules of Grendon and he does it very well. 'But I read the reports; I see what these people have done.'

Grendon is humane; it is positive; it treats prisoners as human beings, no matter how heinous their crime, and it offers them an alternative. 'If you have to have prisons then this is the best way to run them,' says Grendon's governor, Tim Newell.

But there are those who fear that Grendon is used as a fig leaf to cover up the overwhelming failure of our prison system. While Grendon is a success story, it should not distract us from the bigger question: why do we keep on expanding our prison population when we know it is costly and inefficient, and creates more problems than it solves?

12. The abolitionist approach: a British perspective

Joe Sim

> Among social scientists there seems to be considerable disillusionment, and, indeed, a turning away from the goal of abolition – more or less as if it were a youthful and confused prank from the late sixties which the middle aged and wise can hardly uphold. I have, however, never understood why a negative political trend – be it increased armaments or expanded prison systems – should lead one to conclude that the trend in question no longer constitutes a point of fundamental attack and final abolition from a radical position.
>
> (Mathiesen, 1986, p. 84)

The title of this reading, 'The abolitionist approach: a British perspective', will probably seem like an anachronism to many. For those concerned with the daily grind of criminal justice and penal policy, abolitionism is likely to be regarded as an esoteric, academic luxury which is irrelevant to the delivery of penal services both to the confined and to the wider society. The British demand for 'facts' as opposed to historically, theoretically and philosophically grounded analysis, whether of an abolitionist nature or not, is as prominent in the prisons debate as it is in other social policy debates. A number of academics in the UK, no doubt, will have other, but no less critical views. Abolitionists are now regarded as sociological dinosaurs, unreconstituted hangovers from the profound but doomed schisms of the late 1960s, who are marginal to the 'real' intellectual questions of the 1990s. Like Marxism, abolitionism appears to have been left behind on the sandbank of history while the river of modernity – or as many intellectuals would have it, postmodernity – flows progressively forward producing wave after consumerist wave of choice, opportunity and desire. Social formations now need realistic economic and social policies in general, and penal policies in particular, to respond to the new tunes flooding the planet, which in turn require research that is relevant to the service orientation of the newly reformed state and its subjects/customers both inside and outside the walls of the penitentiary.

Superficially, there appears to be strong sociological evidence to support this contention. Abolitionism, it seems, has failed to impact upon the direction of penal policy or the debate on crime and punishment. Indeed, the modern prison, despite 150 years of 'monotonous critique', as Michel Foucault put it, has not only endured but expanded to become materially and ideologically critical in the remorseless struggle to enforce law and maintain order. The institution's presence on the landscape of British society appears to be so deeply embedded that it has become almost naturalised in popular consciousness and state discourse as an immutable barrier, which despite crises and contradictions protects the law-abiding from the swamping encroachment of the desperate and degenerate in the same way that it was thought to protect the respectable from the ravages of first the parasitic delinquent, and then the dangerous classes in the nineteenth century (Garland, 1985). This conception of the prison has continued into the late twentieth century. Whatever social index is taken – the rate of imprisonment, numbers detained, expenditure, time served or judicial sentencing patterns – the prison, despite the occasional drop in the average daily population, is on a relentlessly expansionist course.

[...]

Abolitionism also appears to have been further weakened by the state's strategy for reform, developed in the wake of the furious demonstrations by prisoners in the mid-1980s. Within this discourse the mistakes of the past have been recognised and prison regimes will be modified so that the disasters of the 1980s, such as those at Strangeways (in Manchester, England) and Peterhead (in Scotland) will never be repeated. Even those on the left who might be broadly sympathetic to abolitionists have been highly critical, describing their 'anarcho-communist' position as 'preoccupied with abolishing or minimising state intervention rather than attempting to make it more effective, responsive and accountable' (Matthews, 1989, p. 5).

[...]

The age of improvement?

The debate about the future of the prisons and the criminal justice system in general is now dominated by the issue of state-inspired reforms. It is important to recognise, however, that the movement for reform has been generated not by state benevolence but by the demands made by prisoners in different demonstrations, by grassroots organisations unwilling to accept the 'truth' surrounding the appalling miscarriages of justice that have occurred in the last twenty years, and by pro-feminist organisations demanding changes in the definitions of – and responses to – male brutality towards women. In the light of the major disruption in the prisons during the 1980s two significant reports have been published, *Opportunity and Responsibility* (Scottish Prison Service, 1990) and the Woolf Report (1991). These documents appear to herald a new beginning for prisons in this country. In recognising that change is needed if the deeply damaging events of the 1980s are to be avoided, they propose a number of reforms, including establishing a framework of justice for prisoners, improved conditions, increased contact with the outside, better staff training and, crucially, making the confined responsible for their behaviour through introducing prisoners' contracts. Both documents have been almost uncritically endorsed in the media, and by academics and politicians as the panacea for alleviating the crisis inside.

From an abolitionist perspective there are some serious theoretical and political problems in utilising these proposals as the basis for future penal arrangements. Space does not permit me to provide an in depth analysis, although I have done this elsewhere (Sim, 1991; 1993). However, I want briefly to point to four distinct areas which would form part of an abolitionist critique of the rhetoric of reform contained in these reports.

First, both documents either marginalise or heavily qualify the experiences of the confined. This means that alternative definitions of penal reality remain hidden and subservient to orthodox and state definitions of events. This is important because it allows both reports to transform questions of power, domination and institutionalised intimidation, which have been central to the abolitionist position, into more benign problems of administrative malpractices or individual deviance. There is a classic passage in the Woolf report which illustrates this point. Woolf points out that after the demonstration in Pucklechurch Remand Centre (near Bristol) in April 1990, surrendering prisoners were told that their arms and legs would be broken. The report notes:

> There is no doubt that at the time the inmates were very frightened (I use that word advisedly) and even if the remarks made to them when waiting on the lawn were made in jest, they could, and did, cause considerable fear to the inmates. When considering these criticisms the long hours that management and staff had been on duty should be taken into account. Each member of staff must have been extremely tired and … close to exhaustion.
>
> (Woolf and Tumim, 1991, p. 271)

The second problem also relates to the politics of marginalisation, in this case the failure to deal with or respond to a number of key prison issues that have arisen in the last twenty years: the unfettered discretion of staff, prisoners' rights, the accountability of prisons within a liberal democracy, the financing and cost of the service, women in prison and the sentencing process. For both documents the alleviation of the crisis lies not in confronting these issues but in the development of the responsible prisoner/customer, tied to each establishment by an agreed individual contract. Through this construction the debate is shifted onto the narrow ledge of individualism and social administration and away from wider structural questions concerning power, collective rights and democratic control (Sim, 1993).

Third, the increasing emphasis on coercion and militarisation as strategies for maintaining order means that the proposed reforms, even if they are accepted on their own terms, are unlikely to marginalise the ideological and material support within the state for these strategies. Prisoners will now receive an extra ten years for what is quaintly described as 'prison mutiny'.

As Kenneth Baker has maintained, they must learn that rioting is not a 'cost-free option' (cited in Sim, 1993).

Finally, current reformist rhetoric misses a central issue raised by abolitionists and others in the last two decades, namely that unconditional support for limited change mystifies broader structural questions around the prevailing definitions of criminality that operate in this society, and who is punished as a result of these definitions. The first national survey published by the Prison Reform Trust in December 1991 showed that unemployment, homelessness, lack of education and psychiatric disorders were prevalent in the prison population, that prisoners were overwhelmingly males aged 17–40, that 16 per cent of males and 26 per cent of females came from Afro-Caribbean backgrounds, and that this group was serving substantially longer sentences than white prisoners, in the case of the women over twice as long. The report concluded that imprisonment 'exacerbates those very disadvantages which … led the person into crime in the first place' (Prison Reform Trust, 1991, p. 6).

Historically and contemporaneously, the prison has overwhelmingly contained the detritus generated by this society's hierarchical arrangements. In making this point I am not denying the impact that crimes committed by many of the imprisoned can have, nor am I positing a model of behaviour in which human beings are propelled in a positivist sense by forces outside of their control. Clearly, there are important philosophical and social psychological questions to be discussed concerning free will, responsibility and personal accountability, although given the abject recidivism rate in prisons the institution's supporters can hardly defend its track record in encouraging responsible behaviour in the confined. Having said that, I do want to make the point that today's age of penal improvement is simply reinforcing conventional definitions of criminality, and that the prison of the twenty-first century is likely to operate at an ideological and symbolic level in the active construction and reconstruction of very precise and narrow definitions of criminality and social harm. As abolitionists like Mathiesen have maintained, the prison has to be understood both as a material place of confinement and as an ideological signifier. Not only does the institution encourage and reinforce bifurcation, powerlessness and stigmatisation, but it also establishes 'a structure which places members of one class in such a situation that the attention we might pay to the members of another is diverted' (Mathiesen 1990, p. 138). Distracting attention away from crimes of the powerful and actively constructing particular images of criminality, however fragmentary and contradictory that process might be is, in Mathiesen's view, central to the continuation of the prison and to the reinforcement of a 'pervasive ideological mystification' around crime (Mathiesen, 1990, p. 141). This argument is particularly relevant to the debates around dangerousness. One of the most depressing elements in recent academic debates in criminology, which in my view can be directly linked to the reformist rhetoric of the state, is that in the rush to take crime seriously and to rediscover aetiology, the symbolic place of institutions like prisons as cultural signifiers has been neglected. This continually allows the debate on dangerousness (and crime in general) to take place on a conventional terrain clearly marked out in the discourses of state servants, government ministers, most media personnel and in the common sense of popular consciousness.

[...]

Critics of this position will no doubt say (as they always do) that even if the definition of crimes of the powerful is extended and recognised, abolitionists and other radical critics still fail to confront the fact that there are some dangerous individuals, overwhelmingly men, who in the conventional sense need to he confined. This view can be challenged at two levels. First, [...] many of those involved in the abolitionist movement in Britain have been confronting the issue of violence at least since the early 1980s and have been pointing to the problems that those defined as conventionally dangerous, for example, male rapists, have brought to the lives of particular groups. Second, British abolitionists have never advocated simply 'tearing down the walls' of the penitentiary. Rather they have maintained that incapacitating conventionally dangerous individuals such as rapists through detention does not necessarily guarantee an alleviation of violence, either at an individual or collective level. Imprisoned rapists are likely to be confronted by a prison culture which will do little to change their behaviour, heighten their consciousness or the consciousness of those in the wider society concerning the 'intimate intrusions' which face women on a daily basis (Stanko, 1985). The first major study of imprisoned rapists in the UK supports this argument. It showed that only 32 out of 142 men believed that raped women had been harmed, while less than half displayed any compassion for their victims (*Guardian*, 5 March 1991). While some exemplary work has been done with sex offenders in institutions such as Grendon Underwood and Wormwood Scrubs, supported by individually well-motivated prison officers, which perhaps will be consolidated by the newly formed national system for the treatment of sex offenders, it could be argued that there is a danger that at an ideological level this work and reform simply reassert the 'therapeutic discourse', which conceptualises 'male violence as an irrational act of emotional ventilation' rather than as behaviour based on intentional motivation and the will to dominate (Dobash and Dobash, 1992, p. 248). A similar point has been made in relation to the most recent proposals for reforming police practices concerning domestic violence, which are based on the reassertion of traditional family values (Radford and Stanko, 1991).

My scepticism towards these reforms does not mean resorting to incarcerating the powerful as a way forward. Clearly that would defeat the politics and the objectives of abolitionism by implying that the phenomenon of a 'fair incarceration rate' exists (Thomas and Boehlefeld, 1991, p. 249). It does mean, however, recognising that the operationalisation of power, its interpersonal and structural abuse and its mediation by social class, gender, race and sexuality needs to be responded to; it is *how* we respond that remains the key question for abolitionism. I believe that current reformist proposals, because of their marginalisation of the issue of power, do not come close to addressing the philosophical, sociological, psychological *and* political nuances generated by this question.

Conclusion

[...] [T]he abolitionist argument remains a powerful one, as Willem de Haan's critical dissection of traditional forms of punishment has indicated (de Haan, 1990). Similarly, Pat Carlen's cogent argument for the abolition of women's prisons as 'one small step towards giving the criminal justice and penal systems the thorough shake up they so desperately need' also provides a clear theoretical and pragmatic view of the way forward in this still neglected area (Carlen, 1990, p. 125). As Thomas and Boehlefeld point out, a theoretically refined abolitionism can offer a new way of thinking about the world *and* a vision of the future which contrasts sharply with traditional methods of penality based on incapacitation, deterrence, punishment and rehabilitation. It directly confronts the 'cynicism and anomie' of postmodernism, it reaffirms the argument that prisons don't work 'either as punishment or as a means of ensuring the safety and stability of the commonweal' and it recognises that predatory behaviour needs to be responded to and dealt with within the structural and interpersonal contexts of power and politics (Thomas and Boehlefeld, 1991, pp. 246–49). That vision can be compared with the present situation here and elsewhere, which is evoked in the words of George Jackson: 'The ultimate expression of law is not order – it's prison. There are hundreds upon hundreds of prisons, and thousands upon thousands of laws, yet there is no social order, no social peace' (Jackson, 1975, p. 95). Jackson's posthumous thoughts provide a fitting description of both the politics of British prisons and the increasingly factious and divided nation they help to legitimate and sustain in the late twentieth century.

From 'The abolitionist approach: a British perspective', in A. Duff et al. *(eds)* Penal Theory and Practice: Tradition and Innovation in Criminal Justice *(Manchester: Manchester University Press), 1994, pp. 263–84.*

References

Carlen, P. (1990), *Alternatives to Women's Imprisonment*, Open University Press, Buckingham.

de Haan, W. (1990), *The Politics of Redress: Crime, Punishment and Penal Abolition*, Unwin Hyman, London.

Dobash, R.E., and Dobash, R.P. (1992), *Women, Violence and Social Change*, Routledge, London.

Garland, D. (1985), *Punishment and Welfare*, Gower, Aldershot.

Guardian, 5 March 1991, 29 May 1992.

Jackson, G. (1975), *Blood in My Eye*, Penguin, London.

Mathiesen, T. (1986), 'The politics of abolition', *Contemporary Crises*, 10, pp. 81–94.

Mathiesen, T. (1990), *Prison on Trial*, Sage, London.

Matthews, R. (1989), *Reflections on Recent Developments in Social Control*, paper presented at the British Criminology Conference, July, Bristol.

Prison Reform Trust (1991), *The Identikit Prisoner*, Prison Reform Trust, London.

Radford, J., and Stanko, E. (1991), 'Violence against women and children: the contradictions of crime control under patriarchy', in K. Stenson and D. Cowell (eds.), *The Politics of Crime Control*, Sage, London, pp. 188–202.

Scottish Prison Service (1990), *Opportunities and Responsibility: Developing New Approaches to the Management of the Long-term Prison System in Scotland*, Scottish Prison Service, Edinburgh.

Sim, J. (1991), '"When you ain't got nothing, you got nothing to lose": the Peterhead rebellion, the state and the case for prison abolition', paper presented at the British Criminology Conference, July, York.

Sim, J. (1993), 'Reforming the penal wasteland? a critical review of the Woolf report', in E. Player and M. Jenkins (eds.), *Prisons after Woolf: Reform through Riot*, Routledge, London.

Stanko, E. (1985), *Intimate Intrusions*, Unwin Hyman, London.

Thomas, J., and Boehlefeld, S. (1991), '"Rethinking abolutionism: what do we do with Henry?", Review of de Haan's *The Politics of Redress*', *Social Justice*, 18, 3, pp. 239–51.

Woolf Report (1991), *Prison Disturbances 1990*. Report of an Inquiry by the Rt. Hon. Lord Justice Woolf and His Honour Judge Stephen Tumim, CM 1456, HMSO, London.

Part C

Prison populations

Introduction

In the Conclusion to this reader we will reflect on some of the quantitative data concerning prison populations around the world. Although statistics are useful for comparing different groups within national and international prison populations, Part C is equally concerned with the qualitative experience of life in confinement for some of the flesh-and-blood individuals behind the figures. Limitations of space inevitably result in a set of readings that is highly selective, but our decision to include extracts which reflect the lived experience of incarceration for various demographic groups, the conditions in which they are held, and the abuses and degradations that are routinely inflicted upon them, is made on the basis that, whilst the statistics move onwards and upwards, the reality of imprisonment remains strikingly uniform.

In Reading 13, 'Tougher than the rest? Men in prison', Joe Sim proposes a gendered reading of the literature on men's prison. Like many of the readings to follow in Part D, Sim is concerned with the social order of the prison and the operation of power. But here, we are urged to consider how the prison community is sustained and reproduced 'not only by organisational demands and individual personalities but also through deeply embedded discourses around masculinity and femininity'. As Sim notes, physical violence in prisons frequently endorses dominant cultural patterns, and he employs the notion of 'hegemonic masculinity' (Connell 1987), alerting us to the fact that it is not necessarily the most violent men who are most powerful inside, but that a certain degree of controlled aggressiveness is, none the less, a prerequisite for surviving the physical and psychological rigours of imprisonment. As in any organization, a climate of fear inevitably leads to the exploitation of weaker individuals by more powerful ones and, in prison, the illusion of power often rests on outward displays of intimidation and violence. Although ostensibly about masculinity, then, this reading develops the analysis introduced in Sim's earlier reading on alternative regimes and abolition (Reading 12) and discusses the extent to which some of the pervasive features of life in confinement – violence, predatory sexuality and fear – can be said to support or conflict with the prison's goals of reform, rehabilitation and desistance. In the final part of the extract, Sim reminds us of another institution discussed briefly in Part B, Barlinnie Special

Unit, which is highlighted as an example of a men's prison that challenged the violent, hyper-masculine culture of conventional regimes, and offered an alternative model of imprisonment (see also the description of HMP Grendon in Reading 11). Taking the view that offenders go to prison *as* punishment, not *for* punishment, the staff at Barlinnie attempted to provide inmates with a positive regime underpinned by therapeutic discourses: for example, it was here that (in)famous ex-con Jimmy Boyle began painting, sculpting and writing. But shortly after Sim wrote the piece from which this extract was taken, Barlinnie Special Unit was closed down – arguably a sad indictment of a society that reinforces hegemonic masculine values, not least via the pages of the popular press which heap fear and loathing on the individuals within prison, while at the same time delivering lurid and sensationalized stories about crime to the public at large (for a fuller account of which, see the Conclusion to this volume).

In Reading 14, which is taken from *Analysing Women's Imprisonment*, we turn our attention to female offenders, who now comprise 6.2 per cent of the prison population in England and Wales, up from 3.5 per cent in 1995. Pat Carlen and Anne Worrall raise some important concerns about the imprisonment of women; in particular, the problems of accommodating women and staffing their prisons, of drug use, bullying and violence, and of incarcerating mothers with young children. It is widely recognized that the needs of women in prison are different from those of men, but because of their relatively small numbers their particular problems and requirements are largely overlooked by the Prison Service in favour of a one-size-fits-all policy. Unsurprisingly, the dramatic increase in the female prison population is alarming to many prison commentators and of particular concern is the high numbers of women serving custodial sentences for relatively minor offences such as non-payment of fines and shoplifting. Elsewhere in the full account from which this extract is taken, Carlen and Worrall note in passing that in 1901 there were as many women in prison as there are today and that they made up over 16 per cent of the prison population. Back then, the majority of women were imprisoned for offences of drunkenness and prostitution, small-scale theft and assault, but it is important to note that women could also be confined in other institutions such as reformatories, homes and asylums (Reading 3), suggesting both class and gender biases in the system.

In the final part of Carlen and Worrall's extract, they reflect on the experience of an atypical female prisoner. Ruth Wyner, a middle-class, well educated, professional was sentenced in 1998, and her profound shock – not only at being sent to prison but at the treatment she faced there – brings into sharp relief the difficulty that female prisoners can face in negotiating basic rights like being treated with civility and respect. In particular, it is interesting to note that prison staff could not relate easily to Wyner unless they constructed her as a child-like, emotionally fragile girl. Her persona as an intelligent and articulate middle-aged woman prepared to challenge some of the bureaucratic absurdity inherent in the experience of imprisonment was perceived as threatening and provocative. To illustrate this further, Reading 15 is by Ruth Wyner herself. Taken from her autobiographical book, *From the Inside*, the extract describes the reception process as she was taken from the police cells following her conviction in court, to admission into HMP Holloway. Like this part's first reading by Sim, Wyner's account tells us much about how the behaviour of prisoners and prison staff is located within broader cultural manifestations of gendered power. Whilst many studies of men's prisons characterize staff–inmate relations as being similar to the relationship between parent and child (see Reading 22 by Mathiesen and Reading 24 by Crawley), women prisoners appear especially susceptible to procedures which infantilize and disempower them. Wyner's account also anticipates Goffman's exploration of the processes by which, on entering the institution for the first time, the inmate's sense of self is mortified (Reading 20). After only a few days, Wyner had adopted the persona of a prison inmate and feared that her 'real' self was lost for ever.

The one-size-fits-all policy also adversely affects prisoners from ethnic minority backgrounds who have faced a long struggle in getting the Home Office and Prison Service to recognize their diverse cultural, religious and dietary needs. But arguably the problems facing black and Asian inmates extend far beyond their experience in any given institution. Minority ethnic prisoners are referred to in a number of extracts throughout this reader, and as Ben Bowling and Coretta Phillips point out in Reading 16, a short extract taken from *Racism, Crime and Justice*, ethnic minorities are over-represented not just in prisons, but in the criminal justice system as a whole. Although prison numbers are growing in many parts of the world (by 71 per cent worldwide) it may surprise some readers to find that the prison population in the UK has risen by 15,000 since New Labour came to power in 1997, and has doubled since Margaret Thatcher took office in 1979. Even more surprising, perhaps is that inmates from ethnic minority backgrounds account for much of the overall rise. Whilst the white male prison population rose by 36 per cent between 1985 and 2003, the black population increased by 196 per cent, the South Asian population by 120 per cent, and the Chinese/other Asian by 223 per cent (Cross and Olowe 2003). Similar increases are found among the female prison population which, in the same time period, saw the numbers of black women inmates increase by 474 per cent. Bowling and Phillips highlight some of the possible reasons for the over-representation of ethnic minorities in prison, before going on to discuss racism and racist victimization in prisons. These issues have become particularly salient since the racist murder in 2000 of 19-year-old Zahid Mubarek who was beaten to death by his racist cellmate at Feltham Young Offenders' Institution. After repeatedly bludgeoning Zahid, Robert Stewart scrawled a swastika on the wall of his cell alongside the words 'just killed me pad mate'. According to newspaper reports, in the month before the murder, Stewart had repeatedly made racist gestures and threatened to kill a non-white inmate, but the pair were not separated into different cells (Jewkes 2006). The Chair of the Commission for Racial Equality concluded that Zahid Mubarek's death had been caused by a 'lethal combination of racism and systematic neglect' and that, had the victim been white, he would almost certainly still be alive (CRE 2003).

Reading 17 is taken from *Paramilitary Imprisonment in Northern Ireland: Resistance, Management, and Release* by Kieran McEvoy. It describes what happened to paramilitary prisoners in Northern Ireland at the height of the Troubles in the late 1970s and early 1980s and, in particular, focuses on the implementation of a policy of criminalization in the notorious H Blocks of the Maze prison (formerly known as Long Kesh). Criminalization of political prisoners was achieved through four channels: rule enforcement and the assertion of power; the internalization by staff of propagandist positions; staff brutality and prisoner dehumanization; and hothouse management combined with interference from political ministers. McEvoy describes each of these features in turn, before concluding that the intransigence of the British government resulted in a pyrrhic victory for the authorities; in other words, a victory gained at too high a cost. His descriptions of the conditions in which IRA prisoners were held at the Maze and the processes of criminalization they underwent are reminiscent of more recent discussions about the suspected terrorists held by the American government in Guantanamo Bay, Cuba, and by the British authorities at HMP Belmarsh until December 2004 (see the commentary for Reading 28).

The final extract in Part C concerns the incarceration of children and young people. In Reading 18, John Muncie traces Britain's history of youth detention to the first Borstal, set up in 1908. Only abolished in 1982 (when they were reinvented as youth custody centres) the punitiveness of the borstal system belied its liberal intentions and as Muncie notes – and many prisoner autobiographies testify – for many, a spell in Borstal was simply the first stage in a lifetime spent in and out of prison. The reading, which is taken from *Youth and Crime*, charts the development of young offender institutions (YOIs) and other types of custodial environments for young people, and describes conditions in these institutions, which are strikingly similar to some of the worst abuses that go on in adult prisons as highlighted in the other readings in Part C, including violence and intimidation by staff and inmates alike, drug abuse, and racist victimization. Muncie also reflects on New Labour's policies regarding the punishment of children and young people and, echoing Joe Sim's views (Reading 12), he makes the case against the use of custody for those under 18. He suggests that, since the introduction of the detention and training order (DTO) as part of the Crime and Disorder Act 1998, which incorporates a community service and training element, the government has been able to hide behind a veneer of progressiveness and humanitarianism. However the fact that DTOs also allow for the detention in custody of children as young as 10, and that in England and Wales twice as many children are incarcerated as in Belgium, Portugal, Spain, Denmark, Sweden, Finland, Austria, France and the Netherlands combined (Goldson 2003), causes Muncie and many other commentators to question the morality and appropriateness of the DTO as a penalty to deal with youth offending.

References

Commission for Racial Equality (CRE) (2003) *The Murder of Zahid Mubarek: A Formal Investigation by the Commission for Racial Equality into HM Prison Service of England and Wales. Part 1* (available at www.cre.gov.uk).

Connell, R.W. (1987) *Gender and Power*. Cambridge: Polity Press.

Cross, I. and Olowe, T. (2003) *Prison Population Brief England and Wales, November 2003*. London: Home Office.

Goldson, B. (2003) 'Tough on children ... tough on justice.' Presentation to the European Group for the Study of Deviance and Social Control conference, *Tough on Crime ... Tough on Freedoms*, Centre for Studies in Crime and Social Justice, Edge Hill College, Liverpool: 22–24 April.

Jewkes, Y. (2006) 'Creating a stir? Prisons, popular media and the power to reform', in P. Mason (ed.) *Captured by the Media: Prison Discourse in Popular Culture*. Cullompton: Willan Publishing.

13. Tougher than the rest? Men in prison

Joe Sim

Men in prison

The experience of men in prison has traditionally been tied to understanding the hierarchical arrangements of the institution. These arrangements have been built on the complex horizontal and vertical links established between prisoners and prison officers and between these groups and the white, male technocrats who occupy powerful positions as governors, area managers and state bureaucrats in the Home Office. While this work has generated a number of important sociological insights it has, like the majority of organisational studies, ignored the dialectical relationship between gender and power in prison (Savage and Witz 1992). In particular, it has failed to consider how the social order of the institution has been sustained and reproduced not only by organisational demands and individual personalities but also through deeply embedded discourses around masculinity and femininity. In other words, the daily experience of prisoners can be seen to be consistently and continuously mediated, not simply by their status as numbered and packaged individuals within the formal organisation of a state institution, but more fundamentally, by their relationship with, and expectations of, the other prisoners and their guards as men. A central dynamic of this daily experience and structured within these relationships is the question of violence and its place in reinforcing the hierarchical arrangements inside.

Attempting to understand the mobilisation of violence in prison and its relationship to strategies of domination and subjugation from a gendered perspective requires moving beyond commonsensical, state-defined and, indeed, many sociological explanations which have focused on the role of inadequate individuals, psychopathic personalities or 'bad apples'. Instead a critical analysis means 'drawing distinctions between different situations, which, taken together, comprise a violent institution' (Scraton *et al.* 1991: 66). At the same time, it also means recognising that:

> the acts of violent men in prison, sustained by a culture of masculinity, which idealises and equates personal power with physical dominance, reflects the world outside. Inside, the dominance can be total with nowhere to hide from the bullying of other prisoners. It is concentrated

within a totality of masculinity, the ground-rules heavily underlined by official male authority. Prisoners' violence is often part of the symbol, ritual and reality of a hostile male environment.

(ibid.: 67)

It is important to recognise that the culture of masculinity which has developed inside varies between different prisons. The hegemonic masculinity and the controlled use of violence which prevails in open prisons with its population of older men, middle-class offenders, convicted police officers and those completing their sentences, is of a very different order to the dominant, and often uncontrolled masculinity which operates systemically in young offenders' institutions and detention centres. Here physical violence, psychological intimidation and constant bullying provide the chilling and stark context in which everyday decisions are made, lives controlled and bodies and minds sometimes broken and destroyed. For many young men in these places, and the older men who staff them, violent behaviour is not abnormal but a normal, 'legitimated part of the taken-for-granted' (Morgan 1987: 183–4). This process of normalisation and routinisation underpins and gives meaning to the self-perception of the individual and the perceptions of the significant others in the power networks of the institution. As the account below makes clear, the institution sustains, reproduces and indeed intensifies this most negative aspect of masculinity, moulding and re-moulding identities and behaviourial patterns whose destructive manifestations are not left behind the walls when the prisoner is released but often become part of his 'taken-for-granted' world on the outside:

Violence. I was thinking about it afterwards the other night. Either you understand it or you don't. If you understand it, you find it hard to explain to somebody who doesn't. You've never questioned it, you've always taken it for granted, part and parcel of everyday life. It's normal: what would be abnormal would be if violence wasn't in your life … Before I stopped at the DC [Detention centre]. Now that is violence, real violence a detention centre is. They do things to you at a detention centre, mentally and physically, as bad or worse than anything you could have got sent there for in the first place. Beatings, kickings, humiliations: they heap them on you one on top of another. The idea's to break your spirit, to show you violence doesn't pay, that if you give it out you'll get it back ten times over. So what do you learn? If you haven't got it already, you learn hatred of authority and determination you're not going to let it break your spirit. You're not going to let it win, you're going to show them you're stronger and tougher than they are. If you don't you go under. You come out looking back on it with pride. They didn't break me. I won, I won. It's like graduating from an academy, it's a great feeling. Stay violent you say to yourself; stay violent and you'll win out in the end. You come out bitter at them and what they tried to do, but proud because you didn't let them. You could really call yourself a fully fledged hard man.

(cited in Parker 1990: 86–7)

Confronted by such institutionalised violence, the consequences for individual prisoners can be profound. In March 1992, it was reported that forty prisoners were attempting suicide each month in Feltham young offenders' institution where an 'atmosphere of terror' prevailed. In addition, four prisoners had killed themselves in seven months. One prisoner provided a vivid description of the atmosphere:

> About 70 or 80 boys arrive each day in big buses. You are stripped, given a number, a box of clothes. You are put in a large room with 60 other boys, big guys staring at you. There's a lot of friction when you arrive and you've got to front it out. If you sit in a corner with your head down they will pick on you for sure … if you show fear your card is marked. I've seen guys with fear in their eyes … You get smashed around the head, sent to hospital and you're back on the wing the same night … Some of the boys are so frightened they won't come out of their cells.
>
> (*Observer* 22.3.1992)

In adult, male, long-term prisons there is also a clear hierarchy which has been widely documented in social science and is well established in popular culture. Within both discourses the construction of this hierarchy has been understood less in terms of masculinity and more in terms of organisational demands or the 'natural' differences between offenders. The armed robber and the professional criminal, the epitomes of masculinity, stand at the apex while their antithesis, the child sex murderer, flounders at the bottom. Normal manhood and abnormal perversion live together in the same institution. Understanding the dynamics of this hierarchy from the perspective of prisoners (and prison officers) as men again provides a different analytical starting point. To paraphrase Max Weber both groups are trapped within an iron cage of masculinity which secures not only the reproduction of the material domination of the body but the continuation of oppression within and beyond the walls of the penitentiary:

> All male prisons house men who settle their arguments through fear, intimidation and fighting. Many are convicted for violent assault and present a no-compromise, hard-man image. They gather around them a network of support based on their coercive influence within the prison. Protection rackets, dealing, settling scores and victimisation are the ingredients of the institutionalisation of male violence. The culture of masculinity which pervades male prisons is all inclusive and reinforces hierarchies based on physical dominance … While the prison authorities denounce publicly the activities of a hard core of pathologically violent prisoners, their officers utilize privately the full potential of control which is rooted in their violence. This quite different expression of violence, which dominates interpersonal relations within prison, is also implicitly condoned, if not actively supported and exploited. A clear example of this is the brutal treatment suffered by sex offenders. Their institutionalized brutalisation reinforces their damaged personalities

and does nothing to alleviate the oppression of women. Yet it consumes the energies and reinforces the aggressive masculinity of many prisoners.

(Scraton *et al.* 1991: 66).

Violence and domination in prison can therefore be understood not as a pathological manifestation of abnormal otherness but as part of the normal routine which is sustained and legitimated by the wider culture of masculinity: that culture condemns some acts of male violence but condones the majority of others. It will be condemned only if it transgresses the acceptable limits of masculinity. State servants, for example, will focus their gaze on uncontrollable prisoners who in their view use force indiscriminately, the 'ballbuster' in American prison literature. Such prisoners pose problems for the normal running of the prison and challenge what the official rules call 'good order and discipline'. Seen from a gendered perspective they can be understood quite differently. First, they reinforce popular and professional discourses which equate male violence inside and outside, with individual pathology. Second, they allow the state to maintain that something is being done about violence inside through the removal of these prisoners from normal circulation and into solitary confinement. Third, they normalise violence in that the concentration on these prisoners allows other forms of prison violence to be seen as legitimate, a normal if regrettable part of prison life. In this way the debate on prison violence is constructed on the narrow terrain of psychopathic personalities while the everyday normality of domination, control, humiliation and violence is continually reproduced. These prisoners:

> become the living proof of the assumption that the troubles in British prisons are derived in and orchestrated by the words and deeds of a handful of pathologically violent men. This enables the authorities to affirm the commitment to the traditional criminological classifications of inadequate and violent personalities and to reject the charge of institutionalised violence within harsh regimes. The very celebration of masculinity, then, reduces its most violent manifestations to the level of opportunism and restricts its analysis to the psychologies of a few men. The culture and cult of masculinity which permeates all aspects of life in male prisons … remains dominant and reinforced.
>
> (Scraton *et al.* 1991: 77)

A good example of this point can be seen in relation to the issue of sexuality in prison. A number of recent studies have rightly moved away from the positivist emphasis on the forensic basis of rape in prison to a position which emphasises the relationship between institutional and sexual violence and broader cultures of masculinity. Robert Dumond (1992: 138), for example, has noted how in American prisons highly sexualised terms such as 'Gorilla', 'Daddy', 'Kid', 'Fag' and 'Queen' have become 'sexual scripts which help to define an inmate's orientation within a society which values aggression, power and loyalty – many of the attributes of traditional masculinity in society'. While it is important to focus on the often immense physical and psychological emasculation that is generated by male rape both inside and outside the walls (McMullen 1990) it is also important to recognise that rape behaviour is only one aspect of a broader process of sexual exploitation and coercion which as Betsy Stanko has noted:

> serves to enhance heterosexual masculinity. Inmate power and control can be gained by treating other inmates 'like women', essentially keeping the fear of sexual danger associated with being female. By turning some men into 'women' these inmates use sexuality to dehumanise and degrade fellow inmates. To safeguard an inmate's manhood and manliness an inmate must fend off sexual attacks and be wary of sexual approaches.
>
> (Stanko 1990: 123–4)

The influence that sexually predatory prisoners have is often disproportionate to their numbers in the system. They will generate a deep fear among younger prisoners in particular whose masculinity is kept both under constant surveillance and threat. Jimmy Boyle has described how young prisoners arriving in Peterhead in the mid-1970s would be terrified by the activities of one particular prisoner to the point where:

> some of them would ask for 'protection'. The screws of course thought this all very funny, but personally I felt deeply humiliated that another prisoner could allow himself to be 'used' in this way by them. In his own way he was policing the prison for them and the fact that he was causing conflict amongst the prisoners meant that pressure was taken off the screws. He didn't get away with it completely as some individual prisoners would have a go at him, including some of his group. But he had a frightening effect on prisoners in the main and this gave him some measure of control.
>
> (Boyle 1977: 196)

The organisation and broader power structures of the institution legitimate and facilitate this coercion. At this level many prison officers, for example, will fail to challenge sexual exploitation not only because it divides the prison population against itself (although that is clearly one major benefit for them) but more fundamentally because such exploitation in the words of Bob Connell 'is a form of person-to-person violence deeply embedded in power inequalities and ideologies of male supremacy. Far from being a deviation from the social order, it is in a significant sense an enforcement of it' (Connell 1987: 107). To concentrate on deviant individuals therefore misses this more fundamental sociological point.[1]

[…]

The prison's goals: a gendered reading

The traditional goals of the prison have been built around the institution's power to combine punishment, deterrence, prevention, incapacitation and rehabilitation. The critical sociological response which developed in the 1970s pointed not only to the inability of the institution to do much about crime but also to its role in maintaining and reproducing wider social divisions (Mathiesen 1990). While both positions have generated a range of important work, when scrutinised in terms of gender the differences between them are less apparent than first appears. For example, if the prison was to succeed in its classical liberal goal of rehabilitating male prisoners it could be argued that the definition of success is conceptualised on the narrow terrain of rescuing male law-breakers from behaviour conventionally defined as antithetical to the criminal law and preparing them to live 'a good and useful life' when released. Close links with the family are regarded as central to their rehabilitation. And yet reforming the prisoner so that he can return to normal family life – whatever that means given the breakdown of the traditional nuclear family – fails to take account of the nature of power and its distribution in these micro situations. Deconstructing what a 'good and useful life' means for the women and children in the lives of male prisoners therefore provides a very different perspective on rehabilitation. It should be stressed that this is not an argument for defending the often appalling arrangements for personal contact which currently prevail, nor is it an argument which underestimates the intolerable and harrowing psychological pain that male prisoners feel at particular moments during their confinement (Scraton *et al.* 1991: Ch. 5). It is, however, a position which recognises that the success of the prison is being measured on a narrow philosophical and sociological terrain devoid of gendered power relationships. Similar questions can be asked about deterrence, incapacitation, prevention and punishment.

Radical critiques face similar problems. For example, the correlation between rates of unemployment and rates of imprisonment which has been identified in critical studies since the 1930s is a correlation which is discussed almost entirely in terms of male unemployment. Similarly, the theory that prison distracts attention away from crimes of the powerful and symbolically constructs discourses around good and evil is highly plausible until it is genderised. As a number of feminist writers have noted, powerful men are not necessarily those who occupy the economic and political positions as classically defined in Marxist and Weberian sociology. Those who are the most economically and politically powerless often exert a profound material and ideological influence over the women in their lives through utilising 'everyday violence' (Stanko 1990). Who are the powerful and from what crimes are individuals being distracted therefore become significant theoretical questions when the distraction function of the prison is genderised.

[...]

Challenging hegemonic masculinity

While the analysis in this chapter has pointed to the usefulness of hegemonic masculinity as a theoretical tool for analysing the particular form of gendered order found in male prisons, it is important to recognise that the material and ideological network of power generated by and through hegemonic masculinity inside has not been without its own internal contradictions and challenges. As Bob Connell has pointed out, utilising hegemony as a theoretical concept involves recognising that the relationship between, and the politics of, domination and subordination is very often an incomplete process. Alternative definitions of reality, other strategies and ways of behaving are not simply obliterated by power networks. They are 'subordinated rather than eliminated' (Connell 1987: 184) . Thus, while physical and psychological violence might be a cornerstone of male imprisonment which support dominant cultural patterns and ideologies, they are utilised within a balance of forces in which there is an everyday contestation of power and where there is always the possibility for individual, social and historical change (Connell 1987: 184).

Connell's point is an important one. It is also one which is often forgotten when Gramsci's concept of hegemony is utilised theoretically. Domination is emphasised at the expense of contradiction, challenge and change, both at the level of individual identities and social formations. This position has particular relevance for the study of men in prison, for despite the domineering brutalisation which underpins and reinforces the culture of masculinity inside, this culture has often been undercut by individual and collective strategies of dissent and sometimes by alternative penal policies which have provided a glimpse of the possibility for constructing social arrangements which are not built on violence and domination. I want to explore some examples of this in the last part of this chapter.

First, it is necessary to recognise that not all prisoners are fearless, manipulative and violent hard men. Fear is a constant factor in the daily lives of the majority of prisoners. In a recent study of Peterhead prison, 86 per cent of prisoners interviewed stated that they did not feel safe in prison while 62 per cent indicated that fear was a 'predominant factor' in their daily lives (Scraton *et al*. 1991: 68). While a number of writers have rightly pointed out that the male experience of fear outside prison is very different compared with women (Stanko 1990: 126) and that this fear will often leave men 'isolated and unable to ask for support' (Stanko and Hobdell 1993: 27) it is also important to recognise that frightened prisoners are not always exploited by their fellow inmates. Prisoners who have been beaten or who are frightened of being beaten, will often generate gentler and softer feelings in those observing these events. Interviews with prisoners in Peterhead provided 'poignant accounts of suffering in which the most hardened man identifie[d] with the anguish of another but remaine[d] frustrated and angry at the indifference of the institution and its officers' (Scraton *et al* 1991: 75). Two accounts illustrate this point:

Of all the liberties I witnessed among them was one assault on a young cripple. This particular day his sticks were at surgery being adjusted. He intervened in a slanging match on behalf of another prisoner, the officer seized him by the throat and punched him 3 times or so in the face, the officer said later that he had hit him with a stick. [The prisoner] got 14 days for assault.

The guy has slashed his own face twice in the past couple of weeks. What state of mind is the poor guy in? Not one person has lifted a finger to help him.

(both cited in Scraton *et al.* 1991: 74–5)

Second, some male prisoners make conscious decisions to utilise non-coercive strategies to deal with the encroachment of male and penal power into their lives. These prisoners pose different problems for prison managers. They stand at the opposite end of the masculinist continuum from the 'ballbuster'. Pursuing education classes, attaining an intimate knowledge of prison rules, regulations and standing orders, becoming a 'jailhouse lawyer' and categorically refusing to engage in violent or coercive behaviour are all examples of strategies developed by prisoners which do not necessarily derive from the culture of masculinity inside.

[...]

A third example of this process can be seen in a number of the small units established in British prisons in the last two decades. Space does not allow for a full discussion of these units and the politics behind and within them. I do, however, want to look at them through the lens of gender in order to pinpoint what they can offer as a challenge to the dominant discourses inside. In particular, I want to focus on the Barlinnie Special Unit, opened in February 1973 as perhaps the clearest example yet of the challenge to masculinity in prison.

From the outset the philosophy and practices of the Unit were diametrically at odds with those prevailing in the traditional system where interpersonal confrontation was a daily event. Some of the Unit's prisoners had previously been detained in the notorious segregation unit, the Cages, at Inverness prison where conditions were brutal:

The caged area is approximately 9ft by 6ft. The only moveable objects besides the human body are a small plastic chamberpot – lidless, a woollen blanket and one book that is issued each week. Human contact is made three times a day when the 'screws' enter to search the body of the prisoner ... There is no communication between the 'screws' and the prisoner ... Brutality and abuse of human rights is rife. If a prisoner is particularly awkward then punishment takes the form of leaving his food just out of reach behind the cage bars until it is cold, or he receives it with spittle in it.

(MacDonald and Sim 1978: 23–4)

This regime can be contrasted with that operating in Barlinnie. The most significant aspect of the Unit's work lay in the decentring and deconstruction of violence as central to the repertoire of responses which staff and prisoners had utilised to defend their respective positions in the traditional system. Both groups responded to the others in the Unit not through physical violence and psychological intimidation but through the 'community meeting' where each man was encouraged to examine and articulate his feelings about himself, his life inside and his actions outside the walls (Wardrup 1982: 26). For the prisoners this was a particularly painful experience. They had never been encouraged to shine the searchlight of scrutiny on themselves as individuals or more fundamentally as men. Nor had they been encouraged to take personal responsibility for their actions. According to some accounts this philosophy which demanded personal as opposed to interpersonal confrontation, generated more psychic pain than the physical and psychological brutality they experienced prior to entering Barlinnie.[2] Jimmy Boyle has provided a powerful and highly perceptive account of the pain involved in shedding the layers of psychological skin from his past and the implications this might have for dealing with violent men:

> I have entered a world that has dyed and cast me, like so many others, where certain parts of myself have not been allowed to express themselves; a world that didn't allow my mother to kiss and cuddle me; a world where natural affection was seldom shown. To the present day I am labelled 'Killer' when in fact parts of me were done to death and only now am I discovering them ... to think I am labelled 'Scotland's Most Violent Man'. Is it right that I should think these thoughts or should I do as I have done in the past and fulfil people's expectations of me? Am I doomed to eat raw meat and live in a Cage to satisfy the masses? I come to the present day and watch those very same people who gave me that label say that I am a 'con-man' who is trying to work his ticket out of prison – such versatility I must possess. Could it be that the consequences of someone like me changing would be too much for the establishment to accept?
>
> (Boyle 1984: 148–51)

Another prisoner has also provided a graphic illustration of the internal conflict he endured:

> I was creating crisis after crisis and becoming more hostile towards the community confrontations as they grew more intense in a concentrated effort to modify my behaviour. At this point four of the more experienced members of the community began to work on what can be described as a crash course in maturing me. The understanding and total honesty demonstrated by these men rocked me on my heels and at times became very painful, because each of them in his own way stripped away the masks until I was standing before them, naked in a primitive sense that left me feeling very vulnerable. My values altered to a degree, and while

recognising the futility of submerging myself within the false security of the prison subculture I realised that this was only my first step in what was going to be a long, hard struggle with much more pain to come.

(cited in Carrell and Laing 1982: 25)

Similar views have been expressed by prisoners in Grendon Underwood whose regime emphasises:

the responsibility of prisoners to explore their criminality, to share and express their feelings. To be answerable to each other as individuals and as a community, is we believe a valuable feature and most significant it is social as opposed to anti-social.

(Newman 1991: 21)

While it is important not to underestimate the problems faced by these institutions and to be aware of what Rebecca and Russell Dobash have called the 'therapeutic discourses' (Dobash and Dobash 1992: 248) which often underpin many progressive programmes, it is equally important to recognise that the examples above illustrate the complex and contradictory nature of masculinity in prison and the possibilities for empowerment and change within an often overwhelming network of male and penal power. This approach can be contrasted with the traditional methods utilised in dealing with offenders in general and conventionally dangerous offenders in particular. Incapacitating rapists for example, has not guaranteed an alleviation of violence against women either at an individual or collective level. Such men are likely to be confronted by a culture of masculinity which will do little to change their behaviour, heighten their consciousness or the consciousness of those in the wider society concerning the 'intimate intrusions' which collectively face women on a daily basis (Stanko 1985).

These findings are hardly surprising given the nature of most penal regimes and the discourses surrounding sexuality, masculinity and femininity that prevail within and without the prison walls. In that sense, even allowing for their obsessive secrecy, prisons are not as removed from the body of the wider society as has previously been argued. They are linked to that society by the umbilical cord of masculinity where similarities between prisoners and men outside may be more important than the differences between them in explaining sexual and other forms of violence against women. As one sex offender has noted:

The most common accusation I get is that I've committed my crimes because I like doing them – because … that's the way I get my kicks. But I ask who's getting the real kicks? My case got a centre-page spread in the Sunday newspapers, thousands of extra copies were printed, *and* they exaggerate it for the delight of their readers. And the worst element is that, all the way through, no one asks you why. Oh they'll ask, 'Why did you do this?' But all they're looking for is an explanation which will make sense in their own terms.

(cited in Campbell 1986: 117, emphasis on the original)

Concluding remarks

This chapter has considered the sociological and political implications of a gendered reading of the literature on male prisons. I have concentrated on a number of specific areas but clearly there is scope for developing this analysis through focusing on a range of other areas that are directly related to the micro and macro politics of confinement including: the place of the body in prison culture and hierarchies; sexuality, masculinity and confinement; race and hegemonic masculinity, violence and domination in women's prisons; masculinity, militarisation and the state; the relationship between state violence and male violence and the use of violence as a strategy of resistance. Taken together, these issues raise fundamental questions about the conceptualisation of male imprisonment within social science and the need to reconstruct and transgress the orthodox study of penal power.[3] Such a theoretical shift can provide a more analytical starting point for understanding the behaviour of prisoners as men. At the same time it may also generate strategies for changing their behaviour both within and without the walls of the penitentiary where the culture of masculinity casts a long and profoundly damaging shadow of patriarchal domination over the hearts, minds and bodies of the many women and children whose lives are eclipsed and diminished by its impact.

From T. Newburn and E.A. Stanko (eds) Just Boys Doing Business? Men, Masculinities and Crime *(London: Taylor & Francis), 1994, pp. 100–17.*

Notes

1. It is worth noting that the symbolic attack on the individual's masculinity through sexual exploitation makes it very difficult to gather data on the full extent of this exploitation. Between 1988 and 1993 there were seventeen alleged rapes of juvenile prisoners but as the Prison Reform Trust has noted the shame felt by those subjected to such attacks undermines the gathering of evidence. These reported rapes are therefore likely to be the tip of the iceberg (*Observer* 4.4 1993).
2. The history of the Barlinnie Unit remains to be written. There has been no serious sociological study of its genesis and consolidation or of the antagonism, both official and unofficial, which was directed towards it. The accounts I am referring to come from my personal discussions with staff and prisoners during my visits to the Unit in the mid-1970s.
3. This reflects Cain's (1990) call for the reconstruction and transgression of criminological theory in general.

References

Boyle, J. (1992) *A Sense of Freedom*, Edinburgh: Canongate Press.
Boyle, J. (1984) *The Pain of Confinement*, Edinburgh: Canongate Press.
Cain, M. (1990) 'Towards transgression: new directions in feminist criminology', *International Journal of the Sociology of Law*, 18(1): 1–18.
Campbell, J. (1986) *Gate Fever*, London: Weidenfeld and Nicolson.
Carrell, C. and Laing, J. (eds) (1982) *The Special Unit Barlinnie Prison*, Glasgow: Third Eye Centre.
Connell, R.W. (1987) *Gender and Power: Society, the Person and Sexual Politics*, Cambridge: Polity Press.

Dobash, R.E. and Dobash, R.P. (1992) *Women, Violence and Social Change*, London: Routledge.

Dumond, R. (1992) 'The sexual assault of male inmates in incarcerated settings', *International Journal of the Sociology of Law*, 20: 135–57.

MacDonald, D. and Sim, J. (1978) *Scottish Prisons and the Special Unit*, Glasgow: Scottish Council for Civil Liberties.

Mathiesen, T. (1990 *Prison on Trial*, London: Sage.

McMullen, R. (1990) *Male Rape*, London: GMP Publishers.

Morgan, D. (1987) 'Masculinity and violence' in Hanmer, J. and Maynard, M. (eds) *Women, Violence and Social Control*, Hampshire: MacMillan.

Newman, D. (1991) 'D Wing' in Selby, M. (ed.) *Riot: Reform in Our Time: A Report into Power Sharing*, conference held at HMP Grendon 20–21 August 1991, Springhill: Springhill Press.

Parker, T. (1990) *Life After Life*, London: Secker & Warburg.

Savage, M. and Witz, A. (eds) (1992) *Gender and Bureaucracy*, Oxford: Blackwell.

Scraton, P., Sim, J. and Skidmore, P. (1991) *Prisons Under Protest*, Buckingham: Open University Press.

Scully, D. (1990) *Understanding Sexual Violence*, London: HarperCollins.

Stanko, E.A. (1985) *Intimate Intrusions*, London: Unwin Hyman.

Stanko, E.A. (1990) *Everyday Violence: How Women and Men Experience Sexual and Physical Danger*, London: Pandora.

Stanko, E.A. and Hobdell, K. (1992) 'Assault on men: Masculinity and male victimisation', *British Journal of Criminology*, 33(3): 400–15.

Wardrup, K. (1982) 'The therapeutic community' in Carrell, C. and Laing, J. (eds) *The special Unit Barlinnie Prison*, Glasgow: Third Eye Centre.

14. Analysing women's imprisonment

Pat Carlen and Anne Worrall

Accommodating women prisoners

[...] Because of the small numbers, it is difficult to decide whether women should be accommodated together centrally where it *may*, but rarely *is* possible to provide a greater variety of facilities, or in small groups attached to men's prisons, which might be nearer to their homes but provide much poorer facilities. An example of the latter 'solution' can be found in Western Australia where Aboriginal women from remote areas are located in appalling conditions in remote men's prisons in order to be relatively near their families, rather than being transferred to central Perth where facilities are considerably better (Inspector of Custodial Services, WA 2003). In Hawaii, women were moved into men's prisons precisely in order to access better facilities but the reality was that women had less freedom of movement and ended up with less provision (Chesney-Lind and Rodriguez 2004). In England, increasing numbers of men's prisons are being required to accommodate a small number of women prisoners who invariably become 'second-class citizens' within the prison complexes, having less access to the best jobs, education and recreational facilities than the men – and there is no guarantee that they will end up being any nearer to their families (Carlen 1998).

Architecturally, prisons are not designed with women in mind (though some may argue that they are simply not designed with *people* in mind). Until recently, almost all women's prisons in England (with the notable and disastrous exception of Holloway [...]) were either previously used as men's prisons or were used for completely different purposes historically. All three of the women's open prisons fall into the latter category. Askham Grange and East Sutton Park are stately homes and Drake Hall (now a closed prison) was originally a hostel for munitions workers in World War II. In fairness to Drake Hall, a major rebuild in the mid-1990s did attempt to provide village-type house blocks with green spaces and pathways. Unfortunately, most of the old accommodation remained in use, which rather detracted from the limited but welcomed vision. The approach to accommodating women prisoners has taken one of two forms: women are either considered to be no different from men and have been housed in identical structures, or they have been subjected to a paternalistic belief that if they are in 'nice' surroundings, they will feel less imprisoned. Nothing could be further from the truth. Women from inner London are often desolate and disorientated when located in the unfamiliar rural setting of Drake Hall (in North Staffordshire) and many request to be transferred back to Holloway, despite its worse conditions (Worrall 2000).

The Woolf Report did not consider women's prisons explicitly because no serious collective disturbances have ever taken place in a women's prison in England and Wales. Nevertheless, the implications of his principles for women's prisons, and his advocacy of 'community prisons', were discussed creatively (Nacro 1991; Player 1994; Hayman 1996). In particular, one interpretation of the concept of 'community prisons' was the proposal for a large number of locally-based houses set aside for the purpose, where women would reside (possibly with their children) making use of community facilities and resources to provide their daily regime (Nacro 1991). Examples of such 'transitional' arrangements exist in other countries, such as the Netherlands (see Hayman 1996) and parts of Australia (Carlen 2002) but in this country opposition by campaigning groups (on the grounds that such provision might increase the numbers of women sent to prison) and the general under-funding and neglect of hostel provision for women offenders (Howard League 2000) means that there has been no innovative residential provision for women offenders.

Sexuality and cross-gender posting

Since 1988 the Prison Service has officially adopted an equal opportunities approach to staff posting, which enables women officers to work in men's prisons and men officers in women's prisons (Carlen 1998). Despite this, only 17 per cent of prison officers are female and the proportion of female officers ranges from 3 per cent in one men's prison to 90 per cent in one open women's prison (Liebling and Price 2001). The introduction of female officers to men's prisons has generally been welcomed and viewed as having a 'normalising' effect on the prison environment, though their presence has challenged the male-dominated culture of prisons in much the same way as female police officers challenge 'cop culture' (Liebling and Price 2001; Walklate 2001).

Far less has been written about the impact of male prison officers in women's prisons. In US prisons, there is ample evidence of routine sexual assault of female prisoners by male guards, to the extent that the issue has attracted the attention of Human Rights Watch (Chesney-Lind and Pasko 2004). In her research of women's imprisonment at the millennium in England, Pat Carlen (1998) found that, although women prisoners did not object to male officers *per se*, they were often uncomfortable about their presence in the residential parts of the prison. Many women prisoners have past experiences of violent and abusive relationships with men that make them wary of contact with men in their living quarters. For such women, knowing that male officers are authorised to be involved in their daily routines causes anxiety. The counter-argument is that it might be beneficial for such women to experience men 'who are good role models, because a lot of these women have never met a decent man or a man who can keep his trousers zipped up' (Prison governor cited in Carlen 1998: 142). Beyond that specific anxiety, however, it could be argued that, since all women are socialised into being modest and private about their bodies, the prospect of unknown men being able both to discuss and to view them in various states of (un)dress, health and hygiene, is not unreasonably a matter of concern for them:

> I've no objection to the employment of men in the prison. In some ways it's quite good. Nice to have some male conversation now and then. But I do object when two men do the patrols on the houses at night. Especially at four o'clock in the morning, they either tip the curtain back and shine a torch in, or they actually walk into the room. I don't like that. It could be very awkward.
>
> (Amanda, cited in Carlen 1998: 139)

While the presence of male officers in women's prisons throws the issue of sexuality and sexual relations into sharp relief, there is 'a silence' about the numbers of lesbian officers working in women's prisons (Carlen 1998: 143). There is no evidence to suggest that prison officers in England – male or female, heterosexual or lesbian – are any more sexually predatory than anyone else, but that is not the point. The point is that women who already feel vulnerable by reason of their imprisonment have to contend additionally with a routinised and structured loss of privacy which, quite literally, requires them to be naked before a 'legitimated punitive stare' (Carlen 1998: 142).

Drugs, bullying and violence

The history of women's imprisonment has been a history of the medicalisation of women's problems (Carlen 1983, 1998; Sim 1990) or, as Hannah-Moffat puts it, the power of *pastoralism* – the secular version of concern for the soul of the individual (2000: 8). The rebuilding of Holloway Prison in the 1970s was based on the assumption that women in prison needed medical and psychiatric facilities rather than punishment. Women's prisons were at the top of the prison 'league table' for the prescription of drugs that affected the central nervous system and the psychiatric control of difficult women through medication became one of the main concerns of the campaigning group *Women in Prison* in the 1980s. But, even at the height of this concern, it was acknowledged that prisons were doing no more than reflecting women's widespread dependency on prescribed drugs and that prison doctors were in a 'no win' situation:

> If the prison doctor then stops prescribing drugs which the women have been legitimately prescribed outside s/he is likely to be accused of being punitive. If, on the other hand, s/he continues to prescribe large doses of drugs then s/he is likely to be accused of drugging women solely for penal control purposes.
>
> (O'Dwyer and Carlen 1985: 165)

Increasingly, the view was formed among both those working in prisons and in campaigning groups that women turned to drugs – both prescribed and illegitimately obtained – in order to survive the pains of imprisonment. What was not conceded at that time was that women were themselves *drug offenders*.

The recognition, or over-recognition, of women as drug offenders came with the emergence into professional discourse of anti-discriminatory practice and anti-racism training in the late 1980s and early 1990s [...]. By the mid-1990s, concern about drugs in women's prisons reached the point where the Chief Inspector of Prisons expressed the view, after visiting one women's prison, that it was possible for a woman 'to enter a shoplifter and leave an addict' (cited in Malloch 2000: 7). This level of illicit drug use in women's prisons was leading to bullying, trading and violent sexual assault among women (conducting internal searches on other women) (Malloch 2000). Officers began to view drug-users as the most aggressive and disruptive women in the prison: 'the biggest problem in here isn't the murderers, it's the addicts – they're far more devious' (Malloch 2000: 113).

Levels of substance misuse among prisoners are roughly comparable for men and women (Howard League 2000: 5), though women are proportionately more likely than men to be users of opiates and crack cocaine – the drugs most strongly associated with offending (Home Office 2003; Ramsey 2003). For this reason, the Prison Service Women's Policy Group regards the misuse of drugs as a 'major issue for women in prison' (Stewart 2000: 42) and increasing resources are being made available for drugs treatment in women's prisons. But there is now a danger that courts will send more women to prison precisely because this is the one place in the criminal justice system where such treatment may be available [...]. However, the limited availability of such treatment in prison means that many are simply condemned to an environment of violence and intimidation where their drugs problems worsen rather than improve.

Mandatory drugs testing (MDT) was introduced into prisons in England and Wales in 1995, with little consideration given to its differential impact on men and women (Carlen 1998). Ensuring the provision of an uncontaminated urine sample is a more intrusive process for women than for men – watching women urinate is less socially acceptable than watching men do so! It requires a level of disrespect for privacy that, arguably, comes close to infringing human rights (Smith 2000). MDT may be carried out on prisoners suspected of drugs involvement but it can also be carried out randomly and the legality of compulsory urinalysis has been successfully challenged in Canada (Smith 2000). Although the argument in favour of MDT is often couched in terms of health promotion and the protection of prisoners, it raises the question of the extent to which compulsorily detained people can be subjected to 'further involuntary interventions in their lives' (Smith 2000: 348).

Imprisoning mothers

It is estimated that in England and Wales at least 100,000 children a year experience their father's imprisonment and more than 6,000 children a year are affected by maternal imprisonment (Lloyd 1995). In 1991 the first National Prison Survey interviewed 4,000 prisoners and found that 43 per cent said a family member had criminal convictions, compared with 16 per cent of the general population, and 35 per cent had another family member in prison. Among young prisoners the figures were even higher – 53 per cent had relatives with criminal convictions and 44 per cent had a family member who had been in prison. At the very broadest level therefore having a parent in prison is likely to increase the chances of a child ending up in prison themselves. Pelligrini (1997) interviewed children whose fathers had been imprisoned and she concluded that they went through five stages of adjustment: establishing the meaning of the father's action; acknowledging the separation from the father and adapting daily activities to the new situation; managing feelings elicited by the situation; accepting the father's temporary separation; and re-adjusting to the father's return. The role of the child's mother in ensuring that adjustment was crucial and, although Pelligrini did not interview the children of imprisoned mothers, one cannot imagine that the impact of maternal imprisonment would be any less. The loss of their role as mother is considered by most prison administrations to be a significant 'pain of imprisonment' for women (Woodrow 1992). But this is not just an individual problem for mother and child. The impact of maternal separation on the future well-being of the state and its citizens is also a consideration.

According to a Caddle and Crisp (1997) 61 per cent of women in prison in England in 1994 were mothers. Between them, these 1,000 women had over 2,000 children and nearly one-third of these were under five years old. While men in prison normally expect their children to be cared for by their female partners, women in prison are heavily dependent on temporary carers such as grandparents or other female relations. The same study noted that children of imprisoned mothers were reported as having a variety of behavioural problems resulting from the separation, including becoming withdrawn, sleeping and eating problems, bed-wetting and problems in making and keeping friends.

So administrators of women's prisons feel obliged to find ways of allowing imprisoned women as much contact as possible with their families. This is done in four ways. First, women are afforded a variety of 'temporary releases' to spend time at home. Second, special facilities are made available to enable families to visit women in prison. Bandyup's Family Support Centre is a good example – a well-equipped and well-maintained building just outside the prison. Here, visitors can relax and obtain refreshment after a long journey to the prison. They can also obtain advice and help with any concerns they have. Children can be cared for while parents visit the prison, or collected from a visit half way through. The Centre is run by a non-governmental organisation, which also runs rehabilitation courses for the women, such as offending behaviour courses (Inspector of Custodial Services, WA 2003). Several women's prisons in England run whole day visits for children. Third and most rarely, women are allowed to postpone their prison sentences until suitable child care arrangements can be made. Fourth, and most controversially, women are allowed to keep their children with them in prison up to a certain age.

In England, there are currently four prisons which accommodate mothers with babies – Holloway, Styal, New Hall and Askham Grange – providing 69 places, although there are plans for two further units to be opened in 2004, offering 22 more places. Babies are allowed to stay up to 9 months in the three closed prisons and 18 months at Askham Grange, which is an open prison. The units are staffed by trained prison officers and employ professional nursery nurses. The prison accepts a duty of care towards the baby in relation to health issues. Abroad, there are many variations of provision (Caddle 1998) and the Ter Peel experiment in the Netherlands is often cited as a model of provision. Here, children remain with their mothers up to the age of four years but attend nurseries outside the prison on a daily basis. Similar provision exists in parts of Australia (Farrell 1998; Carlen 2002), although the nursery at Bandyup Prison is considered to be problematic. Here there are no suitably trained staff and the health care centre refuses to provide medical care beyond primary health care. If a child is sick, a relative has to be contacted to collect the child from the prison, which is clearly an unsatisfactory and potentially dangerous situation. Lack of supervision has also resulted in babies being vulnerable to abuse (Inspector of Custodial Services, WA 2003).

The debate about mother and baby units is an unresolved one. It can be argued that a baby has the right not to start its life in prison and there has been much criticism of the standards of care and stimulation in units (Department of Health 1994), although there have been many improvements in recent years (HM Prison Service 1999). Their very existence is also said to encourage courts to send mothers with babies to prison instead of seeking out the alternatives. A study by Catan (1992) compares the development of two groups of babies – one in a unit and one cared for by temporary carers. Although the motor development of the group in the unit was slower, they quickly caught up once the mother was released, and this was off-set by a much greater stability of social environment and continuity of care. Many of the separated babies experienced changes of carers and were less likely to be reunited with their mothers. Even those mothers who did resume care of their babies had difficulties in sustaining the parental relationship.

[...]

Conclusion

Prison authorities often argue that the women they have to deal with are already so damaged that it is extraordinarily difficult for them to achieve anything approaching genuine rehabilitation. One has to sympathise with this argument to some extent. But when Ruth Wyner (2003) was imprisoned under highly controversial circumstances, she found her intelligence, education and management skills wholly inadequate for personal survival. Her profound sense of shock and injustice suffuses her account, as does the evidence of the real and lasting damage caused to her by her imprisonment.

A professional charity worker, Wyner was imprisoned for failing to disclose to the police the names of drug dealers *who had been banned* from the shelter for which she was responsible. Leaving aside the issue of whether or not she should have been imprisoned at all, her story provides an almost clinical case study of the impact of prison on an otherwise 'normal' woman. Her story is one of an assault on identity that affected both her mental and physical health in ways from which she is still recovering. In addition to the routine physical privations detailed in this chapter, it was also clear that the prison was incapable of dealing with her in anything other than a wholly standardised way. As a trained journalist, Wyner offered to be a 'classroom assistant' on the English courses but was apparently told that this could not be allowed ('It seems that as well as being unable to help myself, I am not allowed to help anyone else' [p. 66]). Almost 20 years on, Carlen's observation (above) about 'good prisoners' not thinking themselves better than other women still seems pertinent. Instead Wyner was obliged to attend an art class in which she had no interest and for which she had no aptitude, and to work in the gardens which, as it happened, turned into something of an oasis of sanity for her. That Wyner suffered with migraines and depression throughout her sentence appears to have been a matter of little concern to the medical authorities in the prison. That she was offered an offending behaviour course for drug importers ('"I'm not in for that", I protest. "It's all we have to offer", the probation officer replies' [p. 131]) illustrates the absurdity of inflexible approaches to offender rehabilitation. That, as a Jewish woman, she had to subject herself to a regime of evangelical Christianity in order to live in half-decent surroundings could be viewed as an abuse of Human Rights.

The prison authorities would probably say that Ruth Wyner was a 'difficult' woman because she challenged every perceived incident of disrespect (including being referred to as a 'girl' rather than a 'woman') and she occasionally seems to have stirred up her fellow prisoners. But, by and large, this is an account of a woman trying to be professionally, if not personally, conciliatory – as much for her own survival as for the benefit of others – and feeling herself thwarted on every hand. Presumably, it was her attempt to relate to prison staff in a 'professional' manner that most irritated them. When she was reduced to a crying or giggling 'girl', she was easier to handle.

[…]

From Analysing Women's Imprisonment *(Cullompton: Willan Publishing), 2004, pp. 54–74.*

References

Caddle, D. (1998) *Age Limits for Babies in Prison: Some Lessons from Abroad*. Home Office Research Findings No. 80. London: Home Office.

Caddle, D. and Crisp, D. (1997) *Imprisoned Women and Mothers*. Home Office Research Study 162. London: Home Office.

Carlen, P. (1983) *Women's Imprisonment*. London: Routledge.

Carlen, P. (1998) *Sledgehammer: Women's Imprisonment at the Millennium*. Basingstoke: Macmillan.

Carlen, P. (2002) 'Women's imprisonment: Cross-national lessons', in P. Carlen (ed.) *Women and Punishment: The Struggle for Justice*. Cullompton: Willan.

Catan, L. (1992) 'Infants with mothers in prison', in R. Shaw (ed.) *Prisoners' Children – What Are the Issues?* London: Routledge.

Chesney-Lind, M. and Pasko, L. (2004) *The Female Offender: Girls, Women and Crime*, 2nd edn. London: Sage.

Chesney-Lind, M. and Rodrigues, N. (2004) 'Women under lock and key', in M. Chesney-Lind and L. Pasko (eds) *Girls, Women and Crime: Selected Readings*. London: Sage.

Department of Health (1994) *Inspection of Facilities for Mothers and Babies in Prison*. London: Department of Health.

Farrell, A. (1998) 'Policies for incarcerated mothers and their families in Australian corrections', *The Australian and New Zealand Journal of Criminology*, 31(2): 101–18.

Hannah-Moffat, K. (2000) 'Prisons that empower: Neoliberal governance in Canadian women's prisons', *British Journal of Criminology*, 40(3) 510–31.

Hayman, S. (1996) *Community Prisons for Women*. London: Prison Reform Trust.

HM Prison Service (1999) *Report of a Review of Principles, Policies and Procedures on Mothers and Babies/Children in Prison*. London: HM Prison Service.

Home Office (2003) *The Substance Misuse Treatment Needs of Minority Prisoner Groups: Women, Young Officers and Ethnic Minorities*. Home Office Development and Practice Report 8. London: Home Office.

Howard League (2000) *A Chance to Break the Cycle: Women and the Drug Treatment and Testing Order*. London: Howard League for Penal Reform.

Inspector of Custodial Services, WA (2003) *Bandyup Prison and the Imprisonment of Women in Western Australia*. Perth: Office of the Inspector of Custodial Services.

Liebling, A. and Price, D. (2001) *The Prison Officer*. Leyhill: Prison Service Journal.

Lloyd, E. (1995) *Prisoners' Children: Research, Policy and Practice*. London: Save the Children.

Malloch, M.S. (2000) *Women, Drugs and Custody*. Winchester: Waterside Press.

Nacro (1991) *A Fresh Start for Women Prisoners*. London: Nacro.

O'Dwyer, J. and Carlen, P. (1985) 'Josie: Surviving Holloway and other women's prisons', in P. Carlen, J. Hicks, J. O'Dwyer, D. Christina and C. Tchaikovsky (1985) *Criminal Women*. Cambridge: Polity Press.

Pellegrini, A.M. (1997) 'Children coping with a father in prison: Psychological tasks', in R. Shaw (ed.) *The Child and the Prison*. Durham: North Eastern Prison After Care Society.

Player, E. (1994) *Women's Prisons After Woolf*. London: Routledge.

Ramsey, M. (2003) *Prisoners' Drug Use and Treatment: Seven Studies*, Findings 186. London: Home Office.

Sim, J. (1990) *Medical Power in Prisons*. Buckingham: Open University Press.

Smith, C. (2000) 'Healthy prisons: A Contradiction in terms?', *The Howard Journal*, 39(4): 33–53.

Stewart, C. (2000) 'Responding to the needs of women in prison', *Prison Service Journal*, 132: 41–3.

Walklate, S. (2001) *Gender, Crime and Criminal Justice*. Cullompton: Willan.

Woodrow, J. (1992) 'Mothers inside, children outside', R. Shaw (ed.) *Prisoners' Children – What are the Issues?* London: Routledge.

Worrall, A. (2002) 'Rendering them Punishable', P. Carlen (ed.) *Women and Punishment: The Struggle for Justice*. Cullompton: Willan.

Wyner, R. (2003) *From the Inside: Dispatches from a Women's Prison*. London: Aurum Press.

15. From the inside

Ruth Wyner

I was doing a little yoga on the cold cell floor when they came for me at 9 a.m. The discipline of it was bringing me back to myself a little and I felt annoyed at the interruption. But my life was no longer my own. As I was taken out of the cell I saw a washbasin and asked to use it. They let me splash my face and hands. Though I had brought some clean clothes, I was not allowed to change into them. It seemed as if they were trying to turn me into something dirty.

At the reception desk I was double-handcuffed up, on both wrists and then to the guard. A copper shot me a sardonic look and I involuntarily felt a wave of hatred in response. It wiped away the urge to weep. John came out too and we were taken into the sweatbox (prison transport van). We were each locked into one of the six tiny cubicles. They had hard plastic seats, no seat belts and barely room to move at all. Already it felt hot, stuffy and airless. The handcuffs came off once I was safely secured inside.

As we got underway Cambridge swept past looking beautiful, bathed in the reddish gold of the morning sunlight. I feasted on the countryside; it was like a last supper. All too soon we were overtaken by a grey wall of cloud. After a couple of hours, we stopped at Luton and dropped John off – he was en route to Bedford prison. We wished each other luck. My transport then had to pick up two women from the local court. I was left in a cell with them for a while. Both were heroin addicts. One was on remand and the other, Leanne, was complaining about her eighteen-month sentence for heroin supply. Like many addicts, Leanne's reddened and pockmarked face was evidence of her damaging lifestyle.

'It weren't commercial,' she said. In other words, she had got the heroin to share with friends. I managed to blurt out my tale. My compatriots were shocked and proffered puffs of their fags. Although I had not smoked for ten years, I gratefully accepted.

Bound for Holloway, we were handcuffed up again and boxed back into the van. The other two cracked jokes, which lifted my spirits a little, but I felt uncomfortably dirty, sweaty and sordid, bumping around in the privacy of my cubicle. More tears overtook me. At Holloway prison our transport slowed down to creep past the gates and through a long narrow entrance that spread out into a courtyard. We had only just arrived and already I felt hemmed in. No handcuffs this time: the prison fences were enough.

The prison officer at reception checked and logged my belongings. I must have looked rough. She allowed me to buy a couple of phone cards with what was termed my 'private cash'.

'I should only let you have one phone card, but seeing as it's your first time, you can have two,' she said, adding: 'It's not so bad when you get used to it. See, this girl here came in only yesterday and look at her now.' She pointed to a young woman pushing a mop who could do little but smile at this obvious misrepresentation.

I had the first of many strip-searches to come. This was a terror for me. I thought they would poke around inside my private orifices. To my enormous relief they did not. I got looked up and down and turned around, but was allowed to keep the top or bottom half of my body covered at any one time – an embarrassment nonetheless but a lot better than I had feared.

Then I got locked in a room with six fellow prisoners being booked in with me. Five of them were heroin users and the sixth was on remand for stabbing her violent boyfriend when they had both been drunk. All these women were young enough to be my daughters. The room was large but bare: hard tables and stacked-up chairs, a two-way mirror covering one of the walls so that the officers could see us, but we could not see them. I idly read the notices on the noticeboard, then sat on one of the chairs with my feet up on another. The hours of waiting were endless, and the waves of depression continued. We managed to chat a little, the addicts suffering variously from their withdrawals. I got some inedible sandwiches and a drink of water for my lunch but food seemed unimportant. What was there to keep well for? Anyway, I did not feel hungry, was still deeply traumatized.

Each of us was taken out for a swift health check. The nurse's kindness upset me, though I was grateful for it, and I desperately held back my tears while she gave me a pep talk: 'See it like going to boarding school. There are other women your age in here. You just need to find one friend.' The doctor's evident distaste and ill humour were somehow more palatable.

By 4.30 p.m. I was processed and on D3, the intake wing. Marching through the prison, the décor of it seemed designed to depress; everything was shabby and rundown. I was allocated a place in one of the four-person dorms. To my disappointment, the beds were no better than the one in the police cell and my mattress was badly stained. My locker was smashed in at the back. All the furniture was hard and unrelenting, the lighting dim and the atmosphere heavy.

The wing was built around a corridor, which formed a square with the cells, the staff office, the dining room and the two bathrooms and one shower opening off it. D3 was set in the part of the prison that used to be a hospital, I was told. Another place of pain but also a place of care. The heavy cell door clanged shut behind me; the sound of the keys in the lock was quickly becoming familiar.

'When you get out, you'll automatically jump when you hear a rattle of keys,' Martine, one of my cellmates, knowingly informed me. She was tiny – 5-

foot-nothing tall and barely 6 stone in weight – but fiercely determined. Strong white teeth dominated her shrunken face and with her tiny skinny frame she resembled a starving child. Martine was on remand for shoplifting.

'Banged up at Christmas, for fuck's sake,' she complained. 'Some bastard ripped off my dole cheque. I was only trying to get some food for me and my kid.' An old hand at prison, Martine was the only one of the five addicts I checked in with who had decided not to opt for the prison hospital drug detox.

'They give you nothing that's any help,' she declared, 'and it's twenty-four seven bang-up, surrounded by complete nutters, believe me.' Leanne, my pockmarked friend from the transport, had gone there. I wondered how she would get on.

Martine's defiance felt like a protection for me as well as for her, but she had her own ordeal to come. It started on the first night when she was cold-turkeying badly, tossing and turning and unable to keep still, her legs thrashing the thin blankets into an indiscriminate pile. In the morning she looked weak and pale, her face reflecting the green colour of our worn bedding. She wanted to talk and told me a bit about her chaotic life, how she had been living with her little boy in a bed and breakfast, and had two 6-foot black guys on the go.

'I'm good in the sack,' laughed this tiny wench, going on to give me some unrequested details of her energetic love-making. She also talked about her upbringing, the difficulties she'd had. Her eyes started to swim, but it was only when she spoke of her small son that the tears flowed.

Another bed in the cell was occupied by a beautiful but doleful black American imprisoned for drugs importation, who spent most of her time pretending to read but was really staring at a photograph of her own little boy. We also had the boyfriend-stabber, who would not stop talking. She drove Martine and me to distraction. When you are locked in a cell with someone, there is no escape – except for the American, who got a wing-cleaner's job and was moved out to better quarters. Her bed was taken by an ordinary-looking woman in her late fifties who had stolen £1000 from her employers, the Post Office. She was rigid with fear at being in prison. She had paid the money back and her incarceration would cost the state considerably more than she had stolen in the first place. I wondered why she had not been given a community-service order.

The next to go was the boyfriend-stabber, off to court. At first her bed was filled by a Jamaican woman who was in for importing cocaine and spoke a fast patois that I could hardly understand. Martine had it off to a tee. She had mixed with Jamaicans, she told me proudly, and so could translate. The Jamaican woman had three kids at home and said she took the cocaine on her first-ever trip abroad because she had been told her thirteen-year-old son would be killed if she did not comply. The son was now in hiding with his grandmother.

She painted a frightening picture of Jamaica: of a rule of terror, extreme poverty, and people living in basic shacks. But at heart there was a degree of real civilization. She explained that if someone was hungry they were fed by whoever happened to be around, and if they were homeless they were invited to stay. Our modern British society can hardly boast that level of humanity.

An oddly deluded woman followed the Jamaican; she claimed to be half Russian, which she might well have been, and reckoned she knew the absolute truth, which she most definitely did not, but she drove us mad trying to impart it. From what I could gather, she was in prison for doing the same to a judge, who would not accept a psychiatrist's advice that this woman simply was not well.

These were my fellow sufferers, and I soon learned to join Martine in referring to the prison officers as screws. They were our jailers, and most of them seemed to feel that they had the right to demean their charges as well as lock them up, to inflict further punishment by being gruff and high-handed. I found them fearsome and had not yet come to understand their anxiety, their need to keep us inmates down and in our place, to avoid being destroyed by the huge sea of angst that this dreadful prison created and had to contain.

'Miss, miss, sir, sir,' Martine would shout through the hatch in our door, holding a thin roll-up she had made out of scraps of tobacco. 'Have you got a light, please, miss, please, sir.' Anything for a bit of activity, to lighten the crushing boredom of bang-up.

At Holloway the cells were piled five storeys high and contained a degradation that was previously beyond my imagination. It was as if you ceased to be a person when you got to prison, were not of any import at all. We were just part of the institution's bureaucracy, which in itself was utterly confusing. Everything had to be applied for and waited for, had to fit into the system, whatever that was. Finding out what you were entitled to was difficult enough. Knowing how to get it was the next hurdle. When we were not locked in our cells, I often saw people queuing up, doing things with a purpose, but I did not understand what was going on and no one bothered to tell me. I guess they reckoned I had plenty of time to find out.

My defence systems were struggling to cope with the trauma, the omnipresent anxiety and overwhelming depression. The purpose of this was to punish me, I reminded myself constantly. It was not personal; I was in a system, and had to toughen up. I felt completely disempowered. I did not belong to myself anymore, was merely an object of state custody.

Yoga continued to help. I did a little in the early morning while the others slept and Martine thrashed, finding a space on the floor between my bed and the barred window. A few quiet and concentrated movements – again it was as if I got something of my person back; it brought me into myself, made me feel that I was real, solid, and still there.

Generally, sleep eluded me during the five days I spent at Holloway. I got only fifteen minutes of outside exercise in that time.

'Isn't there some sort of law about getting daily exercise outside?' I wondered aloud. Wearily, the others assured me that there was.

One day, outside exercise was cancelled because it was supposedly too cold outside. We were allowed to walk along the corridor outside the cells for half an hour instead. The sun was shining, bright and strong, and I resented some impersonal authority making decisions for me about whether or not it was too cold to go out, as if I were a child. I could hear seagulls crying to each other and opened a window in the cell to see them whirling about. These windows were made up of strips of smoked glass through which you could not see properly, separated by built-in bars. You could open every other strip and this offered a peculiarly jagged view of the outside world. At this time of year it was too cold to leave them open for long.

Then I heard a blackbird sing. Peering through a window strip I spotted it perched in a tree below, blithely unaware of the value of its freedom. I now understood the acute symbolism that birds had always held for prisoners.

* * *

The prison day was dreary. You were woken at 6.30 a.m. by the screws clanking down the corridor and shouting to us through the hatches to get up. Usually no one stirred. I would do my yoga, if I was not already at it, and then get back into my hard bed. The screws returned at 7.30 a.m.

'Come on, ladies, you should be up and dressed.' We were let out for breakfast in the dining room down the corridor: two slices of stale bread, marge and cereal. On Sunday we got a hard-boiled egg with bread. I made up a sandwich, but eating it seemed to increase the hunger. The night before we were issued with tea-bags and sachets of whitener and sugar, so that we could make something resembling a cup of tea at mealtimes, using hot water from large plastic jugs. Everything was plastic: the plates, the cups and the cutlery.

There was lock-up from around 8.15 a.m. to nearly midday. Once a girl from my cell was taken to 'education'. I was envious, always dying to get out. Gym was sometimes a possibility but sessions seemed to be cancelled more often than not. I managed to get there once and chose to swim madly about in the pool, which was Holloway's pride and joy. My loosened tears mixed with the chlorinated water.

Lunch consisted of a stale sandwich, undrinkable soup, crisps and an orange, and, like all the meals, was a hurried, joyless affair. More bang-up followed, from 12.30 p.m. till dinner at 5 p.m., a hot meal but barely edible. It was best to stuff it down fast, if you could manage to eat it at all, so that you did not taste the food or feel its texture in your mouth. I rarely ate more than a few forkfuls.

Food could not be sent in, but you could buy snacks at the prison canteen once a week, as well as fruit, coffee, tobacco, stationery, toiletries, precious phone cards (at specific times we could make but not take phone calls) and batteries for a radio or Walkman. Everyone had a limit on their weekly spend, regardless of how much money they got sent in. Mine started at £10. At Holloway I got taken to the canteen once, escorted along confusing corridors into a room which had colourful murals on the walls. Tears sprang up from nowhere when I saw them, a little bit of cheeriness in this arid place. I paced around struggling to control myself and the emotion eventually subsided. I am not a person who usually weeps easily and every time it happened I could not bear to let anyone see me, feeling it was a sign of embarrassing weakness.

When my turn at the counter came, I bought a double phone card, shampoo, chocolate, oranges and apples. It came to £10. I did not buy tobacco, then realized immediately that I should have done as I had become a smoker again. A major worry was my Walkman, my one item of luxury, my own special and personal treasure. Inmates were allowed only one set of batteries in Holloway; apparently, lots of them together can be used to make bombs. I resolved to carefully ration the playing of my tapes and to stick to the radio where possible, as it used less power. I kept the Walkman in my bumbag, which the screws had allowed me to keep, along with my stamps and phone cards – the things of worth in here that I was frightened might be nicked. Even so, I could not help noticing that bits of the chocolate kept disappearing from my locker. I suspected Martine, but said nothing. She was better than I was at scrounging tobacco and shared whatever she could get hold of.

Following the screw back from the canteen shop to the cell, I realized I had developed a prison persona: hands in pockets, a slow uncaring walk, shoulders hunched, scowling and grumpy; a woman of few words but always a curse at the ready. It had happened in just two or three days. There I was, Wyner, prison number EH 6524: scared but not going to show it; ready for anything but behaving as if I didn't give a shit. My defences were up, and I knew I needed them, but also I feared that the real 'me' had been destroyed. Would I ever get her back again?

From From the Inside *(London: Aurum), 2003, pp. 16–23.*

16. Racism in prisons

Ben Bowling and Coretta Phillips

The sharp increase in the black prison population is, in part, explicable for the same reasons as the overall upward trend but the fact that the number is increasing at a more rapid rate requires some explanation. It is likely that the younger age structure of ethnic minorities in England and Wales provides part of the answer. This would have had the effect of skewing the proportionality of the prison population, as those entering the risk period for offending behaviour were more likely to be from ethnic minorities. The type of offence for which white and ethnic minorities were convicted would also have contributed to the increase, particularly in relation to drugs offences. Finally, the effects of cumulative disadvantage cannot be ruled out. […] [U]sing the findings from Hood's (1992) study of Crown Court sentencing, the impact of racially discriminatory decisions at sentencing can intensify future criminal justice process outcomes. Thus, some of those black prisoners who were discriminated against by judges in receiving custodial sentences in the 1980s would undoubtedly have faced the courts following further offending, but would then have been eligible for another (and longer) custodial term.

[…]

Racism in prison

The most comprehensive study of 'race relations' in prison to date was commissioned by the Home Office and conducted by Elaine Genders and Elaine Player (1989) in 1985 and 1986. The researchers analysed prison records, conducted interviews with staff and prisoners and observed daily routines in prison. Genders and Player noted that 'race relations' were rarely regarded as a problem by prison officers in two of the prisons where the research was based, largely because of the absence of overt racial conflict and physical confrontations. Indeed, prison staff were highly dismissive of the need for a 'race relations' policy. Notwithstanding this, they reported that rank and file prison officers commonly used racial stereotypes. Black inmates were frequently described as arrogant, lazy, noisy, hostile to authority, with values incompatible with British society, and having 'a chip on their shoulder', because they perceived themselves to be victims of racial persecution. These negative attributes were sometimes presumed to be 'innate' characteristics. Other comments resonated with biological theories of racial inferiority such as an inability to do certain prison jobs and to being unable to undertake further education in prison. In contrast, Asian inmates were perceived as model prisoners being hard-working and polite but also devious and prone to lying (Gordon 1983). Chigwada-Bailey (1997) has drawn attention to the similar way in which African/Caribbean women prisoners are perceived, as troublesome and causing disciplinary problems.

Prison staff interviewed by Genders and Player described the formation of racial groups which they believed provided inmates with a sense of identity and belonging, facilitated shared activities, and increased status and power. Sometimes prison officers felt that this made their job difficult in dealing with disputes, and black inmates, in particular, were regarded as a 'management problem' among 70 per cent, 60 per cent and 40 per cent of prison officers at the three prisons. Staff acknowledged that this meant that black inmates were often treated 'by the book' (that is, formally) more often than their Asian and white counterparts, but prison officers argued that the prisoners were to blame for this situation because of their arrogance and anti-authority attitudes. Not surprisingly, given these views, over half of the uniformed prison officers wanted to limit the numbers of black inmates in any one institution. Asian inmates were cited as the victims of bullying, intimidation and cultural insensitivity.

[...]

Racist victimisation

The racist victimisation of prisoners has also been examined in research undertaken by Burnett and Farrell (1994). Interviews were carried out with 220 African/Caribbean inmates, 75 Asian inmates, 78 inmates from other ethnic minorities and 128 white inmates. One hundred and six prison officers were also interviewed, and of these 11 per cent were from ethnic minorities. In addition, discussions were held with prison managers and specialist staff, including race relations liaison officers and board of visitors members.

Burnett and Farrell (1994) found that one in three Asian inmates, one in four African/Caribbean inmates, one in five of inmates of other ethnic origins and one in eight white inmates said that they had been racially abused or attacked by other inmates over a three-month period. The levels of repeat victimisation were high: for African/Caribbean inmates the average number of incidents during the study period was four and for Asian inmates it was five. Black inmates (44 per cent) were more likely than Asian inmates (33 per cent), 'other' ethnic minority inmates (23 per cent) or white inmates to report that they had been victimised by prison staff. Prison officers that were aware of racially motivated incidents in their establishments were less likely than inmates to perceive them as serious, mirroring the experience of ethnic minorities in the general population with regard to the police. The types of inmate-on-inmate incidents reported varied, with assaults, bullying and harassment being less common than incidents of theft. Racist verbal abuse was the most frequently mentioned.

A complaint form was completed, in only 12 per cent of racial incidents were prisoners actively encouraged to make complaints informally and verbally, a finding confirmed by Jackson (1997). Racial incidents were under-reported largely because victims felt that no action would be taken, or the situation in which the incident arose could not be changed, and because of a fear of being seen as a 'trouble-maker'. It was also the case that prison officers and race relations liaison officers did not always consider the need to record racial incidents, instead preferring them to be 'nipped in the bud'. Where an official complaint had been lodged (including those not related to racial incidents), half of the ethnic minority inmates compared with three-quarters of the white inmates believed that their complaint had not been treated fairly.

A number of recent incidents have also questioned the ability of prison officers to protect ethnic minority prisoners from racist harassment and violence. Four black men who spent three months on remand, despite later having charges dropped against them, issued a High Court writ claiming damages for personal injury after being assaulted by a mob of white inmates (*Birmingham Post*, 25 March 1998). In Parc prison in 1998 there was tension and violence between African/Caribbean and racist white prisoners, after racist graffiti was daubed on the walls (*Times*, 30 May 1998).

From Racism, Crime and Justice *(Harlow: Longman), 2002, pp. 195–205.*

References

Burnett, R. and Farrell, G. (1994) Reported and Unreported Racial Incidents in Prisons, Occasional Paper No. 14. Oxford: University of Oxford Centre for Criminological Research.

Chigwada-Bailey, R. (1997) *Black Women's Experiences of Criminal Justice: Discourse on Disadvantage.* Winchester: Waterside Press.

Genders, E. and Player, E. (1989) *Race Relations in Prison.* Oxford: Clarendon Press.

Gordon, P. (1983) *White Law: Racism in the Police, Courts and Prisons.* London: Pluto.

Hood, R. (1992) *Race and Sentencing.* Oxford: Clarendon Press.

Jackson, J. (1997) *Race Equality in Prisons: The Role of the Race Relations Liaison Officer.* London: Prison Reform Trust.

17. Paramilitary imprisonment in Northern Ireland: resistance, management, and release

Kieran McEvoy

Under the changes introduced by Merlyn Rees, any person convicted of a scheduled offence after 1 March 1976 was to be treated as an ordinary criminal with all special privileges removed. Male prisoners were sent to a newly constructed prison (quickly dubbed the H Blocks, since they were built in the shape of the letter H) erected alongside the compounds in Long Kesh. The legs of each H comprised of wings of twenty-five centrally heated eight-by-twelve-foot cells, a toilet area, and dining, recreation, and handicraft rooms; the central bar of the H was used for medical and administration quarters (NIPS 1977: 8).

With the abolition of Special Category Status Long Kesh thus became two prisons. The compounds, with their Nissen huts, continued to hold the declining number of Special Category prisoners. Anyone convicted of a political offence before 1 March 1976 continued to hold this status. Prisoners convicted of such offences after that date were confined to cells in the H Blocks. In order to signify the new policy direction Long Kesh was renamed the Maze prison although most prisoners and relatives persist to this day in referring to it as Long Kesh.

In the new changed physical conditions of the cellular Maze prison, the implementation of the policy of criminalisation began to take shape. On 14 September IRA prisoner Ciaran Nugent was the first prisoner sentenced under the new regime. Nugent refused to wear a prison uniform and was therefore placed in a cell with only a blanket. The blanketmen were initially few in number and considerably isolated in their cells with only their blankets and a Bible (Taylor 1997: 204). However, over the next months and years Nugent's example was followed by several hundred other Republican prisoners – at any given moment between one-third and one-half of the men arriving at the Maze/Long Kesh – who also went 'on the blanket' (Republican Fact File 1991: 4). [...] [T]hese protests were to be followed by the no wash, dirty protest, and ultimately hunger strike, by Republican prisoners resisting the criminalisation project.

Over the same period, I believe that the implementation of the policy of criminalisation in the prisons came to be characterized by a range of features. Although a number of these characteristics have been constants throughout the history of political imprisonment in Northern Ireland [...], it is arguable that some reached their zenith during this era. It is also clear that a number of these features overlap and indeed, in some instances, appear somewhat contradictory. None the less by conceptualizing each as distinct influences in a thematic rather than chronological fashion, it may be possible to understand better the implementation of the criminalisation policy as a whole. The features which characterized criminalisation included: (i) rule enforcement and the assertion of power; (ii) the internalization of propagandist positions; (iii) brutality, violence, and dehumanization; (iv) hothouse management and political interference. Each is considered in turn below.

Rules enforcement and the assertion of power

The application of prison rules and regulations is clearly one of the key elements of the successful management of a prison system (Loucks 1995). In particular it has been linked to the bureaucratic-lawful notion of prison management, wherein prison life becomes increasingly bureaucratized and codified through the diffusion of power and the atomization of the inmate community (Ditchfield 1990: 9). […] As Liebling argues, staff normally understand that 'the decent thing' to do is selectively to underenforce the law, in order that the smooth flow of prison can continue (Liebling 2000: 345).

[…] British and American prisons were until relatively recently largely free from judicial oversight. The space between the formal legal framework of prisons and actual practices has led some commentators to describe prisons as sites characterized by arbitrariness, unfairness, and discretion (Fitzgerald and Sim 1982: 82). This may involve the application of vaguely formulated rules such as prosecuting a prisoner for 'in any way offending against good order and discipline' (Sparks, Bottoms, and Hay 1996: 182). It may also entail the over-enthusiastic use of prison rules, for example by unnecessarily searching prisoners, an action often viewed as a wind up to the prisoners on the receiving end (McDermott and King 1988). As Livingstone and Owen (1999: 450) have argued, while prisons are extensively rule bound institutions, the authorities can almost always point to a role at some level in the hierarchy to justify any action taken.

The removal of Special Category Status after March 1976 meant that paramilitary prisoners were subject to a set of prison rules applicable to all prisoners regardless of motivation (NIPS 1977: 5). Under Special Category Status prisoners had been exempt from such rules as the obligation to wear uniforms or conduct prison work, regulations which would in any case have been unenforceable in a context where the prison authorities had to negotiate access to the compounds via the prisoners' leadership. However, in the context of cellular accommodation, enforcement of prison rules became a key element in the reassertion of prison officer power and in the determination to ensure that the Maze was run as a normal prison where the same rules were applied as to ordinary prisoners in the system.

[…]

At the Maze, disciplinary proceedings against prisoners rose from 245 offences and 336 punishments in 1975 to 774 offences and 708 punishments awarded in 1976 (NIPS 1977: 41–2). This represented an increase of 216 per cent and 111 per cent respectively. The largest increase in any disciplinary category of offences was insubordination, which rose from 109 in 1975 to 496 in 1976 (NIPS 1977: 41–2) an increase of 355 per cent. In 1977 the number of offences at the Maze rose even more dramatically to 3,548, and the number of punishments rose to 13,038 (NIPS 1978: 42). In 1978 the number of offences was 9,477 (with refusal to work or wear prison uniforms constituting 8,039 offences) and the number of punishments totalling 20,340 (NIPS 1978: 44). While the limitations of recorded disciplinary figures have been highlighted elsewhere (King and McDermott 1995: 98, Sparks, Bottoms, and Hay 1996: 237), and acknowledging that such figures occurred within the context of the prisoners' protests and a steady growth in the population, none the less such huge increases do offer instructive insights into the changed nature of rule enforcement with the introduction of the criminalization policy.

[…] [T]he scale of rule enforcement and disciplinary breaches led to a slightly surreal cycle of charging and repeat offending. During the blanket and dirty protests, prisoners were charged in their cell every 14 or 28 days. An officer would go to the cell of the protesting prisoners, order them to put on a prison uniform and go to work, and upon refusal prepare two charge sheets which were then passed to adjudicating governors. The subsequent adjudications were normally carried out in the corridor in a context of prisoners banging, shouting, and using objects such as furniture, chamber pots, and mugs to create as much disturbance and noise as possible. Protesting prisoners invariably refused to answer the charges and were found guilty. This process was then repeated for each prisoner in 14 or 28 days, with prison staff eventually putting cell mates on the same charging and finding guilty cycle in order to speed the process up.

[…] [T]he prisoners' refusal to wear a uniform and to do prison work were two of the key elements of their protest. While presented within the objective framework of the management of prisons, in effect the enforcement of regulations regarding uniforms and work became the epicentre of the political and ideological struggle between the prison authorities and the prisoners. As it was an offence under the prison rules to leave one's cell improperly dressed, protesting prisoners were confined to their cells for 24 hours per day. Their non-cooperation meant the removal of the three privileged visits per month and the refusal to wear a uniform to the visiting area cost prisoners the fourth visit. Their contact with the outside world was thus limited to one censored letter per week in the first year of the protest (Beresford 1987: 27). After some confrontations with prison officers where furniture was smashed, privileges such as beds and footlockers were removed leaving them with two men per cell, with a mattress, three blankets, and a Bible each.

Such unbending adherence to regulations amongst prison officers during the criminalisation era may be viewed in a number of lights. On the one hand, it may be seen (and is cogently articulated as such by some critical commentators and former prisoners) as the expression of a desire at ministerial and senior management level to crush the political will of

Republican prisoners in particular (Campbell, McKeown, and O'Hagan 1994, Tomlinson 1995, McKeown 1998). Prison staff thus became the instrument of the criminalisation agenda.

On the other hand, some staff have argued to the author that strict rule enforcement came about because staff were often forced to operate without clear guidance from above, particularly in the early days of the criminalisation era. Clearly ministers and prison service senior managers became increasingly preoccupied with the protests in the latter part of the dirty protest and hunger strike era. However, some prison staff have spoken of a 'management vacuum' in the response to the protests and have challenged the notion of top down policy implementation during the criminalisation era. One prison officer argued that they were merely implementing the rules and that 'it wasn't up to us to negotiate a settlement, all we could do was to enforce the rules until the politicians or the NIO made up their mind what to do'. In the context of perceived indecision and a lack of direction in the early days of the protest, it is certainly tenable to argue that individuals from a militaristic and hierarchical institution would resort to rule enforcement as an underpinning philosophy.

Whichever view is closer to the truth, the result remains that rigid rule enforcement during the protests rendered prison disciplinary procedures farcical. Such attitudes and practices exacerbated the protests and placed considerable obstacles in the way of resolving the dispute. By framing the dispute within a maintenance of order paradigm prison staff and management contributed to a context in which pragmatism was seen as weakness, compromise as capitulation, and where the determination of the prisoners to resist was met by an equal determination that they would be defeated.

The internalization of propagandist positions

The distinction between the dissemination of genuinely held beliefs and propagandist positions is often a blurred one. One widely cited definition of propaganda contends that the term propaganda can be used in a non-pejorative or neutral sense (Jowett and O'Donnell 1994). They define propaganda as 'the deliberate and systematic attempt to shape perceptions, manipulate cognitions, and direct behaviour to achieve a response that furthers the desired intent of the propagandist' (Jowett and O'Donnell 1994: 4). However, as Miller (1994: 71) argues, the identification of a propagandist in the real world is a matter of political argument which is linked to specific interests or ideologies. While clearly some commentators from both left and right define propaganda by reference to the source of the information (Curtis 1984, Wright 1991), this does not necessarily mean that such accounts are untruthful (Walton 1997). Rather, propaganda may be seen as the reconfiguration or the repackaging of particular truths, half-truths, or clear lies in order to support a predetermined ideological, political, or organizational position.

While some prison staff and governors suggested that at least in the early days of the criminalisation era ground level staff operated in something of a policy vacuum, others have argued that some staff appeared to internalize and believe in the criminalisation project:

> I would say that there were definitely some of our staff, particularly those recruited in 1976 or 1977 or those who had never worked with paramilitaries in the compounds, who really believed that these people were criminals … I mean they also came into work every day and saw the conditions these people were living in, the shit and piss and the filth and all, conditions entirely created by themselves [the prisoners], and they just thought these are a bunch of animals. (Interview with prison governor, 12 Feb. 1996)

[…] [T]he prisoners' dirty protest in particular resonated with a series of long-standing racist and sectarian discourses linking filthiness and immorality to Irish Catholics. For some of those prison staff recruited from Northern Ireland who came almost exclusively from the Protestant community, such sectarian views may already have existed. At an institutional level, however, the internalization of the criminalisation project by some staff may be linked to the relationship between the self-image of institutions and their occupational culture and working practices.

There is a considerable business and management literature which charts the symbiotic nature of such a relationship (Hampden-Turner 1990, Elwood 1995, Shenkar and Yuchtman-Yaar 1997). Staff may internalize, adapt, or reshape the public perception of what it is they are meant to be doing, even when the origins of that perception are a product of the public relations department (Hatch and Schultz 1997) or was originally envisaged as straight forwardly propagandist. Similarly within criminal justice agencies, some scholars have explored the ways in which organizational self-image based upon discourses of professionalism, impartiality, and upholding law and order are internalized and become *believed* by staff in agencies such as the RUC (Ellison 1997, Mulcahy 1997, 1999). Once insulated from unfavourable discourses by such a self-image, any criticisms may be met with genuine outrage.

The internalization of the criminalisation project by at least some elements of the headquarters and management of the prison service can be seen from their reaction to critical comments at various junctures during the protests. For example, the critical press conference held by the Catholic Primate of Ireland Cardinal Thomas O'Fiaich in July 1978 in which he described the conditions in the Maze as akin to the sewers of Calcutta (Collins 1986: 324), produced the 'furious ill-tempered response' from the Northern Ireland Office […] (O'Malley 1990: 173). Such a reaction was indicative of an institution which had indeed begun to *believe* in its public position.

Similarly at the level of the staff, the public comments in the media at the time and other outlets often displayed a considerable sympathy to the strategy of criminalising paramilitary prisoners. The public position of the Prison Officers Association appeared to fluctuate between criticisms of the government placing their members 'on the front line' and an acceptance that the government could not 'give in to terrorist prisoners'.

Apart from asserting the criminal status of paramilitary prisoners, much of the material produced by the prison service during this era focused upon the preferability of the physical conditions of the new cellular prison when compared to either the compounds or other prisons in Europe. The theme of a modernizing prison system, with excellent facilities being misused and damaged by unreasonable and recalcitrant prisoners, was a basic tenet of the public statements issued during the dirty protest and hunger strikes. The unreasonableness of the prisoners' behaviour was constantly juxtaposed to the reasonableness and professionalism of prison staff and management. For some of the prison officers working on the wings, who were sustained on such institutional discourses, the critical press coverage of the prison service engendered a sense of anger and frustration.

> It used to really annoy me – you would pick up a morning newspaper and read all this Provo propaganda about what was going on in the Maze and about how terrible we all were. We were doing our jobs in terrible conditions, and we were getting murdered in our homes and you still got all this guff about prison officer brutality and all, it was very frustrating. (Interview with former prison officer, 12 Sept. 1996)

At least part of the reason for the frustration of prison staff and managers about their apparent failure to get their story across, was the ineptitude of the prison service's public relations strategy during the protests. The Northern Ireland Office dramatically increased its public relations expenditure during this era. However, much of that increase was spent in the production of relatively crude propaganda leaflets designed for international consumption, including the selective clipping and assembling of montages of supportive journalistic comments (e.g. NIO 1980*a*, 1980*b*, 1981*a*, 1981*b*). One former prison service public relations manager described the quality of public relations during the protests as 'crude and ineffective, particularly to an international audience'.

The improvement in Sinn Fein's public relations skills, albeit with considerably more limited resources (Curtis 1984: 273), the election of Bobby Sands as MP for Fermanagh South Tyrone, and the widespread international criticism of perceived British intransigence (Beresford 1987: 132) has led most commentators to conclude that the prison service lost the propaganda war on the hunger strikes (Miller 1994: 84). Such a feeling amongst some prison staff appeared to add impetus to the sense of isolation and beleaguerment, and reinforced their belief in the criminalisation project.

Brutality, violence, and dehumanization

There are a myriad of reasons offered in the literature to explain why prison officers may resort to violence in the execution of their duties. Some researchers have referred to a 'canteen culture of violence amongst' prison officers where an alarm bell signifying a potentially violent incident leads to 'a frisson of excitement that rushes around the prison like adrenaline' (King and McDermott 1995: 128). Staff violence has also been described as a response to a breakdown in order in a prison (Cavadino and Dignan 1997); a deterrent to, or revenge for, inmate violence (Kauffman 1988: 141); an expression of staff power over the inmates (Abbott 1981); an indication that prison officers may feel undervalued (Fitzgerald and Sim 1982: 123); evidence that prison staff may enjoy *de facto* impunity from prosecution or accountability (Scraton, Sim, and Skidmore 1991) or due to the personality or psychological make up of individual officers.

As discussed above, while Northern Ireland prison staff and management tended to discount allegations of staff violence during the criminalisation protests as 'black propaganda' (NIPS 1980: 17), the truth is that prisoners were indeed subject to harsh beatings, scaldings, and humiliations. The written accounts of the prisoners themselves (Campbell, McKeown, and O'Hagan 1994), the descriptions told to other writers (Beresford 1987, O'Malley 1990, Taylor 1997) and international human rights bodies (Amnesty International 1980) as well as to the current author are fairly consistent. It appears unlikely that many prison officers were held accountable for such actions during that period.

The potential for violent interchanges between staff and prisoners was clearly linked to the protest tactics of the prisoners. For example, when in 1978 the prisoners began their dirty protest, the exchanges over the contents of the prisoners' chamber pots often led to violent clashes (Clarke 1987: 72). The forced washing of prisoners could only be achieved by excessive use of force. In the latter part of 1978 the prison administration introduced wing shifts wherein all men in one wing were moved to an empty wing, the walls and floors of the fouled cells were cleaned, and a pattern of forced moves every 6–7 days was established (Campbell, McKeown, and O'Hagan 1994: 49). The constant rotation of prisoners and an awareness that the prisoners were maintaining communications with the IRA on the outside through comms, provided the rationale for increased use of mirror searches where a number of prison officers would forcibly make a prisoner squat over a mirror while his anus, mouth, scrotum, and other areas were probed.

The brutality and violence of some prison staff during this era may be understood on a number of levels.

At a strategic level, the objective of prison staff was to make the conditions for protesting prisoners so unbearable that they would be forced to come off the protest and join the conforming prisoners. Violence became a tactic designed to defeat the prisoners. Of a total of approximately 700 Republican prisoners held in cellular accommodation at the Maze, the number of protesting prisoners fluctuated from around 300 in 1978 to almost 500 in 1980 (NIPS 1978: 5, Campbell, McKeown, and O'Hagan 1994: 107). As one former prison officer told the author, 'the clear objective was to whittle down the number of protesting prisoners, and increase the numbers on the conforming wings, it was that simple'. Violence and humiliation were entirely consistent with that objective.

There were also a number of possible organizational explanations for the violent conduct of staff. The prison authorities had considerable difficulties in recruiting and maintaining staff members. The dropout rate for prison officers rose dramatically with the introduction of criminalization from one in five in

1975 to one in three in 1976. Given such difficulties, the staff shortages during the 1970s in the prison service (exacerbated by the construction of the labour intensive cellular Maze) led to only the most peripheral screening of recruits (Taylor 1997: 220). Given the poor calibre of some recruits, often placed in the most difficult of working conditions with only minimal training, and an ongoing campaign of assassinations against them and their colleagues, considerable staff violence against prisoners was predictable.

At a more personal level, however, clearly staff brutality was linked to a process wherein the prisoners became dehumanized in the eyes of the prison officers. As discussed above, the dirty protest in particular resonated with sectarian anti-Catholic discourses concerning dirtiness and immorality. Such prejudice dovetailed with the mechanisms used to carry out the cleaning operations, wing shift, and mirror searches, all of which encouraged a depersonalized attitude to the prisoners. In the unreal scatological environment of the protesting wings, prison officers hosed cells and sometimes prisoners at pressures of 160 lbs per square inch (Clarke 1987: 75). […] [W]hen these were replaced by industrial steam cleaners following an infestation of white maggots, lice, and scabies, the prison officers wore aluminium astronaut-like suits to carry out their tasks. As the photographs and accounts of the time highlight, the protesting prisoners, with their long hair and beards, naked, pale, and smelling of excrement, appeared less than human to those officers who were already predisposed to view and treat them as such.

Hothouse management and political and security interference

> The phenomenon I am interested in is the people who have been around for twenty years, and I know most of them, people who made decisions that today we would think that was stupid. But they were all able, well intentioned, rational people who sat down with no particular agenda, well OK their agenda may have been set at some times by ministers, but they came to what they thought were rational decisions. (Interview with former governor, HMP Maze, 20 April 1999)

The fourth element which characterized the management of paramilitary prisoners during the criminalisation era was a fusion of hothouse management with more direct input from ministers in the day to day running of the prisons. This was a scenario in which the already highly pressurized context of staff/inmate relations in the prisons was further complicated by increased interference from political and security sources which obscured the ability to make effective judgements on prison management. 'Hothouse management' was a phrase used by one prominent prison governor to describe decision-making processes wherein managers and policy-makers became so immersed in institutional dynamics, political pressures, and competing security configurations that they appeared to lose sight of broader political realities:

> Decisions during the hunger strikes and dirty protests became so pressurized that looking back on it some of our people took their

eye off the ball. As various people such as the Cardinal and the Irish Commission for Justice and Peace tried to make interventions around issues like civilian type clothing, we had lengthy discussions about what this meant, what would be the consequences in terms of the proliferation of laundry, how would the washing get done and so on, it was crazy but that is how it was. Hothouse management I called it, people under pressure who were not able to see the consequences of their decisions because they couldn't see the wood for the trees. (Interview with prison governor, 12 Feb. 1996)

At least part of the reason for the pressure on prison managers was the extension of ministerial influence deep into operational matters such as the wearing of prison uniforms. The relationship between what constitutes policy (and therefore legitimately falls within ministerial interest) and operational matters is often deliberately obfuscated in the management of prisons (Lewis 1997). Similar tensions have been observed elsewhere between headquarters-based managers and managers within the prisons (Sparks, Bottoms, and Hay 1996: 134–9). However, the argument with regard to the era of criminalisation in Northern Ireland, in particular during the hunger strikes, is that in effect the running of one prison (the Maze) became of such central political significance that it became a political virility test at cabinet and prime ministerial level. Even for those who were predisposed to find a resolution to the stand-off, the direct involvement of Mrs Thatcher in the dispute arguably lessened the room for pragmatic manoeuvrability.

Policy formulation during this period was further complicated by the involvement of the British foreign office, the British foreign intelligence service MI6, and the domestic intelligence service MI5. Given their focus on the international damage to Britain's reputation, the Foreign Office have been widely reputed as having had a generally more conciliatory approach to the resolution of the hunger strike issue. Former Foreign Office Under-Secretary Ian Gilmour has acknowledged a 'difference of emphasis' from their colleagues at the NIO (O'Malley 1990: 197).

MI6, apparently with the agreement of the Foreign Office, had opened a direct line of secret negotiations with IRA representatives during the first and second hunger strikes, taking an apparently less confrontational line than the stated government position (Taylor 1997: 234, 247). Operationally both MI5 and MI6 came under the direct control of the Ulster Security Liaison Committee (comprising representatives of MI6, MI5, the SAS, and RUC Special Branch (Greer 1995: 47–8)). In practice, however, relations were strained and MI5 were considered the more hawkish in their approach to the hunger strikes as with other security-related issues (Block and Fitzgerald 1983). The result of these competing institutional priorities from the security services, and increased cabinet input into policy formulation from a Conservative administration less mindful to compromise, was further to narrow any opportunity for pragmatism amongst prison managers which might have existed.

It would be wrong, however, to view such security and political influence as illiberal impositions from above on an otherwise rational and progressive tier of senior prison managers. At least some prison managers operated within a belief system which did not make them mindful to compromise with the terrorists. Rather, what is being suggested here is that in a hierarchical institution such as the prison service, the impact of such a myriad of influences was to compress policy options, obscure more enlightened alternatives, and internalize a set of discourses which viewed compromise as analogous to surrender.

Conclusion

[...] [T]he hunger strikes ended on Saturday, 3 October 1981, following sustained interventions by the prisoners' families. The view of the prisoners was that they had failed to achieve their demands, in essence that they had lost. However, the pyrrhic nature of the government's victory was highlighted by the widespread international criticism of British intransigence, the emergence of Sinn Fein as a political force, and the granting of at least some of the prisoners' demands within a short period of the end of the protest. Secretary of State Jim Prior announced at a press conference a few days later that prisoners could wear their own clothes, 50 per cent remission was returned, limited free association was granted, and prison work was narrowly defined to include only a small number of activities which prisoners could refuse to do without significant loss of privilege (O'Malley 1990). While the concessions which followed the end of the hunger strikes by no means heralded the reacceptance of political motivation, they did signify that the continued commitment to criminalisation would be tempered by considerably greater flexibility and pragmatism.

The increasingly rigid adherence to the principles of criminalisation as the prisoners stepped up their protest in the late 1970s obscured the origins of the policy as a means of managing political violence. At some stage in the deteriorating spiral of relations a management strategy became transmogrified into a series of ill-defined political principles which inevitably presented obstacles to effective management within the prisons. Unflinching rule enforcement, the internalization of propagandist positions, the dehumanization and brutalization of prisoners, and a lack of clarity in policy formulation interacted with a series of other ebbing and flowing influences on prison management over the period to produce an inflexible and unwielding policy which ultimately failed in its stated objective.

From Paramilitary Imprisonment in Northern Ireland: Resistance, Management, and Release *(Oxford: Oxford University Press), 2001, pp. 233–49 (footnotes omitted.*

References

Abbot, J.H. (1981), *In the Belly of the Beast* (London: Arrow Books).
Amnesty International (1980), *Prisoners of Conscience in the USSR* (2nd edn., London: Amnesty International).

Beresford, D. (1987), *Ten Men Dead* (London: Corgi).

Block, J., and Fitzgerald, P. (1983), *British Intelligence and Covert Action: Africa, Middle East and Europe Since 1943* (Dingle: Brandon).

Campbell, B., McKeown, L., and O'Hagan, P. (1994), *Nor Meekly Serve My Time: The H Block Struggle 1976–1981* (Belfast: Beyond the Pale Publications).

Cavadino, M., and Dignan, J. (1997), *The Penal System: An Introduction* (2nd edn., London: Sage).

Clarke, L. (1987), *Broadening the Battlefield: The H Blocks and the Rise of Sinn Fein* (Dublin: Gill & Macmillan).

Collins, T. (1986), *The Irish Hunger Strike* (Dublin: White Island Book Company).

Curtis, L. (1984), *Ireland: The Propaganda War* (London: Pluto).

Ditchfield, J. (1990), *Control in Prisons: A Review of the Literature*, Home Office Research Study 118 (London: HMSO).

Ellison, G. (1997), 'Professionalism in the RUC: An Examination of the Institutional Discourse', Ph.D. Thesis, University of Ulster.

Elwood, W. (ed.), (1995), *Public Relations Inquiry as Rhetorical Criticism: Case Studies of Corporate Discourse and Social Influence* (Westport, Conn.: Praeger).

Fitzgerald, M., and Sim, J. (1982), *British Prisons* (2nd edn., Oxford: Blackwell Press).

Greer, S. (1995), *Supergrasses: A Study in Anti-Terrorist Law Enforcement in Northern Ireland* (Oxford: Clarendon Press).

Hampden-Turner, C. (1990), *Corporate Culture for Competitive Edge* (London: Piatkus).

Hatch, M.J., and Schultz, M. (1997), 'Relations between Organizational Culture, Identity and Image', *European Journal of Marketing*, 31: 5–6, 356–65.

Jowett, G., and O'Donnell, V. (1992), *Propaganda and Persuasion* (2nd edn., Beverly Hills, Calif.: Sage).

Kauffman, K. (1988), *Prison Officers and their World* (Cambridge, MA: Harvard University Press).

King, R., and McDermott, K. (1995), *The State of Our Prisons* (Oxford: Clarendon Press).

Liebling, A. (2000), 'Prison Officers, Policing and the Use of Discretion', *Theoretical Criminology*, 4: 3, 333–57.

Livingstone, S., and Owen, T. (1999), *Prison Law: Texts and Materials* (2nd edn., Oxford: Oxford University Press).

Loucks, N. (1995), *Anything Goes: The Use of the 'Catch-all' Disciplinary Rule in Prison Service Establishments* (London: Prison Reform Trust).

McDermott, K., and King, R. (1988), 'Mind Games: Where the Action is in Prisons', *British Journal of Criminology*, 28: 3, 357–77.

McKeown, L. (2001) Out of Time: *Irish Republican Prisoners Long Kesh 1972–2000*, Belfast, NI: Beyond the Pale Publications.

Miller, D. (1994), *Northern Ireland: Propaganda and the Media* (London: Pluto).

Mulcahy, A. (1997), 'I'm Not Here to Look Back: I'm Here to Look Forward: The Role of Memory in Debates on the Legitimacy of the RUC', Paper presented at the British Criminology Conference, Queen's University of Belfast, 15–18 July 1997.

Mulcahy, A. (1999), 'Visions of Normality: Peace and the Reconstruction of Policing in Northern Ireland', *Social & Legal Studies*, 8: 2, 277–95.

NIPS (1971–99), *Annual Report of the Northern Ireland Prison Service* Cm (Belfast: HMSO).

Northern Ireland Office (1980a), *H Blocks: The Facts* (Oct.) (Belfast: Northern Ireland Office).

Northern Ireland Office (1980b), *H Blocks: The Reality* (Nov.) (Belfast: Northern Ireland Office).

Northern Ireland Office (1981a), *Day to Day Life in Northern Ireland Prisons* (Mar.) (Belfast: Northern Ireland Office).

Northern Ireland Office (1981b), *H. Blocks: What the Papers Say* (July) (Belfast: Northern Ireland Office).

O'Malley, P. (1990), *Biting at the Grave: The Irish Hunger Strikes and the Politics of Despair* (Belfast: Blackstaff Press).

Republican Fact File (1991), 'Republican Prisoners and the Prison Struggle in Ireland – Criminalisation Defeated by Prison Resistance' (Belfast: Sinn Fein Foreign Affairs Bureau).

Scraton, P., Sim, J. and Skidmore, P. (1991), *Prisons Under Protest* (Buckingham: Open University Press).

Shenkar, O., and Yuchtman-Yaar, E. (1997), 'Reputation, Image, Prestige, and Goodwill: An Interdisciplinary Approach to Organizational Standing', *Human Relations*, 50: 11, 1361–81.

Sparks, R., Bottoms, A., and Hay, W. (1996), *Prisons and the Problem of Order* (Oxford: Clarendon Press).

Taylor, P. (1997), *Provos: The IRA and Sinn Fein: The Book of the BBC TV Series* (London: Bloomsbury).

Tomlinson, M. (1995), 'Imprisoned Ireland', in V. Ruggiero, M. Ryan and J. Sim (eds.), *Western European Penal Systems: A Critical Anatomy* (London: Sage).

Walton, D. (1997), 'What is Propaganda and What Exactly is Wrong With it?', *Public Affairs Quarterly*, 11: 4, 383–414.

Wright, J. (1991), *Terrorist Propaganda: The Red Army Faction and the Provisional IRA 1968–1986* (New York: St Martin Press).

18. From Borstal to YOI

John Muncie

From Borstal to YOI

When the first specialized detention centre for young offenders was formally set up by the Crime Prevention Act of 1908 at Borstal in Kent, it was heralded as a major liberal breakthrough. The separation of the under-21s from adults in their own closed institutions was seen as a major step towards the training of the young criminal. In the spirit of rehabilitation, borstal 'trainees' could be held for at least a year and no more than three years; the regime was based on strict discipline, hard work and drill; it was directed not at the 'incorrigible' but those of 'criminal habits and tendencies' or those associating with 'persons of bad character'. From the outset it attracted criticism for instituting long periods of confinement – up to three years for offences that would not ordinarily attract more than six months (Radzinowicz and Hood, 1990, p. 389). However, it also claimed a remarkable success in preventing reoffending. The first survey in 1915 reported reconviction rates as low as 27 to 35 per cent.

In 1961, the Criminal Justice Act reduced the minimum age for borstal training to 15, and made it easier to transfer young people from approved schools and integrated borstals into the prison system. This integration meant that the training component declined and their regimes became more punitive. The role of borstal as an alternative to prison was undermined, and it was turned instead into a primary punitive institution which acted as a funnel into the prison system. Taylor et al. (1979, p. 65) argued that 'younger and less difficult young people' were increasingly subject to 'tougher punishment'. Partly as a consequence, the reconviction rate which had stayed at 30 per cent throughout the 1930s increased to 70 per cent, suggesting that borstal accentuated forms of behaviour it was designed to suppress. Taylor et al. (1979) described how offers of help were provided inconsistently and arbitrarily withdrawn. Physical and verbal abuse by officers and other inmates was not uncommon. A picture emerged of largely punitive regimes in which retraining was minimal and the possibility of being permanently institutionalized forever present: 'Common humanity, statistical evidence and above all commonsense demand the abolition of the Borstal institution' (Taylor et al., 1979, p. 71).

In 1982 borstals were renamed youth custody centres and in 1988 were included in a wider network of young offender institutions (YOIs). In many respects they now act as mirror images of adult prisons for the young. Following the 1994 Criminal Justice and Public Order Act, the maximum sentence of detention in a young offender institution was increased from 12 to 24 months. The same Act also introduced secure training orders for 12 to 14 year olds who had been convicted of three or more offences which would be imprisonable in the case of an adult. By 2003 three such centres were available.

The 1998 Crime and Disorder Act, abolished these separate sentences and replaced them with a generic detention and training order (DTO). This came into force in April 2000. A DTO can be given to 15 to 17 year olds for any offence considered serious enough to warrant a custodial sentence; and to 12 to 14 year olds who are considered to be 'persistent offenders'. The orders are for between 4 and 24 months. Half of the order is served in the community under the supervision of a social worker, a probation officer or a member of a youth offending team. A custodial sentence of detention (without the training component) is now restricted to those aged 18, 19 and 20. However, for 'grave' crimes, the youth court can pass its jurisdiction to the Crown Court. Under sections 90–92 of the Powers of Criminal Courts Act 2000 (which consolidated those of section 53 of the 1933 Children and Young Persons Act), a 10–17 year old can be detained for a longer period than the normal maximum of two years, at the discretion of the Home Secretary, either in a local authority secure unit or a prison service establishment. The numbers caught in these powers increased from some 100 in 1992 to over 600 in 1999. In addition the Criminal Justice and Police Act 2001 extended the reasons for giving custodial remands from 'protecting the public from serious harm' to 'preventing the commission of future imprisonable offences'.

Conditions in young offender institutions have been a recurring cause for concern. Goldson (1997, p. 83) argues that not only are they 'unsuited to guaranteeing basic standards of safety and welfare, but each day is characterized by a culture of bullying, intimidation and routine self harm'. Between 1990 and 2000, 134 15 to 21 year olds committed suicide in prison. Rates of self harm have escalated with 1,173 recorded instances in 1996/7 alone (Goldson, 2002a, p. 60). The average assault rate in YOIs is over 34 per cent (Prison Reform Trust Press Release, 10 September 2001). As Liebling (1992) established, young offenders are particularly vulnerable to the degrading and debilitating conditions of imprisonment. Young prisoner suicides tend to occur within one month, or at most one year of reception into custody; often when they are on remand, awaiting sentence. Young Offender Institutions also appear to be riddled with individually and institutionally racist practices. The Commission for Racial Equality (2003) discovered high levels of intimidation, discrimination and failure to protect black prisoners epitomised by the murder of 19 year old Zahid Mubarek in 2000 by his cell mate who was known to the authorities to be a violent racist. In one of the first ethnographic pieces of research to test the impact of the Prison Service's anti-racist policies specifically in YOIs, Wilson and Moore's (2003) interviews of 45 teenage boys vividly describe a daily routine of prison officer verbal abuse. Terms such as 'chimp', 'golliwog' 'nigger' and phrases such as 'when I wipe my arse it looks like you' reveal a deeply imbued racism. Yet each of the three YOIs in this study had officially met their performance targets in race relations. For the boys the work of race relations liaison officers and management teams was an irrelevance. None felt racist incidents were worth reporting, if not for fear of retaliation then because none would be taken seriously.

A report by the Howard League (1995, p. 67) concluded in much the same terms as Taylor et al.'s (1979) condemnation of the borstal system: 'an approach which concentrates on incarcerating the most delinquent and damaged adolescents, in large soulless institutions under the supervision of staff with no specialist training in dealing with difficult teenage behaviour, is nonsensical and inhumane'. In 2003 the privately run YOI at Ashfield was condemned as the worst jail in Britain with bullying endemic and staff having lost effective control (*Guardian*, 5 February 2003). Goldson's (2002b, pp. 159–60) research of the experiences of those subjected to secure and penal regimes, whether in the name of welfare or criminal justice, led him to conclude:

> locking up children is spectacularly ineffective ... children invariably leave prison not only more damaged but also more angry, more alienated, more expert in the ways of crime and more likely to commit more serious offences – in fact more of everything that the children themselves and the community need much less of.

Such an argument appears all the more pertinent when applied to girls. There are no dedicated young offender institutions for under 18 year old women. Holding girls in wings of adult prisons has long been condemned but despite repeated promises over 25 years to remove all girls from prison service accommodation, the practice continues. Ironically, it is their small number that means that they appear 'tacked onto' the rest of the system. There is little specialist staff training. Because of the few facilities available, girls are often held further from home, again undermining the possibility of restoring family and community ties. In 1999 86 girls were held in prison; by 2002 there were 120 (NACRO, 2001; Howard League, Press Briefing, 2003). The counterproductive nature of imprisoning children is well known and widely shared. Yet it barely figures in any discussion of a youth justice system which claims to be acting solely on the basis of 'what works'.

Detention centres and boot camps

Detention centres were introduced by the Criminal Justice Act of 1948 and enabled the courts to sentence offenders aged 14–21 to short periods of an explicitly punitive regime. Again this was justified on the grounds that sending young offenders to prison only helped to cement criminal careers, but there is strong evidence that their introduction was also a result of a quid pro quo for the abolition of corporal punishment (Muncie, 1990). Detention centres were established as an 'experiment', but lasted 40 years. Throughout they were dogged by a lack of any precise definition of purpose. Despite significant opposition the only detention centre for girls was opened at Moor Court, near Stoke-on-Trent in 1962. It was closed seven years later because military drill and physical education were not considered appropriate in the 'training' of young women.

Whilst detention centres always promised the delivery of a 'short, sharp, shock', in the 1950s and 1960s their regime was not that far removed from that of borstals. In the 1970s, in an effort to appease those who viewed the entire juvenile justice system as too soft, the Home Secretary announced the establishment of two 'experimental' regimes in which 'life will be constricted at a brisk tempo. Much greater emphasis will be put on hard and constructive activities, and discipline and tidiness, on self respect and respect for those in authority … These will be no holiday camps' (Whitelaw cited in Thornton et al., 1984, para. 1). The regimes were subsequently evaluated by the Home Office's Young Offender Psychology Unit, which concluded that they had 'no discernible effect on the rate at which trainees were reconvicted' (Thornton et al., 1984, para. 8.21). At one centre (Send, for 14–17 year olds) reconviction rates were 57 per cent both before and after the experiment; at the other (New Hall, for 17–21 year olds) the rate rose from 46 to 48 per cent. Doubt was also expressed as to whether the new tougher regimes were actually experienced as more demanding. Indeed some of the activities, such as drill and physical education were comparatively popular; more so than the continuous chore of the humdrum work party which they replaced.

Despite such findings, the tougher regimes were not abandoned but *extended* to all detention centres. In 1985 the rhetoric and political expediency of the 'short, sharp shock' appeared to take precedence over research evaluation or practical experience (Muncie, 1990, p. 61). The political demand for repressive penal policies repeatedly overshadows logical argument. As Harris (1982, p. 248) commented, 'punitive and liberal legislation are judged by different criteria, the latter being immediately at risk when it fails to reduce recidivism, but the former, however ineffective, appearing to a society in which to punish wrongdoing seems natural, to contain an intrinsic logic.'

The experiments in 'short, sharp shock' were formally abolished in 1988 but it took only another eight years for their revival. The introduction of American-styled boot camps in 1996–7 ignored all the lessons learnt in the previous 50 years. The origins of the boot camp lie in survival training for US military personnel during the Second World War. They were introduced in the US from 1983 in response to prison overcrowding and a belief that short periods of retributive punishment would change or deter offending behaviour: 'typically detainees might face pre-dawn starts, enforced shaved heads, no talking to each other, being constantly screamed at by guards, rushed meal times, no access to television and newspapers and a rigorous and abusive atmosphere for 16 hours a day' (Nathan, 1995, p. 2). Such regimes have consistently failed to live up to expectations: the deterrent effect of military training has proved negligible; the authoritarian atmosphere has denied access to effective treatment; there have been occasional lawsuits from inmates claiming that elements of the programme were dangerous and life threatening; they have failed to reduce prison populations; they distract attention from other policies that may work better; and their popularity relies more on an emotive nostalgia for some mythical orderly past than on effectiveness (Parent, 1995; Simon, 1995).

Despite such warnings, the British government decided to go ahead. The first boot camp was opened in 1996 at Thorn Cross Young Offenders' Institution in Cheshire. But instead of a military-based regime, it employed a 'high-intensity' mixture of education, discipline and training. A second camp, opened at the Military Corrective Training Centre in Colchester in 1997, promised a more spartan regime. Aimed at 17–21 year olds, its open prison conditions, however, excluded the most serious of offenders. The notion, too, of handing criminal cases over to a military authority provoked an avalanche of complaints from virtually all sides of the criminal justice process. Each place cost £850 per week compared to £250 per week in other young offender institutions. Despite these misgivings the New Labour government of 1997 was initially reluctant to move for their abolition for fear of being seen to have gone 'soft' on crime. But eventually pressure from the prison service – on grounds of cost, if not effectiveness – was successful in shutting down the Colchester camp barely 12 months after its opening and when only 44 offenders had gone through its regime. Meantime the high-intensity training regime at Thorn Cross continues.

Custodial remands

If an offender under 17 is remanded in custody awaiting trial, then that person should be placed in the care of the local authority. However, if they are deemed unruly, then guardianship is passed to the prison department. As a result whilst no person under 17 can be sentenced to imprisonment as such, the number of juveniles locked up in adult prisons and remand centres has long been a cause for concern. In 1990 15 year old Philip Knight hanged himself in Swansea Prison while awaiting sentence for stealing a handbag. The outcry that followed forced the government to introduce legislation to end such remands, but in 1995 about 1,500 15 and 16 year old boys were still being held in adult prisons: an *increase* of 72 per cent since 1992. Of those 1,500, more than half did not eventually receive a prison sentence. The practice also appears to be significantly racialized. In 1995, in London, 53 per cent of those sent to Feltham Remand Centre were from ethnic minorities, in Birmingham it was 51 per cent, and Manchester 43 per cent (*Independent*, 5 July 1995). In response, the 1998 Crime and Disorder Act placed a statutory duty on local authorities to provide bail support schemes so that juveniles might be removed from the 'corrupting influence' of prison service custody. However, in 2001 the rules governing custodial remand were relaxed to cover persistent minor offending as well as public protection. In September 2002 the total remand population in the juvenile secure estate stood at 653 (NACRO, 2003, p. 10).

Secure units

Young offenders may also find themselves subject to incarceration in local authority or privately run secure accommodation. During the 1970s almost 500 secure units were introduced in community homes with education, youth treatment centres and in assessment centres. The major argument for expanding prison-like conditions within such settings was that their referrals were more difficult than in the past. Millham et al. (1978) and Cawson and Martell's (1979) research, however, concluded that there was no such significant change. Moreover, because at the time the numbers sent to borstal had increased, those in the residential care system were arguably *less* difficult than previously. Confusion also existed over whether the role of a secure unit was to punish or treat or both, or whether they existed simply because no other 'suitable' disposal was available. Harris and Timms (1993) described the situation as one of 'persistent ambiguity'.

In congruence with other custodial disposals, the rate of reoffending was high. Experience of a secure unit also appeared to increase the chance of reoffending for younger children and for those who had not committed offences prior to going in. During the 1980s a number of authorities closed their units partly because of over-provision and partly because of more rigorous conditions attached to gaining a DHSS licence (Harris and Timms, 1993, p. 76). Nevertheless the provision of secure accommodation, not only for offenders but also for runaways, prostitute children and abused suicidal children, rose again in the 1990s to near 300. As Harris and Timms (1993, p. 169) concluded: 'the most potent predictor of high usages of secure accommodation is a local authority's possession of a secure unit.' Any increase in places simply attracts more young people who are considered to be in need of such means of control/protection. Added to this was the proposal, first formally proposed in 1993, just days after the murder of James Bulger, to build five secure training centres for 12–14 year olds to tackle the presumed 'epidemic' of persistent offending, at a cost of between £2,000 and £3,000 per week per child.

Whilst in opposition Labour had been unequivocal in condemning such centres as both expensive and ineffective but the first was opened in Kent in April 1998 as the custodial element of a new secure training order. It was run by a subsidiary of the private security firm Group 4. In the following five years two more units were established, all provided by the private sector. The Youth Justice Board plans to purchase a further 400 places from the private sector by 2005. The existence of such places is widely assumed to be the root cause of an 800 per cent rise in under 15 year olds being sent to custody between 1992 and 2001 (NACRO, 2003). However there is little evidence of their success. Research at one centre (Medway) found that nearly all children reoffended or breached the conditions of the community part of their secure training order (Hagell et al., 2000).

New Labour; new punitiveness

The 1998 Crime and Disorder Act may have promised to break with 'past failures' but the evocation of prevention is present not only in such programmes as parenting classes or drugs education but also in containment in secure environments. As a result despite the (re)emergence of restoration and tougher community penalties, there is also contrary evidence to suggest that the custodial function of youth justice has never been seriously questioned. An ideology of 'popular punitiveness' holds sway, emphasizing the importance of punishing the offender for their wrong-doing in the name of retribution. This strategy of crime control is reflected in the doubling of the numbers of young people incarcerated over the past decade. England and Wales now lock up more young people than any other country in Europe: four times the rate in France, 12 times that in the Netherlands and 160 times that in Norway, Sweden and Finland (Muncie, 2003 [...]); and often in conditions condemned by the Chief Inspector of Prisons as 'utterly unsuitable' and as 'unworthy of any country that claims to be called civilised' (Children's Rights Alliance, 2002). With reconviction rates of ex-prisoners as high as 88 per cent and increasing evidence of inappropriate and brutalizing regimes characterized by racism, bullying, self harm and suicide, it is clear that child incarceration is an expensive failure but nevertheless continues apace (Goldson and Peters, 2000). As a result a compelling case against youth custody has been repeatedly made (see Table 18.1).

The juvenile (under 18) prison population rose from 1,328 in June 1992 to 2,615 in June 2002 driven by a growing tendency to incarcerate the under-15s, ethnic minorities and young women. There was a 175 per cent increase in the use of custody for young women between 1992 and 1996 alone (Worrall, 1999). During the 1990s the average sentence length for 15–17 year olds doubled. Ironically such expansion has been explained not only by a greater willingness for magistrates to resort to custody and with longer sentences as a response to the prevailing climate of popular and political punitiveness (*Independent*, 18 June 2003) but also because the introduction of the DTO with its training component persuaded them this might be a progressive disposal. By making custody appear less harsh, its greater use is encouraged (Goldson, 2002a).

Table 18.1 The case against custody

- Custody fails to prevent reoffending or to act as an individual deterrent. Over 80 per cent of those sent to youth custody reoffend within a two-year period following release.
- The value of custody as a more widespread deterrent is doubtful. Custody is a fairly remote concept for most young people. Paradoxically it is those who know friends who have been in custody who seem most likely to follow suit. Increasing the rate of custody has practically no impact on crime rates.
- A juvenile in custody is making no restitution or reparation to the victim or to the community at large.
- Whilst prisons provide society with immediate 'protection' from the offender, the great majority of juveniles sentenced to custody pose no serious risks to the community. Indeed, they may become a significantly greater danger on their return.
- Over half have prior experience of care or social services involvement. Penal custody exacerbates broken links with family, friends, education, work and leisure, and causes stigmatization and labelling. Rather than reintegrating young people into the communities where they must learn to live, custody results in further social exclusion. Many are discharged without anywhere to live.
- Custody diverts valuable resources from community-based measures of protection and prevention which, in many cases, appear more successful at preventing reoffending.

Sources: Derived from Children's Society (1989, pp. 12–13; 1993, pp. 45–51); Goldson (2002a); NACRO (2003); Monaghan et al. (2003)

From Youth and Crime *(London: Sage), 2nd edn, 2004, pp. 283–90.*

References

Cawson, P. and Martell, M. (1979) *Children Referred to Closed Units*, DHSS Research Report, no. 5, London, DHSS.

Children's Rights Alliance (2002) *Rethinking Child Imprisonment*, London, Children's Rights Alliance.

Children's Society (1989) *Penal Custody for Juveniles – the Line of Least Resistance*, London, Children's Society.

Goldson, B. (1997) 'Children, crime, policy and practice: neither welfare nor justice', Children and Society, vol. 11, no. 2, pp. 77–88.

Goldson, B. (2000b) 'Children in need or young offenders?', *Child and Family Social Work*, vol. 5, pp. 255–265.

Goldson, B. (2002a) 'New punitiveness: the politics of child incarceration', in Muncie, J., Hughes, G. and McLaughlin, E. (eds) *Youth Justice: Critical Readings*, London, Sage.

Goldson, B. (2002b) *Vulnerable Inside: Children in Secure and Penal Settings*, London, The Children's Society.

Goldson, B. and Peters, E. (2000) *Tough Justice*, London, The Children's Society.

Hagell, A., Hazel, N. and Shaw, C. (2000) *Evaluation of Medway Secure Training Centre*, London, Home Office.

Harris, R. (1982) 'Institutionalised ambivalence: social work and the Children and Young Persons Act 1969', *British Journal of Social Work*, vol. 12, no. 3, pp. 247–63.

Harris, R. and Timms, N. (1993) *Secure Accommodation in Child Care*, London, Routledge.

Howard League (1995) *Banged Up, Beaten Up, Cutting Up*, London, The Howard League for Penal Reform.

Liebling, A. (1992) *Suicides in Prison*, London, Routledge.

Millham, S., Bullock, R. and Hosie, R. (1978) *Locking Up Children*, London, Saxon House.

Monaghan, G., Hibbert, P. and Moore, S. (2003) *Children in Trouble: Time for Change*, London, Barnardo's.

Muncie, J. (1990) 'Failure never matters: detention centres and the politics of deterrence', *Critical Social Policy*, no. 28, pp. 53–66.

Muncie, J. (2003) 'Juvenile justice in Europe: some conceptual, analytical and statistical comparisons', *Childright*, no. 202, pp. 14–17.

NACRO (2001) *Girls in the Youth Justice System*, Youth Crime Briefing, London, NACRO.

NACRO (2003) *A Failure of Justice: Reducing Child Imprisonment*, London, NACRO.

Nathan, S. (1995) *Boot Camps: Return of the Short Sharp Shock*, London, Prison Reform Trust.

Parent, D.G. (1995) 'Boot camps failing to achieve goals', in Tonry M. and Hamilton, K. (eds) *Intermediate Sanctions in Over-crowded Times*, Boston, MA, Northeastern University Press.

Radzinowicz, L. and Hood, A. (1990) *The Emergence of Penal Policy*, Oxford, Clarendon.

Simon, J. (1995) 'The boot camp and the limits of modern penality', *Social justice*, vol. 22, no. 2, pp. 25–48.

Taylor, L., Lacey, R. and Bracken, D. (1979) *In Whose Best Interests?*, London, Cobden Trust/Mind.

Thornton, D., Curran, C., Grayson, D. and Holloway, V. (1984) *Tougher Regimes in Detention Centres*, London, HMSO.

Wilson, D. and Moore, S. (2003) *Playing the Game: The Experiences of Young Black Men in Custody*, London, Children's Society/Community Fund.

Worrall, A. (1999) 'Troubled or troublesome? Justice for girls and young women', in Goldson, B. (ed.) *Youth Justice: Contemporary Policy and Practice*, Aldershot, Ashgate.

The prison community

Introduction

What kind of social institution is a prison? What effects does incarceration have on those who experience it? What kind of social relationships are formed between inmates? How stable are relations between inmates and staff? Is power unidirectional or does it flow through prisons in diverse and complex ways? Why is it that prisons, which contain large numbers of people against their will, are not the sites of continuous conflict and disorder? Over the last three quarters of a century, prison sociology has sought answers to these questions and attempted to understand the social organization of the 'prison community', borrowing from anthropology a desire to scrutinize, as if under a microscope, the prison society's distinctive features and relationships. Part D consists of six extracts that explore different aspects of the prison community. The first four are all taken from 'classic' prison studies in the sociological tradition, and are amongst the most influential and most frequently cited works in this field. They focus on the lived experience of confinement for those at the sharp end – prison inmates. The final two readings remind us of a group of individuals who spend much of their lives within prison, and who are fundamental to the quality of life therein, but are frequently rather shadowy, background figures in the literature – prison officers.

Our starting point is Gresham M. Sykes who, in 1958 published *The Society of Captives: A Study of a Maximum Security Prison*. Sykes' influence on academic prison research is immeasurable and his work is still regarded as being of contemporary relevance. In fact, *The Society of Captives* was recently judged to be the most influential book in prison studies of the twentieth century (Reisig 2001). In Reading 19, Sykes discusses the 'pains of imprisonment': five deprivations that are inflicted upon inmates, which constitute the defining characteristics of confinement. For Sykes, the deprivation of liberty, goods and services, heterosexual relationships, autonomy and security, are more than mere frustrations; they are experienced as a set of threats or attacks directed against the very foundation of the prisoner's being. One way for prisoners to diminish the pains of imprisonment described in this extract, however, which Sykes elaborates on later in *The Society of Captives*, is to form a cohesive response to the harshness of prison life. Social solidarity between prisoners manifests itself in the formal and informal codes that develop between inmates and in the special language or 'argot' they use to communicate with each other. It is in such displays of autonomy, tolerated by the prison authorities, that inmates develop ways of coping with imprisonment and the delicate balance of power between staff and prisoners is negotiated. Prison officials might be granted a level of power 'without equal in contemporary society', but even in prison, power is never total.

Sykes' study anticipates the work of Erving Goffman, who is also concerned with the ways in which inmates adjust to the frustrations inherent in the lived experience of confinement. Both were influenced by Robert Merton's (1938) theories on social adaptations to formal social and political structures, and Goffman extends our thinking about the ways in which the structural properties of institutions impact upon, and radically alter, the identities of their occupants. His studies of social interactionism were formulated in mental hospitals and it was here that he first used the term 'total institution' to describe the kind of closed environment where the time and space of the inmate could be completely controlled by an authority. But although not specifically or solely concerned with the prison, Goffman believed that the experiences of inmates in any total institution, be it a prison, monastery, army barracks, boarding school, concentration camp or mental hospital would be similar, and recognizable by their common components. For example, all aspects of life which are ordinarily carried out in different places with different people and with no overall rational plan are, in a total institution, 'rationalized'; that is, brought together in the same place and under the control and direction of a single authority. Activities are further conducted in the company of a 'batch' of others, all of whom are treated alike, and there is a rigid timetable of events to be adhered to. In short, all inmate activities are designed to fulfil the overall, official aims of the institution. This dehumanizing process starts with admission procedures where the new inmate is given a 'clear notion of his plight', a process that provides Goffman with his starting point in Reading 20, taken from *Asylums*. Whilst in the new generation of prisons, greater efforts have been made to be sensitive to the needs of the new inmate, it is nevertheless the case that the demands of efficiency are incompatible with the concerns of individuals who, when they most need it, are given no opportunity to discuss the reality of the world they are entering or their fears concerning any unresolved problems on the outside. These opportunities might come eventually, but at the point of greatest stress to the new inmate, the requirements of the system come before the needs of the individual. Furthermore, as this extract illustrates, for Goffman, the transition from the outside community to the prison is not *just* a matter of officious accomplishment: it carries a symbolic significance that goes well beyond the bureaucratic demands of the establishment. Described by the author as a 'civil death', entry into the total institution involves being subjected to a series of social and psychological attacks which undermine the sense of self.

In Goffman's account, the inmates' sense of exile and wasted time is acutely conveyed and his work is an important precursor of the descriptive studies of mundane interaction produced by Stanley Cohen and Laurie Taylor. *Psychological Survival: The Experience of Long-term Imprisonment*, from which Reading 21 is taken, is a detailed phenomenological account describing the minutiae of everyday life in HMP Durham's E-Wing in the 1960s, and is, like its predecessors in this section, interested in the assaults which imprisonment inflicts upon the inmate's self-identity. Denied access by the Home Office, Cohen and Taylor conducted their research covertly, whilst running an adult education class. Capital punishment had recently been abolished and there were widespread fears amongst politicians and the public that the prison system was now having to cope with what the *Sunday Times* called 'a new breed of prisoner with nothing to lose' (cited in Fitzgerald and Sim 1979: 90). Anxiety was high, and the fact that Cohen and Taylor's students included some of the most newsworthy felons of the time, together with the researchers' arguably unethical means of access, partly accounts for the study's continuing notoriety and longevity.

The extract chosen from *Psychological Survival* considers the 'problem' of time, and the association between time and work/money. Cohen and Taylor suggest that the temporal rhythms of prison life impose particular strains on the individual. Time is different in prison – hence the copious references to 'doing' time, 'marking' time and 'killing' time in the sociological prison research. It might be broadly assumed that the problem for an individual serving life (as the prisoners in this study were) is likely to be one of having *too much* time, but recent research has suggested that individuals serving very long prison sentences live their lives along two very different trajectories (Jamieson and Grounds 2005; Jewkes 2005). In one sense, they do indeed have 'too much' time, and Cohen and Taylor effectively illustrate the amorphous, monotonous, endless nature of time in prison. But whilst prison inmates must find ways of passing significant amounts of unstructured time and of adapting to being caged in a dull, debilitating present, they must simultaneously cope with a sense of their lives being foreshortened. Prisoners serving long or life sentences thus frequently feel a profound sense of time being stolen from them (Jewkes 2005). For the majority of us, work presents a way of passing time but, according to Cohen and Taylor, prison work only exacerbates individuals' sense of dependency and helplessness, and heightens their fears of mental and physical deterioration. Since this extract was written, over 30 years ago, the work offered to prisoners has remained, on the whole, menial, repetitive and poorly paid (on average £7–12 per week). However, the Howard League for Penal Reform has recently advised the government on the benefits of offering prisoners proper employment (the main one being that for prisoners, having a job on release is a key factor in reducing reoffending). As a result, a Home Affairs Select Committee Report, published on 7 January 2005, recommends that prison regimes should support prisoners working a conventional 9am-to-5pm day for a proper market wage, with appropriate deductions to cover the cost of accommodation, food, child support and – as a requirement – reparation for victims (www.howardleague. org). Such an initiative may convince critics like Cohen and Taylor that prison labour can be of greater benefit, to both individual prisoners and regimes, than simply keeping 'idle hands and minds' occupied whilst inmates are out of cell. But for many prisoners still, there remains little job satisfaction in the labour offered to them in prison – if they are lucky enough to have work available to them at all.

Whilst the theme of imprisonment being a painful and disabling experience is a central concern to the first three readings in this part, Reading 22, taken from

The Defences of the Weak by Thomas Mathiesen, departs from the previous three in its findings concerning the responses of inmates to the deprivations inflicted upon them. Like the previous readings, Mathiesen is alert to the fact that prisons cannot be comprehended simply in terms of their formal hierarchies of power, but must also be understood as a network of informal structures and social relations. But whilst Sykes found that the pressures of confinement are substantially mitigated by social interaction, by the taking on of stylized subcultural roles, and by collective adherence to an 'inmate code', Mathiesen found little evidence of the degree of social solidarity which Sykes describes. Indeed, in the extract chosen, Mathiesen argues that 'the world of inmates is … characterized by a surprising lack of peer solidarity'. His themes bear some similarities to those of Sykes – loyalty, fairness, manhood and privacy – but he claims that in the dog-eat-dog environment of the prison (which constitutes a much more 'disrupted' society than that which Sykes writes about) prisoners are essentially weak and lonely individuals, subject to an enforced dependency on their custodians. The extent of their reliance on prison staff for every aspect of their existence renders inmates in a position of psychological, as well as material, weakness: indeed, for Mathiesen, living under the authority of prison staff is itself a 'pain of imprisonment'. Interestingly, in the light of the final two readings in this part, Mathiesen alerts us to the fact that the authority and power wielded by prison officers are unstable because they are born of both bureaucratic procedures and personal responses. The decisions made by staff which impinge directly on the everyday lives and well-being of inmates are officially sanctioned and yet are arbitrary, discretionary and unpredictable.

Of all the relationships that exemplify the unequal distribution of power and resources in prison it is, for Mathiesen, the interface between inmates and officers which is most immediate and which is most strongly implicated in the flow of everyday life inside prisons. Officers perform several roles in relation to inmates: paternalistic guardians; rule enforcers; moral arbiters; and combatants with whom prisoners are engaged in mutual 'wind-ups'. In Reading 23, taken from the *British Journal of Criminology*, Kathleen McDermott and Roy D. King take up this theme, highlighting the extent to which staff and inmates characterize certain aspects of imprisonment as 'mind games' or 'head games'; that is, ritualized competitions for power involving staff 'showing who's boss' and inmates exercising a degree of resistance and autonomy. Although some of the practices referred to in 'Mind games: where the action is in prisons*'* are no longer part of the prison experience (such as 'slopping out' and Rule 43), the apparent arbitrariness of prison officers' decision-making remains a source of frustration for inmates and has been described as the 'hallmark of the English prison experience' (Vagg 1994: 85). Descriptions of 'mind games' are common in the prison literature, frequently viewed as 'sport' by both staff and prisoners, and not necessarily weighted in favour of those who hold officially sanctioned power. Occasionally, however, 'mind games' take a more sinister form (such as the betting games alleged to have been played by staff at Feltham YOI which led to the murder of one prisoner by his cell mate; see commentary to Reading 16 and the introductory commentary to Part E) and, as the authors go on to say later in their study, they can routinely involve prisoners being segregated in solitary confinement, or being 'shipped out' to other prisons (commonly known as being 'ghosted') with little or no prior warning. Violence between prisoners and staff is also not uncommon. But for the most part, the kind of behaviours described in this reading are an accepted, and in some circumstances, even pleasurable, way for inmate and custodian to try to foil each other's game.

Whilst prison officers are mostly consigned to the margins in the sociological prisons literature, a recent book by Elaine Crawley has succeeded in painting a more detailed picture of prison officers, their work, and their lives. In Reading 24, Crawley first outlines the multifarious roles that prison officers might perform, and then discusses their views of prisoners and of the 'right' sort of staff–prisoner relationship. 'Getting it right' is always a delicate balance and, whilst officers tend to use pejorative and stereotypical language when talking about inmates, the relationship between them is invariably more complex, as Crawley demonstrates in her discussion of identification and friendship. She also highlights the difference in staff attitudes to young offenders, compared with adult prisoners, and reminds us that the officer/parent–prisoner/infant analogy is even more pertinent in YOIs where the inmates are children and adolescents. Finally she brings us back to the theme that has underpinned the whole of this part – where power lies in prison. Like McDermott and King, Crawley describes some of the mind games between staff and inmates such as the practice of 'nicking' inmates, or placing them on report. As this extract shows, the 'performance' of power is an integral aspect of the complex horizontal and vertical relationships between prisoners and prison officers with both sides able to change outcomes and make a difference.

References

Fitzgerald, M. and Sim, J. (1979) *British Prisons*. Oxford: Blackwell.

Jamieson, R. and Grounds, A. (2005) 'Release and adjustment: perspectives from studies of wrongly convicted and politically motivated prisoners', in A. Liebling and S. Maruna (eds) *The Effects of Imprisonment*. Cullompton: Willan Publishing.

Jewkes, Y. (2005) 'Loss, liminality and the life sentence: managing identity through a disrupted lifecourse', in A. Liebling and S. Maruna (eds) *The Effects of Imprisonment*. Cullompton: Willan Publishing.

Merton, R.K. (1938) 'Social structure and anomie', *American Sociological Review*, 3: 672–82.

Reisig, M.D. (2001) 'The champion, contender, and challenger: top-ranked books in prison studies', *The Prison Journal*, 81: 389–407.

Vagg, J. (1994) *Prison Systems: A Comparative Study of Accountability in England, France, Germany and the Netherlands*. Oxford: Clarendon Press.

19. The society of captives: a study of a maximum security prison

Gresham M. Sykes

The deprivation of liberty

Of all the painful conditions imposed on the inmates of the New Jersey State Prison, none is more immediately obvious than the loss of liberty. The prisoner must live in a world shrunk to thirteen and a half acres and within this restricted area his freedom of movement is further confined by a strict system of passes, the military formations in moving from one point within the institution to another, and the demand that he remain in his cell until given permission to do otherwise. In short, the prisoner's loss of liberty is a double one – first, by confinement to the institution and second, by confinement within the institution.

The mere fact that the individual's movements are restricted, however, is far less serious than the fact that imprisonment means that the inmate is cut off from family, relatives, and friends, not in the self-isolation of the hermit or the misanthrope, but in the involuntary seclusion of the outlaw. It is true that visiting and mailing privileges partially relieve the prisoner's isolation – if he can find someone to visit him or write to him and who will be approved as a visitor or correspondent by the prison officials. Many inmates, however, have found their links with persons in the free community weakening as the months and years pass by. This may explain in part the fact that an examination of the visiting records of a random sample of the inmate population, covering approximately a one year period, indicated that 41 percent of the prisoners in the New Jersey State Prison had received no visits from the outside world.

It is not difficult to see this isolation as painfully depriving or frustrating in terms of lost emotional relationships, of loneliness and boredom. But what makes this pain of imprisonment bite most deeply is the fact that the confinement of the criminal represents a deliberate, moral rejection of the criminal by the free community. Indeed, as Reckless has pointed out, it is the moral condemnation of the criminal – however it may be symbolized – that converts hurt into punishment, i.e. the just consequence of committing an offense, and it is this condemnation that confronts the inmate by the fact of his seclusion.

Now it is sometimes claimed that many criminals are so alienated from conforming society and so identified with a criminal subculture that the moral condemnation, rejection, or disapproval of legitimate society does not touch them; they are, it is said, indifferent to the penal sanctions of the free community, at least as far as the moral stigma of being defined as a criminal is concerned. Possibly this is true for a small number of offenders such as the professional thief described by Sutherland[1] or the psychopathic personality delineated by William and Joan McCord.[2] For the great majority of criminals in prison, however, the evidence suggests that neither alienation from the ranks of the law abiding nor involvement in a system of criminal value is sufficient to eliminate the threat to the prisoner's ego posed by society's rejection.[3] The signs pointing to the prisoner's degradation are many – the anonymity of a uniform and a number rather than a name, the shaven head,[4] the insistence on gestures of respect and subordination when addressing officials, and so on. The prisoner is never allowed to forget that, by committing a crime, he has foregone his claim to the status of a full-fledged, *trusted* member of society. The status lost by the prisoner is, in fact, similar to what Marshall has called the status of citizenship – that basic acceptance of the individual as a functioning member of the society in which he lives.[5] It is true that in the past the imprisoned criminal literally suffered civil death and that although the doctrines of attainder and corruption of blood were largely abandoned in the 18th and 19th Centuries, the inmate is still stripped of many of his civil rights such as the right to vote, to hold office, to sue in court, and so on.[6] But as important as the loss of these civil rights may be, the loss of that more diffuse status which defines the individual as someone to be trusted or as morally acceptable is the loss which hurts most.

In short, the wall which seals off the criminal, the contaminated man, is a constant threat to the prisoner's self-conception and the threat is continually repeated in the many daily reminders that he must be kept apart from 'decent' men. Somehow this rejection or degradation by the free community must be warded off, turned aside, rendered harmless. Somehow the imprisoned criminal must find a device for rejecting his rejectors, if he is to endure psychologically.[7]

The deprivation of goods and services

There are admittedly many problems in attempting to compare the standard of living existing in the free community and the standard of living which is supposed to be the lot of the inmate in prison. How, for example, do we interpret the fact that a covering for the floor of a cell usually consists of a scrap from a discarded blanket and that even this possession is forbidden by the prison authorities? What meaning do we attach to the fact that no inmate owns a common piece of furniture, such as a chair, but only a homemade stool? What is the value of a suit of clothing which is also a convict's uniform with a stripe and a stencilled number? The answers are far from simple although there are a number of prison officials who will argue that some inmates are better off in prison, in strictly material terms, than they could ever hope to be in the rough and tumble economic life of the free community. Possibly this is so, but at least it has never been claimed by the inmates that the goods and services provided the prisoner are equal to or better than the goods and services which the prisoner could obtain if he were left to his own devices outside the walls. The average inmate finds himself in a harshly Spartan environment which he defines as painfully depriving.

Now it is true that the prisoner's basic material needs are met – in the sense that he does not go hungry, cold, or wet. He receives adequate medical care and he has the opportunity for exercise. But a standard of living constructed in terms of so many calories per day, so many hours of recreation, so many cubic yards of space per individual, and so on, misses the central point when we are discussing the individual's feeling of deprivation, however useful it may be in setting minimum levels of consumption for the maintenance of health. A standard of living can be hopelessly inadequate, from the individual's viewpoint, because it bores him to death or fails to provide those subtle symbolic overtones which we invest in the world of possessions. And this is the core of the prisoner's problem in the area of goods and services. He wants – or needs, if you will – not just the so called necessities of life but also the amenities: cigarettes and liquor as well as calories, interesting foods as well as sheer bulk, individual clothing as well as adequate clothing, individual furnishings for his living quarters as well as shelter, privacy as well as space. The 'rightfulness' of the prisoner's feeling of deprivation can be questioned. And the objective reality of the prisoner's deprivation – in the sense that he has actually suffered a fall from his economic position in the free community – can be viewed with skepticism, as we have indicated above. But these criticisms are irrelevant to the significant issue, namely that legitimately or illegitimately, rationally or irrationally, the inmate population defines its present material impoverishment as a painful loss.

Now in modern Western culture, material possessions are so large a part of the individual's conception of himself that to be stripped of them is to be attacked at the deepest layers of personality. This is particularly true when poverty cannot be excused as a blind stroke of fate or a universal calamity. Poverty due to one's own mistakes or misdeeds represents an indictment against one's basic value or personal worth and there are few men who can philosophically bear the want caused by their own actions. It is true some prisoners in the New Jersey State Prison attempt to interpret their low position in the scale of goods and services as an effort by the State to exploit them economically. Thus, in the eyes of some inmates, the prisoner is poor not because of an offense which he has committed in the past but because the State is a tyrant which uses its captive criminals as slave labor under the hypocritical guise of reformation. Penology, it is said, is a racket. Their poverty, then, is not punishment as we have used the word before, i.e. the just consequence of criminal behavior; rather, it is an unjust hurt or pain inflicted without legitimate cause. This attitude, however, does not appear to be particularly widespread in the inmate population and the great majority of prisoners must face their privation without the aid of the wronged man's sense of injustice. Furthermore, most prisoners are unable to fortify themselves in their low level of material existence by seeing it as a means to some high or worthy end. They are unable to attach any significant meaning to their need to make it more bearable, such as present pleasures foregone for pleasures in the future, self-sacrifice in the interests of the community, or material asceticism for the purpose of spiritual salvation.

The inmate, then, sees himself as having been made poor by reason of his own acts and without the rationale of compensating benefits. The failure is *his* failure in a world where control and possession of the material environment are commonly taken as sure indicators of a man's worth. It is true that our society, as materialistic as it may be, does not rely exclusively on goods and services as a criterion of an individual's value; and, as we shall see shortly, the inmate population defends itself by stressing alternative or supplementary measures of merit. But impoverishment remains as one of the most bitter attacks on the individual's self-image that our society has to offer and the prisoner cannot ignore the implications of his straitened circumstances.[8] Whatever the discomforts and irritations of the prisoner's Spartan existence may be, he must carry the additional burden of social definitions which equate his material deprivation with personal inadequacy.

The deprivation of heterosexual relationships

Unlike the prisoner in many Latin-American countries, the inmate of the maximum security prison in New Jersey does not enjoy the privilege of so-called conjugal visits. And in those brief times when the prisoner is allowed to see his wife, mistress, or 'female friend,' the woman must sit on one side of a plate glass window and the prisoner on the other, communicating by means of a phone under the scrutiny of a guard. If the inmate, then, is rejected and impoverished by the facts of his imprisonment, he is also figuratively castrated by his involuntary celibacy.

Now a number of writers have suggested that men in prison undergo a reduction of the sexual drive and that the sexual frustrations of prisoners are therefore less than they might appear to be at first glance. The reports of reduced sexual interest have, however, been largely confined to accounts of men imprisoned in concentration camps or similar extreme situations where starvation, torture, and physical exhaustion have reduced life to a simple struggle for survival or left the captive sunk in apathy. But in the American prison these factors are not at work to any significant extent and Lindner has noted that the prisoner's access to mass media, pornography circulated among inmates, and similar stimuli serve to keep alive the prisoner's sexual impulses.[9] The same thought is expressed more crudely by the inmates of the New Jersey State Prison in a variety of obscene expressions and it is clear that the lack of heterosexual intercourse is a frustrating experience for the imprisoned criminal and that it is a frustration which weighs heavily and painfully on his mind during his prolonged confinement. There are, of course, some 'habitual' homosexuals in the prison – men who were homosexuals before their arrival and who continue their particular form of deviant behavior within the all-male society of the custodial institution. For these inmates, perhaps, the deprivation of heterosexual intercourse cannot be counted as one of the pains of imprisonment. They are few in number, however, and are only too apt to be victimized or raped by aggressive prisoners who have turned to homosexuality as a temporary means of relieving their frustration.

Yet as important as frustration in the sexual sphere may be in physiological terms, the psychological problems created by the lack of heterosexual relationships can be even more serious. A society composed exclusively of men tends to generate anxieties in its members concerning their masculinity regardless of whether or not they are coerced, bribed, or seduced into an overt homosexual liaison. Latent homosexual tendencies may be activated in the individual without being translated into open behavior and yet still arouse strong guilt feelings at either the conscious or unconscious level. In the tense atmosphere of the prison with its known perversions, its importunities of admitted homosexuals, and its constant references to the problems of sexual frustration by guards and inmates alike, there are few prisoners who can escape the fact that an essential component of a man's self conception – his status of male – is called into question. And if an inmate has in fact engaged in homosexual behavior within the walls, not as a continuation of an habitual pattern but as a rare act of sexual deviance under the intolerable pressure of mounting physical desire, the psychological onslaughts on his ego image will be particularly acute.

In addition to these problems stemming from sexual frustration per se, the deprivation of heterosexual relationships carries with it another threat to the prisoner's image of himself – more diffuse, perhaps, and more difficult to state precisely and yet no less disturbing. The inmate is shut off from the world of women which by its very polarity gives the male world much of its meaning. Like most men, the inmate must search for his identity not simply within himself but also in the picture of himself which he finds reflected in the eyes of others; and since a significant half of his audience is denied him, the inmate's self image is in danger of becoming half complete, fractured, a monochrome without the hues of reality. The prisoner's looking-glass self, in short – to use Cooley's fine phrase – is only that portion of the prisoner's personality which is recognized or appreciated by men and this partial identity is made hazy by the lack of contrast.

The deprivation of autonomy

We have noted before that the inmate suffers from what we have called a loss of autonomy in that he is subjected to a vast body of rules and commands which are designed to control his behavior in minute detail. To the casual observer, however, it might seem that the many areas of life in which self-determination is withheld, such as the language used in a letter, the hours of sleeping and eating, or the route to work, are relatively unimportant. Perhaps it might be argued, as in the case of material deprivation, that the inmate in prison is not much worse off than the individual in the free community who is regulated in a great many aspects of his life by the iron fist of custom. It could even be argued, as some writers have done, that for a number of imprisoned criminals the extensive control of the custodians provides a welcome escape from freedom and that the prison officials thus supply an external Super-Ego which serves to reduce the anxieties arising from an awareness of deviant impulses. But from the viewpoint of the inmate population, it is precisely the triviality of much of the officials' control which often proves to be most galling. Regulation by a bureaucratic staff is felt far differently than regulation by custom. And even though a few prisoners do welcome the strict regime of the custodians as a means of checking their own aberrant behavior which they would like to curb but cannot, most prisoners look on the matter in a different light. Most prisoners, in fact, express an intense hostility against their far-reaching dependence on the decisions of their captors and the restricted ability to make choices must be included among the pains of imprisonment along with restrictions of physical liberty, the possession of goods and services, and heterosexual relationships.

Now the loss of autonomy experienced by the inmates of the prison does not represent a grant of power freely given by the ruled to the rulers for a limited and specific end. Rather, it is total and it is imposed – and for these reasons it is less endurable. The nominal objectives of the custodians are not, in general, the objectives of the prisoners.[9] Yet regardless of whether or not the inmate population shares some aims with the custodial bureaucracy, the many regulations and orders of the New Jersey State Prison's official regime often arouse the prisoner's hostility because they don't 'make sense' from the prisoner's point of view. Indeed, the incomprehensible order or rule is a basic feature of life in prison. Inmates, for example, are forbidden to take food from the messhall to their cells. Some prisoners see this as a move designed to promote cleanliness; others are convinced that the regulation is for the purpose of preventing inmates from obtaining anything that might be used in the *sub rosa* system of barter. Most, however, simply see the measure as another irritating, pointless gesture of authoritarianism. Similarly, prisoners are denied parole but are left in ignorance of the reasons for the decision. Prisoners are informed that the delivery of mail will be delayed – but they are not told why.

Now some of the inmate population's ignorance might be described as 'accidental'; it arises from what we can call the principle of bureaucratic indifference, i.e., events which seem important or vital to those at the bottom of the heap are viewed with an increasing lack of concern with each step upward. The rules, the commands, the decisions which flow down to those who are controlled are not accompanied by explanations on the grounds that it is 'impractical' or 'too much trouble.' Some of the inmate population's ignorance, however, is deliberately fostered by the prison officials in that explanations are often withheld as a matter of calculated policy. Providing explanations carries an implication that those who are ruled have a right to know – and this in turn suggests that if the explanations are not satisfactory, the rule or order will be changed. But this is in direct contradiction to the theoretical power relationship of the inmates and the prison officials. Imprisoned criminals are individuals who are being punished by society and they must be brought to their knees. If the inmate population maintains the right to argue with its captors, it takes on the appearance of an enemy nation with its own sovereignty; and in so doing it raises disturbing questions about the nature of the offender's deviance. The criminal is no longer simply a man who has broken the law; he has become a part of a group with an alternative viewpoint and thus attacks the validity of the law itself. The custodians' refusal to give reasons for many aspects of their regime can be seen in part as an attempt to avoid such an intolerable situation.

The indignation aroused by the 'bargaining inmate' or the necessity of justifying the custodial regime is particularly evident during a riot when prisoners have the 'impudence' to present a list of demands. In discussing the disturbances at the New Jersey State Prison in the Spring of 1952, for example, a newspaper editorial angrily noted that 'the storm, like a nightmarish April Fool's dream, has passed, leaving in its wake a partially wrecked State Prison as a debasing monument to the ignominious rage of desperate men.'

The important point, however, is that the frustration of the prisoner's ability to make choices and the frequent refusals to provide an explanation for the regulations and commands descending from the bureaucratic staff involve a profound threat to the prisoner's self image because they reduce the prisoner to the weak, helpless, dependent status of childhood. As Bettelheim has tellingly noted in his comments on the concentration camp, men under guard stand in constant danger of losing their identification with the normal definition of an adult and the imprisoned criminal finds his picture of himself as a self-determining individual being destroyed by the regime of the custodians.[10] It is possible that this psychological attack is particularly painful in American culture because of the deep-lying insecurities produced by the delays, the conditionality and the uneven progress so often observed in the granting of adulthood. It is also possible that the criminal is frequently an individual who has experienced great difficulty in adjusting himself to figures of authority and who finds the many restraints of prison life particularly threatening in so far as earlier struggles over the establishment of self are reactivated in a more virulent form. But without asserting that Americans in general or criminals in particular are notably ill-equipped to deal with the problems posed by the deprivation of autonomy, the helpless or dependent status of the prisoner clearly represents a serious threat to the prisoner's self image as a fully accredited member of adult society. And of the many threats which may confront the individual, either in or out of prison, there are few better calculated to arouse acute anxieties than the attempt to reimpose the subservience of youth. Public humiliation, enforced respect and deference, the finality of authoritarian decisions, the demands for a specified course of conduct because, in the judgment of another, it is in the individual's best interest – all are features of childhood's helplessness in the face of a superior adult world. Such things may be both irksome and disturbing for a child, especially if the child envisions himself as having outgrown such servitude. But for the adult who has escaped such helplessness with the passage of years, to be thrust back into childhood's helplessness is even more painful, and the inmate of the prison must somehow find a means of coping with the issue.

The deprivation of security

However strange it may appear that society has chosen to reduce the criminality of the offender by forcing him to associate with more than a thousand other criminals for years on end, there is one meaning of this involuntary union which is obvious – the individual prisoner is thrown into prolonged intimacy with other men who in many cases have a long history of violent, aggressive behavior. It is a situation which can prove to be anxiety-provoking even for the hardened recidivist and it is in this light that we can understand the comment of an inmate of the New Jersey State Prison who said, 'The worst thing about prison is you have to live with other prisoners.'

The fact that the imprisoned criminal sometimes views his fellow prisoners as 'vicious' or 'dangerous' may seem a trifle unreasonable. Other inmates, after all, are men like himself, bearing the legal stigma of conviction. But even if the individual prisoner believes that he himself is not the sort of person who is likely to attack or exploit weaker and less resourceful fellow captives, he is apt to view others with more suspicion. And if he himself is prepared to commit crimes while in prison, he is likely to feel that many others will be at least equally ready. […] For the moment it is enough to point out that regardless of the patterns of mutual aid and support which may flourish in the inmate population, there are a sufficient number of outlaws within this group of outlaws to deprive the average prisoner of that sense of security which comes from living among men who can be reasonably expected to abide by the rules of society. While it is true that every prisoner does not live in the constant fear of being robbed or beaten, the constant companionship of thieves, rapists, murderers, and aggressive homosexuals is far from reassuring.

An important aspect of this disturbingly problematical world is the fact that the inmate is acutely aware that sooner or later he will be 'tested' – that someone will 'push' him to see how far they can go and that he must be prepared to fight for the safety of his person and his possessions. If he should fail, he will thereafter be an object of contempt, constantly in danger of being attacked by other inmates who view him as an obvious victim, as a man who cannot or will not defend his rights. And yet if he succeeds, he may well become a target for the prisoner who wishes to prove himself, who seeks to enhance his own prestige by defeating the man with a reputation for toughness. Thus both success and failure in defending one's self against the aggressions of fellow captives may serve to provoke fresh attacks and no man stands assured of the future.[11]

The prisoner's loss of security arouses acute anxiety, in short, not just because violent acts of aggression and exploitation occur but also because such behavior constantly calls into question the individual's ability to cope with it, in terms of his own inner resources, his courage, his 'nerve.' Can he stand up and take it? Will he prove to be tough enough? These uncertainties constitute an ego threat for the individual forced to live in prolonged intimacy with criminals, regardless of the nature or extent of his own criminality; and we can catch a glimpse of this tense and fearful existence in the comment of one prisoner who said, 'It takes a pretty good man to be able to stand on an equal plane with a guy that's in for rape, with a guy that's in for murder, with a man who's well respected in the institution because he's a real tough cookie ...' His expectations concerning the conforming behavior of others destroyed, unable and unwilling to rely on the officials for protection, uncertain of whether or not today's joke will be tomorrow's bitter insult, the prison inmate can never feel safe. And at a deeper level lies the anxiety about his reactions to this unstable world, for then his manhood will be evaluated in the public view.

Imprisonment, then, is painful. The pains of imprisonment, however, cannot be viewed as being limited to the loss of physical liberty. The significant hurts lie in the frustrations or deprivations which attend the withdrawal of freedom, such as the lack of heterosexual relationships, isolation from the free community, the withholding of goods and services, and so on. And however painful these frustrations or deprivations may be in the immediate terms of thwarted goals, discomfort, boredom, and loneliness, they carry a more profound hurt as a set of threats or attacks which are directed against the very foundations of the prisoner's being. The individual's picture of himself as a person of value – as a morally acceptable, adult male who can present some claim to merit in his material achievements and his inner strength – begins to waver and grow dim. Society did not plan this onslaught, it is true, and society may even 'point with pride' to its humanity in the modern treatment of the criminal. But the pains of imprisonment remain and it is imperative that we recognize them, for they provide the energy for the society of captives as a system of action.

[...]

From The Society of Captives: A Study of a Maximum Security Prison (*Princeton, NJ: Princeton University Press*), 1971, pp. 65–79.

Notes

1. Cf. Edwin H. Sutherland, *The Professional Thief*, Chicago: The University of Chicago Press, 1937.
2. Cf. William and Joan McCord, *Psychopathy and Delinquency*, New York: Grune and Stratton, 1956.
3. For an excellent discussion of the symbolic overtones of imprisonment, see Walter C. Reckless, *The Crime Problem*, New York: Appleton-Century-Crofts, Inc., 1955, pp. 428–429.
4. Western culture has long placed a peculiar emphasis on shaving the head as a symbol of degradation, ranging from the enraged treatment of collaborators in occupied Europe to the more measured barbering of recruits in the Armed Forces. In the latter case, as in the prison, the nominal purpose has been cleanliness and neatness, but for the person who is shaved the meaning is somewhat different. In the New Jersey State Prison, the prisoner is clipped to the skull on arrival but not thereafter.
5. See T.H. Marshall, *Citizenship and Social Class*, Cambridge, England: Cambridge University Press, 1950.
6. *American Academy of Political and Social Science*, Vol. 293, May 1954, pp. 99–111.
7. See Lloyd W. McCorkle and Richard R. Korn, 'Resocialization Within Walls.' *Ibid.*, pp. 88–98.
8. Komarovsky's discussion of the psychological implications of unemployment is particularly apposite here, despite the markedly different context, for she notes that economic failure

provokes acute anxiety as humiliation cuts away at the individual's conception of his manhood. He feels useless, undeserving of respect, disorganized, adrift in a society where economic status is a major anchoring point. Cf. Mirra Komarovsky, *The Unemployed Man and His Family*, New York: The Dryden Press, 1940, pp. 74–77.

9. See Robert M. Lindner, 'Sex in Prison', *Complex*, Vol. 6, Fall 1951, pp. 5–20.

10. Cf. Bruno Bettelheim, 'Individual and Mass Behavior in Extreme Situations,' in *Readings in Social Psychology*, edited by T.M. Newcomb and E.L. Hartley, New York: Henry Holt and Company, 1947.

11. As the Warden of the New Jersey State Prison has pointed out, the arrival of an obviously tough professional hoodlum creates a serious problem for the recognized 'bald man' in a cellblock who is expected to challenge the newcomer immediately.

20. Asylums: Essays on the social situation of mental patients and other inmates

Erving Goffman

The inmate world

The recruit comes into the establishment with a conception of himself made possible by certain stable social arrangements in his home world. Upon entrance, he is immediately stripped of the support provided by these arrangements. In the accurate language of some of our oldest total institutions, he begins a series of abasements, degradations, humiliations, and profanations of self. His self is systematically, if often unintentionally, mortified. He begins some radical shifts in his *moral career*, a career composed of the progressive changes that occur in the beliefs that he has concerning himself and significant others.

The processes by which a person's self is mortified are fairly standard in total institutions;[1] analysis of these processes can help us to see the arrangements that ordinary establishments must guarantee if members are to preserve their civilian selves.

The barrier that total institutions place between the inmate and the wider world marks the first curtailment of self. In civil life, the sequential scheduling of the individual's roles, both in the life cycle and in the repeated daily round, ensures that no one role he plays will block his performance and ties in another. In total institutions, in contrast, membership automatically disrupts role scheduling, since the inmate's separation from the wider world lasts around the clock and may continue for years. Role dispossession therefore occurs. In many total institutions the privilege of having visitors or of visiting away from the establishment is completely withheld at first, ensuring a deep initial break with past roles and an appreciation of role dispossession. A report on cadet life in a military academy provides an illustration:

> This clean break with the past must be achieved in a relatively short period. For two months, therefore, the swab is not allowed to leave the base or to engage in social intercourse with non-cadets. This complete isolation helps to produce a unified group of swabs, rather than a heterogeneous collection of persons of high and low status. Uniforms are issued on the first day, and discussions of wealth and family back-

ground are taboo. Although the pay of the cadet is very low, he is not permitted to receive money from home. The role of the cadet must supersede other roles the individual has been accustomed to play. There are few clues left which will reveal social status in the outside world.[2]

I might add that when entrance is voluntary, the recruit has already partially withdrawn from his home world; what is cleanly severed by the institution is something that had already started to decay.

Although some roles can be re-established by the inmate if and when he returns to the world, it is plain that other losses are irrevocable and may be painfully experienced as such. It may not be possible to make up, at a later phase of the life cycle, the time not now spent in educational or job advancement, in courting, or in rearing one's children. A legal aspect of this permanent dispossession is found in the concept of 'civil death'; prison inmates may face not only a temporary loss of the rights to will money and write cheques, to contest divorce or adoption proceedings, and to vote but may have some of these rights permanently abrogated.[3]

The inmate, then, finds certain roles are lost to him by virtue of the barrier that separates him from the outside world. The process of entrance typically brings other kinds of loss and mortification as well. We very generally find staff employing what are called admission procedures, such as taking a life history photographing, weighing, fingerprinting, assigning numbers, searching, listing personal possessions for storage, undressing, bathing, disinfecting, haircutting, issuing institutional clothing, instructing as to rules, and assigning to quarters.[4] Admission procedures might better be called 'trimming' or 'programming' because in thus being squared away the new arrival allows himself to be shaped and coded into an object that can be fed into the administrative machinery of the establishment, to be worked on smoothly by routine operations. Many of these procedures depend upon attributes such as weight or fingerprints that the individual possesses merely because he is a member of the largest and most abstract of social categories, that of human beings. Action taken on the basis of such attributes necessarily ignores most of his previous bases of self-identification.

Because a total institution deals with so many aspects of its inmates' lives, with the consequent complex squaring away at admission, there is a special need to obtain initial cooperativeness from the recruit. [...]

Admission procedures and obedience tests may be elaborated into a form of initiation that has been called 'the welcome', where staff or inmates, or both, go out of their way to give the recruit a clear notion of his plight.[5] As part of this rite of passage he may be called by a term such as 'fish' or 'swab', which tells him that he is merely an inmate, and, what is more, that he has a special low status even in this low group.

The admission procedure can be characterized as a leaving off and a taking on, with the midpoint marked by physical nakedness. Leaving off of course entails a dispossession of property, important because persons invest self feelings in their possessions. Perhaps the most significant of these possessions is not physical at all, one's full name; whatever one is thereafter called, loss of one's name can be a great curtailment of the self.[6]

Once the inmate is stripped of his possessions, at least some replacements must be made by the establishment, but these take the form of standard issue, uniform in character and uniformly distributed. These substitute possessions are clearly marked as really belonging to the institution and in some cases are recalled at regular intervals to be, as it were, disinfected of identifications. With objects that can be used up – for example, pencils – the inmate may be required to return the remnants before obtaining a reissue.[7] Failure to provide inmates with individual lockers and periodic searches and confiscations of accumulated personal property[8] reinforce property dispossession. Religious orders have appreciated the implications for self of such separation from belongings. Inmates may be required to change their cells once a year so as not to become attached to them. The Benedictine Rule is explicit:

> For their bedding let a mattress, a blanket, a coverlet, and a pillow suffice. These beds must be frequently inspected by the Abbot, because of private property which may be found therein. If anyone be discovered to have what he has not received from the Abbot, let him be most severely punished. And in order that this vice of private ownership may be completely rooted out, let all things that are necessary be supplied by the Abbot: that is, cowl, tunic, stockings, shoes, girdle, knife, pen, needle, handkerchief, and tablets; so that all plea of necessity may be taken away. And let the Abbot always consider that passage in the Acts of the Apostles: 'Distribution was made to each according as anyone had need.'[9]

One set of the individual's possessions has a special relation to self. The individual ordinarily expects to exert some control over the guise in which he appears before others. For this he needs cosmetic and clothing supplies, tools for applying, arranging, and repairing them, and an accessible, secure place to store these supplies and tools – in short, the individual will need an 'identity kit' for the management of his personal front. He will also need access to decoration specialists such as barbers and clothiers.

On admission to a total institution, however, the individual is likely to be stripped of his usual appearance and of the equipment and services by which he maintains it, thus suffering a personal defacement. Clothing, combs, needle and thread, cosmetics, towels, soap, shaving sets, bathing facilities – all these may be taken away or denied him, although some may be kept in inaccessible storage, to be returned if and when he leaves. In the words of St Benedict's Holy Rule:

> Then forthwith he shall, there in the oratory, be divested of his own garments with which he is clothed and be clad in those of the monastery. Those garments of which he is divested shall be placed in the wardrobe, there to be kept, so that if, perchance, he should ever be persuaded by the devil to leave the monastery (which God forbid), he may be stripped of the monastic habit and cast forth.[10]

As suggested, the institutional issue provided as a substitute for what has been taken away is typically of a 'coarse' variety, ill-suited, often old, and the same for large categories of inmates. The impact of this substitution is described in a report on imprisoned prostitutes:

> First, there is the shower officer who forces them to undress, takes their own clothes away, sees to it that they take showers and get their prison clothes – one pair of black oxfords with cuban heels, two pairs of much-mended ankle socks, three cotton dresses, two cotton slips, two pairs of panties, and a couple of bras. Practically all the bras are flat and useless. No corsets or girdles are issued.
>
> There is not a sadder sight than some of the obese prisoners, who, if nothing else, have been managing to keep themselves looking decent on the outside, confronted by the first sight of themselves in prison issue.[11]

In addition to personal defacement that comes from being stripped of one's identity kit, there is personal disfigurement that comes from direct and permanent mutilations of the body such as brands or loss of limbs. Although this mortification of the self by way of the body is found in few total institutions, still, loss of a sense of personal safety is common and provides a basis for anxieties about disfigurement. Beatings, shock therapy, or, in mental hospitals, surgery – whatever the intent of staff in providing these services for some inmates – may lead many inmates to feel that they are in an environment that does not guarantee their physical integrity.

At admission, loss of identity equipment can prevent the individual from presenting his usual image of himself to others. After admission, the image of himself he presents is attacked in another way. Given the expressive idiom of a particular civil society, certain movements, postures, and stances will convey lowly images of the individual and be avoided as demeaning. Any regulation, command, or task that forces the individual to adopt these movements or postures may mortify his self. In total institutions, such physical indignities abound. In mental hospitals, for example, patients may be forced to eat all food with a spoon.[12] In military prisons, inmates may be required to stand at attention whenever an officer enters the compound.[13] In religious institutions, there are such classic gestures of penance as the kissing of feet,[14] and the posture recommended to an erring monk that he

> ... lie prostrate at the door of the oratory in silence; and thus, with his face to the ground and his body prone, let him cast himself at the feet of all as they go forth from the oratory.[15]

In some penal institutions we find the humiliation of bending over to receive a birching.[16]

Just as the individual can be required to hold his body in a humiliating pose, so he may have to provide humiliating verbal responses. An important instance of this is the forced deference pattern of total institutions; inmates are often required to punctuate their social interaction with staff by verbal acts of deference, such as saying 'sir'. Another instance is the necessity to beg, importune, or humbly ask for little things such as a light for a cigarette, a drink of water, or permission to use the telephone.

Corresponding to the indignities of speech and action required of the inmate are the indignities of treatment others accord him. The standard examples here are verbal or gestural profanations: staff or fellow inmates call the individual obscene names, curse him, point out his negative attributes, tease him, or talk about him or his fellow inmates as if he were not present.

Whatever the form or the source of these various indignities, the individual has to engage in activity whose symbolic implications are incompatible with his conception of self. A more diffuse example of this kind of mortification occurs when the individual is required to undertake a daily round of life that he considers alien to him – to take on a disidentifying role. In prisons, denial of heterosexual opportunities can induce fear of losing one's masculinity.[17] In military establishments, the patently useless make-work forced on fatigue details can make men feel their time and effort are worthless.[18] In religious institutions there are special arrangements to ensure that all inmates take a turn performing the more menial aspects of the servant role.[19] An extreme is the concentration-camp practice requiring prisoners to administer whippings to other prisoners.[20]

There is another form of mortification in total institutions; beginning with admission a kind of contaminative exposure occurs. On the outside, the individual can hold objects of self-feeling – such as his body, his immediate actions, his thoughts, and some of his possessions – clear of contact with alien and contaminating things. But in total institutions these territories of the self are violated; the boundary that the individual places between his being and the environment is invaded and the embodiments of self profaned.

There is, first, a violation of one's informational preserve regarding self. During admission, facts about the inmate's social statuses and past behaviour – especially discreditable facts – are collected and recorded in a dossier available to staff. Later, in so far as the establishment officially expects to alter the self-regulating inner tendencies of the inmate, there may be group or individual confession – psychiatric, political, military, or religious, according to the type of institution. On these occasions the inmate has to expose facts and feelings about self to new kinds of audiences. [...]

New audiences not only learn discreditable facts about oneself that are ordinarily concealed but also in a position to perceive some of these facts directly. Prisoners and mental patients cannot prevent their visitors from seeing them in humiliating circumstances.[21] Another example is the shoulder patch of ethnic identification worn by concentration-camp inmates.[22] Medical and security examinations often expose the inmate physically, sometimes to persons of both sexes; a similar exposure follows from collective sleeping arrangements and doorless toilets.[23] An extreme here, perhaps, is the situation of a self-destructive mental patient who is stripped naked for what is felt to be his own protection and placed in a constantly lit seclusion room, into whose Judas window any person passing on the ward can peer. In general, of course, the inmate is never fully alone; he is always within sight and often earshot of someone, if only his fellow inmates.[24] Prison cages with bars for walls fully realize such exposure.

[...]

A very common form of physical contamination is reflected in complaints about unclean food, messy quarters, soiled towels, shoes and clothing impregnated with previous users' sweat, toilets without seats, and dirty bath facilities.[25] [...]

Finally, in some total institutions the inmate is obliged to take oral or intravenous medications, whether desired or not, and to eat his food, however unpalatable. When an inmate refuses to eat, there may be forcible contamination of his innards by 'forced feeding'.

I have suggested that the inmate undergoes mortification of the self by contaminative exposure of a physical kind, but this must be amplified: when the agency of contamination is another human being, the inmate is in addition contaminated by forced interpersonal contact and, in consequence, a forced social relationship. (Similarly, when the inmate loses control over who observes him in his predicament or knows about his past, he is being contaminated by a forced relationship to these people – for it is through such perception and knowledge that relations are expressed.)

The model for interpersonal contamination in our society is presumably rape; although sexual molestation certainly occurs in total institutions, there are many other less dramatic examples. Upon admission, one's on-person possessions are pawed and fingered by an official as he itemizes and prepares them for storage. The inmate himself may be frisked and searched to the extent – often reported in the literature – of a rectal examination.[26]

Later in his stay he may be required to undergo searchings of his person and of his sleeping quarters, either routinely or when trouble arises. In all these cases it is the searcher as well as the search that penetrates the private reserve of the individual and violates the territories of his self. [...]

From Asylums: Essays on the Social Situation of Mental Patients and Other Inmates *(London: Penguin Books), 1991, pp. 24–36.*

Notes

1. An example of the description of these processes may be found in Gresham M. Sykes, *The Society of Captives* (Princeton: Princeton University Press, 1958), Ch. iv, 'The Pains of Imprisonment', pp. 63–83.
2. Sanford M. Dornbusch, 'The Military Academy as an Assimilating Institution', *Social Forces*, XXXIII (1955), p. 317. For an example of initial visiting restrictions in a mental hospital, see D. McI. Johnson and N. Dodds, eds., *The Plea for the Silent* (London: Christopher Johnson, 1957), p. 16. Compare the rule against having visitors which has often bound domestic servants to their total institution. See J. Jean Hecht, *The Domestic Servant Class in Eighteenth-century England* (London: Routledge and Kegan Paul, 1956), pp. 127–8.
3. A useful review in the case of American prisons may be found in Paul W. Tappan, 'The Legal Rights of Prisoners', *The Annals*, CCXCIII (May 1954), pp. 99–111.
4. See, for example, J. Kerkhoff, *How Thin the Veil: A Newspaperman's Story of His Own Mental Crack-up and Recovery* (New York: Greenberg, 1952), p. 110; Elie A. Cohen, *Human Behaviour in the Concentration Camp* (London: Jonathan Cape, 1954), pp. 118–22; Eugen Kogon, *The Theory and Practice of Hell* (New York: Berkley Publishing Corp., n.d.), pp. 63–8.

5. For a version of this process in concentration camps, see Cohen, op. cit., p. 120, and Kogon, op. cit., pp. 64–5. For a fictionalized treatment of the welcome in a girls' reformatory, see Sara Harris, *The Wayward Ones* (New York: New American Library, 1952), pp. 31–4. A prison version, less explicit, is found in George Dendrickson and Frederick Thomas, *The Truth about Dartmoor* (London: Gollancz, 1954), pp. 42–57.

6. For example, Thomas Merton, *The Seven Storey Mountain* (New York: Harcourt, Brace and Company, 1948), pp. 290–91; Cohen, op. cit., pp. 145–7.

7. Dendrickson and Thomas, op. cit., pp. 83–4, also *The Holy Rule of Saint Benedict*, Ch. 55.

8. Kogon, op. cit., p. 69.

9. *The Holy Rule of Saint Benedict*, Ch. 55.

10. *The Holy Rule of Saint Benedict*, Ch. 58.

11. John M. Murtagh and Sara Harris, *Cast the First Stone* (New York: Pocket Books, 1958), pp. 239–40. On mental hospitals see, for example, Kerkhoff, op. cit., p. 10. Ward, op. cit., p. 60, makes the reasonable suggestion that men in our society suffer less defacement in total institutions than do women.

12. Johnson and Dodds, op. cit., p. 15; for a prison version see Alfred Hassler, *Diary of a Self-made Convict* (Chicago: Regnery, 1954), p. 33.

13. L.D. Hankoff, 'Interaction Patterns among Military Prison Personnel', *U.S. Armed Forces Medical Journal*, X (1959), p. 1419.

14. Kathryn Hulme, *The Nun's Story* (London: Muller, 1957), p. 52.

15. *The Holy Rule of Saint Benedict*, Ch. 44.

16. Dendrickson and Thomas, op. cit., p. 76.

17. Sykes, op. cit., pp. 70–72.

18. For example, Lawrence, op. cit., pp. 34–5.

19. *The Hole Rule of Saint Benedict*, Ch. 35.

20. Kogon, op. cit., p. 102.

21. Wider communities in Western society, of course, have employed this technique too, in the form of public floggings and public hangings, the pillory and stocks. Functionally correlated with the public emphasis on mortifications in total institutions is the commonly found strict ruling that staff is not to be humiliated by staff in the presence of inmates.

22. Kogon, op. cit., pp. 41–2.

23. Brendan Behan, *Borstal Boy* (London: Hutchinson, 1958), p. 23.

24. For example, Kogon, op. cit., p. 128; Hassler, op. cit., p. 16. For the situation in a religious institution, see Hulme, op. cit., p. 48. She also describes a lack of aural privacy since thin cotton hangings are used as the only door closing off the individual sleeping cells (p. 20).

25. For example, Johnson and Dodds, op. cit., p. 75; Anthony Heckstall-Smith, *Eighteen Months* (London: Allan Wingate, 1954), p. 15.

26. For example, Lowell Naeve, *A Field of Broken Stones* (Glen Gardner, New Jersey: Libertarian Press, 1950), p. 17; Kogon, op. cit., p. 67; Holley Cantine and Dachine Rainer, *Prison Etiquette* (Bearsville, N.Y.: Retort Press, 1950), p. 46.

21. Time and deterioration

Stanley Cohen and Laurie Taylor

Time as a problem

Time is a much more taken-for-granted element of everyday life than is friendship or privacy. We may periodically reflect upon our inability to manage without friends or privacy, we may talk philosophically about the need to seek new friends or dispense with old ones, and consciously reflect upon the merits of gregariousness and isolation. But behind such thinking and planning time ticks away relatively unobserved and unanalysed. We talk of it chiefly as a resource – we do not have enough of it, we cannot spare any for visits to our relations, we must make some so that we can squeeze in this or that activity. We can turn down any engagement on the grounds that we 'simply have no time' and we can become irritated by those who waste time or have time 'on their hands' without using it.

The association between time and money is hardly surprising in a highly industrialized society in which time wasted is often equivalent to money wasted in the great and continuing race for higher productivity. But there are occasions upon which the daily planning and allocation of intervals, the according of hours, days, and weekends to specific activities, breaks down. The sudden loss of a job, the cancellation of an engagement, removal from occupational time-scheduling by holiday or hospitalization, all provide opportunities for absenting ourselves from the obsession with marked time. It is then that time may become an open landscape rather than a set of pigeon-holes.

On these occasions 'past' and 'future' may have a meaning not in terms of time wasted or potential time to use in the future, but rather as parameters which define the present moment. Time then becomes less of an object in its own right. We then recognize that our past is not simply a pile of spent time, it has a personal meaning and significance. In the same way, the future becomes not simply a set of unfilled hours, but it is seen to hold a determinate position in our present existence. It assures us of the finiteness of life and thereby makes a mockery of the customary use of hours and days as steps towards some final goal. Our memory of the past and our recognition of the end of the future throw into relief our everyday human time-scheduling.

But such speculation is quickly ended for most of us. Life, as we say, catches up with us and we become locked back into the round of activities perhaps even persuading ourselves that only by such a self-conscious immersion can we manage to live at all. There is little consideration for those in our society who continually cast doubt upon the need to use time profitably. Much of the hostility felt towards such groups as hippies in contemporary society, is due to their disdain for conventional notions of time and their tendency to alter time perspectives by experiencing only the present and the immediate. One observer of the hippie subculture, Fred Davis,[1] notes how these groups raise doubts about 'the magically rationalistic faith in converting present efforts to future pay off', how their use of 'happenings' and interest in such ideas as astrology are attempts 'to denude the future of its temporal integrity – its unknowability and slow unfoldingness – by fusing it indiscriminately with present dispositions and sensations'. He goes on:

> The hippies' structureless round-of-day ('hanging loose'), his disdain for appointments, schedules, and straight society's compulsive parcelling out of minutes and hours, are all implicated in his intense reverence for the possibilities of the present and uninterest in the future. Few wear watches and as a colleague who has made a close participant observer study of one group of hippies remarked, 'None of them ever seems to know what time it is'.

Such experiences are, of course, linked in these subcultures with the use of mind-altering drugs and indeed a central claim made by proselytizers for such drugs concerns their properties for wholly altering time perspectives.[2] One subject in an L.S.D. experiment reports: 'One of the grossest distortions was that of time perception. Centuries were lived, yet the minute hand of the watch barely moved. My Rorschach took 200 light years, the longest on record.'[3]

Long-term prisoners do not volunteer like hippies for special time experiences, they are not briefly placed outside the normal routines of life like hospital patients or holiday makers, they have instead been given time as a punishment. But they have been given someone else's time. Their own time has been abstracted by the courts like a monetary fine and in its place they have been given prison time. This is no longer a resource but a controller. It has to be served rather than used. The men have described the ways in which they repeated their sentences to themselves – 'twenty years', 'thirty years' – in an attempt to understand the nature of their predicament.

Prisoners are, of course, not the only group who are forced to see time as a problem. For most workers, as one observer notes, '… Time is what the factory worker sells: not labour, not skill, but time, dreary time. Desolate factory time that passes so slowly compared with the fleeting seconds of the weekend'.[4] An industrial sociologist, Donald Roy, has provided a classic account of how a group of factory machine operatives kept themselves from 'going nuts' in a situation of monotonous work activity by a grim process of fighting against the clock.[5]

But the factory worker's day ends, he goes home, he has weekends and holidays, he will eventually retire. And although his time might indeed have been stolen from him he has not been sentenced to a long period in which he is continually and inevitably plunged into considerations about the meaning of time. A long prison sentence is not, however, a short intermission in the real business of life, it is the real business of life.

In these circumstances it is not surprising that the most frequently used metaphor to describe prison experience is a temporal one: serving a sentence is 'doing time' and the most frequent injunction to inmates is to 'do your time and not let your time do you':

> In prison, time accumulates a new dimension. You try to eat it away rather than enjoy it. If a prisoner is having difficulty with his station, if the days are hopelessly long, he is doing 'hard time'. Instead of asking why another is making life difficult one asks 'why are you cutting into my time?' And a frequent answer when one tells of his troubles is 'do your own time' or 'don't press my time'.[6]

The present and the future

Those who dislike speculation about past and future, can usually see an end to the situation which has induced such reflective breaks in the normal scheduling of life; they can consider plans for when they get out of hospital, or prison, or home on holiday. There are still bills to be paid, visits to relations to be arranged, home-coming parties to be organized during those times when one is absent from the normal run of life. The ordinary temporal scheduling of one's affairs is kept in the background of one's mind by the continued operation of such financial, domestic and social matters. When twenty years of one's time is taken away, even these routine matters disappear. The landscape of time, the past and the future, and the actual significance of the present moment insistently occupy the mind. The prisoners in E-Wing found Victor Serge's description of this obsessive state the most accurate.

> The unreality of time is palpable. Each second falls slowly. What a measureless gap from one hour to the next. When you tell yourself in advance that six months – or six years – are to pass like this, you feel the terror of facing an abyss. At the bottom, mists in the darkness.[7]

This unlimited time does not have the same subjective appeal for the prisoners as for the hippie drug user, or the monk or hermit. For as we have said it is not their own time. They did not volunteer for twenty years' self-reflection. And neither do they have a ready-made set of interpretations, a personal ideology to fill the hours of self-reflection. The sophisticated drug-user may be self-consciously using his expanded consciousness of time to construct mental reveries, the hermit and the monk may be conversing with God in their time-free trances, but the long-term prisoner has no such ready-made mystical voyages to take the place of his previous involvement in plans, schedules and routines.

In these circumstances, it is not surprising that the prisoners live for the present – not from some ideological disdain for future planning, but out of necessity. To quote from the experience of one American prisoner: 'You do your time in little daily jerks, living from one microscopic pleasure to the next – from breakfast pancakes to a flash of blue sky ... Try it any other way and you'll be pounding the walls, screaming until your lungs give out.'[8] Richard Byrd, isolated in a polar camp, came to the same solution:

> I built a wall between myself and the past in an effort to extract every ounce of diversion and creativeness inherent in my immediate surroundings. Every day I experimented with new schemes for increasing the content of the hours ... My environment was intrinsically treacherous and difficult but I saw ways to make it agreeable. I tried to cook more rapidly, take weather and auroral observations more expertly and do routine things more systematically. Full mastery of the impinging moment was my goal.[9]

In prison, one also has to find ways of 'increasing the content of the hours' but 'mastery of the impinging moment' has a very different meaning for those who – unlike explorers or even short-term prisoners do not have a clear conception of the future after one survives the treacherous environment. It is all very well to engage in relatively 'meaningless' activities – such as making weather observations – so long as this can be seen as part of a finite period of waiting before release. The long-termer has only the choice between surrendering himself to this meaningless world as a life project or obsessionally thinking about the future – a near certain way of doing hard time.

This discussion leads us to the paradox inherent in the way long-termers deal with the future. In one sense the future is unthinkable. Roy once remarked that, 'If I really thought that I had to do another seventeen years, I'd do myself in.' Other prisoners fight attempts by prison officers to bring home the time factor. Jock said: 'Whenever a screw asks me how long do I think I'll do, I always say, "Oh, about thirty five years", because then he can get no advantage from the conversation. If I say, "Twenty," he'd say, "Oh no, I think it'll be at least twenty five." Really I don't know what any of the figures mean.' The paradox arises in that while the men reject attempts by others to raise the subject, or dismiss thoughts about the nature of the future from their own minds, they are also relying upon ideas about a future life outside to sustain themselves through their temporally undifferentiated days.

For without entertaining the prospect of a life beyond the prison, without literally believing in an 'after life', one has to either face the fact that one's life was over at the moment of entering the prison, or that one's life is that existence which takes place within the prison. The concept of 'my life' is an important one in our culture. Young men look ahead to life, old men look back upon it. People talk about their life being behind or ahead of them. In other words we identify life with particular periods of our existence, with the time between youth and old age, that time before prison, the time which is to come after prison. What appears to be totally unacceptable is the idea that one's life is experienced in prison. One may be serving life, but one is not serving 'my life'. This was certainly true for the men we knew and Farber found it to be the case in his interviews with 'Eight Men Whose Chances of Ever Getting Out Are Slight'. His principal generalization was that *'in not a single case of these men whose chances of ever getting out are negligible is there complete resignation to dying in prison.* That most dismal of all platitudes "Where there is life there's hope" takes on a new freshness.'[10] (Italics in original.)

Marking time

In the circumstances, prisoners who have to sustain their lives in some way look around for ways of marking out the passage of the days, ways of differentiating and dividing time. Psychologists and sociologists have paid little attention to the problems which occur for those whose lives are suddenly emptied of time markers in this total way. Perhaps their involvement in a particularly highly scheduled career structure makes them insensitive to the empty formless years which others have to occupy. At least the only major research into such matters was carried out by Julius Roth, a sociologist who suddenly found himself absorbed by the problem of time-scheduling when he was away from academic life and spending time as a patient in a T.B. sanatorium.[11]

Patients who enter such sanatoria are often surprised to find that they are given no exact date for their release. Lack of information over this matter leads to a frantic activity. Doctors, nurses and other patients are repeatedly questioned and quite ambiguous items of information are treated as significant clues. The demand for a timetable leads the patients to bargain with physicians about the nature and extent of their improvement in order that an earlier release date may be negotiated. Roth's principal concern is to indicate how important career timetables are in most areas of life and to demonstrate the concern which arises when the stages which constitute them are ambiguous or non-existent.

This study by Roth brings out the fact that one obvious benchmark, one way of dividing time, which is built into the sanatorium regimes, is the notion of linear progress. One gets better or stronger; one is able to do things one could not do before. But in E-Wing no such reference to linear progress is possible. Criteria for the positive evaluation of one's progress are not built into the system, and there are no progressive stages of reward and punishment. Though parole is a reward somewhat contingent on good behaviour, most of the men we know see its attainment (realistically) as so remote that it hardly functions as a stage of progress. Indeed, the chances of parole can be almost arbitrarily affected by the sudden appearance of a newspaper item on a notorious criminal. The men in the wing saw any popular reference to them in the Sunday newspapers as setting back even further their chances of remission. They were sophisticated enough to know how much the deliberations of a parole board were eventually influenced by public opinion, despite its avowed concern with the actual individual under consideration.

Unlike the T.B. patients described by Roth, these men have no opportunities for bargaining with the authorities. Their behaviour cannot influence their timetable, there is no room for 'making deals' with their keepers that will help to shorten the stretch or bring an earlier relaxation of restrictions. Unlike hospitals, again, there is nothing in the behaviour of the staff to give the prisoners any clues about when events should occur in the passage of time. The absence and the inscrutability of the Home Office personnel who control a few of the temporal and situational outcomes, are seen as necessary ways of keeping control and preserving security.

The men therefore tend to create stages themselves. They build their own subjective clock in order to protect themselves from the terror of 'the misty abyss'. There are a few achievements which can be used to mark the passage of time. One can engage in mind-building (reading or studying) and in body-building (usually weightlifting). Some of the men talk about an educational career, describing the passage from 'O' levels to 'A' levels to university with an enthusiasm which is rarely found in even those who have a chance of occupationally capitalizing upon the restricted years of specialized study which constitute contemporary secondary education. The significance of weightlifting in this context may be less than we at first thought. It was possible in the wing to find men who agreed that being able to lift extra weights constituted a way of marking out improvements over time, but a somewhat more cynical view came in reply to an article of ours in which we had made this point. An ex-member of the class wrote: 'In my opinion body-building was a bad example because it serves far more potent motives than the need for a concrete progression. Some of the prisoners in question would rather put an inch on their biceps than take a year off their sentence.'

In any case there is a danger in these pursuits of mental and physical targets, for there soon comes a day in which progress is inhibited, in which fewer books are read, fewer essays written and less weights lifted. In normal life we can declare that our interests have declined in such matters and re-invest successfully in foreign travel and golf. For these prisoners the loss of such matters marks the re-entry of unstructured time.

There are other methods of marking time. One can tick off certain fixed, definable periods: days, weeks or months. But this may merely bring home the unreality of time even more forcibly. As Serge writes:

So as not to lose track of the date, you have to count the days attentively, mark each one with a cross. One morning you discover that there are forty-seven days – or one hundred and twenty, or three hundred and forty-seven! – and that it is a straight path leading backwards without the slightest break: colourless, insipid, senseless. Not a single landmark is visible. Months have passed like so many days; entire days pass like minutes. Future time is terrifying. The present is heavy with torpor.

Each minute may be marvellously – or horribly – profound. That depends to a certain extent on yourself. There are swift hours and very long seconds. Past time is void. There is no chronology of events to mark it; external duration no longer exists.[12]

It is the lack of a chronology of events that is most important in Serge's description. Of course, days come and go, but they do not pass as they do on the outside when one is waiting for an event, simply because they are no longer beads on a wire, or counters on a board. They are not progressively used up as one moves toward a goal. They are isolated entities, existing away from the normal cumulative linear context they inhabit. In Roth's words: 'The life prisoner can look forward to Sunday as a welcome break in a dreary routine, but the succession of Sundays does not lead him anywhere.'[13]

In these circumstances, the external clock may be partially abandoned in favour of such subjective markers as changes in mood or feeling. These may have a reality and a temporal meaning which is lacking in the world of clocks and diaries and calendars. Christopher Burney although writing specifically about solitary confinement, captures this transition:

Days in prison are distinguishable only by such rare incidents as from time to time make one of them memorable among its fellows. Although I never lost count of the week or of the date, I followed them subconsciously, and life was divided into longer periods, limited by a state of mind or a physical condition; and it was these more personal symbols than sun or moon which marked out the calendar.[14]

Shorter sentences undoubtedly are managed in more orthodox ways: days are crossed off calendars and hours until release are pencilled on all walls. The techniques for conducting such time management become accepted parts of prison folklore. Leary recalls noticing that the numbers pinned to a trustee's wall signifying the date were removed each day but there was no number for the day on which he was looking at the wall. He asked the prisoner why and the reply was: 'in con terminology when you wake up in the morning that day is over'.[15] There were attempts to advocate variations in such techniques to meet the case of long sentences. When Roland arrived in E-Wing he turned to Paul for advice on the structuring of time. 'How am I going to do twenty years?' Paul, on the basis of three years' experience of an equally long sentence, provided the only reassurance he knew: 'It's easy, do it five years at a time.'

There are of course the 'incidents' referred to by Burney which occur in the wing and which break up the dull passage of time. Many of these are, however, unscheduled and it is therefore not possible to look forward to them or prepare for them. The sudden transfer of a man from the wing or the arrival of a new inmate is typically unexpected. Events which occur in this sudden way are deprived of significance. Once again it is easy to forget how important for our existence is the anticipation of such matters in everyday life. The dull Monday morning becomes acceptable because of the promise of an evening out on Thursday, the long winter is bearable because of an anticipated Easter holiday. Each event by itself may be trivial, even dispensable without great psychic cost, but together they constitute a set of inducements which help to move us forward through time.

Donald Roy's factory workers, spending a day of 'infinitesimal cerebral excitation', repetitively clocking a machine, faced similar problems of marking time: the lunch break, occasional trips to the lavatory or drinking fountain, obviously functioned to 'break the day up into digestible parts'. But Roy soon realized that the men were doing more than this, they were creating 'incidents' and in fact much of their informal activity was devoted to deliberately making new time markers and interruptions in the 'day's long grind'. These were not *just* rest pauses or work interruptions or accentuations of progress points in the passage of time – although they performed this latter function better than a clock:

> If the daily series of interruptions be likened to a clock then the comparison might best be made with a special hind of cuckoo clock, one with a cuckoo which can provide variation in its announcements and can create such an interest in them that the intervening minutes become filled with intellectual content … The group interactions thus not only marked off the time; they gave it content and hurried it along.[16]

The clicker operators called these breaks 'times' and they usually involved the consumption of food or drink: coffee time, peach time, banana time, fish time or coke time. All the themes in the group's interactions, their joking, horseplay, ritualistic conversation provided interaction which captured attention and held interest to make the long day pass.

The routine of E-Wing was so short of events that even our classes became something of an occasion. We were told by the men, quite self-consciously (gently mocking themselves and us at the same time) how they would sometimes make quite elaborate preparations – like 'dressing up' – for our meetings. We were at least outsiders and this they found reassuring. We could pass on in detail the changes in life which were occurring outside, we could interpret changes in the political climate, in drug use, in popular music, in sexual permissiveness. Their ability to assimilate these changes, to approve or accept the widespread use of marihuana or the increased permissiveness of the cinema, provided some type of guarantee that they could rejoin society without too great a strain upon their release. To put it pretentiously, we helped to keep them in gear with external time and in this way provided them with a way of marking time which did not simply refer to the unserved years of their sentence.

But our visits did not of course have the emotional significance or impact of visits from friends and relatives. Such visits were events to be planned for, to be anticipated over days and weeks. Fred Davis talks about the 'accordion effect' that such events produce: a man stretches the time of the event, from the point of its anticipation through to the discussions that follow its occurrence'.[17] With more feeling Serge calls these effects 'exultation': the radiant joy at the expectation of recognition by others, and the fact that 'a fifteen-minute visit is enough to fill long days with expectation and long days with meaning afterwards'.

Unfortunately [...], such events may become increasingly rare as the prisoner moves towards the end of his first decade inside. The joy produced by a visit and the structuring of time which its anticipation allows is not enough to overcome the pains of anxiety which a possible break in that relationship induces.

Work and making time pass

Victor Serge described the 'present' in prison as being 'heavy with torpor'. Days do not go past at their conventional pace. However the adoption of new methods of time-scheduling in this ambiguous situation is not the only problem facing the long-termer. It is not just the division of time which concerns him but the *speed* of its passage. How can it be made to go more quickly? The anticipation of visits or the expectation of letters does nothing about increasing the speed at which time goes. Obsessional concern with such future events may even slow time as anyone who has fixedly waited for a kettle to boil will know.

In everyday life we typically make time go by throwing ourselves into occupational activities. We bury ourselves in our work so that we have no time for 'clock-watching'. This method is not much use even to the average prisoner. It is not much use hoping that a man in Parkhurst's 'tag shop' will become involved in his job of sticking metal ends in to the lengths of green string used to keep files together. It is even less reasonable to suppose that men facing twenty years in jail can lose themselves in repairing sewing machines or making mosquito nets – to name two of the jobs provided for E-Wing men. But people faced with such monotonous jobs in the outside world do, of course, cope. One commentator on the workers' struggle to 'cling to the remnants of joy in work' notes that 'it is psychologically impossible to deprive any kind of work of all its positive emotional elements'.[18] The worker will always find *some* meaning, some scope for initiative, play and creative impulse in the activity assigned to him.

We doubt that this is true for long-term prisoners. The culturally defined meanings of work: learning a trade, making something for one's family, financial incentive are gone. Even if prison jobs were interesting, work for a life prisoner has a very peculiar status indeed: if factory workers have to desperately invest jobs with meaning and time markers, then prisoners without clear meanings or time markers have to try and find them in the work they are given. So their problem is a double one.

In these circumstances it is not surprising to find that only five men out of the forty-two in the Eccleston sample listed work as a way of making time go faster. Ten of the rest saw no ways at all of solving this problem and the others mentioned hobbies, reading, or private study: activities we would regard in the outside world as leisure. When workshops were introduced into E-Wing in 1968 there were references to the fact that the men had done no work for six months and were becoming lazy. Certainly many of them regarded the introduction of the workshops as an additional punishment rather than as an escape from torpor and this was the main reason for the protest and barricade which immediately followed. An editorial comment at this time admitted that the work that was being offered was not interesting or relevant. The real value of the new workshops was that they would 'occupy idle hands and minds, and perpetuate the idea that work, as opposed to idleness, is a requirement of life'. (*Newcastle Journal*.)

The very use of the word 'work' is misleading in this context. As Erving Goffman observed in *Asylums*:

> In the ordinary arrangements of living in our society, the authority of the work place stops with the worker's receipt of a money payment; the spending of this in a domestic and recreational setting is the worker's private affair and constitutes a mechanism through which the authority of the work place is kept within strict bounds. But to say that inmates of total institutions have their full day scheduled for them is to say that all their essential needs will have to be planned for. Whatever the incentive given for work, then, this incentive will not have the structural significance it has on the outside. There will have to be different motives for work and different attitudes toward it. This is a basic adjustment required of the inmates and of those who must induce them to work.[19]

The absurdity of 'work' within the context of the security wing is perhaps most neatly illustrated by the fact that what is a 'job' in one wing – making soft toys – is offered as a hobby in another.

We always found it difficult to maintain a conversation about work with prisoners in E-Wing. They gave the impression that there were other more important matters to be discussed. What job they were doing at the time made little apparent difference to their feelings about life inside. Once again, we are able to turn to Farber for some interesting confirmation of these findings. With the help of prison officials and prisoners he divided up jobs along a good–bad axis and then checked on the relationship between the relative suffering experienced by the prisoners and the quality of the job. There was no link at all. Those with bad jobs suffered no more or less than those with good. He was sufficiently surprised by this result to check up on job satisfaction as well. For perhaps men who had good jobs might *dislike* them and vice versa. But no relationship between degree of job satisfaction and suffering could be found. Farber concludes by saying that 'what would seem to be one of the most important of day-to-day activities bears no relation to suffering. Suffering is related to broader, less immediate aspects of the life situation.'[20]

We have been a little too sweeping, however, in writing off work as a way of speeding up the passage of time. There are a few in prison who feel it to be better than nothing. They admit that it is a self-deception, but claim that there is no alternative. They feel sympathetic to Ivan Denisovich's view: 'How time flew when you were working. That was something he'd often noticed. The days rolled by in the camp – they were over before you could say "knife". But the years never rolled by, they never moved by a second.'[21]

For some time we assumed that these differences in attitude towards the use of work to pass time were idiosyncratic. But behind the cynical view of work may lie a concern about what is involved in passing time in this way. It was the more rebellious members of the group who played down the significance of becoming involved in such activities. In doing this they may have been recognizing the loss of personal autonomy which is involved in fitting oneself to others' schedules. Kathy Calkins, who has conducted a very sensitive investigation into the significance of time in a rehabilitation hospital, reserves the phrase 'time passing' for this particular style of adaptation:

> When time is *passed* (our stress), the patient tends to relinquish a certain amount of control over his own time. Essentially, he fits into the time of others according to their time prescriptions. In this style, the patient voluntarily fills pockets of time outlined by the institution.[22]

For the long-termer to seek to pass time by immersing himself in institutional routines may be to accord some type of legitimacy to the institution. It is to acknowledge that his sentence will be served in accordance with the intentions of the authorities.

The marking and the passing of time are then major elements in long-term prisoners' lives. Time presents itself as a problem. It is no longer a resource to be used, but rather an object to be contemplated – an undifferentiated landscape which has to be marked out and traversed. Conventional markers cannot be used and neither can one's journey be expedited by recourse to conventional methods. Nevertheless the length of the journey continually preoccupies the mind, for only after it has been made, can life be effectively resumed.

There is another preoccupation for these particular time travellers. As the journey proceeds they are accompanied by a number of growing anxieties. Above all long-term prisoners have to learn to live with a constant fear of deterioration.

The fear of deterioration

When Roy arrived to start his twenty-five-year sentence some screws tried to reassure him. 'Look at Dawson,' they said, pointing to the top landing, 'he's been in for nearly twenty years and he's perfectly content.' Roy would not accept this consolation: 'How could I know if he was content? Anyway what was he content *about*?' Roy's fear was that he might lapse into a state of contentment which marked a departure from reality, but which he did not recognize as such.

The long-term prisoners all felt like this. Over the years they have asked us to comment on any signs of deterioration we observed, to record their personality changes, to discuss their cultural inadequacies and their social maladjustments. Not that we are really needed to point out any signs of deterioration. The men we have met are only too ready to do it for each other. One evening they all sat discussing the future programme for the class. The regular group was trying to decide the best dates for a new set of lectures. 'Well, Stan's here on Friday,' said Paul. 'Monday,' said Roy, 'today's Friday, *you're going.*' 'I'm not – anybody could make that mistake. My mother gets the days mixed. There's nothing special about that.'

The incident is trivial but it indicates the obsessive concern with signs of deterioration and the self-consciousness with which such fears were faced. These men felt that all around them were examples of people who had turned into cabbages because they had not been sufficiently vigilant. Every day they encountered an old sex offender who spent hours merely cleaning and filling the teapot, a mindless activity which the old man appeared to be contented with. And this was their problem: at what price would they achieve peace of mind and contentment? Would they start behaving like the old man, as a way of banishing the ghosts of time, the fear of deterioration and not knowing what was happening to them? In other words, would the cumulative result of years of working at something which looked like adaptation, in fact really be a process of learning how to deteriorate?

[...]

From Psychological Survival: The Experience of Long-term Imprisonment (*Harmondsworth: Penguin Books*), 1972, pp. 87–105.

Notes

1. Fred Davis, 'Why All of Us May Be Hippies Someday', *TransAction*, 5 December 1967.
2. For example, Timothy Leary, *The Politics of Ecstasy*, (London, Paladin, 1970).
3. Quoted in Sidney Cohen, *Drugs of Hallucination*, (London, Paladin, 1970), p. 86.
4. Ronald Fraser (ed.), *Work*, (Penguin, 1968), vol. I, p. 12).
5. Donald Roy, ' "Banana Time": Job Satisfaction and Informal Interaction,' *Human Organization*, 18, (1959–60).
6. John Rosevear, 'The Fourth Mad Wall' in Ross Firestone (ed.) *Getting Busted*, (New York, Douglas Books, 1970), p. 234.
7. Victor Serge, *Men in Prison*, (London, Gollancz, 1970, p. 56). It was not only here that the prisoners found Victor Serge most accurate. In our view, *Men in Prison* is the best existing account of survival and resistance in prisons and we have been consistently stimulated by its insights.
8. J. Godwin, *Alcatraz* (New York, Doubleday & Co., 1963).
9. Richard Byrd, *Alone*, (London, Putnam, 1938), p. 109.
10. Maurice Farber, 'Suffering and Time Perspective of the Prisoner', p. 180.
11. Julius Roth, *Timetable*, (Indianapolis, Bobbs-Merrill, 1962).
12. Victor Serge, *Men in Prison*, pp. 56–7.
13. Julius Roth, *Timetables*, p. 99.
14. Christopher Burney, *Solitary Confinement*, (New York, Coward & McCann, 1952), p. 23.
15. Timothy Leary, *Jail Notes*, (New York, Douglas Books, 1970), p. 77.
16. Donald Roy, ' "Banana Time": Job Satisfaction and Informal Interaction', p. 162.
17. Quoted by Kathy Calkins in 'Time: Perspectives, Marking and Styles of Usage', *Social Problems 17*, 6 (Spring 1970).
18. Henri de Man, quoted in Donald Roy, op. cit., p. 160.
19. Erving Goffman, *Asylums*, (Penguin, 1969), p. 10.
20. Maurice Farber in K. Lewin (ed.), *Studies in Authority and Frustration*, p. 174.
21. Alexander Solzhenitsyn, *One Day in the Life of Ivan Denisovich*, (Penguin, 1968).
22. Calkins, 'Time: Perspectives, Marking and Styles of Usage', p. 495.

22. The defences of the weak: a sociological study of a Norwegian correctional institution

Thomas Mathiesen

The problem of peer solidarity

The notion of group cohesion as a necessary but not sufficient condition for peer solidarity is a hypothesis rather than an established fact. In this section we shall see that, whether or not the hypothesis is correct, the world of inmates is at any rate characterized by a surprising lack of peer solidarity. The description will also shed further light on the relative non-existence of cohesive inmate groups.

Among inmates the expression of certain horizontal norms of action, and sanctions on deviance from these norms, may have the function of establishing peer solidarity. This has been pointed out by several other writers. We shall follow Sykes and Messinger's summary of analyses of the inmate social system in American prisons [pp. 5–11] in so far as it fits the Norwegian case.

(a) Loyalty among inmates

A set of norms central to the inmate culture stresses that inmates should be loyal towards each other when they face the staff member. The most important norm in this set may be formulated as follows: 'You should not inform on fellow inmates' [p. 7]. This norm should be adhered to despite personal sacrifices. The following excerpt is indicative:

> You shouldn't go so much up to the doctors. You'll get unpopular among the boys for that.

The statement, made as a piece of advice or a warning during a quarrel between some inmates, is quite typical. The norm against informing is expressed by nearly all inmates, though with somewhat varying strength. Stress on it is consciously intended as leading to solidarity among inmates. Adherence to it is perceived to be in the interest of all inmates when facing staff members as controllers of vital rewards, punishments, etc.[1]

But despite this, there is a widespread belief that informing nevertheless occurs frequently, and there is a widespread fear about this, coupled with ignorance about who the informers are. As one inmate expressed it when caught in a rule-infraction:

> There is a lot of informing in this place. I don't know who does it; I wouldn't like to know, because if I knew, then, –. If X and Y and I here knew it, we would really give them hell …

Informing certainly occurs often enough for us to say that peer solidarity is low, though it is extremely hard to give precise figures about frequency. Inmates have two terms that symbolize these disrupting activities. First of all, there is the more or less 'professional' informer, the *tyster*. He is usually an informer to the police. Rather wild tales are at times told about the rewards that such informers get. These tales appear to a large extent to be unrealistic. However, the important point is that informing of this type is considered to be based on rewards.

There is not much talk about 'professional' informers in the institution. But there is a lot of talk about the 'unprofessional informer', who informs from time to time and under certain conditions. He is known as the *maanser*.

Empirically, several different types of such informing may be found, and frequently they are combined. As a guard put it:

> Do you know that X escaped? I was going in yesterday to get a cup of coffee, and an inmate came over to me. He made some movements as if to imitate a [means of transport]. He said that now X is sitting on the –. They might for example come over and grasp for your keys, and when you tell him that he mustn't do that, the inmate says that many people have keys here, and mentions a name. They probably come to guards they like. If they don't like the guard, they don't say anything. But they often go to the doctor too, perhaps. Take Y, who was released a while ago: inmates here think he got out by informing on others … Often they give us information in order to scorn us; to show that we have been poor guards. They might think they get advantages. They don't get much, but sometimes we give them a little …

The excerpt indicates that the guard perceives several different relationships between informers and staff members. But it is extremely important that from the point of view of inmates, *informing is always viewed as based on a wish for rewards*. They are often uncertain as to how much is actually given.

Though informing certainly takes place, there seems to be an exaggerated fear of it. The exaggeration may partly be a consequence of the feeling of unpredictability relating to the distribution of important benefits and burdens: sudden changes in staff policy are often difficult to explain, and may in part be explained as a consequence of informing.

Exaggeration of the occurrence of informing is probably the root of the ignorance about who the informers are; an ignorance that seems to persist despite the extremely effective channels of communication among inmates (to be dealt with later). There is, in fact, not only ignorance about who are informers at any moment in time, but also about who may become informers in the future. This is reflected in the following excerpt from a conversation between two inmates:

> *Inmate 1*: If I were going to escape, I wouldn't tell it to anyone.
> *Inmate 2*: No, you can't say anything to anyone here, not even to your best friend.
> *Inmate 1*: Couldn't I have informed on you if I had wanted to? About things that are hidden and so on?

The widespread belief in the frequent occurrence of informing for rewards is taken by inmates (non-informing as well as informing) as a clear indication that private interests are not sacrificed for interests common to the rank as a whole.

(b) Fairness

Despite the fact that staff members may applaud and adhere to norms of loyalty in other social settings, such norms clearly negate many of the formal purposes and plans of staff members in the institution. In other words, they imply cultural dissensus between inmates and staff. We view institutionalized cultural dissensus as a necessary condition for peer solidarity […], and the many deviations from the norms of loyalty are particularly disruptive.

Yet, some other norms among inmates also have, if institutionalized, the function of establishing peer solidarity, though they do not so clearly imply cultural dissensus between the parties. They may be called 'supplementary norms', and they have solidarity as a more or less latent function.

First of all, mention must be made of a set of norms that is closely related to the norms of loyalty. The set in question stresses that inmates should be fair towards each other, in the sense that they should not abuse one another, steal from one another, etc. […]. Norms stressing loyalty and fairness may be said to be two subcategories of a more general category of norms. However, while the norms of loyalty cover the direct relationships between inmates and staff members, the norms that we have chosen to call the norms of fairness cover only relationships between inmates themselves. Yet, indirectly, these norms are important for staff-inmate relations: if they are broken, inmates are presented with a fresh indication of the pursuit of quite private interests rather than common ones.

The norms of fairness are perhaps most important in connection with property rights. Again, the 'small' things in life – plastic money, coffee, tobacco – are highly valued. In this connection, two particularly important ways of being unfair towards fellow-inmates, thus flouting the norms, should be mentioned.

First of all, a certain amount of stealing takes place.

> He is a bad fellow-inmate; a rotten fellow inmate … He steals from the others. X had ten crowns in real money in his wallet … and Y went in alone, stayed there a while and came out again … Later X was going to play cards for money, and then the money was gone … It's difficult

to complain about it, since human money is really not allowed in the institution.

Such occurrences, even if not frequent, loom large in the minds of inmates. In so far as stealing occurs, inmates gain the impression that private interests are being pursued.

Second, though gambling may be indulged in according to the inmate code, direct abuse of others is negatively evaluated. Yet such abuse certainly occurs.

Such occurrences are important, because the victim as well as bystanders feels the threat of standing alone, without support from the only category of persons from which they can expect support. According to inmates themselves, the loss of some material goods becomes a rather small problem compared with this threat. As one inmate expressed some of this:

> If he had taken something from someone outside, that's one thing. But to do it to one who's in [the same situation], and who doesn't have anything … I had asked him to be particularly careful with it … It was a gift [I had got]. The money, that's not the most important thing.

In more general terms, perhaps the presence of the swindler to a certain degree becomes a source of problems in the inmate world. The swindler as a type is relatively intelligent, suave, apparently nice, open, and friendly. These traits are necessary if he is to perform his criminal acts in a satisfactory way. The swindler is often a source of much genuine good humour. But still, from the point of view of other inmates, if the swindler is unfair towards others and hides his real intention, he may be unfair towards fellow-inmates as well. The possibility of unpredictable pursuit of private interests is again open.

In short then, the norms stressing loyalty and fairness are broken, indicating that private interests are often not sacrificed for common ones. Facing such threats, many inmates act as if they ask themselves, 'Is *anybody* here willing to sacrifice his private interests?' A negative answer to this question is further substantiated by some other features of the inmates' situation.

(c) Manhood

A third set of norms among inmates stresses that the inmate should be sexually completely normal and robust. Potency in its various forms is the best sign of normality and robustness. In this connection, the number of illegitimate children is at times jokingly viewed as a favourable criterion.

This set of norms clearly has a complex psychological background, which is only partly related to the problem of peer solidarity. However, in so far as the norms are flouted, it provides a dangerous threat to peer solidarity. It supports the impression that other rank members pursue private and dangerously deviant interests. This, interestingly enough, appears at times to be the case from the point of view of the sexually deviant as well as the normal, though our data on this point are by no means conclusive. And the norms appear to inmates to be flouted very frequently.

The fact that there are sexual deviants among inmates is well known. While this is the case in most institutions, the treatment-oriented institution is characterized by an over-representation of such criminals. The ensuing fear of homosexuality and related sexual deviations is so great that the category of inmates appears to the participants to be splintered into small segments pursuing quite personal and unacceptable interests while in the institution.

The actual number of manifest homosexual relationships is probably not very great in our institution, though it is difficult to get a close estimate. Typically, relationships are started by older, active homosexuals who have been in the institution for a while. Such homosexuals make initial contacts with newcomers by giving them small gifts and invitations for coffee. The initiator may finally find a companion, either a manifest homosexual or one who claims to go along for 'kicks' or some type of compensation. The following excerpts from interviews with the active and the passive partner in a relationship are indicative of some of the feelings and alleged motives involved:

> My only friend is X. Now he has been moved to another cell-block. He didn't want to himself, because he liked it where he was, but he was ordered to move. Our friendship was not tolerated. There is nothing unclean in our relationship, we talked that over very early … We find the positive values in each other, which make life worthwhile … I help him with the things I know better … We used to eat dinner together and then make a good cup of coffee afterwards.

> Yes, about my relationship to Y, I'm fed up with him … He wants me to feel sorry for him … he wants everyone to feel sorry for him. He gives gifts, as all those guys do … it's tobacco, coffee, and so on. And he makes dinner, and wants me to eat in his room. And then he says, 'I dreamt about you last night.' He is a fluteplayer – he wants … it that way.

But while manifest homosexual relationships are perhaps not extremely frequent, at least two factors make for the impression that the norms of manhood are frequently flouted. First, the active homosexuals have in their search contacted many other inmates, thus creating in the minds of these others a picture of a population marred by sexual deviation. Second, the constant presence of some such relationships, more or less free for all to see, is probably a permanent reminder of homosexual and other deviant tendencies in oneself. This holds even for criminals not incarcerated for such offences. In a closed institution for men, the self-perception of manhood is dangerously undermined by long abstinence from heterosexual relationships and association with women. This threat is made even more pronounced through the presence of actual homosexual relationships. The possibility of deviant sexual tendencies in oneself makes the inmate suspicious of similar tendencies in others, even if there are no observable indications of them. Thus, in its pure form, the surrounding world appears unpredictable with respect to sexual inclinations.

The importance of homosexuality and related types of sexual deviance may perhaps be said to be reflected in the number of names symbolizing its various forms. The 'sweeper' (*soper*) is the general name for the homosexual. Other terms describe more specific types of sexual crimes. Thus, 'sugar', is the man who prefers children. 'White sugar', the man who prefers little girls, is obviously less dangerous to his fellow inmates than the man with the opposite inclination, 'brown sugar'. These and other terms are used by quite a few inmates.

(d) Privacy

But are there no ways of remedying these deep cracks in peer solidarity?

As in other situations of conflict, the inmates as participants in one party to a conflict may actively try to make themselves and others overlook or forget the disruptive differences that exist between them, making common interests in relation to the adversary stand out more clearly.

In this connection, mention must be made of another set of norms stressing that certain parts of the life of inmates should not be argued about and inquired into by fellow-inmates. The clearest and most important example of this set of norms is the one stressing that you should not ask questions about the criminal background of fellow-inmates. In general, while questions about the man's role as inmate seem allowed, questions about intimate matters are frowned on. As one man expressed it:

> It's not considered good taste to ask what a man sits for. Only if you're old friends … [But] you can very well ask how long a man has been sitting and how long he's got left.

The importance of the norms banning intimate questions becomes clear when we remember that inmates are subjected to forced living with others and lack of privacy in many spheres of life. But the institutionalization of such norms may, under some conditions, also have the function of making the participants overlook as irrelevant at least some disruptive differences.

Unlike the norms stressing loyalty, fairness, and manhood, the norms of privacy are not frequently flouted. Inmates claim that they are infrequently asked and do not themselves ask questions about private matters. However, the fact that the norms are adhered to does not seem to aid peer solidarity. Some crucial conditions for their doing so are not present.

Though direct questions, etc. about criminal and other background characteristics are not frequently asked, inmates know with extremely great precision what crimes other inmates have committed as well as other background information about them. As one inmate expressed it:

> Often we know everything about a man before he arrives; how old he is, whether he has a wife and children, what he had done, that his wife wants to divorce him, and so on … There is an awful lot of lying here … and you have to go along and say 'yes' and 'no' and pretend that you believe it. X said to me: 'If I had done what Y has, I wouldn't agree

to castration, I would simply be sitting here.' But that's exactly why X is here for such a long time …

There appear to be several channels through which inmates get information about each other. Conscious leakage from staff members is only one of them. In addition, inmates have considerable contact with staff members, especially guards […], and may therefore easily get fragments of information from them that may later be assembled into a meaningful picture.

Information is also gained through inmates who come back from furloughs or who have been released for a while, or who are newcomers to the institution. These contacts with the outside give inmates information about the criminals who are coming and how released criminals behave. Information gained through these channels enables inmates to predict with astonishing accuracy, for example, when released inmates will return.

Further, a specific kind of 'intuition' should be mentioned as a possible 'process' through which information about others is gained. As an inmate expressed it:

Here we know everything that happens. It happened to me once when I was awaiting trial that the boys said to me that 'you'll be released tomorrow at noon'. Then they'd say they were just joking, but the next day, sure enough, I was released … I don't know why – we go into an office and hear a part of a telephone conversation, or –. It's as if we have a sixth sense. It's like animals when they're in danger.

Such references to 'intuition' or a 'sixth sense' may represent a way to prevent oneself from revealing sources of information. But in part, they seem to indicate an unusually high degree of willingness to draw conclusions from very little data. Prior extensive knowledge of the institution makes for a high degree of correctness in the predictions.

The information gained through these and other channels is spread accurately and swiftly through the institution. But it is characteristic that much of it does not reach the surface of direct face-to-face interaction. Although questions, particularly about criminal background, are not often asked directly, and correct information is often not given directly, there is an undercurrent of questions, answers, and information about fellow-inmates: A gets information about B through C and about C through B, B gets information about A through C and about C through A, and so on. We do not want to assert that this indirectness in spreading information is complete. For example, persons who have committed very 'normal' crimes, such as certain property crimes, may say so frankly, though even they are rarely asked directly. Yet, the indirectness is sufficiently great to warrant special attention.

[…]

In short, then, inmates are asked by their fellows to be loyal, fair, manly, and unquestioning. These norms are, of course, acceptable aspects of culture in many settings outside prison walls or fences. Outside, people feel that they should in many contexts be loyal towards each other, that they should be fair towards each other, that a man should be a man in a more restricted sense, and that one should not nose into other people's private lives. We suggest that the inmate has internalized these norms outside, and that he brings them with him when he comes into the correctional institution. But inside, the inmate is presented with a series of problems of living, including staff distribution of benefits and burdens. These problems, we suggest, constitute an unusual magnification of the problems of living that Norwegians meet in a variety of settings outside the institution. Therefore the code of norms, the 'raw material' for which is brought in from the outside, stands out in relief. And inside, some of the norms (those focusing on loyalty) negate many aspects of the formal programme of the institution and its staff. While the staff members, as Norwegian citizens, also normatively expect loyalty from their fellows in many settings, this is not what they expect normatively between inmates in the institutional setting, because it hinders their programme. In this sense we are presented with a cultural dissensus. […]

Staff distribution and what inmates experience as illegitimate patriarchalism constitute an important problem of life for many. If peer solidarity were established and maintained among inmates, it would in turn constitute an effective defence against the staff. For example, if a staff member then tried to reward some inmates and not others, as part of what he saw as a highly legitimate programme of individual treatment, this would be met by sanctions on the part of inmates: the inmates in question would, for example, sacrifice their rewards for the sake of their less lucky fellow-inmates. In effect, this would mean that the staff member could not expect to get his decisions executed and in turn that the inmates would feel that the illegitimate patriarchalism had been reduced; that staff power was less personal, more limited, and thereby more legitimate. In short, in the struggle over decision-making about rewards, punishments, and other benefits and burdens the inmates would make considerable headway: the staff member's ability to regulate through distribution such benefits and burdens would be greatly circumscribed, according to staff member and inmates alike.

It is important that the inmates are to some extent aware of this defensive function of solidarity. Some claim that if solidarity were established, 'things would be different'. We shall see later that this feeling by no means appears to hold throughout the inmate category. But in any case, things are not different; *peer solidarity is low.* Informing certainly takes place. To some degree unfairness and sexually deviant practices make for further disruption. The deviant back stage of the participants is free for all to see, making identification with one's fellows in terms of rank membership close to impossible.

[…]

From The Defences of the Weak: A Sociological Study of a Norwegian Correctional Institution *(London: Tavistock), 1965, pp. 124–34.*

Note

1. When reference is made below to 'common interests', we are primarily thinking of limitation of staff ability to manipulate benefits and burdens.

Reference

Sykes, Gresham M. and Messinger, Sheldon L., 'The Inmate Social System', *Theoretical Studies in Social Organization of the Prison*, Social Science Research Council, New York, 1960, pp. 5–19.

23. Mind games: where the action is in prisons

Kathleen McDermott and Roy D. King

Confinement Games

The walls of British prisons confine people in a world that is necessarily unreal. It is a world where the routine form of address from prisoners to staff is 'boss' – 'Can I have an application for change of labour, boss?' – for the staff control all, or most, of the formal avenues to power, privilege and possessions. But it is a world where the 'boss' is also required to discharge domestic responsibilities of feeding, clothing, supervising the spending of pocket money, and so on, normally associated with the (typically female) role of parenting young children. It is hardly surprising that both staff and prisoners – most of whom would probably wish to present themselves in a rather more macho image – find themselves involved in mind games that seek solutions to some of the dilemmas posed.

It is appropriate to start with one of the most basic prison rituals – going to the lavatory – for in some prisons, especially locals, this provides a mechanism through which everyone's stereotypes are first built up, then reinforced and finally confirmed.

It is an all too familiar occurrence that the bell rings on the fours landing, to be met by a shout from an officer on the ones 'stuff it up your arse'. More usually an officer is on the landing when the bell rings, but that does not mean that the prisoner will be allowed out of the cell to attend to his needs. Mike was just one of many prisoners who told us:

> There's one bucket for three men. We don't even get a bucket each. It's just possible to bring yourself to piss in the bucket – but anything else? – no way. But what do you do when they don't answer your bell? Sometimes I've had to wait an hour and a half to get a response. Some screws just don't bother. They expect us to live like animals, wallowing in our own filth. In the end you just do it and chuck it out the window. We used to wrap it in newspaper – now we use prison issue underpants.

From what Officer Atkins told us it is not difficult to see how such attitudes develop among the staff:

Up there (on the landings) you can go all day without speaking to anyone except cons. Even if there are staff on, you've heard everything that everyone else has to say. It's either the same old jokes or else you keep shut up. You'd like to read – and you do – but you can't get stuck into a good book because of all the bells going. You can read – but you end up saying 'I'll come as soon as I've finished reading this chapter'. Or 'I'll get your bell later'. Or just 'let him wait'. The less you do in this job the less you want to do, until, in the end, you don't want to go down that end of the landing even though it's your job, and that's *all* your job is.

But refusal to answer bells also comes about because staff begin to see prisoner requests as actually unreasonable, or even 'wind ups'. The request 'open up my cell, boss' may be met with 'you should go at the proper time' or 'you've only just been banged up – why didn't you go earlier?'. If you have answered six bells already, the seventh may be the one that exhausts your patience – and yesterday's experience all too easily feeds today's habit.

Not all staff react in this way, but so universal is the experience (virtually all prisoners have been three'd up at some time and virtually all staff have worked as landing officers) and so powerful is the imagery and the cultural support that there is near unanimity in the stereotyping: staff are callous zoo keepers, indifferent to, or enjoying, the indignities suffered by their charges; prisoners are no better than animals who don't deserve proper sanitation (or other facilities) which they would only abuse, because they already abuse those facilities which they have got. To be fair, most staff and most prisoners were quite prepared, in their direct dealings with us, to make exceptions to this judgement. But in doing so they explicitly acknowledged the stereotype as an important part of their experience. And their preparedness to admit exceptions to us was rarely exercised when in the company of their peers.

Throwing 'shit parcels' out of the window is, of course, partly functional relieving the necessity for those prisoners to spend time with the stench. But it is also a gesture of hatred, anger and contempt. Someone else has to clear it up. And using prison clothing as the wrapper brings the issue back to where it properly belongs – the prison authorities. This unwholesome version of 'pass the parcel' is resisted by the staff. It is not them who clear up the mess, though they have to organise other prisoners to do it each morning on what is often euphemistically called the 'Chief's party'. And in the end it is prisoners who suffer from the shortages in kit supply.

Nevertheless the message is got across – and occasionally with some drama. The ultimate degradation in this bizarre process occurs at slopping out. In prisons where there is reasonable access to the recesses through most of the day this is a far less repulsive business than in the crowded local prison. Staff and prisoners are quite skilled in avoidance rituals that minimise the possibility of friction – but the upturned bucket, depositing its contents over the head of the uncircumspect officer, is the final move in this particular game. In times of crisis human excreta can become a powerful weapon – as in the so called 'dirty protests'. In some U.S. prisons, during lock down situations, staff are issued with oilskins before they walk the range because of what can be thrown through the open grille work.

Association games

Pass the parcel is just one of the survival games, developed in close confinement under insanitary conditions. At the other extreme are survival games that take place in situations where prisoners are given greater physical and social space and which show both staff and prisoners in a different light.

Once prisoners spend time outside their cells and engage in a variety of activities their encounters with staff, with other prisoners, and with more or less arbitrary rules which govern their lives, increases. Leaving specifically security matters on one side, it would be fair to say that the further up the security scale one goes the more laid back staff become in their interaction with prisoners. They are less obtrusive, less hectoring, and more prepared to absorb abuse before they react. When they do react, the action is designed to 'cool out', to defuse, to deflect, rather than to confront. It is a game of *diplomacy*. After all, how do you order 100 men to stop watching television or to leave the football field and to return to their cells?

Developing inter-personal skills can be essential to staff survival on association – both to avoid an immediate assault in the heat of the moment, and in the longer term to avoid scores being settled in a future riot. But their use constitutes a delicate game, because often staff are trapped in a situation where they have to bear the brunt of prisoners' frustration but are powerless to relieve it. Sometimes inexperienced assistant governors (AGs), who insist on the authority of their office, or principal officers who have become distanced by promotion, have to be rescued by the skills of front line staff who 'know the prisoners' and 'how to handle them'. Jim, volatile, highly strung, but personable and well liked, was screaming at the wing AG who had just 'knocked back' his home leave application: 'if my mother dies while I should be out there, I'll hold you personally responsible. And when I get out I'll fucking kill you.' As the AG retreated behind his role so Jim became more angry. It was a basic grade officer who knew Jim and Jim's sense of irony, who said 'come on Jim, you know she's as tough as old boots. She's not going to die. She's had you on a string all this time, she's not going to let you off now.' Eventually Jim smiles, and a difficult situation is retrieved.

Prisoners usually know when they are being 'handled' in this way, and, on reflection, are usually grateful for it. But there are other situations where staff skills are used to fob them off, and where the technique is acknowledged though hardly welcomed. In the local prison it is easy for staff to say no, because the answer to nearly all questions is no. It is not so easy in the associated regime of training prisons, where staff develop an acute perception that 'a refusal often offends'. In this setting the aim of staff is to hold the line. Some staff develop a capacity to resist the pressures themselves. Thus one senior officer told us: 'I tell them you play ball with me and I'll play ball with you. Of course, I don't tell them it's my ball and they can only play when I want them to.'

For most staff, however, the art is not to say no oneself, but to get someone else to say no. In this way the line is held without landing staff carrying the can. This is what some staff refer to as the *sloping shoulders game*. The landing officer refers the matter to the senior officer, the senior officer to the principal officer, and the principal officer to the AG. This can be a counter productive process because the further away from the landings the decision is made, the more likely are management to say yes. Then landing staff may be left with a situation in which they have simply invited more requests. The sloping shoulders game is best played by staff when they can safely refer the matter to someone whom they know is bound to say no. Thus any officer knows that the answer to the request 'Can I take my guitar to the workshop today?' is 'no'. But by saying 'well, I'll just see about that' and then calling the workshop, where the instructor immediately says no, the consequences of the refusal are passed elsewhere. Not surprisingly this does not bring pleasure to workshop instructors who may feel ill-used.

Not all prison staff develop these techniques and skills. As Officer Browne says:

> This job is all about getting through the day, getting home safe, and keeping the place locked up … if you can't hack it on the landings, and you want to be 'excused cons' you go for promotion. If you have a relationship with the cons you probably don't want promotion anyway. But many screws can't be bothered and you just become a machine doing it for the money.

For staff the pressures of working on the landings can be considerable, and for those who do not develop good survival skills the temptation to find a staff detail whereby they are 'excused cons' may be overwhelming. Even those who do develop good techniques from time to time subscribe to the philosophy that 'happiness is door shaped'.[1]

The strains of association tell on prisoners as well as staff. Ever since Sykes (1958) it has been a familiar adage that one of the pains of imprisonment is being with other prisoners. The greater the levels of association, and the more laid back the staff in supervising, the more powerful those pains may be. In extreme cases 'no go' areas develop whereby staff, for example, do not supervise the TV rooms from inside, or do not move out of the office on the 4's landing, or do not patrol the recesses, thereby tacitly approving sexual exploitation, wheeling & dealing, and strong-arming of various kinds. When a new principal officer told his senior officer in the wing office 'Right I'm going to the 4's, and I'm going to check the recesses, then I'm going to do that on all the landings, and then I'm going in to the TV room and change the channel', the senior officer replied 'yes sir, right sir, it's your wing sir'. They were, of course, at one level, joking. But they were also acknowledging that this would be remarkable behaviour. And when prisoners told us 'you can't take a shit or a shower in comfort here' they were referring to the anxiety that prisoners had for their own safety whenever they go to the recess. Some prisoners, in these circumstances, prefer to do their time behind their doors. It is well known that certain classes of prisoner, particularly nonces, grasses, and debtors may choose, or be forced by other prisoners, to spend all or parts of their sentences on Rule 43 – in segregation for their own protection. Beatings are not uncommon, 'executions' are certainly not unknown.

There are many ways for prisoners to make out in their contacts with other prisoners – but if you are not to be bought and sold and if you are not to seek the protection of staff one way is playing *charades*. An example of this was provided by Dave Butcher. A repeated sex offender himself, he was anxious to avoid the label of 'nonce'. He was ruefully aware of their place in prison culture: 'What would we do without nonces? Someone has to take the blame for everything.' A prisoner had once called him a nonce in the workshops, testing him out for the label – and though very slightly built he had challenged his accuser to a fight in the showers. He knew he would lose, and after taking a few punches he went down. But he earned respect for the challenge and he certainly avoided the far worse beating that might have come from three or four prisoners setting out to get him in his cell, or in the recess.

But long term survival is in the head as much as in the body and depends on one's capacity to act a role. Reasoning correctly that what prisoners could do to him was much worse than what staff could do to him, Dave turned the laid back stance of staff and their preparedness to absorb abuse to his own self-protective advantage. Choosing his moment, in a very public situation, he would shout threats at the staff. Mostly nothing would result, though the worst might be a few days in the block. Far more important was the impression left with prisoners that one did not mess with someone able to take the staff on in that way.

Some prisoners, especially 'domestic' life sentence prisoners, however, are, or at least feel themselves to be, even more in the power of staff than of prisoners and this dramatically affects the way in which they behave on association. Lifers are continually under review as to how they are coping, their actions and reactions to the unreal world they inhabit being used as a gauge to judge their eventual fitness for release. At no time is a release date actually certain, because there is always the possibility that a particularly bad incident in the prison could cause the Parole Board to reconsider, just as there is always the possibility that post release behaviour, which yet falls short of a criminal offence, could result in a recall to prison. In a world of such uncertainty, life sentence prisoners feel themselves to be peculiarly dependent upon the staff and on getting good reports. When faced with the inevitable wind ups that constitute doing time the lifer cannot afford the luxury of ill-considered responses. Indeed he knows that whatever he does it will be open to interpretation. If he explodes, his report may say that he cannot cope with frustration. Indeed worse may happen – he may be transferred back from open to closed conditions or from a training to a local prison to cool off before he is 'tested out' again. If he keeps his own counsel, the reports may say that he is withdrawn and cannot come to terms with his offence. Finding an acceptable public face brings many lifers subserviently close to staff. Not surprisingly, lifers like to distance themselves from the games played by short term prisoners. And not surprisingly, either, staff like having lifers around as a stabilising influence.

Security games (hide and seek)

Prisons are about keeping prisoners in custody. They are also about keeping undesirable persons and things outside, at least in part the better to maintain control inside. Security games are played within an elaborate framework of bureaucratically devised rules which govern the frequency of inspections of 'locks, bolts and bars', of body and cell searchers, of cell changes for high risk prisoners, and so on. Since staff (and prisoners) know that these rules are not always rigorously applied, and that there are other, more effective, ways of achieving these ends but which are not countenanced by the rules, they presume that the real function of the rules is to get officials off the hook while holding staff to account should things go wrong (cf. Irwin, 1980). In the circumstances staff settle for limited objectives and prisoners accept that the price of reaching a reasonable accommodation most of the time is that occasionally they are caught 'bang to rights' and take a fall. In addition to the routine procedures all staff are expected to submit security information reports (SIRs) to enable the security team to keep a finger on the pulse.

Part of the security game involves the process of covert intelligence gathering, with all the ploys and double ploys that have become associated with the world of espionage.[2] Informers are cultivated by the security team, and paid 1/2 oz of tobacco out of the 'Chief's slush fund'. Prisoners grass each other up by posting notes in the box at the time they post their regular mail. Such information is rarely free: sometimes the intention is simply to gain a good report, or to express fear or repulsion at what is being planned; sometimes it offers a convenient way to use the system to settle a score with another prisoner; occasionally it can be an elaborate attempt to cover something even more threatening by diverting attention elsewhere. But informers can be discarded by staff, with all the consequences that entails, as well as cultivated, so it can be a dangerous game.

As we review our fieldnotes we have more data on security related incidents than any other single matter. Space dictates that we limit ourselves to a single illustration, and we have chosen the cell search, or *hunt the thimble*, because it touches on a wide range of issues.

Cell searching is a delicate matter. It could not be otherwise. As far as prisoners are concerned the cell is home. Where your home is, and if necessary with whom you share it, are at least as important inside prison as outside. In training prisons, where the overcrowding and squalor of the local is no longer the over-riding concern, attention turns to questions of furnishing, decorations and possessions. Within the limits of prison supplied furniture, and what is permitted on the privileges list, a landing of otherwise identical cells can become surprisingly individualised. Hobbies, books, papers, family photographs or pin ups, may be stored carefully away, piled in corners, or extravagantly displayed. All prisoners, but especially long-term prisoners who may have accumulated more goods and invested more effort in their cells, feel more or less protective about 'their' space, and see staff presence, for whatever purpose as an unwarrantable invasion of privacy. But the ultimate contempt is for searching officers who, in a classic of role reversal, are described as 'burglars'.

Searching officers, charged with implementing bureaucratic rules as to the frequency of cell searches, the nature and number of permitted items, the proper disposition of cell furniture in relation to the cell walls and windows, and so on, are acutely aware of their image. It would be surprising if there were not some process of accommodation to make an otherwise impossible job more tolerable. In fact, there is a tacit understanding, among staff and prisoners, that although the rules exist as a backdrop they will not normally be enforced to the letter. As one searcher told us:

> Normally we let them keep bits and bobs they are not supposed to have … we know what is going on but it is not possible to operate on the basis that you take everything. I know they hate us – we are the most hated men in any prison – but we try to be fair. So long as nothing is too much out of order then we don't mind too much.

In practice, other things being equal, this means that for routine cell searches (as distinct from those triggered by tip-offs or SIRs) attention is focused only on 'heavy items' – money, drugs, weapons, escape equipment. Prisoners are either allowed to retain things they have borrowed or else these are returned to their rightful owners; some obviously pilfered items might be confiscated but without further action; and for most other extras a blind eye is turned. In many cases the act of searching may be no more than a reassertion by staff that the cell is not private territory.

[…]

From 'Mind games: where the action is in prisons', British Journal of Criminology, 1988, Vol. 28, no. 3, pp. 357–77.

Notes

1. Throughout our fieldwork we worked long hours, as did prison staff at that time. Our fieldwork took place immediately before the implementation of Fresh Start which reduced the dependence on overtime working. One of the most unnerving moments of our research was when *we* found ourselves looking at our watches wondering when it would be time for lock-up, so that we could go 'off-duty'.
2. Goffman has intriguingly applied the game analysis to the world of spying in his *Strategic Interaction*, (1970).

References

Goffman, E. (1970) *Strategic Interaction*. Oxford: Basil Blackwell.
Irwin, J. (1980) *Prisons in Turmoil*. Boston: Little Brown and Co.
Sykes, G. (1958) *The Society of Captives: A Study of a Maximum Security Prison*. Princeton: Princeton University Press.

24. Doing prison work: the public and private lives of prison officers

Elaine Crawley

What do prison officers do?

There is much more to being a prison officer than simply being there. In addition to their primarily custodial tasks – such as locking up and unlocking prisoners, providing meals, checking locks, bolts and bars, maintaining discipline, regulating visits and the flow of prisoners to and from work – the modern prison officer is also expected to change prisoners' behaviours and outlooks and to provide him or her with care. Prison work also demands a range of interactional skills, including an ability to communicate, a willingness to negotiate and to engage in what Hay and Sparks (1991) call a 'creative use of the self'.

The moment that offenders step within the prison walls they will find that certain roles are lost to them by virtue of the barrier that separates them from the outside world (Goffman 1968: 24). Moreover, as Goffman notes, the process of entrance into the prison also typically brings with it other kinds of loss and mortification: finger-printing, the removal of personal effects, the issuing of prison clothing, the assigning of a number and a cell allows the prisoner 'to be shaped and coded into an object that can be fed into the administrative machinery of the establishment, to be worked on smoothly by routine operations' (*ibid.*: 26). Stripped of his identity kit, the prisoner will find it difficult to present his usual image of himself to others. Prison officers, however, must get to know these prisoners *as individuals*; they must learn their foibles, personal circumstances, dispositions and ability to deal with incarceration. This knowledge (the latter in particular) is necessary for the smooth running of the regime, for security purposes and for the safety of staff and other prisoners. In order to carry out their job effectively, prison officers should be able to assess, with a fair degree of accuracy, the prisoners in their charge.

Most of my interviewees were keen to emphasise the numerous (and varied) roles a prison officer might be required to perform on any one day. Their list included 'locus parentis' (parent role), mentor (role model), counsellor (in the event of bad news), teacher, social worker, comedian (every officer noted the importance of having a sense of humour), psychologist (recognising when a prisoner is not acting like his or her usual self), filing clerk, probation officer (officers are now involved in through-care), fire-fighter (some staff are trained to use breathing apparatus and fire-fighting equipment), tourist guide (giving guided tours of the prison to outside visitors), stock controller (ensuring an adequate supply of toilet rolls, plastic cutlery, laundry and so on), security guard and, finally, police officer (dealing with disciplinary actions). As we shall see, however, not all officers perform all these roles. On the contrary, some officers are prepared to do little more than the last three. I was, none the less, struck by the range of tasks that prison officers are *asked* to perform, and the sheer volume and variety of prisoner inquiries and requests. Some of these requests are extraordinary – or at least they are extraordinary given the context in which they are made – and they are illustrative both of the needs of individual prisoners and of the varied nature of the prison officer role. For example, one evening in the Vulnerable Prisoner (VP) Unit at HMP Wymott, a nurse from the hospital approached a senior officer to discuss a prisoner's request for a bra. It transpired that the prisoner, a man in his early thirties, was in the process of undergoing sex-change hormone treatment (which had begun prior to his sentence) and had complained to officers that he had 'leaking breasts'. In addition, the prisoner had requested that the upper part of his body should be searched by female officers and the bottom half by male officers (he had been denied permission to have his male genitalia removed surgically whilst still a prisoner). Although there was some incredulity about this state of affairs and, it must be said, a fair amount of ribaldry, on the whole the uniformed staff (the majority of whom were men) seemed to take this situation in their stride. Generally, however, much of the prison officer's day is taken up with more mundane matters.

[…].

Prison officers have a tendency to speak of prisoners (and prisons) in terms of certain recurrent metaphors. The metaphors that officers use for prisoners are revealing of the contempt in which they are held i.e., 'vultures'; 'bodies'; 'animals' (as in 'feeding the animals'); 'scum'; 'toe-rags'; 'inadequates'; 'children'; 'dangerous children'. Many officers also characterise prisoners in stereotypical vein; prisoners from Liverpool, for example, are invariably seen as 'gobby (mouthy) Scousers' and perceived as the worst-behaved prisoners while black prisoners are often seen as 'quick to play the race card'. All this seems to suggest that prison officers have a very 'fixed' view of prisoners; in reality, however, relationships between officers and prisoners are much more complex. To take such (metaphorical) descriptions at their face value is to adopt a 'distal'[1] analysis of prison life. As we shall see, some officers do admit to liking certain prisoners and to being sympathetic to their feelings of frustration, anxiety and regret. Likewise some prisoners admit to liking certain officers, and understand that they are 'only doing their job' (numerous prisoners, all prisons pers. comms.). In all the prisons in this study there was some degree of friendly rapport between staff and prisoners (although the degree of rapport differed markedly across prisons and between wings). At Lancaster Farms, Garth and Wymott, some officers reported that their relationships with certain prisoners were closer than they ever imagined could be the case when they first started working in prisons. Indeed, one or two of these officers admitted that with certain prisoners they were 'almost friends' (see below). This should not, perhaps, strike us as surprising, given that many officers and prisoners have similar socio-economic backgrounds and share similar interests and experiences.

Generally speaking, whether an officer can 'identify with' a prisoner (in terms of sharing interests and values) depends, in part, on the kind of prison in which the officer works, and the age and background of the prisoner. Identification depends to a lesser extent on the nature of the prisoner's offence. That is not to say, however, that a prisoner's offence has no bearing on the relationship; while many officers are willing to maintain a low level of social distance with prisoners who have committed (what officers perceive to be) 'normal' crimes – theft, forgery, burglary, minor assault and so on – they often maintain a high social distance with those who have committed certain offences (particularly sexual offences against children), particularly those who then complain about prison life: 'you get the ones that have booted somebody and put him in a wheelchair, and then they're moaning if their chips are cold. It really pisses me off that does' (male officer, Garth).

Adults and young offenders

There is a marked difference between the ways that officers speak about adult prisoners and the ways they speak about young offenders. While adult prisoners are generally seen as wanting little to do with uniformed staff except with regard to prison-related issues', young offenders are often seen as 'needy' – as 'craving contact with staff':

> Working with YOs is a different ballgame altogether from working with adults. Adults generally get on with it, and then occasionally they blow – and then boy do they blow. But YOs, they don't *think*; they need to keep asking staff questions all the time, and they're always pitching for a quick fight – then it's all over Also, staff have to physically run round after YOs a lot more, so they're more tiring in that sense. (Senior officer, Lancaster Farms)

Working with young offenders can also be emotionally demanding: 'In an adult situation, threats have to be taken much more seriously. YOs on the other hand blow hot and cold all the time; they're up and down all the time and we go up and down with them' (officer, Lancaster Farms).

It was clear from my conversations with prison officers and from their written reports on individual prisoners that imprisonment can be particularly frightening, lonely and stressful for young offenders. Officers told me that many of the young men imprisoned at Lancaster Farms, Portland and Stoke Heath were often tearful and anxious as well as aggressive; on every wing, observation books were replete with comments about the distressed state of so-and-so, and on numerous pages staff had pinned notes from prisoners threatening self-harm or informing staff of threats they had received from other prisoners. Some young prisoners barely cope with imprisonment; as this officer observed: 'some of them cry on coming out of their cells in a morning until they are locked up in the evening. It's hard to know what to do about it really' (officer, Lancaster Farms).

Comments such as this highlight the fact that these prisoners are *children*. Officers' reflections on the day-to-day behaviour of prisoners barely into their teens make this glaringly apparent. Elaborating on his remark that the prisoners at Portland 'seem to be getting younger these days', an officer on night duty commented: 'I get a lot of little squirts in here now. At night, you can hear 'em downstairs. They're like a lot of little budgies fluttering about.'

The immaturity of many young prisoners is reflected in this officer's subsequent description of their behaviour at night; during one of his patrols of the wing, he had had to censure, in something of the style of a boarding school house master, two young men who were having a pillow fight: 'There they were whacking each other with pillows. One of the 'em said "He's messed my bed up Sir". I said to 'im "Well make it again and get back into it!"'

There is general agreement amongst officers that young offenders are noisier and more boisterous than adult prisoners, even at night when they are locked up. Throughout the evening, especially on long summer evenings, the grounds of each of the young offender institutions in this study resounded with the noise of prisoners calling to each other from cell windows. Some of it is general banter but much of it is offensive and abusive; there is bullying of other inmates and encouragement of others to bully. Even at Lancaster Farms, where officers made great efforts to stamp out bullying, I was told that prisoners regularly force weaker prisoners to sing nursery rhymes out of cell windows, and that those who refuse to do so are likely to be punished, i.e. assaulted later. During association, or on the way to gym and/or work, young offenders routinely shout obscene comments about other offenders' families and make arrangements as to who will 'get it' next. These were alien activities to officers used to working with adults. As this senior officer working at Lancaster Farms put it:

> YOs are a lot noisier and more hassle, especially at night. At Long Lartin, you could patrol around at night and its lovely and peaceful. Here it's like a rough blooming council estate! [At Long Lartin] You might get a buzz of conversation if you're lucky, early on, but *here*…
> […]

Resentment of prisoners' rights

Amongst uniformed prison staff, questions about just desert and legitimate expectations are to the fore. That prisoners 'have too many rights' – indeed 'more rights than staff' – and 'get too much' (most officers hold fast to the principle of 'less eligibility'[2]) was a familiar refrain amongst officers working in every prison in this study. In terms of the former, officers' claims that

management 'cares more about prisoners than they do staff' was well
rehearsed; in terms of the latter, a significant proportion of uniformed staff
were of the view that prisoners were being 'pandered to' whereas officers
have to make do with what they are given. Food is a particular focus of
attention in the discussion of prisoners' rights. That prisoners are allowed a
choice of menu is a particular irritation for many officers. Take, for example,
this remark from an officer who had recently returned from control and
restraint[3] training: 'It's gone ridiculous now…We went on a C&R Advanced
and we just had a cold packed lunch. You had no choice of meals. *Inmates*
get one though!' (Senior officer, Moorland). Similarly, this time from a senior
officer at Lancaster Farms: 'Prisoners should only get two choices – take it
or leave it!'

Most officers who hold such views believe that the general public shares
their sentiments:

> The prisoners here have got more rights than I have. They've got
> entitlements for everything…In my opinion you've got a prison system
> that doesn't reflect the views of the majority; they reflect the views of do-
> gooders. Prison Reform Trust, Howard League and so on – pro-criminal
> groups…Why *should* they have rights? They should have *privileges*, and
> they should *earn* them. (Senior officer, Lancaster Farms)

Such resentments are part of the more general and long-standing resentment,
on the part of many officers, that prisoners are viewed more favourably than
they are, not only by prison reformers and the courts but also by their own
managers. Whether or not the latter is the case is, in a sense irrelevant; what
is important is that most officers *believe* it to be the case (for a discussion of
this in the American context, see, for example, Dilulio 1987). In short, what
is important is how the officer (as social actor) defines the situation; as the
American sociologist W.I. Thomas observes, 'if men define situations as real,
they are real in their consequences'.

Generally speaking, officers feel that most prisoners do not appreciate their
efforts; on the contrary, there is a common perception that any kindness they
show is 'mistaken for weakness'. Officers may attempt to protect themselves
by deliberately increasing social distance:

> I came into this job thinking of prison officers as rough, strict and
> treating everyone like dirt. I thought I'd be the one to treat prisoners
> well. But it didn't work out like that. They just thought I was soft. The
> only thing they responded to was [my] being hard. I was as cynical as
> the rest of them within twelve months.

Those who do make efforts for prisoners are often disappointed when
prisoners let them down. One officer, for example, reported that he had
spent a great of time trying to persuade a local builder to employ a young
offender who was due for release. He was eventually successful and the
prisoner accepted the job but on the first day failed to turn up. Unfortunately

(but perhaps unsurprisingly) such disappointments foster further cynicism amongst officers, along the lines of 'I won't bother in future'.

Getting the staff–prisoner relationship 'right'

[...]

How officers interact with prisoners is dependent on a range of situational and social factors, including the type of prison in which these interactions take place, the category and type of inmate (sex offender, lifer or whatever), staffs' prior work experiences and the occupational cultures of particular prisons, to which every officer is expected to subscribe. For some officers, getting staff–inmate relationships 'right' means helping and supporting inmates (Rutherford's 1993 Credo Three) while for others it means keeping a distance between 'us and them', either for reasons of efficiency (Credo Two) or to express a view that prison is for the punitive degradation of offenders (Credo One). In the prison setting, working credos dictate both the quality of the staff–inmate relationship and the approach that officers take to the job itself:

> A lot of people come into the job and they've got this view of prisoners, and it doesn't help…Some of them see inmates as the lowest of the low – as the scum of the earth. But you can't tar them all with the same brush…Some of them *are* very dangerous people, but some of them are okay. You try and do what you can for them. (Senior officer, Garth)

Drawing the 'line': friendly but not friends

Virtually all the officers in this study referred to the 'line' that must exist between officers and prisoners, but there was a great deal of discrepancy about where that line should be drawn, even between officers working in the same prison. For example, according to one male officer working at Garth: 'He's a prisoner and I'm a screw. End of story.' In contrast, another observed: 'You can get to know them better than your family. I know it sounds stupid but…' Numerous officers claimed that their relationships with inmates *were* friendly, and that they were glad of this. They were equally keen to stress, however, that this did not mean that officers and inmates were *friends*; on the contrary they made a sharp distinction between these two modes of emotional engagement and stressed the inappropriateness (and potential dangers to security) of the latter relationship. Being friendly with inmates assists in day-to-day order maintenance; it 'oils the wheels' of the system. Being friends, on the other hand, suggests equality of status between two individuals and a state of mutual obligation; in the prison setting, where power and authority are supposed to lie with the staff, officers must 'draw the line' at becoming too close to individual prisoners in case mutual obligation threatens both their authority and the security of the prison. Indeed, one of the central criticisms that male officers make of women working in men's prisons is their tendency to become intimate with the prisoners (that female officers 'get off with the cons' was a commonly made remark). The 'trick' was to develop a relationship whereby staff and inmates could recognise each other's predicament and 'rub along' on a day-to-day basis with the minimum of friction.

While it was a common refrain amongst officers that 'you can be friendly but you can't be friends' since to become friends with a prisoner is to 'leave yourself wide open to all sorts of things', several officers admitted that they *were* 'almost like friends' with prisoners or that they would have been friends had they met in different circumstances. As this (relatively young) senior officer reflected:

> I've known inmates that, if this hadn't been a prison, me and him would have been good friends. [Talking about a lifer that he had got to know, he added] We had a lot in common. He was the same age as me, he had the same interests, we got on really well...Yeah, you could say firm friends.

With certain prisoners and in certain circumstances, officers found that the placing of the 'line' was especially problematic, not least because they have to rely on the co-operation of inmates on a day-to-day basis. For example, 'trusty' or 'red band' prisoners given the job of cleaner tend to get numerous 'perks', such as extra association and extra food as informal 'payment' for doing certain helpful tasks. Getting these perks, however, can lull these prisoners into thinking that they have a different sort of relationship with staff than other prisoners do. While officers are often prepared to cajole trusted prisoners, they are unwilling for the line to be moved too far:

> Sometimes they have to be cajoled a bit...given the benefit of the doubt. For example, if they are late out of bed in the morning, you'll just say come on, shake a leg but you won't put them on report or anything like that. But then sometimes you'll go in and they'll be just lying in bed with their arms folded behind their head and treating you like a mate – *that's* when you've got to draw the line 'cos they're getting too familiar. (Senior officer, Lancaster Farms)

Power in prisons; negotiation and coercion

Most prison officers (particularly those working with long-termers) concede that control – and hence order – is achieved most successfully through positive staff–prisoner relationships. Not all staff are happy with this state of affairs, however; as I stated earlier, some officers do not desire a positive relationship and would prefer it if prisoners simply spent more time 'behind their doors'. In all the prisons in this study, a significant number of staff were of the view that order in their own establishment was being achieved only because management were 'appeasing' (or 'pandering to') prisoners. [...] It can be noted, however, that what counts as 'appeasement' for one officer is perfectly reasonable negotiation for another.

Who holds the power? Negotiation and appeasement

The question of where power resides, then, is one of perennial concern to prison officers. Some officers felt that in the prisons in which they are working, or in which they had worked in the past, 'the balance of power has tipped the wrong way'. Dispersal and high-security training prisons were a popular target in this respect:

> It's all a balance [between keeping control through rules and encouraging the co-operation of inmates]; it's just that at long term prisons, the balance is very much in favour of the prisoner. The management will give in to the prisoners at every conceivable opportunity, because in their eyes, that is the best way of keeping things quiet. In the middle of it, you've got, normally, totally demoralised staff, because the criminal is treated as king. (Senior officer, Lancaster Farms)

The belief that the 'criminal is king' in such prisons is held by many prison officers, particularly those with experience of working in regimes that are necessarily more relaxed. Many officers feel that a liberal regime is more difficult to work in for two main reasons. First, officers in long-term prisons have much more *sustained* contact with prisoners (prisoners at Garth in particular spent a great deal of time out of cell). Secondly, long-term prisoners tend to be much more informal, and *more familiar with*, uniformed staff than are prisoners in other regimes. During my period of fieldwork at Garth, there was some debate amongst staff about whether the prison was controlled by staff or by prisoners. One morning, as I sat talking to a group of staff on one of the wings, an officer who had recently transferred from a dispersal remarked that his colleagues' claim to be 'in control' was mistaken, and that in his view the low level of confrontations between themselves and prisoners was due more to their lack of awareness of the true extent of rule-breaking than to their being in control. In short he felt that his new colleagues were being 'conned'. He went on to argue that if they *were* more aware of the extent of prisoners' rule-breaking there would be a higher level of staff–prisoner confrontation at Garth. The officers vigorously disagreed with this officer's assessment, and a (rather heated) discussion ensued. The new officer eventually conceded that he might be mistaken – that his definition of the situation might stem from 'dispersal paranoia' and his anxieties from Garth's combination of relatively relaxed regime, low staffing levels (relative to a dispersal) and high proportion of newly recruited staff. In addition, the officer claimed to have heard numerous horror stories (some true, some less so) still circulating about Garth. Up until fairly recently Garth had a reputation across the service as being a confrontational prison, where assaults on staff were common and staff morale, in consequence, was low. The officer remained concerned about Garth staff's reputation for 'wanting to get on with everybody' just to avoid trouble.

Working with long-term prisoners does place different demands on prison officers. On the whole (there were a few exceptions) Garth's uniformed staff were relatively relaxed, informal and friendly to prisoners (as the

Chief Inspector of Prisons (HMCIP 1997) put it, they have 'a light and easy manner'). Indeed, they made particular efforts to maintain a relaxed regime because they realised that the prison was also home to the men serving their sentences there: 'A lot of these that are here, it's like ten years, fifteen, lifers...It's like livin' with 'em really. You've got to keep, er, some sort of decent atmosphere going.'

In common with staff working in many other long-term regimes, Garth officers were much less officious, less provocative and more accommodating than many of the officers working in the young offender institutions. A paragraph from fieldnotes I made at Garth serves to illustrate this:

> At one point, there was play-fighting between some of the officers (basic and senior grade) and a couple of inmates in the wing office. They were throwing a board rubber at each other. The senior officer snatched an empty plastic bottle from one of the inmates and stamped on it. It made a hell of a bang when the top blew off! After a bit of a scuffle, the same inmate pulled the senior officer's tie off (they are the clip-on type) and pretended to bash him over the knees with a long perspex ruler he'd found on the desk. After a few minutes, the officers looked like they'd had enough and needed to 'pull back' a bit. The senior officer started talking to the other officers about various tasks that needed doing and the inmates, having got the message that the time for horseplay was over, wandered out of the office.

The 'good' officer

For some officers, the above scenario would have been unthinkable since the 'good' officer never lets the prisoner up close. When asked what skills they thought a 'good'[4] officer needs, officers listed, in no particular order, 1) confidence; 2) the powers of persuasion (having the ability to sell sand to an Arab is how one officer described herself); 3) calmness (interestingly, however, one officer commented that being *too* calm can actually provoke prisoners – he was thinking specifically of those officers who stare calmly ahead while reciting the rules); 4) being a good team-player (officers quickly get to know the officers who are afraid of confrontations and who cannot be relied upon when 'trouble' arises); 5) being a good communicator (being prepared to talk to prisoners and to explain things); 6) being assertive when necessary (and recognising when it *is* necessary); 7) being a good listener – 'You've got to be like a sponge really'; 8) being mentally tough (as opposed to being physically tough. An officer who is 'mentally weak' was regarded as being vulnerable to the pressures of both prisoners and fellow officers); 9) having patience; 10) being fair (most officers said that it is important to be fair in dealings with prisoners); 11) liking people; 12), having 'common sense'; and 13) having a sense of humour (the latter two skills were perceived as vital by virtually every officer in this study).

The personal qualities and skills of uniformed staff do, of course, impact upon the nature of staff–prisoner relations. Numerous officers commented on the need to strike a balance between friendliness and inflexibility; as one senior officer working at Wymott reflected:

> You have to be approachable, but it doesn't do to be too familiar. On the other hand, it does not do to be constantly nicking, or putting on a basic regime, inadequate or awkward inmates. [You have to] nurture him, show him the way; you have to be able to lead the horse to water and make him drink. This takes skill.

Prison officers' views on what makes a good officer differ markedly, even within the same prison. Compare these responses from two male officers working at HMYOI Portland:

> You've got to have good ears for a start, and be able to listen to a lad. And you've got to be fair, and if you promise to do something, you've got to get back to them. Sometimes they'll ask me to spell something – well I might not be able to spell it, but I'll go and get a dictionary …

In contrast: 'I think one of the best skills you can have is being able to look an inmate in the eye and say No.'

In the eyes of some officers, then, a 'good' officer is one who sees the prison world in purely 'black and white' terms and who maintains order through sticking to the rules. No *means* No, rules are there to be obeyed and the 'line' between 'Them and Us' is sharply drawn at a point which demands little prisoner–staff interaction and hence rarely entails negotiation. In the eyes of others, 'good' officers are those who are flexible and who apply the rules appropriately and at their own discretion. Retaining credibility in the eyes of prisoners involves being seen as someone who operates in a fair and professional[5] manner; who recognises prisoners' pains and their lack of autonomy to ameliorate them. There were difficulties, however, associated with being seen as the officer most likely to help prisoners:

> One of the main rules is if an inmate asks you to do something, you sort it. 'Cos if you don't, there's your credibility gone. They'll say [to other inmates] 'Don't go to him he's fucking useless!' But it can go the other way as well; they'll only come to *you* and then you've got the fly-round-the-jam pot syndrome. (Male officer, Garth)

Being a good communicator was seen by many as crucially important for conflict prevention and reduction. According to this ex-dispersal officer: 'I've never been assaulted, even though I've dealt with big guys with fighting backgrounds. Your ability to survive is your ability to talk to inmates. It's all about communication.'

Interestingly, the vast majority of my interviewees were of the view that the skills of social interaction – being 'good with people' – are skills that cannot be learnt simply through a training course. On the contrary, they argued that being able to get on with people is not a learnable skill. This is one such comment:

[Can officers be trained in getting on with people, do you think?] The ability to get on with people is something that is natural. I would say that would be down to the person's *personality*. It's a difficult question is that. I would say, I would say it would be very hard to train somebody like that. (Male officer, Lancaster Farms)

Similarly, when I asked a principal officer (YOI) what, in his view, makes for a professional prison officer, he replied: 'The ability to relate to, and deal with difficult, truculent people. This can only be gained by experience of life and by working with prisoners. It cannot be taught.'

Negotiation is something that does not come easily to some prison officers. These officers, many of whom were recruited from the military, believe that *dictation* is more appropriate to the prison officer role. In contrast, some officers are willing to negotiate even with very young prisoners, and on significant issues such as wing transfers. Here is an extract from my fieldnotes (Lancaster Farms) to illustrate the point:

A female senior officer has just been asked if she will swap one of her prisoners with one from a different wing. After studying the roll board for a few minutes, she selected a prisoner's name and told another officer to instruct him to pack his things. A few minutes later the prisoner came to see her in the office, pleading to stay on the wing on the ground that he had a good cleaning job which he would lose if transferred. The inmate begged and pleaded – he promised 'to be good and to be a good cleaner – only please can I stay on this wing Miss?' The interaction between this officer and this young prisoner was fascinating: she eventually said 'Alright, I'll try to find somebody else but I'm not promising. I'll get back to you.' There was then some discussion between herself and two other officers, during which they consulted the roll board again. Some minutes later the senior officer had indeed found someone else to move instead, and the prisoner was called back in. On being told he could stay on the wing after all, the prisoner, thrilled to bits, punched the air. As he went out of the office, smiling broadly, the senior officer shouted after him 'But you'd better behave yourself!'

Many officers rely on their sense of humour, their skills of persuasion and their ability to communicate effectively and fairly with people who may feel angry, anxious or depressed. These officers are acutely aware that prisoner co-operation often depended upon their ability to persuade and cajole; indeed they could rely on very little else. As one female officer put it: 'You've got to be good at talking. At Styal you had one officer to twenty-three women, and all you had was your radio and your gob.'

Every officer has his or her own way of controlling prisoners. They have two ways of maintaining control on a routine basis – formal and informal. The informal way necessitates the officer using his or her individual personality; some use humour (Dilulio's 'clowns') while some command respect based on their reputation for being 'firm but fair' and calm under pressure (Dilulio's 'statesmen'). The formal way, in contrast, involves routinely 'nicking' prisoners for every infraction of the rules. Many officers prefer informal methods; not only does this obviate the need for 'paperwork', as the following remarks illustrate, but the ability to deal with infractions informally is a matter of honour and pride:

> I always think when I put somebody on report I've abdicated my responsibility to the governor – it means that I can't cope [with that particular inmate or situation] – I've given up. A younger, less experienced officer might say [of the inmate who's getting up his nose] 'Well I'll have him', and go out of his way to get him. Older staff will just 'clock it' and deal with him at a later point, perhaps to the officer's advantage. (Male senior officer, Wymott)

Similarly:

> Nicking a prisoner amounts to getting someone else [i.e. a governor] to do your work for you. The best officers are good at taking the inmate on one side and letting him know that he's been clocked. (Male principal officer, Portland)

And again:

> Some officers place every act of indiscipline on report. Basically, if you've got to put people on report all the time, you're not doing your job right. Some prisoners you threaten, some you kid along, and some you can just tell. Knowing which are which comes from experience. [In my view] The worst sort of person you can have on any wing is one that's nicking prisoners all the time. (Male senior officer, Garth)

Officer–prisoner negotiation is illustrated in the following extract from my fieldnotes. It describes a (rather amusing) incident that occurred as I was 'shadowing' an officer on the (low visibility) wings at Garth:

> During wing patrol, an officer was looking for a certain inmate in order to bang him up. He looked around on the wing, shouting for him, but to no avail. I accompanied the officer on his search; we looked in doorways, in various rooms, in empty cells, etc. Eventually we passed a toilet, and the officer said he would have a look to see if he was in there. To my amazement, as the officer walked in, the inmate jumped out. He'd been hiding behind the door. The inmate thought it was funny, but the officer didn't. He said to the inmate, 'I've got some good news for you – me and you are going to see the governor in the morning' [meaning at adjudication]. 'Oh no, fuck off!' moaned the inmate. 'No, I'm not being pissed about' said the officer, and locked him in his cell. Later on, when he had been unlocked, the inmate came into the office, 'cap-in-hand', to ask if he could 'have a word' with the officer. Pleadingly, he asked the officer he had annoyed if he could do some cleaning or something instead of getting nicked. He was apparently due

for his Cat C board and appearing before the governor would spoil his chances of being recategorised. In reply to his request, the officer clearly wanted to make him stew a bit, and said he would 'see'. When the inmate had gone out, I asked the officer what he would do, and he replied that he would get him to polish his boots or something instead! Clearly there is power being performed here; while the officer clearly has the 'upper hand' in the negotiation, the inmate felt that negotiation was a possibility; that he might be able to persuade the officer to deal with the matter informally.

[...]

From Doing Prison Work: The Public and Private Lives of Prison Officers *(Cullompton: Willan Publishing)*, 2004, pp. 95–115.

Notes

1. The distinction between 'distal' and 'proximal' thinking has a long history in intellectual inquiry. Distal thinking privileges results and outcomes, the apparently 'finished' and 'complete' things or objects of thought or action. The distal is what is preconceived, what appears already constituted and known, what is simplified and distilled. 'Proximal' thinking, in contrast, deals in the continuous and unfinished (see Cooper and Law 1995 for a fascinating discussion of the distal/proximal debate). The distal approach to social inquiry is analogous to the view from a telescope; one can see far-away places and things but only in a certain degree of (fixed) detail. The proximal approach is analogous to what can be seen beneath a microscope. Here we find that fixed, biological structures are not fixed at all; rather they move, divide and merge. We see, in short, the structures of biological life *in process*. In the same way, a proximal approach allows the sociologist of the prison to see prison structures, relations and interactions as they develop, change and reproduce.
2. The principle of 'less eligibility' transformed penal policy (and hence prison conditions) in the mid-nineteenth century. Essentially, prison officials came to believe that the prisoner – (re)constructed as feckless, incorrigible (and hence dangerous) – should not be so well looked after that his circumstances corresponded to his non-criminal counterparts. He was, in fact, deemed 'less eligible' for warmth, food, clothing and rest than the 'deserving poor'.
3. Control and restraint (C&R) is a *defensive* method of physically dealing with prisoners. It uses controlled actions aimed at minimising physical injury, according to laid-down rules of authority and accountability (Barclay *et al.* 1994: 161).
4. An interesting discussion of officers 'at their best' can be found in Liebling and Price (2001).
5. Numerous officers mentioned being 'professional' but none really knew what they meant by it. They found it easier to discuss what made an officer *unprofessional*, i.e. 1) discussing inmates' offences in front of other inmates; 2) writing adverse reports because you don't like somebody; 3) always being late; and 4) offending against the discipline code.

References

Barclay, A., Skerry, K., Sneath, E. and Webster, R. (1994) 'Management of dissent in prison', in E. Stanko (ed.) *Perspectives on Violence*. London: Quartet Books.
Cooper, R. and Law, J. (1995) 'Organization: distal and proximal views', *Research in the Sociology of Organizations*, 13: 237–74.
Dilulio, J. (1987) *Governing Prisons*. New York, NY: Free Press.
Goffman, E. (1968) *Asylums*. Harmondsworth: Penguin Books.
Hay, W. and Sparks, R. (1991) 'What is a prison officer?', *Prison Service Journal*, summer issue.
HMCIP (1997) *HM Prison Garth: Report of a Full Inspection 9–13 June*. London: Home Office.
Liebling, A. and Price, D. (2001) *The Prison Officer*. Leyhill: HM Prison Service.
Rutherford, A. (1993) *Criminal Justice and the Pursuit of Decency*. Oxford: Oxford University Press.

Part E

Current controversies

Introduction

There are numerous controversies currently afflicting the prison service which could have been included in this final part of the reader. For example, one of the most shocking allegations about prison culture to have emerged in recent years was a finding of the inquiry into the racist murder of Zahid Mubarek in Feltham Young Offenders' Institution in 2000. According to an officer at the prison who was so troubled by what he witnessed that he contacted the Commission for Racial Equality, Mubarek had been put in a cell with a known white racist psychopath as part of a game played by staff. In a perverted take on a gladiatorial theme, prison officers would put two adversaries in the same cell (white and ethnic minority, weak and strong, or two bullies) and bet on the outcome (www.zahidmubarekinquiry.org.uk).

Although homicides in custody are relatively uncommon (an average of two per year), 42 per cent of victims are killed by their cellmate (Prison Reform Trust 2004) and the murder of Zahid Mubarek was clearly predictable and therefore avoidable. Diagnosed at the age of 13 with a personality disorder and excluded from secondary school, Mubarek's killer had grown up experiencing many of the most common characteristics of social exclusion. These characteristics are illustrated in the first contribution to Part E, Reading 25, which is a table produced by the Social Exclusion Unit (part of the Office of the Deputy Prime Minister) in 2002, and reproduced in the Prison Reform Trust *Factfile* of December 2004. For example, compared with the general population, prisoners are 13 times as likely to have been in care as a child, 10 times as likely to have been a regular truant from school and 13 times as likely to have been unemployed.

That prisoners frequently experience a lifetime of social exclusion taking many different forms sadly means that the statistics on self-inflicted deaths in custody (numbering 95 in 2004, including 13 women) are unsurprising. Alison Liebling has been researching and writing about suicides in prison for over a decade and in the first substantive reading of Part E, 'Suicides in prison: ten years on', given as a Perrie Lecture in 2001 and reproduced in the *Prison Service Journal* in November of that year, she reflects on her research and where it has taken her since her doctoral thesis on the subject was published in 1992 (Liebling 1992). In Reading 26, Liebling highlights the predominant risk factors in suicide and self-harm generally, including adverse life events, poor interpersonal relationships, weak attachment to education and employment, alcohol and drug misuse, and socioeconomic disadvantage. Thus, whilst deaths in custody share common characteristics with suicides in the population at large, this reading emphatically underlines the fact that the prison population has been 'carefully selected to be at risk' of suicide. In contrast to the psychological literature on suicide which has dominated the field, the research carried out by Liebling throughout her career is notable for the rich, ethnographic data she provides about this most sensitive of subjects. The extracts from interviews with serving prisoners who have attempted suicide or witnessed the self-inflicted deaths of friends in prison are frequently disarmingly frank and almost unbearably poignant. Thus, not only does this reading provide detailed information about external, structural factors that play a role in individuals' decisions to take their own life, but it also sheds light on the inner worlds and self-perceptions of these vulnerable individuals. As such, Liebling's work continues the tradition of prison ethnography initiated by Sykes, who describes the 'pains of imprisonment' in Reading 19, and has inspired many others to undertake sociologically imaginative research in prisons.

One of the biggest differences between Sykes' influential 1958 study and contemporary research into prison cultures and communities is the overwhelming presence of drugs in today's prisons. Drugs, and the ruthlessly dog-eat-dog environment they engender, have arguably destroyed any likelihood of the kind of inmate solidarity which Sykes claims is one of the key factors in coping with imprisonment. According to the Prison Reform Trust *Factfile* already mentioned, the omnipresence of drugs in prisons can be partially explained by the Prison Service's failure to meet its targets. This failure is evident in the figures for getting prisoners on to drug treatment programmes, and also for such prisoners successfully completing the programmes (Prison Reform Trust 2004). In fact, it is estimated that just 10 per cent of prisoners receive treatment for their drugs use. Along with Sparks and Bottoms (Reading 9) and Liebling (Reading 26), Ben Crewe is another scholar whose work is located within the ethnographic tradition of research into the internal dynamics of everyday life in contemporary British prisons. Like the previous piece, Reading 27, 'The drugs economy and the prisoner society' is a Perrie Lecture that was reproduced in the *Prison Service Journal*. Based on a ten-month period of research (involving observation and interviewing) at a Category C training prison for men, this piece describes the extent to which heroin is the 'key motor of social dynamics in prison'. Crewe highlights the paradoxical influence of the drug: heroin is both despised as a 'dirty' drug that stigmatizes its users, and simultaneously venerated as a means of earning privilege and respect for dealers. He also notes that the benefit afforded dealers – known in prison jargon as 'powder power' – is a transient and often false mark of status. But perhaps Crewe's most interesting finding, given public perceptions about the properties of heroin being debilitating and all-consuming (perceptions that are usually informed by government-funded advertising campaigns warning young people of the perils of taking Class A drugs), is that many inmates are able to manage their use of the drug. Some use heroin to make their sentence more bearable but wean themselves off it before returning to the community, whilst others arrive at prison with a habit and use their prison sentence as an opportunity to 'get clean'. Unfortunately, the impact of imprisonment on drug use is difficult to establish in precise terms, although it appears that drug misuse is a problem that many inmates import with them into prison from the community. A study for the Home Office found that 47 per cent of recently sentenced males had used heroin, crack or cocaine in the 12 months prior to imprisonment, and 73 per cent of prisoners had taken an illegal drug in the year before entering prison (Ramsay 2003). It has been further estimated that at some inner-city prisons, eight out of ten men are found to have Class A drugs in their system on reception, a figure that is repeated amongst new arrivals at HMP Styal, a local women's prison (Prison Reform Trust 2004). Meanwhile, a report by the Social Exclusion Unit (2002) found that 77 per cent of released inmates admitted taking drugs since leaving custody.

Another problem linked (along with drug misuse) to suicide and self-harm in prison is that of mental illness amongst prisoners. Mental illness is over-represented in the prison population (64 per cent of male and 50 per cent of female sentenced prisoners have a personality disorder, and psychotic disorders are represented in prison at 14 times the level as in the general population for men, and 23 times the level for women; Prison Reform Trust 2004). The difficulties associated with poor mental health that face prisoners are under-researched, and relatively little knowledge about the lives of inmates suffering from psychotic disorders exists outside the psychological and psychiatric fields. What we can say with some certainty, however, is that prison regimes do little to address the mental health needs of prisoners. According to a study released by the Office for National Statistics, three quarters of inmates in England and Wales have personality disorders and 6,175 are psychotic. Furthermore, the Prison Reform Trust reports that 28 per cent of male sentenced prisoners with evidence of psychosis spend 23 or more hours a day in their cells – over twice the proportion of those without mental health difficulties (Prison Reform Trust, 2004). Disappointingly, however, prisoners are twice as likely to be refused treatment for mental health problems inside prison than outside. Because the majority of individuals with mental health problems are not receiving adequate (or, indeed, any) treatment in prison, and because of the recent focus on offenders with dangerous and severe personality disorder (DSPD) in political and media discourses, the reading chosen to represent issues surrounding mental illness is primarily concerned with those at the sharp end of risk assessment. Specifically, Reading 28 'Radical risk management, mental health and criminal justice' by Philip Fennell, is concerned with the convergence of the mental health and criminal justice systems, and the drive to manage risk through preventative detention. This convergence of penal and medical discourses is an attempt to bridge the gap between clinical and actuarial assessments in a new programme of treatment for the most dangerous offenders, but Fennell highlights some of the problems associated with attempts to control so-called 'risky populations'. He describes the processes by which it is decided whether an offender who is diagnosed with a mental illness will be either detained in prison or referred to a hospital, and concludes that risk management has replaced treatment. Finally, Fennell discusses the ethical implications of these processes, arguing that, in fact, the ethics of the penal and psychiatric systems are mutually eroded by their convergence, and that we are, in effect, returning to a nineteenth-century model of citizenship and human rights when it comes to the mentally ill.

The other factor in our decision to include this extract is that it highlights another issue that is becoming a common feature of penal policy in England and Wales: that of indeterminate sentencing. As Fennell says, there has been a move away from the notion of proportionality between offence and sentence towards greater use of 'protective' custody. 'Imprisonment for public protection' is an indeterminate sentence imposed on offenders convicted of serious (i.e. sexual or violent) offences carrying a maximum penalty of 10 years or over who are assessed by the court as posing a significant risk to the public. There are also a number of age-related variants, including 'detention during her majesty's pleasure', an indeterminate sentence that can be imposed on children aged between 10 and 18. The use of indefinite detention has been much in the news in recent years due to the cases of the suspected terrorist detainees held without trial at Belmarsh and other penal establishments for three years until a law lords ruling in December 2004 that their detention was unlawful. The behaviour of several of the men deteriorated rapidly and a commission set up to review their cases in January 2005 ruled that it was the indefinite nature of the imprisonment that was a detriment to mental health, engendering 'a growing state of dependency and institutionalisation' (*Guardian* 1 February 2005).

Reading 29, 'Life as a woman', is also concerned with indeterminate sentencing, and simultaneously returns us to the themes outlined in Sykes (Reading 19). In this extract, though, it is the gendered pains of imprisonment that are the focus (see also Sim, Reading 13). Co-authored by Stephanie Walker and Anne Worrall, a life-sentence prisoner and academic prison researcher respectively, the article – which, like the first two substantive readings in this part was published in the *Prison Service Journal* – argues for a new understanding of women's experience of life imprisonment, taking account of the unique deprivations associated with women's incarceration and their responses to them. Around 15 per cent of suicides and 46 per cent of self-harm incidents in prison are committed by women, despite the fact that they make up only 6 per cent of the prison population (Prison Reform Trust 2004). Walker and Worrall's decision to focus on the gendered pains of imprisonment amongst those who are living the experience thus reminds us that prison sociology can only give voice to the survivors, but earlier in the article from which this extract is taken, they criticize what they see as the 'outward bound' mentality of the prisoner coping literature, arguing that, in women's prisons, the over-riding expectation that prisoners should find ways of coping is incompatible with inmates' own expectations: some simply do not want to cope or see why they *should* cope. The study, undertaken between 1994 and 1996 in four women's prisons, consisted of interviews with 47 of the 111 women who were at that time serving life sentences, and 49 prison officers. The chief finding was that the most significant gender-specific pains of indeterminacy revolve around women prisoners' status as mothers or non-mothers, but that their responses to pains of imprisonment more generally may be gendered. Losing control over time – the ultimate sanction of life imprisonment – has even more profound consequences for women than those outlined by Cohen and Taylor in Reading 21, because losing control over time for a woman means losing control over her fertility and her relationships with her children. Thus, echoing Goffman (Reading 20), the interview data illustrate that an indeterminate life sentence is more than a loss of liberty; it is an assault on the prisoner's very being.

Reading 30 by James B. Jacobs examines prison labour in the USA. This extract is taken from a collection of essays on prison labour in 15 different countries, edited by van Zyl Smit and Dunkel (1999): *Prison Labour: Salvation or Slavery?*. Throughout the development of the modern prison there has been discussion of various issues concerned with the notion of 'less eligibility'. For example, should labour be productive or unproductive? How many hours should prisoners labour? Should their labour contribute towards the upkeep of prisons? Should prisoners be put to labour at all when large sections of the 'free' population are unable to find employment? If they do not work, how should prisoners occupy their time? Is it right that they be afforded the kinds of consumable goods and opportunities for leisure that most of us occupy our 'free' time with? In relation to these issues, Jacobs presents us with the two spectres that, he argues, haunt American penology (and which have their counterparts in the UK, Europe and Australasia). On the one hand are liberal concerns about prisoners being forced to labour by profit-obsessed managers and, on the other, conservatives express fears that prisoners spend most of their time idle – watching television, playing sport or working out in the gym. Jacobs argues that the factory or full-employment prison is simply unrealistic in the USA for a number of reasons. These include infrastructure, location, inadequate capital, an unreliable and irresponsible workforce, safety and security being prioritized over industry, legal and political impediments and the sheer size of the US prison population. Jacobs argues that concerns regarding work and full employment have taken the discussion away from hard questions: namely, if prisoners are not working then what should they be doing all day? He asks whether it is a 'matter of indifference to penologists whether prisoners watch TV soap operas and game shows or meditate or play board games?'

The final reading (31) resonates with many issues raised elsewhere in this reader (the mental health implications of indefinite detention and solitary confinement, prison conditions, the exercise of discipline, questions of legitimacy and fairness, amongst others). In 'Prisoners' rights in the context of the European Convention on Human Rights', Stephen Livingstone is concerned with prisoners' 'enthusiastic' take-up of recent legislation that was not designed with their circumstances in mind. This reading could have been placed in other parts of this collection but 'current controversies' was chosen for two reasons. First, the European Commission and Court of Human Rights have made some important decisions that have impacted on prison law, particularly in the UK. Secondly, the 'public' would regard the issue of prisoners' rights as a controversial issue, as witnessed by a recent BBC Ceefax poll which found that 95 per cent of respondents thought that prisoners' should not be allowed to vote. Reports in the broadly right-wing British media suggest that prisoners' have more than enough rights already and that prison conditions should be more severe and 'rights' should be curtailed (see the Conclusion to this volume). In this extract Livingstone examines the application of the European Convention on Human Rights to specific areas of prison life, focusing on prison conditions and discipline. The full article from which this extract is taken also examines communication with the outside world and release from prison. With regard to prison conditions and discipline, Livingstone argues that judicial involvement has been uneven and a human rights approach still leaves considerable discretion to the prison authorities.

References

Liebling, A. (1992) *Suicides in Prison.* London: Routledge.

Prison Reform Trust (2004) *Prison Reform Trust Factfile.* December 2004 (www.prisonreformtrust.org.uk).

Ramsay, M. (ed.) (2003) *Prisoners' Drug Use and Treatment: Seven Studies. Home Office Research Findings* 186. London: Home Office.

Social Exclusion Unit (2002) *Reducing Re-offending by Ex-prisoners.* London: SEU.

25. Social characteristics of prisoners

Many prisoners have experienced a lifetime of social exclusion. The Social Exclusion Unit has found that compared with the general population, prisoners are thirteen times as likely to have been in care as a child, thirteen times as likely to have been unemployed and ten times as likely to have been a regular truant.

Characteristic	General	Prison population
Ran away from home as a child	11%	47% of male sentenced prisoners
Taken into care as a child	2%	27%
Regularly truanted from school	3%	30%
Excluded from school	2%	49% of male and 33% of female sentenced prisoners
No qualifications	15%	52% of men and 71% of women
Numeracy at or below Level 1 (the level expected of an 11-year-old)	23%	65%
Reading ability at or below Level 1	21–23%	48%
Unemployed before imprisonment	5%	67%
Homeless	0.9%	32%
Suffer from two or more mental disorders	5% of men and 2% of women	72% of male sentenced prisoners and 70% of female sentenced prisoners
Psychotic disorder	0.5% of men and 0.6% of women	7% of male sentenced prisoners and 14% of female sentenced prisoners
Drug use in the previous year	13% of men and 8% of women	66% of male sentenced prisoners and 55% of female sentenced prisoners
Hazardous drinking	38% of men and 15% of women	63% of male sentenced prisoners and 39% of female sentenced prisoners

Source: Social Exclusion Unit Report Reducing Re-offending by Ex-prisoners, *July 2002, reproduced in Prison Reform Trust* Factfile, *December 2004.*

26. Suicides in prison: ten years on

Alison Liebling

> Social death begins when the institution ... loses its interest or concern
> for the individual as a human being and treats him as a body – that is,
> as if he were already dead.
>
> (Shneidman 1973: 159)

When I read this, I could hear the words of so many officers, telling me
'we lock up 300 bodies on this wing', or I was reminded of the 'body book'
signed at reception when the police handed over a prisoner. A first ever
Thematic Inspection had been carried out on 'Suicide in Prison' in 1984. This
had been inspired by three hangings within 12 months at HMP Swansea, and
a 'lack of care' verdict brought by an inquest jury following the suicide of a
young prisoner at Ashford Remand Centre. In Scotland, a series of suicides at
Glenochil young offenders complex resulted in a detailed report on the then
current suicide prevention procedures (SHHD 1985). Dr Derek Chiswick, a
forensic psychiatrist and main author of the report concluded: 'this is not a
psychiatric problem, it's a management problem.'

It was in this context – of growing concern, increasing numbers, an
especially rapid increase in the numbers of young prisoners taking their
own lives, and some revisiting of suicide prevention procedures that I
began the research I conducted for my PhD degree. I had been working in
young offenders' institutions – a Detention Centre and two Youth Custody
Centres, interviewing staff and prisoners as part of a Home Office funded
study of throughcare. I had been struck by the prevalence of self-injury, the
helpless and sometimes angry reaction of staff, and the use of strip cells for
those considered at risk. Some prisoners thought attempting suicide was a
prison disciplinary offence. It had been a criminal offence until 1967. Those
considered at risk carried a large red 'F' on their files – this stood for 'felo-
de-se': the murder of oneself.

The late 1980s and early 1990s witnessed dramatically increasing suicide
rates in prison, particularly amongst the young. What was often overlooked
was the dramatic increase in suicide amongst young males in the community:
those in lower socio-economic groups were particularly at risk. Large groups
amongst the prisoner population share those characteristics associated

with increased suicide risk in the community: adverse life events, negative interpersonal relationships, social and economic disadvantage, alcohol and drug addiction, contact with criminal justice agencies, poor educational and employment history, low self-esteem, poor problem-solving ability, impulsivity, and low motivational drive. Whilst the media blamed overcrowding and prison conditions, the prison population was also carefully selected to be at risk. Prisons like Risley, Brixton, and Leeds suffered from apparent epidemics. Was this a problem of conditions, demographics, imitation, psychiatric disorder, manipulation, lack of care, prison culture, inactivity or management?

[...]

Main findings: understanding vulnerability and suicide risk

Depression and anger. What it was, I was thinking all about the family and what was going on all around me, and with me not having any letters for a week or two, I just thought, well there's no point in me being here, no-one cares about me.

(Suicide attempter)

There was no hope, no light at the end of the tunnel. Once you're in the system you'll never get out of it; the only way out of it is to become dead or anonymous, because that's the only way they will ever leave you alone. That's the only way you can start to rebuild a life, because once you've been in this system and they know all about you they will arrest you for things you don't do. They will put you inside a prison for things you don't do and they will generally fuck up your life all the time.

(Suicide attempter)

The first study I want to briefly relate took place in four closed Young Offenders' Institutions between 1988 and 1990 (Liebling 1992) and the second took place in three local/remand centres and one closed training prison between 1990 and 1992 (Liebling and Krarup 1993). In the first study, interviews were carried out with 50 prisoners who had attempted suicide and 50 prisoners drawn randomly from the general population within the same establishments. In the second study, interviews were carried out with 62 prisoners who had attempted suicide and with 80 prisoners drawn randomly from the populations in the same establishments. Interviews were long and semi-structured and included detailed questions about prisoners' backgrounds, their criminal justice histories, their experiences of imprisonment and their plans for release. Questions were also asked about suicide attempts, suicidal thoughts and prisoners' explanations for such events both in their own case and on behalf of other prisoners in general.

A number of important and consistent differences emerged in both studies between the two groups and these differences were most marked in the accounts prisoners gave of their experiences of imprisonment. Most of these results could not have been obtained by using recorded information. In the descriptions we obtained of prisoners lives, backgrounds and criminal justice histories, the significant differences to emerge between the suicide attempters and a comparison group were differences of degree. The presence or absence of family breakdown, violence, local authority care and previous offending, and the pattern of their education and employment histories were similar. However, the degree (frequency and consequences) of family violence, the reasons for placement in local authority care, the reasons for prolonged absences from school, and the period spent in the community between custody were significantly different. Suicide attempters were more likely to report multiple family breakdown, frequent violence leading to hospitalisation, local authority placement as a result of family problems (as opposed to offending), truancy as a result of bullying (as opposed to boredom or peer pressure) and very short periods spent in the community between custody.

In terms of their criminal justice histories, suicide attempters had a slightly earlier start and slightly higher numbers of previous convictions. Many of those in the suicide attempt group spent less than three months in the community between sentences. Successful coping in prison reflected in part, prisoners' lives in the community.

Suicide attempters were found to have fewer qualifications from school than comparison groups. This is particularly significant as many were unable to read and write without difficulty. They were frequent truants and they were significantly more likely to have been involved in violence at school, including having been the victims of bullying. They were more likely to have been in local authority care, and this was slightly more likely to have been for family or behavioural problems than for offending behaviour alone. They were more likely to have received psychiatric treatment, both in and out of hospital, and they were more likely to report major alcohol and drug problems. More of the suicide attempters had injured themselves before coming into custody: only a quarter had not injured themselves in any way before their sentence. Suicide attempters were more likely to report experiences of sexual abuse (this was especially common amongst both groups of female prisoners (see Liebling, 1992) and amongst young male suicide attempters). On a range of background characteristics, then, suicide attempters could be differentiated from comparison groups, using a dimensional approach.

Once in prison, the scale and quality of the differences between the two groups were clearer. On most questions relating to the prison experience, the suicide attempters both were and saw themselves as considerably worse off than their peers:

> Hell. I live a hell every time I close my eyes and go to sleep. I live a hell every time I get up in the morning and have to face this lot. I live a hell every time I look at people in here shouting nonce and beast and every time I go for me meal … Every time I see somebody sitting here crying because his wife's left him and he can't have contact with his kids, or he wrote a letter and the letter's got lost, or nobody writes to him, or somebody stands there and slits his face open because of what he's in for. Bleak, isn't it?

> (Suicide attempter)

They were less likely to be engaged in activities, less likely to have a job in prison, and less likely to report being able to get anything constructive out of what they did. They were more likely to report difficulties with other prisoners and with staff:

> Yes. I was shocked. I wasn't even thinking about any violence in prisons. I just got beat in, on A wing, in the dinner queue. One of them came over and saw me crying against a locked door they took – me over the hospital.
>
> (Suicide attempter)

> Some (of the staff) are all right, they do communicate with you. But they can say hard things. They'll turn round and say to you: 'Go and sit with the other outcast', things like that, which isn't very nice. I know these people have to work here and the place must become very dull for them as well, I respect that … but they say things like, 'I bet you he's never had a good woman in his life'. That hurts.
>
> (Suicide attempter)

They were less likely to enjoy PE or use the gym, and were more likely to pose disciplinary problems. They were least likely to be receiving regular or helpful contact from outside, either from families and friends or from the Probation Service, although many of the comparison group of prisoners also found this aspect of prison life especially painful:

> How can you think big of yourself when you're not getting no visits? There's some guys in here who think because they're getting visits and you're not, that you're some kind of Joey for them.
>
> (Prisoner: comparison group)

> Yes. It would make it easier for me (to receive more visits) because I'd know then that there is somebody out there who cares, whereas when nobody comes to visit me, my head automatically thinks, there's no-one who cares about me, there's no point in being here.
>
> (Suicide attempter)

> Well, a woman from the Samaritans came after I slashed up, to talk to me. She asked me why I did it. I said I was bored and depressed, and lack of contact with the family. It helped a bit, but not that much. She asked me to write to her. It has crossed me mind a few times to write.
>
> (Suicide attempter)

Visits were described in detail as major events – with anxious anticipation, frequent disappointment, and feelings of being 'gutted' when they were over, or when visitors failed to turn up. Handling the emotional roller-coaster of visits was a skill, and was linked to a capacity to immerse themselves in activities.

Most important in terms of understanding their immediate vulnerability to suicide, and linked to this general capacity to handle prison life, suicide attempters were unable to occupy themselves when left alone in their cells:

> Alone. I felt so alone, you know? Four walls, nobody there.
>
>   (Suicide attempter)

> I suppose there must be ways (of passing the time) but I just don't bother. I could read, but there again, I can't be bothered. I just can't get into it.
>
>   (Suicide attempter)

> There's nothing. It's not just boredom; it's problems outside (too) … And when you ask for someone to talk to, you can't get no-one … Then you sit here. You think, what's the point?
>
>   (Suicide attempter)

It was this sense of there being nothing, this dependence on 'sustaining external resources', which left some groups of prisoners unable to cope in conditions of confinement and isolation. In addition to being the group least able to occupy themselves constructively when alone, the suicide attempt group were also most likely to end up in those locations within the prison most likely to involve longer than average periods of isolation (for example, health care centres, segregation units, and vulnerable prisoner units). Suicide attempters found many aspects of the prison situation more difficult to cope with than comparison groups of prisoners drawn randomly from the same populations. Their vulnerability, characterised by a history of adverse life circumstances followed by persistent problems in 'coping', was exposed by many different aspects of the prison world, from activities and relationships to planning for the future:

> It's all sorts of things, like. I could say things that are still happening from years ago … I know there are other people in here like me, you know, who've been through what I've been through, but like, I've been in care from age six to 16, and from 16 I've been in prison, with the exception of five months. So, like, when I tell them I need to be taught the basic things of life, they turn round and say to me, it should be up to me to go out and learn these things. But how can I when I don't know what the things are to learn? When I go to someone else, they just say the same things in different words. I've just got fed up with it.
>
>   (Suicide attempter)

> Since I did it last time, I have thought about doing it again. I've even thought about overdosing. These people, right, they think, 'Oh, he's trying to commit suicide, he's daft, he don't know what he's doing'. But we think – I've done it – we know what it feels like to be hurt, they don't. All they're thinking is, 'He's daft'. They don't know what you're going through. They don't know what your mind's thinking. You can't

talk to no-one in here, so you take it out on yourself, and that's why the majority of people commit suicide in prison, because they can't talk to no-one.

(Suicide attempter)

Their release plans were poor and unrealistic, and they avoided thinking about outside and the future.

Background factors were less significant than cognitive appraisals of the current situations. In other words, it was less 'who they are', and more 'what they think and feel', that counted. Many badly wanted help:

What I really need is psychological help ... Understanding would be a better word. Understanding, rather than paying £250 a week or whatever it is, just to keep somebody like me in prison. But they've never once tried to sort my head out, or rehabilitation, which they could probably do for half that amount ...

(Prisoner)

Those who are most vulnerable are exposed to a highly demanding environment in which survival skills are highly valued and indications of weakness or helplessness may bring about verbal and physical abuse, theft, taxing, sexual violence and psychological torment.

The role of prison staff

Prison officers were crucial in the handling of prisoners at risk. They could be of immense practical help – facilitating phone calls, job changes, home leave, discussing possible work opportunities on release, parole procedures and psychiatric referrals. They could also be helpful in personal ways:

They cheer you up ... just in the way they speak to you and take time to speak to you.

(comparison group)

Prisoners complained that staff were always busy and that there weren't enough of them – this was in 1988, before the onset of managerialism and market testing. Prison officers complained bitterly about paperwork, and were sceptical of the relationship between paperwork and the causes of and solutions to suicidal feeling. They complained about lack of communication, particularly between themselves and the health care centres. The main problems were lack of feedback from the hospital, their unwillingness to accept prisoners thought to be at risk on to the hospital, the lack of adequate instructions given to staff on the wings on the prisoner's return, and the generally low level of information sharing that went on. Hospital staff felt that staff expected the hospital to provide a refuge for discipline and control problems, and that officers sometimes over-reacted to prisoners in distress and were too keen to 'send their problems to us'.

235

Both sides wished they had more 'half way houses' where discipline and medical expertise could be shared, despite the fact that neither side ever suggested that suicide risk might lie somewhere between discipline and medical concerns. Relationships were better where health care staff appeared regularly on wings, for example, to give out treatments. There was a clear barrier, reminiscent of 'shared working' between prison and probation staff in the old days, where officers thought the hospital could pick and choose their clients, kept themselves empty wherever possible, and received extra privileges for doing less work. Prison staff lacked confidence in dealing with suicide risk, and tended to underestimate the painfulness of prison. They felt procedures worked best when 'it's all avoided by letting him have a cry on your shoulder' (Senior officer).

Reflections on current developments

My feeling is that far too many of these points remain relevant today than I would like to believe. There have been some major developments – including what looks like a first downturn in the figures. There is much better quality information – suicide verdicts are no longer used as the basis for research or management information. Research has flourished, and is started to become more integrated instead of the separate studies we used to see. The ending of the use of strip cells (if indeed it has been ended) is symbolic of a generally less punitive response to vulnerability. The use of suicide investigations has been valuable – and a recent Masters' thesis conducted by Gordon Morrison, the Controller of Wolds, has helped to capitalise on the learning from these very useful procedures.

The recent expansion of SASU and its reincarnation as the 'Safer Custody Group' is a most welcome development. It is clear that alongside a clearly stated commitment to reducing suicides, resources have followed. Regimes in prison have improved in most places, and prisoners no longer routinely spend most of the day locked up (although there are some important exceptions). Likewise, I would argue that relationships with staff and the role of the prison officer more generally, have improved, for various reasons. It is just possible that in the theoretical model that myself and colleagues are continuing to develop, the prison is making a less obvious contribution, but the vulnerability of the population continues to increase. We still do not know enough about individual psychological survival in prison. (Have markedly improved regimes resulted in a less gruelling and more constructive experience of imprisonment for prisoners?) We cannot assume this, without evidence. Is there a clear relationship between regime provision and suicide risk? What is the relationship between prison conditions and the prison experience? These are the questions we have to ask next.

From 'Suicides in prison: ten years on', Prison Service Journal, *no. 138, November 2001, pp. 35–41 (references unavailable).*

27. The drugs economy and the prisoner society

Ben Crewe

Heroin and prison culture

With remarkable consistency, experienced prisoners claim that it is heroin that is chiefly responsible for the erosion of a former culture of solidarity and cohesion amongst prisoners. The following quote captures general sentiments:

> Smack – that's what's changed things a lot in prisons. People would never steal from people or grass each other up. Now that's just commonplace: grassing and co operating with staff. (…) It's lowered general morals in the prison system. Proper heroin addicts have got no morals, y'know, they'd steal from their mum, they can't be trusted with anything. (…) So there's a kind of general mistrust around the place. (…) The violence levels have gone right up because of drugs. It was unusual for someone to get slashed up. There was fights (…) but now people are getting slashed up and set fire to just over nothing, five or ten pounds (debt). There's a lot more debt now in prison than ever before. And big debts as well. (…) People sell their clothes now in prison, which you never saw, for drugs, and all their belongings. People work for other people in prison for drugs now. They'll spend their life cleaning someone else's cell out for drugs, or whatever else they have to do. General moral standards have gone downhill, because of heroin. (…) it's hardened people's feelings towards their fellow prisoners. If someone's ill or poor or in a mess – a few years ago people would've gone to them and said 'here you are mate, here's some tobacco', or a phonecard, 'get yourself sorted out'. Now they say 'oh, he's a smackhead, forget him'. (So) people's good nature to other prisoners has got less and less. (…) Heroin culture has destroyed the humanity that was to other prisoners, that's gone now. That's why I think there's more slashings and whatever, because people don't look at each other as humans anymore, especially if they're smackheads – that's all they are: they get that label and they're finished.

Between them, then, heroin users and dealers violate almost every element of the prisoner code of conduct. The heroin economy, and the debt that it generates, is linked to bullying and exploitation, grassing, and stealing from cells. Heroin users are seen as manipulative and phoney, undermining general levels of trust and breaching norms about behaving without front or pretence. They are considered volatile, unpredictable and confrontational, in ways that add to the stress of everyday life. Their behaviour brings the attention of officers onto other people's activities. And their dependency, desperation, and physical degeneration are considered insulting to the collective dignity of the inmate community.

Heroin use and stigma

It is for all these reasons that heroin users in prison are stigmatised – albeit less than in previous years, when being a heroin user or dealer could result in being violently ostracised from a wing (Duke 2003).[1] Users recognise this stigma, often acknowledging in private the shame that they feel about having to sell their clothes, work for other prisoners, and steal or beg from others in order to feed their consumption. 'It makes you into a worse thug than you already were', one prisoner commented, remorsefully (fieldwork notes, 2002).

However, while 'smackheads' are certainly at the bottom of the prisoner pecking order (within the mainstream community), drug use itself is tolerated (or perhaps accepted as inevitable) provided that it does not interfere with the lives of other prisoners, or come to suggest vulnerability, immorality or lack of control. Such distinctions are partly based on views brought into prison from outside communities, where heroin dependence is associated with weakness and 'dirtiness', and where there is great distaste for the kinds of acts perpetrated by addicts.

Many prisoners will be candid about their drug consumption, but will downplay its extent and try to distance themselves from the identity attached to hardcore users: 'I smoke heroin, but I'm not a smackhead' is a common refrain. Prisoners differentiate between those drug users whose use dominates their lives, and those for whom it is an occasional and controlled pursuit. Indeed, whilst being unable to control your drug use is a mark of being unable to handle incarceration, some credibility can be gained from being able to afford heroin and knowing where to find it.[2]

Heroin dealing and power

It is through drug dealing, though, that significant status and power can be amassed. Prisoners repeatedly described the influence and comfort that being a drug supplier can afford:

Drugs run every prison. (…) When you've got heroin, you're up there. You're one of the men. If you've got a constant flow of heroin, your prison life can be very comfortable.

God, y'know, heroin in prison is the most powerful thing. It's the most powerful thing in prison, you can get anything done. You can get somebody stabbed, you can get somebody slashed, whatever you want with heroin.

Power? Power's drugs. Drugs is power.

Clearly, those prisoners directly dependent on drugs are most susceptible to the power that drugs bestow upon dealers. However, non-users are also affected by the ability of drug dealers to accumulate other tradable commodities such as tobacco, and pay others to settle scores. They can also be drawn into the violent politics of the drugs economy if their friends find themselves in debt.

In an environment in which personal possessions often represent status, as well as currency, prisoners whose involvement in the drugs trade allows them to build up belongings are held in high regard. One interviewee said:

I was just admiring the way they done it, (…) They got the whole wing under control (and) they had everything (…) chocolate bars, boxes of brand new trainers and tracksuits all hangin' up.

Another aspect of the respect assigned to drug dealers relates to the 'nerve', ambition and contacts that they are assumed to have in order to be able to secure their supplies. As one prisoner reported, dealers get 'respect for getting the gear in the first place (…) They must be big people if they can get drugs into jail'.

However, it is important to identify the true nature of the 'respect' that drug dealing brings. Largely, prisoners recognise that it is born out of fear rather than genuine admiration. They also note that it is often only a temporary form of power, which resides in the drugs themselves, rather than in any aspect of character, and which therefore dissipates somewhat when the drug supply itself runs out. The term 'powder power' encapsulates what is, in fact then, a form of proxy or 'dummy respect'. It signifies both the false friendship that drug users give dealers in order to get hold of heroin, and the disrespect that dealers can show to users in the knowledge of the power they hold over them.

Many prisoners therefore take exception to drug dealing not only because it leads to forms of exploitation, and undermines notions of equality, but also because it allows otherwise 'ordinary' prisoners to climb the social hierarchy and boost their social image. Such complaints often have racial overtones, as well as connotations about masculine prowess. Thus, there is some disdain about the rising social power of Asian prisoners, who have traditionally been a relatively weak grouping, but whose involvement in the drugs economy is transforming their collective status: 'They're not powerful people – they're like matchsticks!', exclaimed one prisoner, 'but they have power, through the drugs they bring in.'

However, it would be wrong to suggest that prisoners can simply ascend the pecking order through the provision of drugs. A prisoner who without heroin is weak is unlikely to be able to hang onto his stock. In this respect, it is necessary either to already have some degree of physical or social clout, some other source of status, or to make smart alliances with powerful prisoners, in order to be able to operate as a dealer. Drugs alone are unlikely to enable a very weak member of the inmate community to become very powerful.

The opposite trajectory is more likely, as a result of drug use. Another reason why heroin is begrudged, particularly by experienced prisoners, is that it has corroded traditional sources of status and distinction among prisoners (such as age, physical strength, staunchness and offence):

> You can still be an armed robber, but if you're a smackhead as well then the two don't go, do they? (…) You'll get comments like, 'he used to be top brethren, but he's a smackhead now.' (…) You've got a weakness. And if people know you've got a weakness, it can be exploited. (People) can buy your loyalty because of your weakness. (…) You're not staunch no more, because people can buy you.

> There is no hierarchy no more. Whoever brings in the most drugs is the hierarchy now.

> If you can get drugs in, you're somebody, in prison. (…) You can be the biggest rapist on earth. But as long as you're bringing smack in, it doesn't matter what you've done.

> Someone may be physically strong, they may be strong willed, they may be a bit of a bully, but because they're on the brown, people will frown upon them.

> Heroin means you can have a 23 year old selling to a grown man, who's licking their arse.

Heroin's presence on a wing also shifts the terms on which prisoners associate with each other. Drug users are not really loyal to each other, nor do they trust each other, but they are 'loyal to each other's company' (Larner and Tefferteller 1964: 14): they will associate with each other pragmatically in order to acquire and consume heroin. Former affiliations are often, therefore, abandoned. As one prisoner summarised, then, this has altered the conditions of social interaction:

> You can have a senior heavy armed robber type who'll be hangin' around with a house burglar, simply because they both take smack, whereas in the old days you wouldn't get that: people were drawn to each other because of what they were in for.

Overall, then, heroin's impact on prisoner power and social relations is complex. In some respects, it distorts and supplants traditional relationships. In other ways, it amplifies existing inequalities and expands the conventional hierarchy, making some vulnerable prisoners all the more indebted, ostracised and stigmatised, and increasing the power available to certain prisoners whose position in the prisoner world allows them to command the drugs trade.

Motivations for drug use and drug dealing

Accumulating goods, services and status while in prison are some of the main motivations for dealing. Prison drug dealers are often dealers outside too, and many claim that continuing is a means of offsetting the material deprivations of incarceration, and living a life that corresponds, at least a little, to their lifestyle outside. Suppliers also take pride in 'beating the system', as one former dealer highlighted:

> I got my victories by selling drugs. (...) They paid me £11 a week. If I wasn't working they paid me £3 a week. I lived well above that. I could have what I wanted. (...) When a screw came in my pad and saw it overflowing with food and tobacco and just everything, that was good enough for me.

The appeal of heroin consumption is generally discussed in terms of sanctuary, diversion and relief: 'it brings the walls down', 'it's like being wrapped up in cotton wool', 'every single weight on your shoulders just seems to disappear.' However, it is important to note the different patterns of drug use inside and outside prison. Not least, many prisoners report that they use heroin *only* when in prison. Furthermore, they appear to manage their consumption quite consciously – reducing it in the months before release to ensure that they do not risk adding days to their sentences, or leave with a taste for heroin.

In contrast, many prisoners whose offences are addiction-related use prison as an opportunity to get clean. For them, the experience of imprisonment is of a different nature from other prisoners. Firstly, they are more likely to talk of having 'real friends' in prison than other prisoners, who generally regard prison 'associates' as much less trustworthy and sincere than their 'proper friends' outside, and consider it reckless to put faith in people met in the artificial context of incarceration. In contrast, ex-addicts see their prison identities as 'real' and reliable and their outside selves as inauthentic, and project this view onto others:

> I'll be able to trust (other prisoners) in a jail scenario, but otherwise, I don't know, they could get out of jail and change totally. I know that I would. I change when I get out. It's not as if I come in prison and put a mask on. I come in prison and I revert to me. This is the real me. Outside, I'm totally false (...) It's a chemical lifestyle I lead outside. My whole character changes.

241

Secondly, because of their experiences as addicts outside prison, some prisoners find confinement a relatively less painful phenomenon than freedom. Often, they describe imprisonment as an 'opportunity', or a 'relief' from the chaos, misery and immorality of their lives outside. The kinds of degradations documented by prison sociologists in the past, for example, the deprivation of power and control, are considered less arduous than those that accompany addiction on the streets, as this interviewee describes:

> (Outside) I don't have control of my life, heroin has a control over my life. I hand the reins to heroin (…). It's in prison that I can find I'm able to control my life more … and I'm happy, I'm happier. (…) How can a prison have power over you when you're in no rush to go beyond the boundaries of the gates. Cos I'm not. If I was to go out there, I would end up in a bigger state (of addiction) than I've ever been in.

For this cohort, then, prison provides a respite from drugs (rather than vice versa): a chance to improve their physical and psychological health, and the state of their personal relationships.

Interventions and further research

The practical and policy implications of these findings are by no means self-evident, and academic sociologists are not always the best people to assess them. A number of suggestions and notes of caution can nonetheless be offered.

First, as is clear to most practitioners, interventions need to be institutional as well as individual, and they need to be well-planned and balanced. If prisoners use drugs to relieve stress and boredom, and to escape temporarily from reality, then decent, constructive regimes are likely in themselves to reduce demand. At the same time, however, open regimes may increase supply by allowing drugs to more easily enter and circulate. Likewise, if prison wages are higher, this may increase demand for drugs by making more currency available for prisoners tempted to consume. However, there may be less motivation for suppliers if there is less need to substitute canteen food for poor quality meals, and if there are alternative, legitimate ways of establishing status within the prison community.

Establishments do have some scope to shift the terms on which status is assigned. Certainly, prisoners suggest that the kudos attached to violence is greater in some prisons than others, and those changes in modes of control and in officer culture have reduced it across the prison system as a whole. Decreasing the status of drug dealing might be more complex. If prison staff raise the stakes or revel too openly in their successes in combating drugs, this might make dealers, who tend to hold relatively anti-authority attitudes, all the more determined. Officers might also be careful not to appear to legitimise or enhance the status of drug dealers by acknowledging their power – even if only through the banter that can be part of the game between security staff and suspected dealers.

Similarly, since powerful prisoners are often involved in drug networks, there are dangers in mobilising them in order to control wings. That is, giving privileged wing-jobs and perks to influential prisoners, in return for them 'keeping the wing quiet', may be very imprudent. Even if a wing run along these lines appears calm, it may actually be the case that drugs are rife, but that a loose (and illegitimate) order is being maintained through collusion between officers and drug dealers who are keen to protect their markets by preventing overt and excessive disorder.

There are also dangers to be aware of in taking advantage of the lack of trust and loyalty that heroin engenders, and that exists between heroin users in prison. Prison sociologists have long noted that some level of solidarity is beneficial not just for prisoners, in terms of helping them to alleviate the pains of imprisonment, but also for prison administrators, who might otherwise face a much more unruly, discontented and self-interested prisoner population (Sykes 1958). It may be tempting for prison administrators to promote a culture of informing in order to eradicate heroin, and therefore promote greater harmony and safety within the prisoner community. However, this may itself undermine levels of trust and solidarity between prisoners, in ways that create an equally damaging and isolating environment. Moreover, prisoners may be very reluctant to grass on drug dealers, not only because this may be highly dangerous for them, but also because it can be self-incriminating, especially in a prison where admissions of drug use are dealt with in highly punitive ways.

However, in the same way that the official language about bullying has built upon, and been absorbed into, prisoner discourse, it is not implausible that a campaign against prison drug dealing could harness the antipathy felt by many prisoners about the presence of drugs within the system.

Given the stigma attached to drug use, compared to the more ambivalent status of dealing, it may be easier to tackle drug demand than supply. This requires a degree of understanding about the attractions and contexts of drug-taking. Prison staff need to recognise the ambivalence about heroin consumption felt not only by non-users, but also by users themselves, who are often full of shame about selling their clothes or getting family members to fund their habits. They may be unlikely to express this to officers, or want to discuss with them the intensity with which they may desire heroin when it is available. Again, this will be the case all the more if prisoners feel that drug use is dealt with only punitively or dismissively, rather than with some level of sympathy and support. It is also worth staff being aware that, although heroin users in prison may appear to be collectively powerful, as individuals they are often isolated, with few proper friendships. Labels that simply deride and condemn them may increase their vulnerability, and push them further towards narcotic means of coping.

Staff should also be conscious that there exist different patterns of demand and behaviour amongst prisoners in relation to heroin. If drugs are consumed in prison as a way of easing the pains of confinement, then there are certain times during a sentence when this temptation is likely to be greatest: at its beginning, and in its middle-phases, when the prisoner is most isolated from the outside world, and most psychologically dependent on forms of support within the prison.

For recovering addicts, who often desist entirely while in prison, stability, support and resettlement are critical. Constructive activity may be seized upon with relish; prison friends and peers – often in similar positions – can be excellent sources of mutual support. It is unhelpful if officers believe (as prisoners sometimes – and often wrongly – think that they do) that 'druggies are druggies' or 'junkies never change', when these may actually be the prisoners most receptive to rehabilitation. Equally, it may be unwise to encourage prisoners to present themselves only as helpless victims if this risks undermining their sense of agency and self-esteem.[3]

[...]

From 'The drugs economy and the prisoner society', Prison Service Journal, No. 156, November 2004, pp. 9–14 (references unavailable).

Notes

1. 'In the old days if you knew somebody who had smack, you'd go and have a chat with them, quietly, on the side. [And say] "Make sure nobody else gets it. You will take it. Nobody else will. You alone will take it. You won't knock any of that stuff out. If you go knocking it out, we'll knock you out".'
2. As one prisoner commented: 'It is [stigmatised], yeah. But it's also, it's also a status symbol to them. Somebody that can be seen to be running about, and eventually get the prize, i.e. a bag of smack [...] they'll come out and walk about the wing, scratching their nose, "yeah, I'm a gangster man, I can afford smack, and I know where to get it".'
3. Promoting helplessness as the key means to gain support or escape sanctions is also dangerous because it encourages prisoners who do not have drug problems to present themselves as if they do (see also Shewan and Davies 2000). A small number of interviewees reported that they had claimed, on entry into prison, to have drug abuse issues, because they believed that providing the prison with 'something to address' made it more likely that they could appear 'corrected', and therefore worthy of parole and other benefits.

28. Radical risk management, mental health and criminal justice

Philip Fennell

[...]

Convergence [between the mental health and criminal justice systems] is driven by the Government's desire to be able to manage risk through preventive detention. In the penal system it is marked by a strong move away from the notion of just deserts and proportionality between offence and sentence toward greater use of so called protective (that is, indeterminate) sentencing, once the province of the psychiatric system. In the psychiatric system convergence is marked by such developments as the broadening of powers to detain on grounds of risk to other people and the erosion of patients' rights to confidentiality of medical information by the introduction of duties to share information about patients thought to be high risk.

Since before the Lunacy Act 1890 a prime concern of mental health legislation has been the protection of patients from wrongful or unduly prolonged use of powers to detain and treat compulsorily. The Mental Health Act 1959 introduced the Mental Health Review Tribunal (MHRT) to provide review of the lawfulness of and continued need for detention. The Mental Health Act 1983, partly prompted the adverse ruling of the European Court of Human Rights in *X v United Kingdom*[1] increased the frequency with which patients could apply for discharge, gave them rights to second opinions if treated compulsorily, and added to those due process rights a welfare entitlement by giving patients subject to long term powers of detention a right to after care following discharge.

That concern for rights in the sense of due process rights and latterly patient entitlement to treatment has been replaced by a concern for human rights in a much broader sense. This embraces not only the rights of patients to protection against arbitrary use of State therapeutic power (the due process rights under Arts 5–7 of the Convention and the right of sanctity of the person under the right of respect for privacy in Art 8), but also the human rights of victims or potential victims of mentally disordered people to protection of their right to life under Art 2 and to protection against inhuman and degrading treatment under Art 3. [...]

Radical risk management

The social control of so called 'risky populations' has always been a goal of criminal justice policy,[2] but lately it has become an increasingly overt preoccupation.[3] Since the early 1990s mentally disordered people in general, let alone those who have committed criminal offences, are increasingly portrayed as a risky population. A steady procession of inquiries into homicides by former psychiatric in-patients has increased the association in the public mind between mental disorder and dangerousness, leading to increasing demands for protection from crime particularly crimes committed by mentally disordered people, although a survey of homicides since the 1950s shows that homicides by mentally disordered people have not increased (Taylor and Gunn, 1999). This in turn has resulted in a role redefinition whereby risk management has assumed increasing centrality in the role of psychiatrists and other mental health professionals, and philosophies of risk management now permeate decision-making in both the psychiatric system and the penal system.

Risk management may be defined as the identification, assessment, elimination or reduction of the possibility of incurring misfortune (Castel, 1991). As Nikolas Rose has put it, risk management 'operates through transforming professional subjectivity':

> It is the individual professional who has to make the assessment and management of risk their central professional obligation They have to assess the individual client in terms of the riskiness they represent, to allocate each to a risk level, to put in place the appropriate administrative arrangements for the management of the individual in the light of the requirement to minimise risk and to take responsibility, indeed blame – if an untoward incident occurs. It appears that it is no longer good enough to say that behaviour is difficult to predict and 'accidents will happen'. Every unwelcome incident may be seen as a failure of professional expertise: someone must be held accountable [Rose, 1997].

[...]

Beck also writes of the 'technocratic authoritarianism' which can result where the presence of the technology to manage risk creates a political expectation that it will be used, whatever the consequences in terms of expense or interference with other fundamental values. An example of this kind of expectation is the Government's statement in the *High Risk Patients* Volume of the White Paper that:

> There is no single answer to the problem of dangerousness. No society can ever be completely free of the risk of serious harm. But where there are deficiencies in the provision of specialist services, as in the case of dangerous people with severe personality disorder (DSPD), the public rightly expects the Government to take action [Home Office, 2000, para 1.8].

The action which the Government proposes is to remove 'weaknesses' in the law. This involves broadening immensely the scope of the concept of detainable mental disorder, broadening the powers of psychiatric detention under civil powers, rendering mental health professionals accountable for their decisions not to implement compulsory care, and allowing detention of personality disordered offenders as long as there are treatments which can manage the behaviours consequent upon the disorder, even if they cannot treat the core disorder. As the Government put it:

> This approach will provide the unambiguous authority to detain individuals who would fall within the DSPD group where appropriate interventions are offered to tackle the individual's high-risk behaviour. In all cases treatment will be delivered in an appropriate therapeutic environment [Home Office, 2000, para 3.7].

These proposals entail the further expansion of powers of preventive detention, the ultimate risk management mechanism of both the penal and the psychiatric system to protect society from dangerous offenders. Both the penal and the psychiatric system provide for detention in different levels of security. In both sectors great reliance is placed on strategies of 'graduated relaxation of security'. Patients and prisoners who start in high security are gradually tested in conditions of lesser security before release to the community through probation or supervised after-care. Both sectors concern themselves with the management of risk to the public, and risk management becomes more difficult once a patient or prisoner leaves detention and is made subject to community supervision.
[...]

Prisoners and patients: converging legal status?

[...] In 1991 Gunn *et al* carried out a study of 5% of the male prison population and found that 1% were diagnosed schizophrenic, and 10% personality disordered (74% of whom required psychiatric treatment) (Gunn *et al*, 1991). Although the growth of forensic psychiatry as a specialism has been dramatic, from two consultants in 1962 to 70 consultants in 1992 (Home Office, 1992, para 2.8), the capacity of the health service to absorb mentally disordered offenders is limited. On 31 March 2000 there were 12,900 patients detained in hospital, of whom 1,305 were detained in high security hospitals, 10,200 in other NHS hospitals, and 1,400 in private mental nursing homes. The number of court admissions increased from 1,500 in 1988–89 to 2,110 by 1994–5, but then fell back to 1,900 in 1998–99 and more steeply to 1,600 in 1999–2000 (DoH, 2000, para 3.9). Whilst the penal system has the capacity to absorb large numbers of offenders, the ability of the health service to do so is limited by three main constraints: the lack of facilities, the reluctance of the psychiatric profession to become involved in treating those whom they do not believe are likely to respond to treatment, and competing demands for health and social services budgets.

For Convention purposes, offenders detained under the Mental Health Act system of hospital orders and restriction orders are patients detained on grounds of unsoundness of mind. Until the ruling of the European Court of Human Rights in *X v United Kingdom*,[4] the Home Secretary, a Government minister, retained control over the discharge of restriction order patients. Restricted patients could have their cases referred to a Mental Health Review Tribunal, which could advise the Home Secretary on suitability for discharge, but the Home Secretary was not bound by their advice. The European Court of Human Rights held that Art 5(4) entitles everyone detained on grounds of unsoundness of mind to seek review of the lawfulness of their detention before a court or tribunal. In order to be a competent court for the purposes of the Art 5(4), the Mental Health Review Tribunal had to be given the power to discharge restricted patients if the conditions which justified the initial detention were no longer met. The judicial body had to have the final say regardless of the minister's view.

In order for a psychiatric detention to remain lawful for the purposes of Art 5 there must be objective medical evidence of unsoundness of mind of a kind or degree warranting confinement. The most disturbing aspect of the ruling in *X v United Kingdom* from the Home Office's point of view was the possibility that an offender who was given a hospital order with restrictions for a serious offence would be entitled to seek discharge before a Mental Health Review Tribunal after only six months in hospital, and might be discharged after a comparatively short period of detention if the unsoundness of mind which originally justified the detention was no longer present. Offenders committing crimes meriting 10 or 15 years in prison might be found no longer to be mentally disordered to a degree warranting detention shortly after admission, and might then be discharged after only a few months' detention.

Mental disorder has a very broad meaning under the Mental Health Act 1983, including mental illness, psychopathic disorder, mental impairment and severe mental impairment. An offender who is mentally disordered may be detained in prison or in hospital. Which route they follow, therapeutic or penal, depends on whether they are identified, by psychiatrists willing to treat them, as being mentally disordered within the meaning of the 1983 Act. In the case of patients with mental impairment or psychopathic disorder, the doctors must consider that medical treatment is likely to alleviate or prevent deterioration in their condition (in short that they are treatable). Section 37 of the 1983 Act allows for the detention of mentally disordered offenders in hospital under hospital orders. It is important to recognise that the system of hospital orders requires no causal connection between the mental disorder and the offence. The only relevant considerations are the offender's mental condition at the time of sentencing. Detention may be prolonged by the psychiatrist in charge of the patient's treatment, the responsible medical officer, who may furnish a report to the hospital managers 'renewing' the authority after six months and thereafter at annual intervals. Hospital order patients may be discharged to the community subject to 'supervised discharge' under ss 25A–25J of the Mental Health Act 1983.

If an offender is given a hospital order and the Crown Court feels it necessary to impose restrictions on discharge because of the need to protect the public from serious harm, it may impose a restriction order. Restrictions may be imposed for a prescribed period, or without limit of time. This has the effect of requiring the leave of the Home Secretary via the Home Office Mental Health Unit before the patient can be granted leave, transferred to another hospital, or discharged. At the end of 1995 there were 2,482 mentally disordered offenders detained in hospital subject to Home Office restrictions on discharge, more than in any of the previous 10 years.[5] Restriction order patients may be subject to conditional discharge, which means that they remain liable to recall to hospital at any time during the currency of the restriction order.

From a risk management point of view, therapeutic detention of offenders under the Mental Health Act has the advantage that it is potentially indefinite. It can extend until the offender is deemed well enough to leave hospital. The Mental Health Act offers the possibility of extending detention beyond the duration of whatever prison sentence is proportionate to the gravity of the offence. But after *X v United Kingdom*, detention under the Mental Health Act could not guarantee that the offender would spend a minimum period in detention. Worse still, it opened up the possibility that people with psychopathic disorder would have to be discharged if they were no longer treatable, even if they still posed a risk to the public.

The legal status of prisoner means that for Convention purposes a person is detained following conviction of a criminal offence (Art 5(1)(a)), and in these cases it is possible to stipulate a minimum period to be served in detention which is proportionate to the gravity of the offence. In *Thynne Wilson and Gunnell v United Kingdom*[6] the European Court held that in the case of discretionary life prisoners it was allowable for a criminal court to impose a minimum tariff period of detention to reflect the gravity of the offence and the culpability of the offender, and for detention to be extended beyond that period if the prisoner remained dangerous. [...]

Whilst a hospital patient has the right under the Mental Health Act to seek review of detention after the first six months of detention, a life prisoner has to wait until the tariff period has expired before becoming entitled to review. The tariff period is the part of the sentence which reflects the gravity of the offence. The legal status of prisoner has always had advantages over that of patient if the goals of policy are to ensure that an offender will be detained for a minimum period commensurate with the gravity of the offence and the level of blameworthiness. Following *Thynne* it was clear that the Convention represented no obstacle to extending detention beyond the tariff period on grounds of dangerousness, as long as there were opportunities for review. The possibility of indefinite detention on grounds of dangerousness, which used to be the advantage of patient status from the risk management point of view, was now available in relation to prisoners.

Conclusion

Foucault has written evocatively of the development and refinement of a 'carceral network' where deviancy and delinquency can be controlled through the development not just of penal institutions but other institutions aimed at cure and reformation, and the development of surveillance mechanisms in the community (Foucault, 1977). The hallmark of these developments is that risky individuals who pose a threat to the social fabric can be detained and monitored, and that legal mechanisms exist to move them from one set of institutions to another with relative ease if the risk management dictates. The proposed arrangements for DSPD individuals represent the apotheosis of the cross fertilisation of risk management and therapeutic strategies between the penal and the psychiatric systems which I have described as a convergence. They would allow the indefinite detention usually associated with the psychiatric system, but without the requirement of treatability beyond the stipulation that behaviour consequent upon the disorder can be managed. In other words, risk management becomes treatment.

The convergence of the penal and the psychiatric systems continues apace, and the ethical dilemma is if and where a boundary line can be drawn between therapy and preventive detention or 'growing old in custody'. Jeremy Bentham's Panopticon, the model upon which both the penitentiary and the asylum system were based, enabled a large number of inmates to be supervised with relative ease from a central point. The new system into which we are moving is increasingly characterised by controls exercised from an institutional base, where patients can be detained if necessary, and where they can be brought by force by specialist teams of paramedics for compulsory treatment. Those posing a risk will be tracked in the community. Supervisors in the community will assume responsibility for ensuring that patients receive community care.

What are the likely consequences of the convergence I have described in terms of the relationship between therapist and patient? Increasingly psychiatrists are becoming involved in decision-making about risk in the penal system, whether sitting as medical members of the various panels of the Parole Board, or giving expert evidence on risk before those panels. The Modernised Care Programme Approach suggests a significant role for the police in what has traditionally been health and social care decision-making about risk management and community care. The ethics of health care are based around the primacy of therapy (*primum non nocere*) key notions such as respect for autonomy, informed consent and confidentiality. The ethics of criminal justice and risk management afford primacy to deterrence, retributivism, social protection, selective incapacitation and recognition of the rights of victims. The erosion of the boundaries between the medical world with its values and the criminal justice system with its own very different concerns results in the concept of confidentiality being redefined to accommodate the information sharing requirements of effective risk management. Most notably, however, the proposals will greatly limit therapeutic discretion, the discretion not to disclose medical secrets, and the discretion not to detain being significant examples. It has always been a principle of the psychiatric system that a psychiatrist cannot be legally required to accept a patient under his care and custody. This principle remains, but where there is risk, it will be uncomfortable for the mental health professionals under the new proposals if they have to give reasons for not taking compulsory powers. The proposals are designed to encourage defensive medicine in the name of risk management. Just as there is a calculus of risk, so too there is a calculus of rights. The liberty rights of the mentally disordered person have to be balanced against the right to life and protection against inhuman and degrading treatment enjoyed by potential victims, reflected in expedients such as the right of victims and their families to make representations to the Mental Health Tribunal considering the patient's discharge. At the moment the balance is moving towards risk management and away from patients' rights.

This all has consequences in terms of the citizenship rights of mentally disordered patients. The Richardson Committee tried to promote principles of non-discrimination by bringing the regime of powers regarding mentally disordered people as close as possible to the common law powers to treat people with mental incapacity without their consent. In short they tried to use general medical law as their starting point. The current proposals take criminal justice models of risk management as their starting point. As such their philosophy bears many of the hallmarks of late 19th century thinking about the status of mentally disordered people. In 1890 the authors of Pope's *Treatise on the Law and Practice of Lunacy* said this:

> Possessed of physical force without a regulating mind, and subject to the natural instincts untutored by discipline and uncontrolled by fear or punishment, some classes of the insane threaten continual danger to those with whom they are brought in contact ...

> So far as they are irrational, the insane, though in the state are not of the state. On the other hand, though not of the state, the insane are yet in the state. Hence the state has relations with them, though not those which it has with its citizens proper [p xiv].

The tenor of these proposals is that people with a mental disorder are not citizens proper in a number of senses. First, they may be detained on grounds of risk on the basis of a very broad concept of mental disorder. Secondly, the proposals are stigmatising in drawing a constant association between mental disorder, risk and criminality, and in subjecting mentally disordered people to regimes of surveillance and liability to detention which are outside the framework of the criminal law, but which are based on criminal justice and penal models rather than general medical law.

From N.S. Gray, J.M. Laing and L. Noaks (eds) Criminal Justice, Mental Health and the Politics of Risk *(London: Cavendish), 2002, pp. 70–2, 80–3, 95–7.*

Notes

1. (1981) 4 EHRR 188.
2. See, for example, Kellow Chesney's discussion of the Victorian preoccupation with 'the dangerous classes'.

3. The most obvious example being the Government's proposals in relation to *Dangerous People with Severe Personality Disorder*, discussed […].
4. (1981) 4 EHRR 188.
5. One difficulty in assessing the scale of the use of therapeutic disposals is that the Home Office issues statistics of mentally disordered offenders which are collected by calendar year and which cover mainly restricted patients. Meanwhile, the Department of Health collects statistics by financial year of all admissions to psychiatric hospitals, including those of the many offenders admitted without restrictions.
6. Series A, No 190, Judgment of 25 October 1990.

References

Beck, U. 'From industrial society to risk society: questions of survival, social structure and ecological enlightenment' (1992) 9 Theory, Culture and Society 91.

Castel, R. 'From dangerousness to risk', in Bruchell, G., Gordon, C. and Miller, P. (eds.), *The Foucault Effect: Studies in Governmentality*, 1991, Hemel Hempstead: Harvester Wheatsheaf.

Chesney, K. *The Victorian Underworld*, Pelican.

Department of Health, 2000, *In-patients Formally Detained in Hospitals under the Mental Health Act 1983 and other Legislation, England: 1988–89 and 1994–95 to 1999–2000*, Statistical Bulletin 2000/19, London: HMSO.

Foucault, M. *Discipline and Punish: The Birth of the Prison*, Sheridan, A. (trans), 1977, New York: Pantheon.

Gunn, J. Maden, A. and Sinton, M. 'Treatment needs of prisoners with mental disorder' [1991] BMJ 303.

Home Office, *Review of Health and Social Services for Mentally Disordered Offenders and Others Requiring Similar Services* (The Reed Report), Chairman Dr John Reed, Cm 2088, 1992, London: HMSO.

Home Office, *Reforming the Mental Health Act: Part II High Risk Patients*, TSO 2000, Cm 5016–2, 2000, London: HMSO.

Pope, H.M.R., *A Treatise on the Law and Practice of Lunacy*, 1890, London: Sweet & Maxwell.

Rose, N. 'At risk of madness: law, politics and forensic psychiatry', paper delivered at the Cropwood Conference on The Future of Forensic Psychiatry, St John's College, Cambridge, 19–21 March 1997.

Taylor, P. and Gunn, J. 'Homicides by people with mental illness: myth and reality' (1999) 174 Br J Psychiatry 9.

29. Life as a woman: the gendered pains of indeterminate imprisonment

Stephanie Walker and Anne Worrall

Indeterminacy is incompatible with a managerialist approach to imprisonment. Increasingly complex rules and procedures are employed to mask and neutralise the inherent uncertainty of life imprisonment. But the rational despair of lifers cannot be managed by rules and procedures, even if these are subject to the changes recommended by penal reformers. The pains of indeterminate imprisonment are specific to that experience and are structured by the (gendered) loss of a world for which lifers are not allowed (because they have forfeited the right) to grieve. This unique study *of* female lifers *by* a female lifer argues for a re-orientation of understanding of women's experiences of life imprisonment. That understanding must take account of the relationship between time and the reconstruction of 'womanhood' under conditions of intensive and prolonged surveillance. It must confront the refusal of many female lifers to perceive 'coping' as a virtue and it must question the complex morality of requiring 'bereaved' women to 'address their offending behaviour' in a context where time is torturously unstructured and where goals and priorities are forever subject to the vagaries of law and order crises.

Introduction

A life sentence is a sentence like no other. The ultimate weapon in the penal armoury of England and Wales,[1] its uniqueness lies in its indeterminacy, a feature which sets it apart from even the longest determinate sentence. In populist punitive discourses it remains the Other of the capital punishment debate – the overly lenient and undeserved escape from death for those who have taken or endangered the lives of 'the innocent'. In 1998 there were 3,934 life sentence prisoners in England and Wales (Home Office, 1999). The number of prison receptions sentenced to life imprisonment has increased by 61 per cent since 1987. Lifers are also being detained for longer: in 1987 the average length of time served before release was 11.2 years; in 1998 it was 14.2 years. The population of female lifers has increased from 74 in 1987 to 137 in 1998
[…].

The pains of indeterminacy

Much has been written about the 'pains of imprisonment' experienced by both men and women, particularly those serving long sentences who, in addition to those losses experienced by all prisoners (for example, privacy, autonomy, heterosexual relations, family contact, personal security and so on) also experience a great fear of physical and mental deterioration. (see, for example, Flanagan, 1995). What, in our view, remains relatively unexplored are the losses specifically associated with indeterminate sentences – the losses that become more, rather than less, difficult to bear with time. For women, many of these losses are bound up with motherhood. Even – perhaps especially – those women who do not have children suffer extensive gender-specific loss as the result of a life sentence. We have identified those gendered pains as:

- The biological clock
- Losing children
- (You don't stop) Being a Mum

Other pains of indeterminacy may appear to be gender-neutral in the sense that they apply to both male and female lifers, but the impact of those pains and reactions to them may be gendered. We have identified these pains as:

- Suffering for men behaving badly
- Lack of understanding of the life sentence
- Living under the microscope
- The apparent irrelevance of time

The biological clock

Matthews (1999:40) argues that the relationship between time and biological rhythms is closely linked on a daily basis in prison, but that the relationship between the body and seasonal changes is 'muted and less relevant' than outside prison. Yet, for women of child-bearing age, those seasonal changes are crucial. A life sentence can prevent a woman from becoming a mother. This simple biological fact makes a life sentence a greater punishment for women than for men:

> Men can do a life sentence and come out and still have a family, but a woman can't come out at 40 or 50 and start a family.
>
> (Ruth)

Of the women in our study, 14 had no children and at least ten of these were likely to be uncertain about their chances of child-bearing on release. Only four of the young offenders, with relatively short tariffs, could be reasonably certain of being able to start families after their release.

The ability to bear children is central to the social construction of womanhood and is increasingly viewed as a human right (Articles 8 and

12 of the European Convention on Human Rights) regardless of her ability to *rear* children. Although there is much public debate about the lengths to which society can go, ethically, to enable a woman to bear children, there is no debate at all about the circumstances under which a woman may be prevented from bearing children, especially her first child. Yet women serving life sentences and other very long determinate sentences may be thus prevented without any challenge or even discussion (Howard League, 1999). Male life sentence prisoners, on the other hand, are already anticipating the introduction of the Human Rights Act in October 2000 by seeking the right to inseminate their wives artificially (*Guardian*, 30 June 2000).

Losing children

All prisoners run the risk of losing contact with their children, to a greater or lesser degree. The longer the sentence, the greater that loss of contact, but the additional pain inflicted by a life sentence on children and parent alike is uncertainty and an inability to plan as a child is growing up.

> I mean, they talk about when I'm going to come home and what they want us to do ... But I try and talk to them as if to say 'Well, Mummy will be a lot older by then, and you'll be in a big school, high school, and maybe you'll be at college', and things like that ...
>
> (Sarah-Louise)

It is perhaps unsurprising that the strain of this uncertainty leads those who are caring for the children to try and 'stabilise' the situation, often by minimising or stopping contact:

> He's living with his Dad ... My husband doesn't want me to see him.
>
> (Bernadette)

> I don't have any contact with my children ... After the first 12 months in Shelley, the contact stopped.
>
> (Jessica)

> I've had no visits at all, and I wrote to them every week ... but the letters started being returned, so now I limit it to Christmas and birthday cards ... which are returned.
>
> (Lauren)

It might be argued that these are problems experienced by children with either parent in prison, but there are additional problems for children whose mother is in prison. The most obvious one is the greater uncertainty about continuity of care. Whereas the children of imprisoned men usually remain in the care of their mothers, the children of imprisoned mothers have lost their principal carer and are far more likely to experience major disruption in their caring. Caddle and Crisp (1997) found that only nine per cent of the children of women in prison remained in the care of their fathers. A similar proportion were taken into local authority care and the rest had temporary carers, mostly grandparents or other female relatives. Although we have no evidence, we suspect that the percentage of the children of female lifers being looked after by the local authority or adopted is likely to be higher than in the general female prison population:

> They're adopted … After spending four years seeing them, and then to be told 'you can't see them', and not being given a chance to explain to them what was going on, I feel bitter …
>
> (Toni)

> The eldest ones are adopted … I think about them every day, but I know the people they're with really do care and love them …
>
> (Linda)

One of the reasons for this, of course, may be that the children's father has been the victim:

> Women lifers are mainly in prison because of a man. Our children are out there with nobody. It's our husbands who have been killed. Our children have lost both parents …
>
> (Lauren)

(You don't stop) being a mum

If loss of contact with her children is a woman lifer's greatest fear:

> I wonder if they'll let me fade out of their lives in years to come … You worry that, over 15 years, will they fade out of *my* life?
>
> (Rose)

then coping appropriately with visits, year in and year out, is probably the next greatest cause of anxiety:

> I need those visits but I've also got some rather unpleasant scars through my children grabbing hold of me and screaming 'Mum, mum, mum – I don't want to leave you, Mum' … I've come upstairs and just couldn't handle it, so I've picked up a razor …
>
> (Sam)

> After a time they say it gets better having visits, but it doesn't. It just gets harder. So in the end you think to yourself 'why do I put myself and my children through this by seeing them so often?' So you tend to cut your visits down.
>
> (Cassie)

The women talked extensively of their feelings of inadequacy as mothers, of the pain of separation, knowing their children are growing up without them and unable to forgive themselves for leaving their children (cf. Boudin, 1998). Feelings of worthlessness, helplessness and emptiness were widespread:

> When you come into prison, they forget to tell you how to stop being a Mum.
>
> (Kelley)

In her study of male lifers, Sparks (1998) talks briefly about the men's feelings for their families. It was clear that most of the men wanted and valued the support of their families but their concern appeared to be about what their families could do for *them*, rather than vice versa. It may simply have been an artefact of the interview questions, but there was no mention at all of fatherhood.

Suffering for men behaving badly

This research took place at the time of the Whitemoor and Parkhurst attempted escapes. The women lifers who were interviewed were outraged at the deprivations they experienced in the subsequent security clamp-down:

> Why should us women have to pay for something that's the men's fault? Because it's very rare a woman lifer will try to escape. Women lifers don't do that. We're entirely different to men.
>
> (Marion)

> How many female riots have you heard of? How many prisons are trashed by women? How many women stand up in groups and become aggressive? It doesn't happen.
>
> (Jane)

> It's *always* men who mess the system up and it's *always* women who suffer.
>
> (Yvonne)

> With the shopping trips and everything else stopped, it's down to the men isn't it? Because they took the piss and got screws to go out and buy them loads of food ... the reason the clothes are being taken away from us is because of the men, isn't it?
>
> (Rayma)

This profound sense that they were no longer trusted through no fault of their own was epitomised in the introduction of handcuffing for any journeys outside prison. Women who had been trusted on outside visits and trips for years were shaken and humiliated by the new regulation:

> When we have to go out to hospital we have to be handcuffed, which is very, very shameful ... I felt so ashamed ... I'd never, ever been handcuffed, and it was a feeling of hurt as well, of having the trust that had been built up after so many outside trips just whipped away from you for no reason at all ... apart from the Parkhurst and Whitemoor incidents.
>
> (Lauren)

In portraying women as, yet again, the victims of men's behaviour, there is a danger that women's agency will be lost (cf. Pearson, 1999). Women are undoubtedly as guilty as men of colluding with the smuggling of drugs into prison (Chief Inspector of Prisons, 1997) and thereby provoking obsessive security consciousness. The point to be made here is that a particular group of women who had been trusted for years was suddenly subjected to excessive security measures as a result of specific, physical, behaviour by men that no-one honestly believed would be imitated by these particular women. The punitive impact of Woodcock and Learmont is now recognised as falling disproportionately and inappropriately on women prisoners (Chief Inspector of Prisons, 1997; Prison Reform Trust, 2000).

Lack of understanding of the life sentence

Confusion about the intricacies of the life sentence may be as widespread amongst male lifers as amongst females, if Sparks's (1998) study is anything to go by. However, the reason we have been unable in this study to distinguish between those serving mandatory and those serving discretionary life sentences is that so many of the women themselves were unclear. When asked which type of sentence they were serving, 16 apparently did not know. In addition, confusion over the nature and purpose of the tariff and the various stages of sentence was widespread. Several women believed that their tariff date was their release date:

> The longest I would serve, which I have in black and white, is six years ... They can't give me more than six years. They can't, can they? I've got it down there in black and white, and they can't, can they? They can't go back on their word. [The latter comments made in response to the researcher explaining that this is not what the tariff means.]
>
> (Priscilla)

Others had listened to rumours and myths:

> I've heard that if you stay out of trouble for ten years you can ask for the licence to be ripped up. But I don't know, is that true? Does it get ripped up?
>
> (Sam)

Yet others displayed utter confusion about the process of the life sentence, causing the researcher a few (though not many!) ethical qualms about using her role to explain the process to some of the women:

> I know you've got to do a first stage, and then you do a second stage, but the only thing they haven't told me … they say you normally do three years at your first stage, but with my tariff being so high – because I haven't asked this question, and nobody's even come to tell me either – does that mean that I have to do a lot longer on my first, because of how long the tariff is, before I'll be able to go on to my second stage?
>
> (Sarah-Louise)

Living under the microscope

Lifers are subject to more constant monitoring and surveillance over a greater period of time by more people than are any other group of prisoners. The women spoke of finding it difficult to 'be themselves'[2], knowing their actions were monitored and that whatever they did would be written about in reports. They talked about feeling wary of what they said, for fear of their words being misinterpreted, and knowing that one error could result in a 'blotted copybook' that would remain with the woman for a long time:

> You're here for x number of years. You lie once and that's it – your credibility is totally out the door.
>
> (Gill)

Non-conforming behaviour is pathologised, even when that behaviour is intrinsically neutral, such as choosing not to spend time in the association room or not to eat in the dining room:

> I don't eat prison food – I never have. I think the system perceives that to be an eating disorder … It's noted in reports here that I do not eat in the dining room.
>
> (Jane)

> You won't ever see me in the TV room because there's crowds of people in there and I don't like crowds … I've been told by various screws that this is not a good idea – that I should be associating.
>
> (Sam)

As Sapsford commented, 'anything he (sic) does may count as a symptom' (1983:19). Carlen identified many years ago that a 'good' female prisoner is one who 'opens up' to staff and 'doesn't think she is any better than the other women' (1983: 102). Such scrutiny over years has the effect of undermining any previous confidence a woman might have had in her own sense of identity:

> Basically, I'm happy with myself, but riddled with guilt because so many people *aren't* that I don't understand how I can possibly be OK … You know, they make you question your whole personality and everything – every aspect of your identity – comes under the microscope, and you just don't know who you are any more.
>
> (Jane)

The apparent irrelevance of time

Although the women felt themselves to be under constant scrutiny and required to examine themselves over and over again, this pressure was perversely juxtaposed with a perceived lack of urgency on the part of 'the system'. Women spoke of the agonisingly slow speed at which 'the system' works and the consequent perception that 'they' don't care. Women were told at reviews that they had to 'address' certain areas of concern, only to find that assistance in doing so was not viewed by staff as a matter of priority:

> They say they're going to address certain areas and then you don't see anybody from one lot of 12 months to the next.
>
> (Jessica)

> There's an anger management course I'm meant to go on and a drug course and I've been inside three years now and none of it's taken off, no-one's seen me. They've all said I've got to do this but no-one's referred me to anyone.
>
> (Ziggy)

Reports were not submitted on time and women felt their sentences were being unnecessarily prolonged because of the failure of senior staff to work efficiently to a time-scale. The absence of regular reviews often distorted any sense of 'progress':

> You have to chase around for so much … I said to them 'Look, I've got to have F75s done after three years, and then another lot of F75s done. three years after that, because my last lot of F75s, which will make it nine years, will be my LRC [first parole hearing]'. I had to tell them that. But if we don't push, things don't get done … If my F75s don't get done on time … well, I'm going over that nine years, aren't I?
>
> (Freda)

Lifers, it seemed, were not going anywhere, so getting things done 'later' was just as good as getting them done 'sooner':

> You're doing a life sentence, so time is irrelevant it doesn't matter. There's no time scale on things … And there's no date for things to be done by, so they can just drag it out as long as they want to.
>
> (Jane)

What the women may not be aware of is what Carlen has identified as the erosion of prison officers 'professional discretion' - a necessary tool in volatile situations requiring sensitive rule interpretation and innovative management (1998:112). She cites an officer who talks specifically about the problems of lifer management:

We used to feel we could give the women some guidance about how they were doing in prison ... but now we're all at sea on everything. You cannot give an opinion on anything, anything may happen from day to day. And I think that, as a result, the prisoners have less confidence in us. They see the way we're treated, and they know that sometimes we are no more knowledgeable about what's going on in the system than they are.
(Prison Officer cited in Carlen, 1998: 112–13)

Coming to terms with a life sentence

So total is the transformation of the existence of those on whom life imprisonment is imposed that it may be defined as the involuntary leaving behind of one world for another: the world which was theirs is replaced by a world which is alien, holding nothing familiar, nothing certain, to which they might otherwise anchor themselves.

Their vulnerability exposed, the combined forces of helplessness, powerlessness, fear and despair lay ready in wait to occupy the place vacated by that which gave meaning and purpose to life. For, in the forfeiting of one world for another, it is the entirety, the sheer scale, of that which is missing which, by its very absence, has the most crushing impact. Both Cohen and Taylor (1972) and Sapsford (1983) draw a parallel between the plight of displaced peoples, whose lives are destroyed and have then somehow to be rebuilt and that of the life sentence prisoner. For those in receipt of a life sentence, the overwhelming feeling is one of abject loss – even, in a sense, the loss of themselves.

The issues of loss for the life sentenced women in this study were so acute and all encompassing that their characteristics parallel those of bereavement. The women have 'lost' their lives, as they knew them, and only the shell of their existence remains. Time, as we have seen, means everything (the biological clock) and nothing (the irrelevance of time). They grieve for the loss of the world of which they were a part and which continues to exist without them. They can still see it, hear about it and read about it. The 'outside world' can still impact on them directly when there is a law and order crisis, or when a journalist (or researcher!) wants to provide it with education, entertainment or titillation (see, for example, the recent BBC series *Jailbirds*).

Jose-Kampfner (1990) suggests that the experience of life imprisonment may share characteristics with the experience of terminal illness. We recognise that some may find this analogy offensive insofar as lifers have, at least at a superficial level, chosen the path that has led to life imprisonment in a way that most terminally ill people have not. On the other hand, those who are dying are seen as worthy of love and support, while lifers are often not only denied that love and support, but are seen as having forfeited the right to 'grieve for the loss of themselves and their outside world' (1990:112). Building on the widely accepted stages of grieving (Kubler Ross, 1969), Jose-Kampfner argues that female lifers (should be allowed to) experience (not necessarily sequentially) denial, anger, depression, mourning, acceptance and hope. The prison environment, however, is uniquely unsuited to such a process. It is not our intention here systematically to explore each of these stages but we would argue that an understanding of bereavement and the grieving process is essential to an understanding of the experiences of female (and maybe all) lifers.

The process of 'coming to terms' with a life sentence entails an acceptance of several things: the rightness of the verdict, the rightness of the life sentence, the rightness of the tariff and, finally, the reality of imprisonment. All this involves a devastating admission of guilt to oneself and an acceptance that one is a totally and irreversibly changed person. One can never go back to being the person one once was, nor is there any hope of a brighter future for many, many years – if ever. Boudin (1998), herself a long-term prisoner, argues that 'this crisis is potentially an opportunity for enormous growth if it is faced, growth in a woman's ability to develop emotionally, growth in her ability to parent her child' (1998:105). But this can only be done within the supportive environment of feminist therapeutic group work, where women can work through the conflicts of shame, guilt and failed motherhood.

Sapsford (1983:85) acknowledges the emotional 'floundering' of most lifers at the beginning of their sentences, but goes on, nevertheless to argue that, with a few exceptions:

> ... all of the sample [of 60 life sentence prisoners] found a way of dealing acceptably with the sentence ... a clear distinction is apparent between men whose activities are directed chiefly at planning for the time after their release, those whose activity is seen as purely 'internal to the prison' – men who are climbing the ladder of prison jobs and privileges, or becoming expert at prison 'fiddles', or undertaking educational programmes or a hobby task purely for its own sake – and a third group who appear to be just waiting out their sentence and making no plans. (Sapsford, 1983:87-88)

Sapsford also identifies a 'small' fourth group of – recently arrived – lifers, who cope by being pre-occupied with appeals 'and have not yet come to terms with prison as an inescapable reality' (1983:88). In our study, only ten women had *not* been through the appeals process. We found women still pre-occupied with appeals after many years because they believed themselves to be either innocent of any crime or, more frequently, innocent of a crime requiring a life sentence. They had 'come to terms' with prison as an inescapable reality – but an unjust one.

> I was totally wrongly convicted. I wasn't even there.
> (Samantha – three years into a 12 year tariff)

I'm here not because I've committed a crime. I'm here because the jury concluded that 'she must have done it'.

> (Emmanuel – two years into a 15 year tariff)

I know what I did but it wasn't like what they said.

> (Mary – two years into a 15 year tariff)

They think you've deliberately gone out to plot and take someone's life. They can't understand when you say you didn't.

> (Gill – three years into a 13 year tariff)

I don't believe I should have got a life sentence for what I done. I believe I deserved a sentence, but not a life sentence.

> (Linda – three years into an eight year tariff)

Perhaps Sapsford's apparent faith in the objective justice of the life sentence is a reflection of a more trusting penal era – certainly it was an era uncomplicated by such things as the recognition of miscarriages of justice (Wilson, 1999) and domestic violence.

I'm in the middle of appealing now ... Emma Humphries getting out has given me a bit more of a chance, because violence in the home was not looked at.

> (Toni – having served five years of a 16 year tariff)

I went for two appeals and I was knocked back on both of them. That group that's fighting for Sara Thornton, they've got a lot of letters belonging to me ... I've seen the governor and he told me three and a half years ago that he'd get me a solicitor, and he never did. I said to him, 'it's wrong to keep me in here for something I haven't done' and I explained everything to him ... but I'm still waiting.

> (Tracey – having served seven years of a 12 year tariff)

I've tried to appeal, yeah. The solicitor that I had was crap. I mean, he was sat in Shelley telling me that I was not a murderer and that I shouldn't be there, you know ... They made a real cock-up of all the evidence and everything. They just didn't expect me to get life.

> (Lisa – having served five years of an eight year tariff)

Despite these protestations of innocence, most realised, like Rose (into her third year of a 15 year tariff) that appealing is 'just another game'. When that game ends in failure, however, the next 'game' is the appeal against tariff:

I've appealed twice and got turned down. I'm thinking of appealing against my tariff.

> (Ziggy – having served three years of a 12 year tariff)

The judge at my trial said I should only serve ten years, the Lord Chief Justice agreed and the Home Secretary put two on. So I'm trying to get them two off. I don't know whether it's easy or not. I don't know. I wrote to everybody after I lost my appeal.

(Carole – having served seven years of a 12 year tariff)

The pretend games

Even when the women themselves had 'come to terms' with the reality of their sentence, they found themselves having to play multiple 'pretend games' for the benefit of families and friends. Visiting time was the most difficult time:

You play the 'pretend' game. You get real good at that. You do your face, do your hair and you pretend that they haven't come after hours of travelling. You pretend that they haven't got up at three o'clock in the morning to get to Shelley in time for a visit. They play the game and you play the game.

(Rose)

I don't allow them to know what's going on in prison. I never do and I'm sure that's quite common with everybody.

(Ruth)

You can't tell them. It's not fair on them. It's hard enough for them to understand that one of their children is actually doing a life sentence – it's bad enough doing a prison sentence, but actually doing a *life* sentence.

(Linda)

But for a number of the women, the hardest aspect of the 'pretend' game was being unable openly to grieve for their victim. Caz had killed her daughter:

It's the guilt that gets to me more than the actual prison sentence. I'll never get over the death of my daughter, never. I have a lot of hate for myself.

Jessica, who killed her husband, was asked if she thought it would help to talk to someone about her feelings:

I'm sure it would help but I can't … I just cannot talk to people … When I talk about him, the bad things come out about, you know, how he was, and then I feel so bloody disloyal, because I loved the guy. It just seems wrong that I'm knocking him and he's dead – through my fault.

The exquisite pain of feeling obliged to deny the range of negative emotions usually regarded as 'normal' in bereavement is exacerbated in another way. In order to address their offending behaviour, the women were required to re-live their offence again and again at review boards. Many of the women spoke of the distress of having to re-live the offence repeatedly:

> There's so many people that you have to keep repeating your case to … This happens all through your sentence and in the end it's like a monologue. You take all feeling out of it to cope with it, so you probably come across as this uncaring bitch who couldn't give a shit about what they've done … You've said it so often it doesn't even sound real to you any more.
>
> (Linda)

Re-living the offence made the women feel as if they were never going to be able to put it behind them:

> You try to climb the ladder and it's like they keep knocking you down.
>
> (Shirley)

> I feel like a broken record … After that I get really depressed … They say to me 'Oh? you can talk to a befriender'. I say 'I can befriend myself I don't want no one to come so you'd better leave me alone' … It's like you have a scar where you get stabbed and it start to heal and some man come and stab you again and the wound get deeper … I says 'don't you realise what you're doing to people?' they say 'it's our job' … I says 'I'm not blaming you, I'm not blaming no-one. I'm just telling you the way I feel after it and what kind of effect it has on people'.
>
> (Jaimie)

> Yeah, they've always brought it up that I haven't accepted enough responsibility for my crime … Don't they realise, these people, that it's because you do accept responsibility for what's happened that it's so hard to talk about?
>
> (Louise)

Almost every woman had an impassioned story to tell of the way in which she was repeatedly expected to re-live her crime, the subsequent profound depression and the extent to which such torturous demands prevented her from moving on and rebuilding her life:

> Waiting for reviews, waiting for reports, you tend to revert to the time of your offence because everything's thrown back up in your face and you have to deal with it. And you *have* to deal with it as it was *then*, and not as it is now. You deal with how you felt *then* which puts you back in that time warp.
>
> (Jane)

In a 'normal' bereavement, the bereaved person is encouraged gradually to rebuild their lives. They are not expected to forget their loss but time is seen as the great healer and with the passing of it, there is some hope that the worst of the pain will diminish. Not so with the lifer:

> To continue to feel that worthless for x number of years isn't … a healthy option. No, it doesn't diminish. The system doesn't allow it to diminish either … They drag up, you know, the *old* hurt, that *old* feeling. So you never have anyone to help you deal with the *new* hurt and the *new* feelings, because that's irrelevant … You'd think they'd realise, wouldn't you?
>
> (Jane)

Conclusions

Our discussion has not been primarily about the politics of life imprisonment. We have avoided mentioning Myra Hindley and Rose West (neither of whom were part of our study anyway), we have avoided the debates about 'whole life' tariffs and the abolition of the mandatory life sentence (Penal Affairs Consortium, 1994). We have been concerned to give voice to some of those 140 women who are daily facing the contradiction of lives that are both extremely and mundanely (un)predictable under a system which is both extremely and mundanely (un)predictable. As Jamie says of the review board, 'I'm not blaming you, I'm not blaming no-one. I'm just telling you the way I feel after it and what kind of effect it has on people'.

The construction of the 'responsible life sentence prisoner' is dependent on tariff setting, sentence planning, risk assessment, addressing offending behaviour and, above all, public acceptability. Within this model, time is not *done, killed or wasted*, but *managed*. Yet, even if the system were working efficiently and effectively, (which it is not), indeterminacy would undermine this model, not simply because there is no predictable end to the sentence, but because the uncertainty is an intentional feature of the whole experience. It makes time both crucial and irrelevant. It makes every aspect of 'becoming responsible' more difficult. A life sentence encourages every inclination towards self-pity, every sense of injustice, victimisation and unresolved grief. It militates against the very accountability and reconstruction to which it aspires. For women, whether or not they are mothers, this experience appears to have a strongly gendered and domestic dimension. Whatever Pearson (1998) would have us believe, women are not 'getting away with murder'. On the contrary, women who commit murder are never allowed to 'get away' with, or from, it at all. Some would argue that this is as it should be – but let us not pretend that we are doing anything other.

From 'Life as a woman: the gendered pains of indeterminate imprisonment', *Prison Service Journal, 2000, no. 132, pp. 27–37 (references unavailable).*

Notes

1. Many other countries have also abolished the death penalty and this sociological study aims to provide a framework of understanding that has international currency. Nevertheless, it is recognised that women's experiences of life imprisonment are also dependent on the social, economic and political climates of the society in which they are imprisoned.
2. As Carlen points out, however, 'being yourself' is something of a double-bind. One prisoner retorted: 'They tell you to be yourself … If I was myself in here I'd never be off report' (1983: 102).

30. United States of America: prison labour: a tale of two penologies

James B. Jacobs

Introduction

Two spectres haunt American penology. The one that keeps liberals up at night is the picture of sadistic profit-obsessed managers driving prisoners in forced labour (enforced by brutal whipping) beyond the levels of human endurance. The spectre that keeps conservatives awake at night is the image of idle prisoners spending their days watching television, listening to music, smoking marijuana, lifting weights and playing basketball. The first vision anguishes about the risk that prison labour will deteriorate into a system of punishment, exploitation and even torture; the second is vexed about the anomaly that citizens pay taxes to support idle prisoners; it thus focuses on the relationship of prison labour to social equity.

There have certainly been periods in American history when the exploitation and abuse of prison labour justified the liberals' concerns. The greatest abuses occurred in the American south in the nineteenth century and, in some cases, into the twentieth century (Sellin, 1976). Prisoners were often leased out to private entrepreneurs who worked them unmercifully, sometimes to death, in mining, agriculture, road works and in other jobs (Cvornyek, 1993; Fierce, 1994; Lichtenstein, 1996). Even when the prison officials retained managerial control, there were outrageous abuses. That the prisoners oppressed by this penal slavery were almost all black reinforces liberals' anxiety about current calls to reintroduce hard labour.

Brutal labour more or less came to an end in the post-World War II period as a consequence of both ideology and the prisoners' rights movement (Garland, 1990). The southern plantation prisons, vilified in film, journalistic portrayals and lawsuits, were essentially dismantled. The southern prisons, epitomized by those of Texas, were forced to adopt the northern model of imprisonment that was characterized by greater bureaucracy and much less labour. However, in the last few years, legislatures in several southern states have voted to reinstate 'chain gangs' thereby rekindling liberals' fear that, under the guise of work programmes, prisoners will once again be abused (Curriden, 1995). The reinvested chain gangs are so recent that I am not aware of any scholarly assessments. My prediction, however, is that there is more symbolism here than reality. In large part, this is because prison officials no longer have the stomach or the disciplinary tools for implementing hard labour. Furthermore, such programmes will be given tough scrutiny in the courts and in the mass media.

We now come to the second spectre, the one of prisoners sitting around doing nothing, wallowing in indolence. As study after study and commission after commission have shown, American prisons suffer from pervasive idleness. Only a small percentage of prisoners are 'employed' in any serious sense of the word. For the most part, they serve their time in their cells watching television and listening to music on headphones or on the tiers talking and 'hanging out'. If they are fortunate, they may go to the gymnasium or the recreation yard an hour or two a day. They sleep much and do little. This idleness is not treated as a component of the intended prison regime but as an unintended, albeit unavoidable, consequence of too many prisoners and too few jobs.

The vast majority of prisoners who do have jobs work in institutional maintenance, carrying out chores that keep the prison functioning. In theory, such work is compulsory; there is no right to refuse. In practice, however, there are far more prisoners than jobs. They sweep, scrub, mop and wax. They work in the laundry, in the kitchen and on the prison grounds. Such jobs are neither challenging nor interesting, and they usually last only a few hours a day. But they get the prisoner out of the cell house and into a position, if he wants to, to wheel and deal in prison intrigues and rackets.

A very small minority, perhaps 5–10 per cent of prisoners, work in 'industries'. These industries are often laughably antiquated, using machinery dating back decades. The so-called 'industries' bear no resemblance to a modern factory. To the observer, the inmates work very slowly; there is much 'featherbedding'. There is no hustle and bustle, no sense of time pressure; the atmosphere certainly does not suggest productivity. There is an extraordinary amount of 'down time' because foremen are not available, supplies have not arrived, orders have not come in, machinery is broken, the prison is on lockdown and so forth.

The most work-intensive prisons in American history were the southern plantation-type prisons that sent hundreds of prisoners off to the fields every day to pick cotton, plant alfalfa and so on. Agricultural work was the ideal unskilled labour. By expanding acreage more prisoners could be accommodated and the produce could be consumed by the prisoners themselves and by inmates of other state institutions. Modest capital and practically no technical skill were needed to implement or supervise these agricultural operations. The guards, drawn from the rural areas in which prisons were located, knew all about the way farms are supposed to operate. But these were the very labour programmes that resembled slavery and generated charges of ghastly abuse.

These plantation systems did not survive the prisoners' rights movement of the 1970s. The modern advocates of rehabilitation excoriated agricultural labour because it was completely divorced from what the mostly urban prisoners would do upon release. They denounced agricultural work as demeaning and irrelevant. Moreover, it was a kind of hard manual labour that looked to the critics a lot like punishment. In any event, the critics put their faith in treatment, therapy and education, not work. The courts proscribed the hard punishments, such as whipping, isolation and physical abuse, that had been used to compel inmates to work. Eventually, many of the prisons (like Stateville in Illinois where field research was carried out in the early 1970s) sold off their agricultural lands (Jacobs, 1997).

While liberals favour *meaningful* work and job training (as long as proper safeguards are established) for its rehabilitative effects and conservatives believe that work is a moral imperative, neither pundits nor penologists face up to the practical difficulties of providing acceptable work opportunities, especially in the face of the massive increase in the number of prisoners currently overwhelming prisons in the USA. Just as political discourse has not accepted the reality that significant unemployment is an endemic feature of modern capitalist economies, those who engage in prison policy debates do not recognize that a very high rate of unemployment is endemic to the organization and operation of American prisons. Indeed, there is a certain naivety among legislators, reformers and penologists when it comes to making grandiose recommendations regarding the employment of prisoners.

It is not difficult for prison commentators of all political persuasions to pay homage to the ideal of a prison alive and humming with productively employed inmates. Like motherhood and apple pie, work, especially 'meaningful well-remunerated work', is a symbol that commands universal obeisance. According to the ideal, prisoners should work away at tasks that are meaningful, interesting and remunerative. They develop good work habits, a powerful work ethic and improve their human capital, acquiring skills that will be utilized upon release. Prisoners who are absorbed in work will not become bored, alienated, frustrated, restless or rebellious. Therefore, the full-employment prison (like the full-employment society) is safe because busy inmates are contented (or at least preoccupied) inmates. This same belief in the social value of work undergirds all criminology and is the most common (at least liberal) recommendation for addressing the crime problem.

This picture becomes even more appealing when we add the claim that the value of the prisoners' labour will pay for or at least substantially defray the cost of running the prisons, a cost which has become a real drag on state and local government. The working prisoners will contribute to their room and board, make restitution to their victims, pay off their fines and pay their taxes. No matter how expensive (or perhaps *because* of how expensive) prisons become and how large a share of the government budget they consume, politicians continue to talk about the self-financing prison.

According to the ideal's advocates, once the costs and benefits are properly explained, no interest groups will oppose this vision of the productive, full-employment prison. The most likely opponents, free-world workers and free-world companies, will realize that prison industries will not displace private sector firms or will do this so marginally as not to be noticed. By judiciously choosing which industries to establish, the prison officials will manage not to compete with private sector businesses. Likewise, by paying the prisoners a minimum wage or even prevailing wage, union opposition will be allayed. Thus the legislature and the taxpayers will be happy.

The bitter reality

Unfortunately, the full-employment industrial prison, no matter how often it is conjured, has not even begun to materialize. Nevertheless, penologists, liberal reformers and moral conservatives continue to pass laws proclaiming that prisoners should work, that prisons should be self-supporting, and that free-world workers and businesses should not be displaced. Some academic commentators blame the seemingly intractable problem of prisoner idleness on lack of will. They argue that prisons could be transformed into 'factories within fences' simply by making a strong political and moral commitment. Some years ago the then Chief Justice Warren Burger was much applauded for urging the complete restructuring of American prisons around the concept of productive work. Likewise, in a leading review of scholarship on prison labour, the criminologist Gordon Hawkins wrote:

> The implementation on a national basis of the concept of the industrial prison would present economic problems. But the principal barrier over the years to the profitable employment of prisoners has been neither the conditions of the labour market, the prevailing mode of production nor any other aspect of the economy. The principal barrier to a rational solution to the problem of prisoners, work and prison has been the persistent influence on penal policy of the principle of less eligibility. (Hawkins, 1983: 120)

I disagree with Hawkins. I believe that the idea of a factory prison, at least in the US context, is utterly unrealistic. This is not, of course, good news. But unless we face the reality, we will not be able to experiment with different models of the day-to-day routine of imprisonment.

The obstacles to establishing viable work regimens in prison hardly need recounting. With respect to 'industrialization', the prison suffers the same problems as some underdeveloped countries. First, there is the problem of infrastructure. The typical prison is at least several decades old and was not designed to serve as a modern-day factory. Such essentials as water, electricity and basic physical plant are inadequate to support a serious factory operation. Modern factories in the USA today typically have enormous square footage, are frequently purpose-built, including reinforced foundations, appropriate lighting and electrical wiring and good access to transport. Even so, competition is fierce, markets are fickle and there is certainly no guarantee of success.

A second and related problem is location. Prisons are usually located in rural, sometimes remote, areas. Thus they are far from suppliers, repairmen, customers and auxiliary service providers. More important, prisons are usually located far from large labour markets. Consequently, prisons have a major problem recruiting and retaining competent staff to serve as foremen, teachers and executives. Competent industrial foremen are much in demand in the private sector. Prisons are a 'tough sell'. There are many obvious drawbacks to spending one's working life in prison. The working conditions are very unpleasant and even dangerous, and there is little chance of developing a social life around one's co-workers. Such a position does not carry high status or prestige and will not advance one's career.

A third problem is inadequate capital. It takes a lot of money to establish, nurture and operate a successful business. To produce high-quality products requires good and modern equipment which has to be upgraded, repaired and replaced. And over the past two decades American businesses and industries have become increasingly capital-intensive. Thus factories need continuous access to capital markets. They borrow money from banks, sometimes float bonds and sometimes offer stock. Prisons industries must depend upon unstable government financing which, among other things, can only be counted on one year at a time, if that. In recent years, many state governments lurch from fiscal crisis to fiscal crisis and even demand across-the-board mid-year cuts in operating and capital budgets.

A fourth major obstacle to establishing a viable industrial programme in prison is the unreliable and irresponsible workforce. Despite some romantic claims that our prisoners are diamonds in the rough and as qualified for work as free-world persons, that is hardly true. The prisoners are grossly undereducated, irresponsible, non-cooperative, prone to be drug abusers and, most importantly, unsocialized into the world of work. The majority have never held a real job; there is a great deal of hostility or, at best, indifference to work. In addition, they are constantly exposed to the frustrations and tensions of prison life, including sexual deprivation, gang conflict, physical insecurity, lack of privacy, and so forth. This is not a contented workforce.

Prisoners' motivation to apply themselves to their tasks is not likely to be high. Most prisoners do not see themselves as settling into a '9 to 5' working life upon release. Furthermore, prison officials can do little to motivate hard work with attention to accuracy and quality. Pay is poor, indeed so poor (for example, $0.50–$0.70 an hour) as to convey the message that the work is not valuable and not worthwhile. Opportunity for 'advancement' is quite limited. For reasons discussed above, and because of antiquated technology and machinery, it is almost inconceivable that the prison factory will equip a prisoner with skills necessary to compete in the outside job market. The inmates' main motivation is probably to avoid the boredom of sitting in the cell house or to qualify for remission time. The motivation to work may even be perverse: to enjoy opportunities for gang banging, socializing and so on. Some prisoners may even take malicious pleasure in sabotaging the industrial enterprise.

Even under the best of scenarios, jobs are not as important to prisoners as they are to free-world persons. The job rarely comes first. Sometimes prisoners leave the prison for days, weeks or months in order to appear in court. On particular workdays they may be absent because of visits from family, friends or lawyers. Prisoners who may be in key positions in the industrial enterprise may voluntarily and sometimes involuntarily transfer to other prisons. (Of course, they may also be paroled or otherwise reach the end of the prison sentence.)

A fifth problem is 'intervention of the state'. Even under the most optimistic assumptions, industry will never be more than a secondary or tertiary (at best) organizational goal. Prison officials will always consider industry a lower priority than safety and security. Thus the prison suffers from frequent lockdowns which may shut down all activity for an indefinite period. The prison workplace is subject to unannounced searches and periodic shutdowns in the name of security. Sometimes prisoners are 'incarcerated' (sent to the segregation unit) for rule violations on and off the job or reclassified as not qualified to serve in an industry. The industries almost by necessity will have potential weapons lying around, so security staff will not permit some inmates to work there. All this causes delays and unpredictability that would try the patience of even the saintly customer.

The sixth problem is a whole slough of legal and political impediments to prison industries. In the USA prison-made goods have been banned from inter-state commerce (The Hawes-Cooper Act (1929), 49 U.S.C. s.60; Ashurst-Sumners Act (1935) and the Sumners-Ashurst Act (1940), 118 U.S.C. 1761, 49 Stat. 1134). Furthermore, the elaboration of free trade institutions at the international level has led to prohibitions on the export of prison-made goods (see Cowen, 1993). Most states limit the market for prison goods to state agencies and institutions, but this does not necessarily mean that government agencies have to make their purchases from prison industries. Some laws provide a caveat that government agencies must buy from the prisons only when the prison products are less expensive. It is also possible for government agencies to avoid purchasing from prison agencies by describing their desired purchase needs in a way that would exclude the prison products; or they can argue that the prison product is inadequate and/or does not meet their needs. In other words, it is not easy to force shrewd government officials to become purchasers. Ultimately, to be dependable customers, they will have to be convinced of the superiority of the prison-made product.

Politically, with people already insecure about their jobs, it is not surprising that unions, politicians and people generally will be hostile to the displacement of free-world jobs by prison industry. A number of states have placed restrictions in their laws regarding work release and prison industries to the effect that inmates should not be employed in industries, crafts and skills that compete with free-world industry in the region. This means that prison industry will have to succeed in businesses which no entrepreneur has seen as possibly profitable. It is utterly unrealistic to imagine the US federal and state prison systems, not to mention gaols, employing even a substantial fraction of their 1.4 million inmates in industrial-type production.

The seventh problem is that the massive increase of prisoners in the USA over the last two decades has seriously exacerbated the situation. The prison population has practically quadrupled. There were not enough jobs before and the situation has only worsened by orders of magnitude.

Thus it seems that prison industry is likely to be no more robust in the future than it is today. Indeed, the danger is that the modest amount of prison industry we have today will dwindle in absolute terms, as it already has in terms of the proportion of inmates involved. UNICOR is even now under serious threat in Congress. In this environment it is difficult to tell whether demands that UNICOR pay inmates the minimum wage are sincere or simply a cynical way of dismantling federal prison industries. A minimum wage is completely unrealistic unless it is no more than an accounting gimmick that would register a transfer of funds into the inmate workers' accounts and then register a reverse transfer back to the prisons for room and board.

Conclusion

The obstacles to establishing a full-employment productive prison seem formidable. The prisons have not been located, constructed or configured with industrial production in mind. The prisons lack capital and access to capital. Prison officials lack expertise in and strong commitment to business. Security concerns significantly affect the way prisoners can be assigned and how workshops can be run. The pool of prisoners from which workers must be recruited is uneducated, unskilled, unreliable, unmotivated and undisciplined.

The amazing thing is that there are any success stories (Federal Prison Industries (UNICOR, 1995). Indeed, so formidable are the obstacles that one might wonder whether claims of success by the Federal Prison Industries (FPI) or UNICOR could withstand rigorous evaluation. Moreover, to this author's eye, it is incredible that certain European countries seem to have succeeded in establishing viable prison industries. If true, it is important to determine whether this success can be explained by differences in these countries, national economies, size of prisoner population, absence of a large pool of unskilled low-wage labour, quality of prisoners or by other factors.

It is fascinating that penologists, beyond recommending in a general way productive work, have not focused on what prisoners should do all day. Is it a matter of indifference to penologists whether prisoners watch TV soap operas and game shows or meditate or play board games? The universal obeisance to work and full employment has completely diverted us from looking the hard questions in the eye.

From D. van Zyl Smit and F. Dunkel (eds) Prison Labour: Salvation or Slavery? *(Aldershot: Ashgate), 1999, pp. 269–79 (footnotes omitted).*

References

Cowen, Jonathan M. (1993). One Nation's 'Gulag' Is Another Nation's 'Factory Within a Fence', Prison-Labor in the People's Republic of China and the United States of America. *UCLA Pacific Basin Law Journal* 12: 190 ff.

Curriden, Mark (1995). Hard Time. *ABA Journal* 81: 72 ff.

Cvornyek, Robert L. (1993). *Convict Labor in the Alabama Coal Mines, 1874–1928.* Unpublished PhD thesis, Columbia University.

Federal Prison Industries (UNICOR) (1995). *Annual Report.* Washington: Government Printing Office.

Fierce, Mifred, C. (1994). *Slavery Revisted: Blacks and the Southern Convict Lease System, 1865–1933.* Brooklyn College, African Studies Research Center.

Garland, David (1990). *Punishment and Modern Society.* Chicago: University of Chicago Press.

Hawkins, Gordon (1983). Prison and Prison Industries. In *Crime and Justice: An Annual Review of Research,* edited by Michael Tonry and Norval Morris. Chicago: University of Chicago Press.

Jacobs, James (1997). *Stateville: The Penitentiary in Mass Society*. Chicago: University of Chicago Press.

Lichtenstein, Alex (1996). *Twice the Work of Free Labor*. London and New York: Verso.

Sellin, Jonathan T. (1976). *Slavery and the Penal System*. New York: Elsevier.

31. Prisoners' rights in the context of the European Convention on Human Rights

Stephen Livingstone

Introduction

Unlike the European Convention for the Prevention of Torture and Inhuman or Degrading Treatment or Punishment, or the United Nations Convention against Torture, the European Convention on Human Rights (ECHR) was not designed with the specific circumstances of imprisonment in mind. However prisoners soon became enthusiastic users of this international treaty. In its early years a substantial proportion of the applications received by the European Commission on Human Rights[1] came from people in detention (Fawcett, 1985: 63). Many of these applications, and an even higher proportion that have gone on to be decided by the Court, emanate from the United Kingdom. The reason for this is not immediately clear but it may well be that the lack of judicial supervision of the execution of sentences in the United Kingdom has encouraged a greater volume of prisoner litigation and stimulated a more sympathetic response from the European Court. The availability of a judge to control issues such as home leave or early release in countries such as France or Germany may have provided prisoners with a more immediate outlet for grievances. However the United Kingdom is not the only country whose prison system has come under scrutiny from Strasbourg as regards conformity with human rights standards. Important decisions have also been rendered in respect of such diverse countries as Austria, Belgium, Italy and Turkey. With the Council of Europe having already identified the state of the prisons as a major cause for concern when considering the accession to the Convention of several Eastern European states, notably Russia (Council of Europe, 1994: 282), it will be no surprise if prisoners in these countries too invoke the Convention to challenge their conditions of imprisonment.

Prisoners lose far more cases than they win in Strasbourg, the overwhelming majority of applications being ruled inadmissible either as failing to satisfy procedural conditions or as 'manifestly ill founded' under Article 35(3). However, significant victories have been won which have had an important impact on issues such as prison discipline, communication with the outside world and release procedures.

276

Application of the ECHR to specific areas of prison life

Prison conditions

[...] [T]he main way in which the Strasbourg Commission and Court have examined issues of overcrowding, lack of facilities, violence and poor medical care is through the lens of the Article 3 prohibition on torture, inhuman or degrading treatment or punishment. In the past decade a number of the Court's decisions have offered increasing protection to all detainees against deliberate treatment which poses a serious threat to bodily integrity. Thus the Court has recognized that some forms of ill-treatment in custody can reach a level sufficiently severe to be described as torture (*Aydin* v. *Turkey*, 1997; *Selmouni* v. *France*, 1999). It has also observed that any use of force against a detainee, which is not strictly necessary to prevent injury to self or others 'diminishes human dignity and is, in principle, an infringement of the right set forth in Article 3 of the Convention' (*Ribitsch* v. *Austria*, 1995: para. 38). Furthermore it has stressed the need to provide effective means of investigation and redress where an applicant claims that they were mistreated in custody (*Assenov* v. *Bulgaria*, 1998). Although most of these cases have concerned detention in police custody the principles would appear to have the same application when it comes to treatment in prisons.

They also apply in respect of deaths that raise questions as to State responsibility. The Court has increasingly stressed that the State's Article 2 obligation to protect life includes both an obligation to take reasonable steps to prevent death, even at the hands of third parties (*Osman* v. *United Kingdom*, 1998) and an obligation to investigate deaths in suspicious circumstances (*Kaya* v. *Turkey*, 1998; *Tanrikulu* v. *Turkey*, 1999). When combined with the Article 13 right to a remedy, the Court has indicated that where someone has been killed in contravention of Article 2 the State is obliged to ensure that an investigation is conducted which is capable of leading to the identification and punishment of those responsible. These observations have relevance not only to the relatively few occasions that prisoners are killed by prison staff in Europe, but also to the far more frequent occasions when prisoners take their own lives. In the wake of the *Osman* case, where the Court indicated that a State could be found to be in breach of Article 2 where it failed to take reasonable steps to avert a known risk to an identifiable person, the Commission has recently admitted an application which concerns the suicide of a prisoner in the United Kingdom (*Keenan* v. *United Kingdom*, 1998).

However, while the Court has shown itself willing to develop the standards of protection for those in detention at what might be called the higher end of the spectrum, it has remained reluctant to extend the scope of Article 3 at the lower end to cover more routine conditions produced by neglect. The Strasbourg institutions clearly start from the premise that Article 3 was not intended to find the inevitable deprivations resulting from everyday conditions of imprisonment as constituting inhuman or degrading treatment. They have also shown a willingness to take the rationale for conditions into account. As a result, as Phillippa Kaufmann points out, 'where measures are imposed for security, disciplinary or protective purposes, the Commission has shown a remarkable tolerance, irrespective of the effects of their stringency and the effects on the health of the victim' (Kaufmann, 1999: 457). On few occasions have prisoners been able to assert that the conditions they were detained in amounted to a violation of their human rights. This is especially so where the applicant is not detained for politically related reasons.

Thus it is only in the case of political detainees, such as the *Greek case* (1969) and *Cyprus v. Turkey* (1982), that the Commission and Court have been prepared to find breaches of Article 3 in relation to things like overcrowding or inadequate medical treatment. In the former, holding some prisoners two to a very small basement cell for periods between 30 days and nine months without any recreation and virtually no light was recognized to reach the appropriate level of severity. Where, on the other hand, one is dealing with prisoners remanded or convicted in respect of criminal charges, the Commission and Court have frequently taken the view either that the conditions are insufficiently severe or that a prisoner has not spent enough time in them for this to amount to inhuman or degrading treatment. In *Reed v. United Kingdom* (1983), for example, spending three weeks in a cockroach-infested cell was held not to be enough, nor was being held overnight in a cell containing the stale smell of urine and faeces of an earlier occupant (*X v. United Kingdom*, 1979b). In the *Tekin* case (1998) the Court found a breach of Article 3 where the applicant was held for four days in a police cell in freezing conditions and with little food and water. However he was also subject to regular beatings and the decision leaves it unclear whether the neglect or physical mistreatment alone might amount to inhuman or degrading treatment. In *McFeeley v. United Kingdom* (1981) the Commission was prepared to conclude that the conditions of those on the 'dirty protest' in the Maze Prison in Northern Ireland did amount to degrading treatment. The applicants were living for months on end in cells smeared with excrement, conditions which the Commission described as 'self-inflicted debasement and humiliation to an almost sub-human degree' (*McFeeley*, 1981: para. 45). However here too the Commission concluded that there was no breach of Article 3 in that the applicants had brought these conditions upon themselves, although it indicated dissatisfaction with the 'inflexible' approach of the Government to resolving the dispute.

Solitary confinement is another area where applicants have tried and largely failed to secure the Court's intervention. In *Krocher and Muller v. Switzerland* (1982) the applicants were detained for several months in cells 8.4 square metres under constant surveillance by CCTV and in permanently lit cells. For the first month of this isolation they were denied access to lawyers and families, exercise was limited to 20 minutes a day for the first three months and for up to six months they were denied access to radio, TV and newspapers. In concluding that such conditions did not amount to a breach of Article 3 the Commission was clearly influenced by a lack of medical evidence indicating that these conditions caused severe suffering and by the fact that the regime was progressively improved. In the United Kingdom case of *Hilton* (1976), the applicant was detained in solitary confinement for 23 hours a day and deteriorated in the course of his imprisonment from an apparently normal prisoner into one so depressed that he would roll around in his own excrement. Although four members of the Commission dissented and took the view that it was unacceptable that any prison system should reduce a man to this state, the majority decided that there was no breach of Article 3, noting that the applicant was a disruptive prisoner with a history of personality disorders which the authorities had at least tried to help.

It has been notable in these cases that neither the Commission nor the Court has drawn much on the standards developed by the CPT (Peukert, 1999: 88–90). Indeed in one case, that of *Aerts* v. *Belgium* (1998), a majority of the Court concluded that there was no breach of Article 3 in respect of conditions in a specific prison which the CPT had described as inhuman and degrading. This has led some to despair of the Court ever intervening in a significant way to condemn prison conditions in Europe as being inconsistent with the Article 3 standard. However it must be remembered that, as the Court has often observed, the Convention is a 'living instrument' and that nowhere is this more true than in the interpretation of Article 3. Practices which might once have been viewed as entirely consistent with it, such as corporal punishment (*Tyrer* v. *United Kingdom*, 1978) or capital punishment (*Soering* v. *United Kingdom*, 1989) have subsequently come to be seen as problematic. The recent decision of *D* v. *United Kingdom* (1997), where the United Kingdom was found to be in breach of Article 3 where it sought to deport a prisoner terminally ill with AIDS to St Kitts, despite the lack of adequate medical facilities or family support on the island, is an excellent example. It indicates once again the positive character of the Convention obligations and suggests that States could be in breach of Article 3 where they fail to respond adequately to the medical needs of those in custody. This is an area where the Convention authorities have given conflicting indications in the past.[2] In the coming years the Court will in all probability have to deal with an increasing number of Article 3 challenges to prison conditions in countries such as Russia or Ukraine, where difficulties of overcrowding and poor health care conditions are already well known. It seems unlikely that the Court will be unable to offer any remedy to the unfortunate applicants in these sorts of cases.

Prison discipline

The major decision of *Campbell and Fell* v. *United Kingdom* (1984) had a very significant impact on the formal prison discipline system in British prisons. This case arose from the disciplining of a number of prisoners following a major disturbance at Albany prison. Several of the prisoners received punishments of lengthy periods of loss of remission,[3] in one case a total of 570 days. They subsequently sought to challenge the procedures followed in respect of these punishments. One of the issues they raised was the fact that they were prohibited from being represented by a lawyer before the Board of Visitors which adjudicated on their case. The Court concluded that this was contrary to Article 6(3)(d) of the Convention, having adopted a purposive approach to the definition of 'criminal charge' in the Convention and rejected the United Kingdom's arguments that this provision was not applicable as the applicants were facing disciplinary rather than criminal proceedings. The court took the view that the classification of an offence under domestic law was not decisive and that it should also have regard to the nature of the offence itself and the potential punishment. Here it was especially struck by the fact that the prisoners risked an unlimited loss of remission and that one of them had actually been punished by a loss of 570 days' remission. Noting that any punishment involving a deprivation of liberty was likely to bring the sanction into the sphere of a criminal charge the Court observed that 'by causing detention to continue for substantially longer than would otherwise have been the case, the sanction came close to, even if it did not technically constitute, deprivation of liberty' (*Campbell and Fell*, 1984: 157).

The decision in *Campbell and Fell* was quickly seized upon by a number of English courts who ruled that domestic law too required that prisoners be allowed legal representation when facing especially serious disciplinary charges (Livingstone, 1995: 172). This led the Government to reduce the number of days' loss of remission that Boards could order as punishments in discipline cases and hence reduced the value of having Boards, as opposed to prison governors, adjudicate on disciplinary charges. It thus began a process which would lead, by 1992, to the removal of adjudication powers from Boards of Visitors in English prisons (Livingstone, 1994). However the Court in the *Campbell and Fell* case could have brought this about even earlier had it accepted the Commission's view that a Board of Visitors was not a sufficiently 'independent' tribunal to satisfy the requirements of Article 6(1). The Court's refusal to do so made it very unlikely that it would hold that disciplinary adjudications by prison directors, the more usual practice throughout Europe, would fall foul of this requirement of Article 6.

Indeed, post *Campbell and Fell*, the Strasbourg authorities have had little to say on the methods by which order and discipline is maintained in prison. In one case the Commission concluded that a loss of 18 days' remission did not amount to a sufficient penalty in order to bring the disciplinary proceedings within the scope of 'criminal charges' as conceived by Article 6 (*Pelle* v. *France*, 1986). Cases such as *Kiss* v. *United Kingdom* (1976) suggest that even 180 days' potential loss of remission would not be sufficient to amount to a criminal charge and hence invite the detailed procedural protections of Article 6. Even if, as a pre-*Campbell and Fell* decision, this must be treated with some caution it would appear true that the Court is prepared to allow disciplinary penalties which involve prisoners spending significantly longer periods in prison to be ordered without the tribunal in question having adhered to any of the requirements for a fair hearing set out in the Convention. Moreover methods of maintaining order and discipline within the prison environment are not limited to the use of formal disciplinary hearings in respect of alleged rule infractions (Sparks et al., 1996). Prison authorities may resort to removing prisoners from general association, transferring prisoners between prisons, denying them certain privileges or subjecting them to certain restraints. Although often perceived by prisoners as imposed in an arbitrary and unfair manner few of these activities appear to implicate Convention rights. Efforts have been made to include them, for example by suggesting that transfer may infringe Article 8 where a prisoner is moved a long way from their family or that lengthy periods of removal from association may be in breach of Article 3. However these have all tended to fall at the Commission stage. As a result the impression is left that the Court is prepared to accept that justice in prison remains a fairly rough sort of justice. Providing the penalties involved are not egregious the Strasbourg authorities have not required the imposition of procedural requirements that might apply in some outside disciplinary environments.

[…]

From 'Prisoners' rights in the context of the European Convention on Human Rights', Punishment and Society, Vol. 2, no. 3, 2000, pp. 309–10, 313–17.

Notes

1. In its original format the Convention provided for all applications to be considered by the Commission, whose task was to decide whether the application was admissible and, if so, whether a friendly settlement could be reached between the parties. Only if such a settlement was not forthcoming might the case go on for decision to the Court. With the coming into force of Protocol 11 in 1998 the Commission has been dissolved and the Court now makes decisions on both admissibility and merits. For an outline of the procedure see Starmer (1999: 695–714).
2. In *Hurtado* v. *Switzerland* (1994), failure to x-ray a suspect with a fractured rib for six days was held to breach Article 3. However in *Lockwood* v. *United Kingdom* (1991) a medical officer's delay of four months before seeking a second opinion in a case of a suspected tumour was held not to involve such a breach.
3. At the time in the United Kingdom system, prisoners sentenced to determinate sentences were automatically entitled to one-third remission (e.g. they would only be required to serve four years of a six-year sentence). Such remission could only be lost on conviction by an administrative hearing of a disciplinary offence.

References

Council of Europe (1994) Report on the conformity with European human rights standards of the Russian Federation, *Human Rights Law Journal* 15: 250–87.

Fawcett, James (1985) 'Application of the European Convention on Human Rights', in M. Maguire, J. Vagg and R. Morgan (eds), *Accountability and prisons: Opening up a closed world*, pp. 61–78. London: Tavistock.

Kaufmann, Phillippa (1999) 'Prisoners', in K. Starmer, *European Human Rights Law*, pp. 453–91. London: LAG Books.

Livingstone, Stephen (1994) 'The changing face of prison discipline', in E. Player and M. Jenkins (eds) *Prisons after Woolf*, pp. 97–111. London: Routledge.

Livingstone, Stephen (1995) 'The impact of judicial review on prisons', in B. Hadfield (ed.) *Judicial review: A thematic approach*, pp. 167–86. Dublin: Gill & Macmillan.

Peukert, Wolfgang (1999) 'The European Convention for the Prevention of Torture and the European Convention on Human Rights', in R. Morgan and M. Evans (eds) *Protecting prisoners: The standards of the European Committee for the Prevention of Torture in context*, pp. 85–102. Oxford: Oxford University Press.

Sparks, Richard, Tony Bottoms and Will Hay (1996) *Prisons and the problem of order*. Oxford: Oxford University Press.

Starmer, Keir (1999) *European human rights law*. London: LAG Books.

Cases

Aerts v. *Belgium* (1998) Decision of the Court, 30 July.
Assenov v. *Bulgaria* (1998) Decision of the Court, 28 October.
Aydin v. *Turkey* (1997) 25 EHRR 251.
Campbell and Fell v. *United Kingdom* (1984) 7 EHRR 165.
Cyprus v. *Turkey* (1982) 4 EHRR 482.
D v. *United Kingdom* (1997) 24 EHRR 423.
Greek case [1969] Yearbook 1.
Hilton v. *United Kingdom* (1976) 4 D & R 176.
Hurtado v. *Switzerland* (1994) Series A No 280-A.
Kaya v. *Turkey* (1998) 28 EHRR 1.
Keenan v. *United Kingdom* [1998] EHRLR 648.
Kiss v. *United Kingdom* (1976) 7 D & R 55.
Krocher and Muller v. *Switzerland* (1982) 34 D & R 24.
Lockwood v. *United Kingdom* (1991) 15 EHRR CD 48.
McFeeley v. *United Kingdom* (1981) 3 EHRR 161.
Osman v. *United Kingdom* (1998) Decision of the Court, 28 October.
Pelle v. *France* (1986) 50 D & R 263.
Reed v. *United Kingdom* (1983) EHRR 114.
Ribitsch v. *Austria* (1995) 21 EHRR 573.
Selmouni v. *France* (1999) Decision of the Court, 28 July.
Soering v. *United Kingdom* (1989) 11 EHRR 439.
Tanrikulu v. *Turkey* (1999), Decision of the Court, 8 July.
Tekin v. *Turkey* (1998), Decision of the Court, 9 June.
Tyrer v. *United Kingdom* (1978) 2 EHRR 1.
X v. *United Kingdom* (1979a) 14 D & R 246.
X v. *United Kingdom* (1979b) 15 D & R 242.

Conclusion: prisons, public opinion and the 'new punitiveness'

A deep cultural attachment to the prison?

The final part of this reader is called 'Current controversies' and was perhaps the most challenging section to compile, simply because there are so many contentious issues currently blighting the prison system. The fact that official estimates predict a prison population of anything between 91,400 and 109,600 by the end of this decade is controversial enough, and the dramatic rise in the numbers of offenders being sent to prison and, in particular, the growing use of short custodial sentences over the last 20 years, has resulted in chronic levels of overcrowding in prisons. This, in turn, has led to further problems. Overcrowding has been linked to lack of safety for those who live and work in prisons, as well as bullying, suicide, self-harm and mental health problems amongst inmates. It results in fewer opportunities for rehabilitative work due to a lack of supervision, and inmates are confined to their cells for longer (23 hours a day in some prisons), causing greater tensions both amongst prisoners and between prisoners and staff. At the time of writing (spring 2005), 76 of the 139 prisons in England and Wales exceeded their Certified Normal Accommodation (CNA), the most overcrowded being Leicester, which was holding 361 prisoners in accommodation intended for 191 (that is, 189 per cent occupancy). Meanwhile, 22 per cent of the prison population 'double up' in a cell designed for one person (www. howardleague.org). The worst prisons for overcrowding are local prisons like Leicester (which hold high numbers of remand prisoners) and dedicated remand centres. So bad is the situation that many remand prisoners have, in recent years, been confined in police cells where conditions are even more inadequate than in prisons (Cavadino and Dignan 2002). In short, some of the poorest conditions are to be found in custodial environments holding high numbers of people who have yet to be actually convicted.

One of the solutions to prison overcrowding, introduced in 1997, was a prison ship moored in Portland Harbour, Dorset. A former troop ship in the Falklands war, HMP Weare housed 400 men serving the last nine months of their sentence but was soundly criticized by many, including Her Majesty's Chief Inspector of Prisons, for its unsuitability as a prison and its lack of opportunities for prisoners to undertake activities that might reduce their likelihood of reoffending. One of the initiatives that helped Home Office ministers to make the decision to close HMP Weare (at least for the time being) was the opening of a new prison at Peterborough in March 2005. With a capacity to hold 840, including 360 women, Peterborough is the eleventh privately operated prison in England and Wales – itself a subject of some controversy (see Reading 7). On the whole, though, building new prisons seems to have little effect on the problem of overcrowding: of the 13 new facilities built in the last ten years, 9 were overcrowded by the end of 2003.

So why has the UK – in line with most other western societies – come to develop such a deep cultural attachment to the prison? Why does the UK lock more people up than any other country in Europe? What of other societies: how do they deal with offenders? What role does the UK's popular media play in influencing public perceptions about the kinds of places prisons should be? These are some of the questions we will be addressing in this final section of *Prison Readings*. But, first, let's consider the global prison population.

A global phenomenon

According to the most recently available statistics (Walmsley 2005), the world prison population currently numbers over 9 million people. Heading the table is the USA with 2.08 million (or 714 prisoners per 100,000 of the national population), followed by Russia (0.76 million or 532 per 100,000 of the population) and China (1.54 million or 118 per 100,000 – although both these figures relate to sentenced prisoners only, and do not include those on remand or those in 'administrative detention'). In Europe, the UK tops the prison population table with new peaks being reached in 2005 of 75,320 for England and Wales (142 per 100,000 of the population), 6,742 for Scotland (132 per 100,000) and 1,275 (72 per 100,000) for Northern Ireland. By way of comparison, France's prison population stands at 55,028 (91 per 100,000 of the national population), Sweden's at 6,755 (75 per 100,000) and Norway's at 2,975 (65). Meanwhile, in Australia the rate per 100,000 is 117 and in New Zealand it is 168.

The fact that America leads the world prison population table is of great concern to many prison experts. Recent academic discussions of American prisons have tended to be dominated by the twin concepts of the 'Supermax' and 'mass imprisonment'. As we saw in Reading 10, supermaxes are purpose-built prisons where inmates are held in maximum security conditions, in conditions not unlike their Victorian predecessors (see the Introduction to this volume and Reading 5). The pointless cruelty of the treadwheel, crank and harsh dietary regime may have disappeared, but their modern equivalents – physical isolation, sensory deprivation and minimum food requirements – are equally intended to break the prisoner's spirit and will (Pratt *et al.* 2005). The stripping away of all human characteristics and individual personality traits has long been a core rationale of official attitudes to prisoners, particularly at the point of reception into custody when they have to be 'processed' with as much efficiency as possible (Reading 20). However, the supermax takes this administrative task to new depths of impersonal brutality, particularly in those American states where it converges with death row. Here, the two monoliths of America's 'cruel and unusual punishment' system (Jarvis 2004) confine inmates to a protracted period of liminality, not only underlining their social exclusion in the most potently symbolic fashion, but also forcibly suspending future expectations about their lifecourse (Jewkes 2005). It is arguable that all custodial environments are repositories for the fears and anxieties of the wider social group, but the convergence of America's supermax and death row almost certainly represent the most graphic illustrations of 'toxic waste management', at least in contemporary advanced Western societies (Lynch 2005; cf. Douglas 1966). Indeed, Lynch (2005) argues that the use of supermax isolation for death-row inmates is intended to 'prime' the condemned prisoners for death, creating a pliable population more willing to meet their fate. Meanwhile, for those who are not destined for execution, the supermax is experienced as a kind of purgatory, a state of limbo somewhere between life and death (Lynch 2005). Comparisons with the Nazi concentration camps used in the Second World War are obvious here, both institutions being a literal manifestation of the human desire to eliminate pollutants in order to organize the environment and restore order (Douglas 1966; Jewkes 2005). As Lynch implies, the notion of reducing 'sociologically and psychologically rich human beings into a kind of untouchable toxic waste' is anathema in so-called civilized, late-modern societies (2005: 79).

The other monument to extreme punishment in the USA, 'mass imprisonment', refers to a phenomenon that has emerged during the last 20 years, which has two essential characteristics; first, the sheer number of people in prison; and, secondly, the social concentration of imprisonment's effects. 'Imprisonment becomes *mass imprisonment* when it ceases to be the incarceration of individual offenders and becomes the systematic imprisonment of whole groups of the population' (Garland 2001: 1–2). Both of these aspects of incarceration apply to the current situation in the USA. The fact that the population of America's jails and prisons now exceeds 2 million prisoners for the first time ever, with 1 in 75 of all men inside, is an 'unprecedented event in the history of the USA and, more generally, in the history of liberal democracy' (Garland 2001: 2). The social group most disproportionately targeted are young black males from large urban areas, for whom imprisonment has become part of the socialization process; 'a regular, predictable part of experience, rather than a rare and infrequent event' (Garland 2001: 2). Although an extreme example, the disproportionate and discriminatory incarceration of minority groups is not geographically bounded, as we saw with regard to the UK in Reading 16, and as others have shown in relation to many countries around the world (such as the excessive rate of Aboriginal imprisonment in Australia; see, for example, Midford 1992; Brown 1998).

Amongst many criminologists and penologists, there is a concern that, in matters of penal policy, where the USA leads, other English-speaking nations follow. The 'great American carceral boom', as Wacquant (2005) has called it, certainly has been dramatic; an exponential growth that has seen the prison population rise from 176 per 100,000 inhabitants in 1971 to 714 inmates per 100,000 inhabitants today, a figure that bears comparisons:

> To gauge how extreme this scale of confinement is, suffice it to say that it is about 40 per cent higher than South Africa's at the height of the armed struggle against apartheid and six to twelve times the rate of the countries of the European Union, even though the latter have also seen their imprisonment rate rise rapidly over the past two decades. During the period 1985–1995, the United States amassed nearly one million more inmates at a pace of an additional 1,631 bodies per week, equivalent to incorporating the confined population of France every six months (Wacquant 2005: 5).

Whilst these trends are exceptional in the western world – indeed, Garland (2001: 1) has described them as a 'pathological phenomenon' – it could be argued that they are once again merely a more excessive version of what is occurring in England and Wales where the same period has seen the prison population almost double from 40,000 since 1971. And, given the endemic overcrowding problems already mentioned, it seems hopelessly naive to believe that criminal justice systems can do anything more ambitious than managing a seemingly permanent prison population – far less maintain any pretence of transforming criminal subjects as their nineteenth-century counterparts attempted to do (Caplow and Simon 1999). But what do we know about the flesh-and-blood individuals behind the statistics? As many of the readings in this collection have shown, there have been significant trends in recent years, including increases in the numbers of people with serious mental health problems being sent to prison, increases in the proportion of women and individuals from ethnic minority backgrounds and increases in the remand population. What is clear is that in all advanced, Western countries – and this also applies to the federal states of countries like America and Australia – prison population rates do not appear to be directly linked to the amount of crime being committed in that jurisdiction. What is also apparent is that in most advanced, Western societies (and certainly all English-speaking countries) it is the poor and the disadvantaged who are most likely to face a prison sentence. As we saw in Reading 25 social exclusion can be a lifelong experience.

Accompanying the growth of the prison population has been a range of situational and social control measures which have crept back into the logic of imprisonment (Morgan 1997). These trends are a small part of what has been coined the 'new punitiveness' (Pratt *et al.* 2005) which, in their most extreme manifestation (barring capital punishment), involve prisoners being locked up for all but one hour a day and denied access to exercise, education, behavioural therapy programmes and association with others. The punitive turn encompasses a much greater range of penal developments introduced across the Western world, including indefinite detention strategies (see Readings 28 and 29), shaming punishments such as registers for sex offenders, the return of chain gangs in America and, of course, the supermax (Reading 10), as well as broader criminal justice strategies such as zero-tolerance policing, 'three-strikes' laws and massive investment in electronic surveillance technologies (Pratt *et al.* 2005). All these measures, in turn, have an effect on public attitudes to crime and justice which, in recent years, have most notoriously been manifested in vigilante-style 'direct action' against those who offend (or – as in the case of assaults on individuals erroneously thought to be paedophiles in the community – those perceived to have offended).

But as we have argued in the Introduction and throughout this reader, many of these punitive 'innovations' bear remarkable similarities to the conditions of the mid-nineteenth century, when inmates were subjected to prolonged periods of isolation, military force was called upon to quell prison protests and early forms of surveillance were introduced, such as the photographing of convicts to trace repeat offenders, all of which beg the question: just how 'new' *is* the 'new punitiveness'? Furthermore, as Hinds (2005) has pointed out, there is much greater diversity across the penal estate in America than there was even just 30 years ago, a trend that can also be observed in the prison systems of, for example, Britain and Australia. Furthermore, punitiveness cannot simply be measured in terms of numbers of people locked up. In countries that have lower prison populations than the UK, there may be aspects of penal procedure and organizational practice that mask the punitive behind the seemingly progressive. For example, Italy has one of the lowest rates of convicted prisoners in Europe, and has a reputation for leniency and measures of mercy and conditional forgiveness but, at the same time, its conviction and custody rates of foreign-born offenders are increasing and it has one of the highest average detention periods (Nelken 2005). Canada, meanwhile, has a reputation for being moderate and progressive (for instance, prisons are becoming smaller and a 'needs' discourse is being introduced, explicitly directed at specific prison populations such as women and inmates from minority ethnic backgrounds). However, the implementation of liberal measures that appear to empower prisoners by allowing them to participate in therapeutic and cognitive behavioural programmes designed to change them has been found to reinforce a punitive rhetoric (Moore and Hannah-Moffat 2005). Like their counterparts in the UK and elsewhere, these treatment programmes are part of a neoliberal policy which casts the onus of responsibility on to the individual prisoner. Punishment becomes a social contract, but one where the inmate first has to acknowledge responsibility for what he or she has done.

By contrast to these apparently tolerant societies, Russia's prison system has a reputation for being closed, overcrowded and an assault on human rights. It carries a hangover from the days when the Soviet system used imprisonment to manufacture a deviant population which could be trained in the disciplines of labour and production. Yet it is making headway in its efforts to modernize (of course, it would be fair to say that – when the starting point for modernization is the appalling conditions of the concentration camp colonies that characterized the Soviet Union's penal landscape for nearly a century – small improvements have relatively profound impacts). Russia now appears to be responsive to international penal thinking, the numbers of people sent to prison is falling and there has been some success in reversing the human rights abuses of the past (Piacentini 2004; see also Reading 10). However, Russia may continue to have much in common with other countries that have undergone major political reform; South Africa being a prime example, where overcrowding remains acute, prison gangs and organized criminals continue to terrorize their fellow inmates, and the implementation of human rights initiatives is slower than the introduction of legislation that ultimately results in unmanageably large prison populations (van Zyl Smit 1998).

One of the most interesting penal experiments of recent years has taken place in Finland which, in the last four decades, has gone from being amongst the highest prison populations in Europe to the lowest and where, even in the most 'secure' closed prisons (such as Hämeenlinna, 60 miles from Helsinki) the regime is strict but not oppressive, with plenty of opportunities to work and study. Meanwhile in Finland's open prisons, inmates are free to come and go as they please, so long as they check in at night, and they have access to a sauna, tennis court and the prison garden (Younge 2002). Yet, like other Scandinavian countries, Finland's young people appear to have a weaker commitment to the progressive policies of their parents' generation and there are fears that the low imprisonment rates and high tolerance levels characteristic of this region may be in jeopardy (Bondeson 2005). These emerging signs of strain are, to a significant degree, fuelled by an expanding and increasingly strident media who are perceptibly changing public views of crime and punishment (Younge 2002). This scenario – a hard-line media that over-reports serious crime and exaggerates the risk of victimization – does, of course, raise questions that are similarly being rehearsed in the UK about where ordinary people – the public – get their ideas about prison from, and what the relationship is between public opinion, penal policy and prison reform in the UK.

Like the countries of Scandinavia, there is an ever-present tension between prison reformers' demands for humane and rehabilitative punishments and public expectations about what prisons should be like, which are frequently shaped by the popular press. It is somewhat ironic that the British tabloids persist in falsely painting a picture of prisons as holiday camps, given that the UK sends offenders to prison *as* punishment and not *for* punishment. As the readings in this collection demonstrate, many academic criminologists are troubled by the creeping punitiveness in penal policy (to the point of arguing the case for abolition; see Reading 12). Even some of the seemingly most liberal innovations in prison regimes may not be as generous as they appear at first sight. For example, whilst the degrading act of 'slopping out' was abolished following a recommendation by Lord Woolf in 1991, some prisoners still do not have adequate 24-hours-per-day access to toilets, and few would argue that integrated sanitation is ideal in an 8 × 10 ft cell shared by more than one man. To take another example derided by much of the popular press as an example of British justice being 'soft' on convicted criminals, the introduction of in-cell television across most of the prison estate at the turn of this century may not be the luxury it is frequently presented as. True, the introduction of media into prisons undoubtedly affords prisoners unprecedented access to information and entertainment, grants them a semblance of public participation, and returns to them membership of some of society's democratic processes. Yet, as one of us has suggested elsewhere, it is arguable that media are being used undemocratically within the walls of many prisons (Jewkes 2002). Personal media – like letter writing, phone calls, personal possessions allowances, family visits and numerous other perceived 'perks' – are highly effective devices of social and behavioural control which can be employed as a reward or punishment, as a bartering tool and as a conduit of power. Thus, whatever pleasures are to be found in incentives and earned privileges (see the Introduction to this volume) such as personal televisions, they will always be tempered by the demands of the institution and used, not only as a lever for securing compliant behaviour, but as a means of undermining the individual inmate in relation to structural power. Perversely, then, the introduction of in-cell TV into prisons may be reproducing disadvantage and deprivation. As earlier lock-up times are introduced, educational programmes are cut back, opportunities for inmates to associate with others are reduced and some inmates are effectively coerced into having – and paying for – their televisions, it is difficult to avoid the conclusion that incentives and earned privileges have one great, unspoken advantage as far as prison authorities are concerned, and that is to normalize the regulation and surveillance of inmates. In other words, innovations such as in-cell television – for all its acknowledged advantages to inmates – is being used as the 'sweetener' which is intended to conceal or compensate for emergent security and control measures and create a docile and passive prison population. For the prison service then, the gradual introduction of the kind of privileges that the British tabloid press whip themselves into a lather about may simply serve to ensure that the embedded practices of imprisonment – however undemocratic, unpopular or unpleasant – are accepted as natural to inmates over time (Jewkes 2002).

Media representations and public opinion

A key aspect, then, of the 'new punitiveness' is the more active role that the public are expected to perform when it comes to the exercise of justice. Whilst this widening of the democratic process is usually thought of as a sign of progress, in matters of penal policy it results in a populist agenda that is virtually indistinguishable from the new politics of law and order whereby politicians are constantly trying to out tough each other and convince the electorate that *they* are the party most equipped to protect people in times of heightened risk (of terrorist attacks, random murderers and rapists, hospital super-bugs, etc.). Explanations of the relationship between actual crime rates and punitive public sentiments are contested (Caplow and Simon 1999), but there is little doubt that the recent expansion of penal sanctions has failed to generate much public debate (with the possible exception of the unlawful detention of terrorist suspects on both sides of the Atlantic although, even in these cases, whilst there *has* been a shift in public opinion since the notorious pictures from Abu Ghraib were published, the rights of the detainees remain a deeply unpopular cause; *Financial Times* 28 August 2004). In the UK the tension that exists between penal policy and media-informed public opinion is most evident in the tabloid newspapers where the clearest public manifestations of the new punitiveness (such as the 'naming and shaming' of offenders from paedophiles to the individuals suspected, but not convicted, of the racist murder of Stephen Lawrence) are reflected and reinforced in unrestrained tones.

Mediated discourses concerning prisons and prisoners are similarly poised between administrative decision-making and populist sentiment, as they have been since at least 1862 when the moral panic over garrotting seized the public imagination. Political and media institutions invariably lend themselves to a single analysis; on matters of crime and punishment they function together, with dominant media representations mirroring the rhetoric of 'official' leaders and then communicated to audiences in such a way as to satisfy public appetites for retribution. Whilst fictional media portrayals of imprisonment are, on the whole, character driven and are likely to engage viewers at a relatively superficial level (see Jewkes 2006 for a fuller discussion of representations of prisons on television), news reporting taps into and reinforces cultural fears of 'otherness', fervently demonizing and stigmatizing those who are already socially excluded (Greer and Jewkes 2005). Of all the likely contenders for society's fear and loathing, prisoners are viewed as detritus by large segments of the British press's readership and thus frequently induce a lazy contempt amongst journalists. On the whole, the grim and frequently inhumane conditions of their incarceration only reach public attention if accompanied by a sound-bite from a statement by Her Majesty's Inspector of Prisons in language that will appeal to the popular press (Jewkes 2006). There are exceptions, of course. Generally, the 'quality' press are better at reporting on prison conditions than the tabloids, and the *Guardian* deserves praise for its investigative reports and editorials (including those by Erwin James, written whilst he was serving a 20-year sentence) which have brought numerous 'unpopular' prison issues to the attention of its readers, amongst them overcrowding, racism amongst inmates and prison staff, drug addiction, mental illness and suicide (www. guardian.co.uk/prisons). But in the popular press, coverage of these issues is sparse and, on the whole, reporting of prisons and prisoners tends to reflect the tabloid media's view of a criminal justice system which is soft on crime and which prioritizes the requirements of offenders over those of victims. In general, popular press reporting about prisoners and prisons tends to fall into one or more of five thematic groups.

Tabloid tales: five 'types' of prisoner

The five-fold typology within which prisoners are constructed by the popular press consists of celebrity prisoners, pampered prisoners, sexual relations in prison, lax security and abuses or assaults on inmates. The most salient of these themes, especially in the tabloids, is that of 'celebrity' which is usually predicated on the offence(s) for which the prisoner was sentenced. In accordance with the news values that shape the selection and construction of stories generally, individuals whose crimes meet a certain threshold of horror, or whose offences are explained by reference to their sexuality or sexual deviance, and involve multiple victims and/or child victims, frequently achieve a macabre kind of celebrity (Jewkes 2004). Of particular note in this regard is Ian Huntley who, since the death of Myra Hindley in 2002 and the release of his former partner Maxine Carr in 2004, has become Britain's most newsworthy inmate. Many stories concerning Huntley are vehicles for the press to censure the Prison Service (e.g. when staff at Woodhill Prison failed to spot that an undercover *News of the World* journalist had gained a job as a prison officer and taken photographs of Huntley and his cell in April 2004). But Huntley also carries the dubious distinction of being a 'filler' for the tabloids on quiet news days and a stock narrative concerns the friendships he's formed in prison with other tabloid folk devils (e.g. 'Baby Killer makes friends with Ian Huntley', *News & Star*, 3 November 2004; and 'Huntley's new pal is serial slayer suspect', *People* 7 November 2004).

The second theme framing press coverage of prisons is that of pampered prisoners. As we have already seen in relation to in-cell TV, stories which characterize prisons as 'holiday camps' in which inmates enjoy advantages they do not 'deserve' fuel the tabloid media's view of a criminal justice system which is soft on crime. Reporting on a favourite figure of hate, the *Sunday Mirror* writes:

MAXINE Carr enjoyed an extraordinary festive knees-up behind bars … During a day of astonishing antics Carr:

- RELISHED her role as prison celebrity, teasing warders and basking in the attention of fellow inmates
- TOLD jokes and took part in party games including Pictionary and bingo.
- ENJOYED a hearty meal, including turkey and Christmas pudding.
- BOASTED about how much she was looking forward to her 'new life' once she's freed.

Her festive joy was in sharp contrast to the devastated lives of the families of Huntley's 10-year-old victims, Jessica Chapman and Holly Wells. While they could only reflect on their terrible loss, Carr was letting her hair down. (*Sunday Mirror* 28 December 2003).

A third theme is that of sexual relations in prisons. Interestingly, consenting sex amongst male prisoners remains a taboo subject for the media, yet sex amongst women prisoners is the subject of much speculation and scrutiny. Evidence of, or allusions to, lesbian relations between inmates are overwhelmingly presented as 'proof' of their guilt and as justification for their demonization at the hands of the press (Jewkes 2004). Most infamous in this respect were the photographs published in 1995 showing Myra Hindley and Rose West holding hands in the high-security wing of Durham Prison, but 'inappropriate relationships' is a pervasive – if tenuous – theme in a great many news reports about women in prison. For example, the account of Maxine Carr's Christmas in Holloway goes on to report that 'she greeted warders by hugging them' and 'ran her hands through their hair – shocking fellow prisoners'. One reported: 'She is really touchy-feely. Maxine caresses their hair – it's quite horrid' (*Sunday Mirror* 28 December 2003). Another highly newsworthy story – and one that further indicates the low status afforded women in the patriarchal popular press – is that of the prison officer who forms a sexual relationship with an inmate. Such stories regularly involve two women, but a variation on the same theme is the story of the naive female officer who allows herself to be duped into having an affair with a calculating and controlling male inmate.

Whilst the three categories mentioned so far are easily dismissed as a trivialization of prison matters, the final two themes that determine and structure news stories about prisoners cannot be regarded as mere media froth, although they are subjects that may be graphically sensationalized. The fourth is security – or to be more precise, lack of security. Given the relative infrequency of prison riots, reports about lax security usually take one of two forms: either prisoner escapes, or suicides and attempted suicides:

Dead shooting suspect was taken off suicide watch. The man accused of shooting dead his estranged wife and her sister at a family barbecue killed himself in prison three days after being taken off suicide watch, it was revealed today ... The 39-year-old had dismantled a disposable razor and cut himself repeatedly with the blade while in his single cell (*Guardian* 21 June 2004).

Outrage after drug smuggler flees prison. One of Scotland's most notorious drug smugglers has escaped from an open prison after serving just six years of a 21-year sentence. Roderick McLean, the king-pin behind a plot to smuggle £10 million of cannabis into the country, was originally classified as a dangerous Category A prisoner at Saughton jail in Edinburgh. But he was subsequently moved to an open prison in England that does not even have a perimeter fence. It has now emerged that McLean walked out of the prison two months ago and has not been seen since (*Scotsman* 29 December 2003).

Once more, an acquaintance with the processes of news production helps us understand why most escapes and deaths in custody are not considered newsworthy. Suicides and attempted suicides usually only reach the pages of the press if the story conforms to several cardinal news values – e.g. it concerns a particularly notorious ('celebrity') inmate, thus meeting the required 'threshold' for inclusion, and is reduced ('simplified') to an event that was both 'predictable' and therefore preventable. The suicides of Fred West and Harold Shipman are notable examples. The more general trend, however, is for prison suicides to go unreported, and few newspaper readers may be aware that there were 95 self-inflicted deaths in prisons in 2004, including 13 women. The suicide in that year of a 14-year-old believed to be the youngest person to die in British custody – is not included in official figures because he died at a privately run secure training unit (www.howardleague. org/press). Similarly, escapes generally only feature in the national press if the inmate concerned is well known or is especially dangerous. They are more likely to be reported in the local press (i.e. newspapers proximate to the location of the prison from which the prisoner absconded), but, again, only if the escapee represents a danger to the public or if the story constitutes a 'filler'. In any case, the press relies on contacts within the police or Prison Service to feed them information about security lapses, which may not be forthcoming. In relation to the Scottish incident, prison reform campaigner Mark Leech reports that, when he questioned the service's Director General about why the public were not advised that a dangerous prisoner was at large, he was told, 'We have a duty to keep in custody those committed by the courts but we do not have a duty to inform the media of every escape' (www.PrisonToday.com).

The final theme underpinning reports of prisons is the abuses and assaults inflicted on prisoners by staff or by other inmates. Of all the themes, this is the least salient, and generally stories about victimization in prisons will be reported only when an official inquiry has taken place. Like crime news more generally, the appearance of a story about an assault in prison is dependent upon editorial judgements being made about the victim, with some victims being considered more worthy than others (Jewkes 2004). And, again, in common with wider media constructions, a story will always be more newsworthy if the victim's relatives make themselves part of the story (Jewkes 2004). But, aside from a few notable examples where a family campaigns tirelessly to keep a case in the public eye, most assaults and abuses remain hidden behind prison walls. Like previous examples, the exception to this invisibility is attacks on notorious or 'celebrity' inmates, which tend to be widely reported.

That assaults on inmates are sometimes tolerated by those with the authority to intervene, and are then regarded as suitable fodder for the popular press, is a depressing indictment on societal attitudes towards prison inmates. Unfortunately, as many of the extracts throughout *Prison Readings* have underlined, such attitudes – on the part of politicians, administrators, prison service personnel, the popular media and general public alike – have a long and cyclical history, continuing to stigmatize a population which is already at the margins, and which rarely has a right of reply.

References

Bondeson, U. (2005) 'Levels of punitiveness in Scandinavia: description and explanations', in J. Pratt *et al.* (eds) *The New Punitiveness: Trends, Theories, Perspectives.* Cullompton: Willan Publishing.

Brown, D. (1998) 'Penality and imprisonment in Australia', in R.P. Weiss and N. South (eds) *Comparing Prison Systems.* Amsterdam: Gordon & Breach.

Caplow, T. and Simon, J. (1999) 'Understanding prison policy and population trends', in M. Tonry and J. Petersilia (eds) *Prisons*. Chicago, IL: University of Chicago Press.

Cavadino, M. and Dignan, J. (2002) *The Penal System: An Introduction* (3rd edn). London: Sage.

Douglas, M. (166) *Purity and Danger: An Analysis of Concepts of Pollution and Taboo*. London: Routledge & Kegan Paul.

Garland, D. (ed.) (2001) *Mass Imprisonment: Social Causes and Consequences*. London: Sage.

Greer, C. and Jewkes, Y. (2005) 'Images and processes of social exclusion', *Social Justice*, 32.

Hinds, L. (2005) 'Crime control in Western countries, 1970 to 2000', in J. Pratt *et al.*, (eds) *The New Punitiveness: Trends, Theories, Perspectives*. Cullompton: Willan Publishing.

Jarvis, B. (2004) *Cruel and Unusual: A Cultural History of Punishment in America*. London: Pluto.

Jewkes, Y. (2002) *Captive Audience: Media, Masculinity and Power in Prisons*. Cullompton: Willan Publishing.

Jewkes, Y. (2004) *Media and Crime*. London: Sage.

Jewkes, Y. (2005) 'Loss, liminality and the life sentence: managing identity through a disrupted lifecourse', in A. Liebling and S. Maruna (eds) *The Effects of Imprisonment*. Cullompton: Willan Publishing.

Jewkes, Y. (2006) 'Creating a stir? Prisons, popular media and the power to reform,' in P. Mason (ed.) *Captured by the Media: Prison Discourse in Popular Culture*. Cullompton: Willan Publishing.

Lynch, M. (2005) 'Supermax meets death row: legal struggles around the new punitiveness in the US', in J. Pratt *et al.* (eds) *The New Punitiveness: Trends, Theories, Perspectives*. Cullompton: Willan Publishing.

Midford, R. (1992) 'Imprisonment: the aboriginal experience in Western Australia', in M.K. Carlie and K.I. Minor (eds.) *Prisons Around the World: Studies in International Penology*. Dubuque, IA: Win. C. Brown.

Moore, D. and Hannah-Moffat, K. (2005) 'The liberal veil: revisiting Canadian penality', in J. Pratt *et al.* (eds) *The New Punitiveness: Trends, Theories, Perspectives*. Cullompton: Willan Publishing.

Morgan, R. (1997) 'Imprisonment: current concerns and a brief history since 1945', in M. Maguire *et al.* (eds) *The Oxford Handbook of Criminology* (revised 2nd edn). Oxford: Oxford University Press.

Nelken, D. (2005) 'When is a society non-punitive? The Italian case', in J. Pratt *et al.* (eds) *The New Punitiveness: Trends, Theories, Perspectives*. Cullompton: Willan Publishing.

Piacentini, L. (2004) *Surviving Russian Prisons: Punishment, Economy and Politics in Transition*. Cullompton: Willan Publishing.

Pratt, J., Brown, D., Brown, M., Hallsworth, S. and Morrison, W. (2005) *The New Punitiveness: Trends, Theories, Perspectives*. Cullompton: Willan Publishing.

van Zyl Smit, D. (1998) 'Change and continuity in South African prisons', in R.P. Weiss and N. South (eds) *Comparing Prison Systems*. Amsterdam: Gordon & Breach.

Wacquant, L. (2005) 'The great penal leap backward: incarceration in America from Nixon to Clinton', in J. Pratt *et al.* (eds) *The New Punitiveness: Trends, Theories, Perspectives*. Cullompton: Willan Publishing.

Walmsley, R. (2005) *World Prison Population List* (6th edn). London: HMSO.

Younge, G. (2002) 'Land of the free', in Y. Jewkes and G. Letherby (eds) *Criminology: A Reader*. London: Sage.

Index

The abolitionist approach: a British perspective 58, 98–103
abuse
  prisoners' negative evaluation of 196
  see also assaults; rape; sexual abuse; verbal abuse
acceptance, of life sentence 262
accordion effect 188
Adam Smith Institute 61
admission procedures 175
adult offenders, working with 211–12
Aerts v. Belgium (1998) 279
agricultural labour 269
Albany regime 56, 79–80, 82
Alma Dettingen military barracks 61
Analysing Women's Imprisonment 106, 121–7
ancillary services, contracting out 60
appeals, preoccupation with 262–4
appeasement 216–17
architectural design, prisons 5, 6
artificial insemination, prisoners' wives 252
Ashfield 152
Asian inmates 136
assaults
  media coverage 293
  in young offender institutions 151
  see also sexual assaults
Assenov v. Bulgaria (1998) 277
association games 204–6
Asylums: Essays on the social situation of mental patients and other inmates 160, 174–9, 190
autonomy, deprivation of 168–70
Aydin v. Turkey (1997) 277

Baker, Kenneth 53, 100
Bandyup's Family Support Centre 125
Barlinnie Special Unit 105–6, 116
basic regime 9
Belmarsh 88
bereavement, female lifers 266
biological clock 254–5
black males, disproportionate imprisonment 297
blanketmen 138
Blundeston 6
Boateng, Paul 55
The body of the condemned 18–21
boot camps 153–4
Borstal 150–2
bridewells *see* houses of correction
Britain
  dispersal policy 86–7
  interest in Supermax 86, 88–90
brutality, towards political prisoners 143–6
Buckley Hall 63
bureaucratic staff 169–70
Burger, Warren 271
Byely Lebed 88–9

Cages unit, Inverness 116–18
Campbell and Fell v. United Kingdom (1984) 279–80
Can prisons be legitimate? Penal politics, privatization and the timeliness of an old idea 56, 71–7
Cane, Edmund du 4, 33
capital, obstacle to a viable work regimen 272
carceral network 250
Carnarvon Committee 51, 54

categorization, of prisoners 7–8
celebrity prisoners 291
cell searching 207–8
Chapters on Prisons and Prisoners 45
charades 206
Chatham Convict Prison 4
Chesterton, George Laval 22
children
   imprisonment of 152
   loss of 255–6
   maternal imprisonment 125
   right to bear 254–5
Children and Young Persons Act (1933)
   151
civil death 175
Clay, John 15, 40–1, 46, 48
clock towers 5
coercion 100
Colchester boot camp 154
communication, between prisoners 53
confinement
   Borstal 150
   marginalisation of experience 100
   mid-Victorian prisons 53
   see also solitary confinement
confinement games 202–4
conservative fears, idle prisoners 227,
   268, 270
construction of prisons, contracting out
   60
contaminative exposure 178–9
Continuous Assessment Scheme 87, 89
contracting out *see* privatization
contracts, prisoners' rights 9
control
   maintaining 219–20
   see also situational control; social
      control
Control Review Committee (1984) 85
controversies, current 223–7
correctional institution, Norway 193–201
corruption, prevention of 31
countryside, and crime 46
covert intelligence gathering 207
cracksman 49
crime, and countryside 46
Crime and Disorder Act (1998) 151, 154,
   156
Crime Prevention Act (1908) 150
crime rates 89
criminal classes 47–8
criminal justice

ethics 250
   histories, suicide attempters 232
   radical risk management 245–52
Criminal Justice Act (1948) 152
Criminal Justice Act (1961) 150
Criminal Justice Act (1991) 63, 76
Criminal Justice and Police Act (2001)
   153
Criminal Justice and Public Order Act
   (1994) 153
criminal statistics 89
criminal subculture, identification with
   165
criminalisation, political prisoners 138–47
cross-gender posting, prison staff 122–3
culture, of masculinity 110, 111
   see also criminal subculture; prison
      culture
custodial remands, young offenders
   154–5
Cyprus v. Turkey (1982) 278

D v. United Kingdom (1997) 279
dangerous and severe personality
   disorder (DSPD) 225, 250
dangerousness 101–2, 246
DCMF prisons 63–4, 65
death penalty 2
deaths in custody
   application of ECHR 277
   lack of media coverage 292–3
deep-end institutions 61
*The defences of the weak: a sociological
   study of a Norwegian correctional
   institution* 72, 162, 193–201
dehumanization 147
delivery of services, privatization 61, 74
deprivations 164–72
design of prisons, contracting out 60
detention
   protection of prisoners 277–8
   psychiatric 247–9
detention centres 151, 152–4
   see also young offender institutions
detention and training orders (DTOs)
   151
deterioration, fear of 191–2
deterrence 27, 32, 250
dictation 219
dirty protest 140, 142, 144
disciplinary proceedings, Maze prison
   140

discipline *see* prison discipline
Discipline and Punish 14
dispersal policy, Britain 84–5
dispersal prisons, Britain 84–5
disturbances *see* riots
Doing prison work: the public and private lives of prison officers 165, 209–21
Drake Hall 121, 122
dress *see* uniforms
drug dealing and use
   interventions and further research 242–45
   motivations for 241–2
   and power 238–41
   see also heroin
drug offenders, female 134
drugs testing 134
The drugs economy and the prisoner society 224–5, 237–44
due process rights 245

economics, female crime 36
educational qualifications, suicide attempters 232
enhanced regime 9
ethics
   criminal justice 250
   health care 250
ethnic minorities
   disproportionate and discriminatory imprisonment 285
   officers' ability to protect 137
Europe, experience of supermax 84–8
European Convention on Human Rights 276–81
ex-prisoners, stigma 54
exultation effect 188–90

factory workers, and time 182–3, 188
fairness 195–6
families, female prisoners' contact with 125–6
fear 116
Federal Prison Industries 275
Feltham Remand Centre 111, 154
female lifers 253–67
   biological clock 254–5
   experience of motherhood 256–7
   increase in prison population 253
   irrelevance of time 260–1
   life under surveillance 259–60
   loss of children 255–6

pains of indeterminacy 254
pretend games 264–6
sentences
   coming to terms with 261–4
   lack of understanding of 258–9
suffering from men's bad behaviour 257–8
female offenders, as victims
structure 36
female prisoners
   accommodating 121–2
   drugs, bullying and violence 123–4
   influence on treatment of 35–7
   Ladies Prison Associations 32–5
   male guards 122–3
   mothers 125–6
   separate system 31–3
   silent system 30–1
   see also female lifers; girls
female prisons, experience of 129–34
female warders, prison discipline 34–5
feminist thinking, penal policy 36
feminist writers, imprisonment and punishment 15
financing, contracting out 60
Finland, open prisons 288
first-night units 7
food
   mid-Victorian prisons 52
   resentment of prisoners' rights 213
formal control 219–20
Forsythe, William 32, 37
free market, privatization 64–6
friendliness, towards prisoners 214–5
From Borstal to YOI 150–6
From the Inside 106–7, 129–34
Fry, Elizabeth 33–5
full employment prison
   ideal 270
   obstacles to 271–4
   as unrealistic 227
Full Sutton 87
functional austerity, prison facades 5
the future, dealing with 184

gaols 2, 3, 13
Gardner, Sir Edward 62
Garth 216–17, 220–1
ghosted 163
girls, imprisonment 152, 153
good officers 217–21

goods
   prohibitions on export of prison-made
      273
   and services, deprivation of 165–8
Gordon, Mary 36
gothic revival designs, prison facades 5
Grendon 57–8, 94–7, 102
*Grinding men good? Lancashire's prisons at
   mid-century* 15–16, 39–43

Hansbrow, Captain 42
Hawkins, Gordon 271
health care, ethics 250
health service, capacity to absorb
   mentally disordered 247
hegemonic masculinity 110
   challenging 123–7
heroin
   appeal of consumption 241
   dealing and power 238–41
   prison culture 237–8
   use and stigma 238
   see also drug dealing and use
heterosexual relationships, deprivation
   of 167–8
hierarchy
   drug dealing 239–40
   male long-term prisons 111
High Risk Patients 246
Hill, Frederic 42
Hilton v. United Kingdom (1976) 278
Holloway Prison 123
Holyoake, Frederick 47
Home Affairs Select Committee (1987) 58
Home Affairs Select Committee (2005)
   161
homicides
   in custody 223
   statistics 89
homosexual relationships 197–8
homosexual tendencies, activation of 168
homosexuals 167–8
hothouse management 147–9
houses of correction 2, 3, 13
Howard Association 32
Howard, John 13
Howard League 152, 161
Howard, Michael 64
human rights
   bearing children 254–5
   concern for 245
   treatment of prisoners 85

   see also European Convention on
      Human Rights
Human Rights Act (2000) 255
humiliation, in total institutions 177–9
hunger strikes 146, 147
Huntley, Ian 291
Hurd, Douglas 61–2

identity *see* self-conception
identity equipment, loss of 176–7
ill-treatment, in custody 277
immaturity, of young offenders 212
imprisonment
   deprivations of 164–72
   duration, Preston 28
   indeterminate *see* indeterminate
      imprisonment
   long-term *see* long-term imprisonment
   mass 297
   measures to alleviate conditions 7
   use of, mid-Victorian era 51
   utopian realist politics 76–7
   young offenders
      case against 157t
      rates 156
   see also prisons
improvement, the age of 99–102
Incentives and Earned Privileges (IEP)
   scheme 8, 9
indeterminate imprisonment 226,
   253–7
individuality, female prisoners 34
industries, prison labour 269
informal control 220
information, about other inmates
   199–200
informational preserve, violation of
   prisoner's 178
informers 207
informing 193–5, 243
infrastructure, as an obstacle to a viable
   work regimen 271
institutional racism, young offender
   institutions 151–2
institutional reflexivity 76
institutionalised violence 111
International Covenant on Civil and
   Political Rights 85
interpersonal skills, prison staff 204–5
intimidation, young offender institutions
   151
intuition 199

Inverness, caged area 116–18
Italy, prison system 287

Kaya v. Turkey (1998) 277
kindness, misunderstood for weakness
    213
Kirkdale 41, 42, 43
Kiss v. United Kingdom (1976) 280
Knight, Philip 154
Krocher and Muller v. Switzerland (1982)
    278

Ladies' Prison Associations 33–5
Lady Visitors 35–6
Lancashire's prisons, nineteenth century
    39–43
Learmont Inquiry 86, 88
legal impediments, as an obstacle to a
    viable work regimen 273
legal representation 279–80
legitimacy
    penological debate 76–7
    in prison regimes 79–83
    of prisons 71–3
    privatization 73–6
Legitimacy and order in prisons 56, 79–83
lesbian officers 123
less eligibility 33, 227
liberal concerns, prison labour 227, 268,
    270
liberal regimes 216
liberty
    deprivation of 164–5
    rights, mentally disordered offenders
        251
life sentences 251
*Life as a women: the gendered pains of
    indeterminate imprisonment* 228, 259–67
lifers
    dependence on staff for good reports
        206
    right to inseminate wives 255
    see also female lifers
listening schemes 7
local prisons 3, 6, 8
location of prisons
    as an obstacle to a viable work
        regimen 271–2
    changes in 5
Long Kesh 138
Long Lartin regime 54, 78–9, 80
long-term imprisonment 183–94

dealing with the past and future
    185–7
fear of deterioration 193–4
marking time 187–91
time as a problem 183–5
working and making time pass 191–3
long-term prisoners, working with
    218–19
long-term prisons, hierarchy in 111
losses, imprisonment 166–74, 256, 257–8,
    263
loyalty 195–7, 242
Lunacy Act (1890) 247

maanser 196
McFeeley v. United Kingdom (1981) 280
male guards, in women's prisons
    122–3
male violence 102, 109–19
    therapeutic discourse 102
management, contracting out 61
managerialism 74
mandatory drugs testing (MDT) 124
manhood 198–200
masculinity
    challenging hegemonic 115–19
    culture of 110, 111
mass imprisonment 287
Maze prison 138, 139–41, 148, 280
media
    introduction in prisons 290–1
    and public opinion 291–2
    see also tabloids
men
    in prison, experience of 109–13
    see also prisoners
mental disorder
    legal definition 250
    in prison population 227
mental health, radical risk management
    245–52
Mental Health Act (1959) 245
Mental Health Act (1983) 245, 248, 249
Mental Health Review Tribunal (MHRT)
    245
mental health system, convergence of
    penal system and 245–52
mental incapacity, female prisoners 36
mentally disordered offenders
    detention 247–9
    liberty rights 251
    social situation 174–9

MI5 146
MI6 146
militarisation 100
Military Corrective Training Centre 154
Millbank Penitentiary 3, 4
Mind games: where the action is in prisons
  162–3, 204–10
minimum wages 273–4
Modernised Care Programme Approach
  250
modernity, institutional reflexivity 76
moral hospitals, prisons as 41
moral reform 31–2
mortification, of the self 175–9
mother and baby units 126
motherhood, as female lifer 256–7
mothers, imprisonment of 125–6
Mountbatten Committee 5, 6
Mubarek, Zahid 107, 223

National Prison Survey (1991) 125
negotiation 216–22
neoclassical designs, prison facades 5
New Jersey State Prison 164–72
New Labour, new punitiveness 156
new penality 74
new punitiveness 156, 286–7, 289–90
nicking 20
non-conforming behaviour, pathologised
  259
normalisation, of violence 110, 112
Northern Ireland Office, public relations
  expenditure 143
Norwegian correctional institution, peer
  solidarity 193–201
Nugent, Ciaran 138

offences, re-living 265
Offences against the Person Act (1861) 2
O'Fiaich, Cardinal Thomas 142
open prisons, Finland 288
operation of prisons, contracting out 61
Opportunity and Responsibility 99–100
organizational issues, violence of prison
  staff 146–7
Orthodox accounts, imprisonment and
  punishment 4, 14
Osman v United Kingdom (1998) 277
overcrowding 283–4

pains of imprisonment 114, 164–72,
  253–67

pampered prisoners 291
Panopticon 250
Paramilitary imprisonment in Northern
  Ireland: resistance, management and
  release 107–8, 138–47
Parkhurst 91
pathology, male violence 112
patriarchalism, illegitimate 200
Paul Onesiphorus, Sir George 31
peer solidarity 193–201
Pelle v. France (1986) 280
penal policy
  American carceral boom 285–6
  current 1–2
  feminist thinking 36
penal reform 33, 99–102
Penal Servitude Act (1853) 3
Penal Servitude Act (1857) 4
Penal Servitude Act (1864) 4
penal system, convergence of psychiatric
  system and 245–52
Penitentiary Act (1779) 2
Pentonville 3, 4, 5, 40, 45
personal defacement 176–7
personal disfigurement 177
personal media 289
personal qualities, prison officers
  217–18
personality disorders 225, 250
Perth prison 4
Peterborough 6, 284
Peterhead 115
physical incapacity, female prisoners
  36
pickpockets 48–9
plantation systems, prison labour 269
poachers, treatment of 46
political impediments, as an obstacle to
  a viable work regimen 273
political prisoners
  application of ECHR to prison
    conditions 278
  criminalisation 138–47
    brutality, violence and
      dehumanization 143–5
    hothouse management and
      political and security
      interference 145–7
    internalisation of propagandist
      positions 141–3
    rules enforcement and the
      assertion of power 139–41

The Politics of Abolition 72
Poor Law Amendment Act (1834) 33
popular punitiveness 156
power
    assertion of 139–41
    heroin dealing 238–41
    and legitimacy 77
    in prisons 216–22
Powers of Criminal Courts Act (2000)
    151
Preston House of Correction 15
    inspection of 46
    reformatory system 22–9, 40–1, 42–3
pretend games, female lifers 262–5
prison authorities, legitimacy of actions
    82–3
*The prison chaplain: memoirs of Reverend
    John Clay* 15
prison community 159–63
prison conditions
    application of the ECHR 277–9
    newspaper reports 290
    see also overcrowding
prison culture, and heroin 237–8
prison discipline
    application of the ECHR 279–81
    challenging, mid-Victorian prisons
        52–3
    female warders 34–5
    see also prison regimes
prison gangs 89
prison issues, marginalisation 100
prison labour 268–74
    making time pass 189–91
    political prisoners' refusal to do 140
prison officers
    ability to protect ethnic minorities 137
    failure to challenge sexual
        exploitation 113
    negotiation and coercion 215–21
    resentment of prisoners' rights 212–14
    roles and tasks 209–12
    staff-prisoner relationships 214–15
    verbal abuse towards young offenders
        151–2
    working with offenders 211–12
    see also lesbian officers; prison staff
Prison Officers Association (POA) 64,
    142
prison populations 105–8
    as an obstacle to a viable work
        regimen 273

current numbers 284
female lifers 253–4
mental illness in 225
predicted numbers at the end of the
    decade 283
young offenders 156
*Prison privatization: panacea or Pandora's
    box?* 55–6, 60–70
prison reform, social control 39–43
Prison Reform Trust 94, 101, 224, 225
prison regimes
    legitimacy in 79–83
    liberal 213
    mid-Victorian 52–3
    religion in 14, 24–6, 28
    see also separate system; silent system
prison services, contracting out 60–1
prison ships 284–5
prison staff
    brutality, violence and
        dehumanization 143–5
    cross-gender posting 122–3
    handling of suicide risk 234–5
    internalisation of criminalisation
        agenda 141–3
    interpersonal skills 204–5
    refusal to answer bells 202–3
    see also prison officers
    from the report for 1846 22–6
    from the report for 1847 26–9
prison transfers 280–1
Prison on Trial 72
'Prison Works' speech 7
Prisoners 16, 45–9
prisoners
    as an obstacle to a viable work
        regimen 272
    behaviour 90
    challenge to discipline 52–3
    criminal classes 47–8
    degradation of 165
    dress 23–4
    identification with criminal subculture
        167
    influence of sexually predatory 113
    metaphors for 209
    need for legitimation from 81–2
    officers' identification with 211
    pickpockets 38–9
    relationships with officers 214–15
    self-examination by 23
    social characteristics 229

social situation 174–9
solidarity 159–60, 193–201
tabloid typology 290–3
types of 7–8
use of non-coercive strategies 114
working classes 43–5
see also ethnic minorities; ex-prisoners;
   female prisoners; lifers; long-term
   prisoners; mentally disordered
   offenders; political prisoners;
   young offenders
prisoners' rights
   contracts 9
   officers' resentment of 212–14
Prisoners' Rights in the context of the
   European Convention on Human Rights
   227, 276–9
prisons
   emergence of modern 13–16
   from eighteenth to twenty-first
      century 1–7
   gendered reading 105–6, 109–19
   Lancashire's nineteenth century 39–43
   legitimacy 71–3
   media in 288–9
   mid-Victorian experience 51–4
   privatization 60–7
   racism in 135–6
   theoretical approaches and emerging
      trends 55–8
   types of 7–9
   see also correctional institution;
      detention centres; imprisonment;
      open prisons; supermax; total
      institutions
Prisons Act (1865) 3
privacy 198–200
Private Finance Initiative 64
privation, mid-Victorian prisons 52
privatization
   free market theory 65–7
   legitimacy 73–6
   meaning and forms of 60–5
professional informers 194
professional thieves 38–9
Project Quantum 64
propagandist positions, staff'
   internalisation of 141–3
protection, of prisoners 277–8
psychiatric detention 248–9
psychiatrists, involvement in decision-
   making 250

psychological pain, male prisoners 114
psychological problems, deprivation of
   heterosexual relationships 167
psychotic disorders 225
public execution 2, 18–20
public knowledge, of prisons 5–6
public opinion, and media 289–90
public relations
   expenditure, NI Office 143
   skills, Sinn Fein 143
punitiveness
   Borstals 152
   see also new punitiveness

Quaker Society for the Improvement of
   Prison Discipline 34–5
quality press reports 290

racial groups 136
racial incidents, under-reporting 137
racism
   in prison 135–6
   young offender institutions 151–2
Racism in prisons 107, 135–7
racist victimization 136–7
Radical risk management, mental health and
   criminal justice 225–6, 245–52
Radzinowicz Committee 8, 86
rape behaviour, in prison 113
rapists, imprisonment of 102, 118
reconviction rates
   Borstal 152
   therapeutic communities 57
Reed v. United Kingdom (1983) 278
reformatory systems
   young offenders, Mettray 20–1
   see also separate system; silent system
rehabilitation, female prisoners 126
relationships
   staff–prisoner 214–15
   see also heterosexual relationships;
      homosexual relationships
religion, prison regimes 14, 24–6, 28
religious education, female prisoners 34
remand centres 8
Renzi, Revd G. de 30
reoffending, secure units 155
resentment, of prisoners' rights 209–11
respect, assigned to drug dealers 239
responsible life sentence prisoners 266
restrictions orders 249
retributivism 250

revisionist accounts, imprisonment and
    punishment 4, 14–15
Ribitsch v. Austria (1995) 277
Richardson Committee 251
rights
    to liberty, mentally disordered
        offenders 251
    see also human rights; prisoners'
        rights; victims' rights
riots
    New Jersey State Prison 170
    nineteenth century prisons 4
*The Rise and rise of supermax: an American
    solution in search of a problem* 56–7,
    84–92
risk management, radical 286–7
rituals, mid-Victorian prisons 52
robbery, statistics 91
routinisation, of violence 101, 103
Rule 43 206
rules enforcement, political prisoners
    139–41
Rumbold, Angela 63
Russia, prison system 88, 287–9

Safer Custody Group 235
sanitoria, marking time in 185–6
secure training orders 151
secure units, young offenders 155–6
Securicor Ltd 61
security
    categories 7–8
    deprivation of 171–2
    facilities, supermax *see* supermax
    media coverage 292
    political interference 147–9
security games 207–8
selective incapacitation 250
self, mortification of 175–9
self-conception, imprisonment as threat
    to 164, 166, 167, 169
self-examination, by prisoners 23
Selmouni v. France (1999) 277
separate system 14
    official adoption of 42
    Preston House of Correction 22–9, 40,
        41, 42–3
    purposes 31–3
services *see* goods and services; prison
    services
sexual abuse, suicide attempters 232
sexual assaults, on female prisoners 122

sexual deviants 197–8
sexual exploitation 113
sexual frustration 167–8
sexual relations, taboo subject for media
    291–2
sexuality
    cross-gender posting 122–3
    in prison 112–13
sexually predatory prisoners, influence
    of 113
shallow-end institutions 61
shit parcels 202–3
silent system 14, 30–1
    Preston House of Correction
        40–1
    supporters of 41–2
Sinn Fein, public relations skills 143
situational control 82
slopping out 203–4
social characteristics, prisoners 229
social control
    prison reform 39–43
    risky populations 246
social disadvantage
    female crime 36
    prison population 101
social interaction, skills 218
social protection 250
social solidarity, between prisoners
    159–60
*The Society of Captives: a study of a
    maximum security prison* 159–60
Soering v. United Kingdom (1989) 279
Softly does it 57, 94–7
solidarity
    benefits of 243
    see also peer solidarity; social
        solidarity
solitary confinement
    application of ECHR 278–9
    marking of time 187
solitude, periods of, Pentonville 3
Special Category Status 138, 139
Special Unit Selection Committee (SUSC)
    88
staff *see* prison staff
standard regime 9
standards of living, in prisons 166
state intervention, as an obstacle to a
    viable work regimen 272–3
statistics, criminal 91
stealing 195–6

stigma
   ex-prisoners 54
   heroin use 238
Strangeways 63
Straw, Jack 65
subjective clocks 186
substance misuse 124
substitute possessions 176–7
suffragettes, experience of imprisonment
   36–7
suicide 230–7
   current developments 236
   institutionalised violence 111
   lack of media coverage 282, 293
   role of prison staff 234–5
   vulnerability profile 236
   vulnerability and risk 231–5
   in young offender institutions 153
Suicides in prison: ten years on 223–4,
   230–9
Super-enhanced regime 9
supermax 84–92
   European experience 86–90
   impersonal brutality of 284–5
supplementary, private prisons as 75–6
supplementary norms 195
surveillance
   in the community 250
   experience of female lifers 259–60
swindlers 196

tabloids
   false depiction of prisons 288
   typology of prisoners 290–3
Tanrikulu v. Turkey (1999) 278
tariff period 249
technocratic authoritarianism 246–7
Tekin v. Turkey (1998) 278
Ter Peel experiment 126
terminal illness, life imprisonment as
   261–2
Thatcher, Margaret 63, 148
therapeutic communities 57–8, 94–7
therapeutic detention 247–9
therapeutic discourse 102
thieves in law 88
Thorn Cross 154
Time and deterioration 160–1, 181–92
time, long-term imprisonment
   dealing with the past and future
      183–5
   irrelevance of 260–1

marking 185–9
as a problem 181–3
total institutions 160, 174–8
Tougher than the Rest? Men in prison
   105–6, 109–19
training component, Borstal 150
training prisons 8
transportation 2, 3, 4, 13–14
Treatise on the Law and Practice of Lunacy
   251
Tyrer v. United Kingdom (1978) 279
tyster 194

Ulster Security Liaison Committee 148
uniforms
   political prisoners' refusal to wear 140
   Preston House of Correction 22–3
United States of America: prison labour: a
   tale of two penologies 268–74
unprofessional informers 194
unsoundness of mind, patients detained
   on grounds of 248
utopian realism, politics of imprisonment
   76–7

verbal abuse, young offender institutions
   151–4
verbal responses, humiliating 177–8
victimization
   media coverage 293
   racist 136–7
victims' rights, recognition of 250
Victorian prison lives 16, 45–9
Victorian prisons 3, 4, 6
   experience 51–4
   see also Lancashire prisons
violence 109–19
   American prisons 89, 90
   towards political prisoners 143–5
   see also male violence
visiting time, pretend games 264
visits, marking time 188–9
Vologda 88

Waddington, David 63
Weare 283–4
The Well-ordered prison: England 1780–
   1865 16, 51–4
Whig accounts, imprisonment and
   punishment 4, 14
Whitemoor 84, 87
Williams, William John 41–2

Windlesham, Lord 63
women *see* female prisoners
Women, crime and custody in Victorian England 15, 30–7
Women in Prison 123
Woolf Report (1991) 8–9, 72, 81, 100–1, 122
work *see* prison labour
working classes, prisoners 45–7
Wormwood Scrubs 102
Wymott prison 210

X v United Kingdom 245, 248, 249, 278

young offender institutions
    assaults 151
    conditions 151
    suicide 231–5
    see also boot camps; Borstal; detention centres
Young Offender Psychology Unit (Home Office) 153
young offenders
    case against imprisonment 157t
    custodial remands 154–5
    new punitiveness 156
    prison population 156
    reformatory system, Mettray 20–1
    secure units 155–6
    working with 211–12
Young report 62
youth custody centres 151
Youth Justice Board 155